Children
of the Great
Depression

W9-DGJ-296

The University of Chicago Press

Chicago
London

Children of the Great Depression

Social Change in Life Experience

Glen H. Elder, Jr.

The University of Chicago Press, Chicago 60637
The University of Chicago Press, Ltd., London

International Standard Book Number: 0-226-20263-1

Glen H. Elder, Jr., is professor of sociology
at the University of North Carolina
and research professor at the Institute for Research
in Social Science.
[1974]

Contents

Tables

Figures

Foreword

Depressions, wars, and periods of extreme social ferment often produce major reorientations of society. That the life course of individuals may also be reshaped by such periods of crisis is apparent from personal experience and from biographical studies. Some lives are cut short or stunted, while others find purpose and opportunity to achieve beyond all prior imaginings. In periods of crisis, the element of chance seems to play a major role in influencing life outcomes. At such times, we can hardly specify an expectable life course beyond the immediate impact of the crisis. The task of delineating "net effects," of tracing out the various patterns of impact, response, and ultimate influence, seems almost insuperable. Only by combining historical, sociological, and psychological perspectives with detailed, longitudinal data on individual experiences, orientations, and behaviors can such an analysis be accomplished. This is precisely what Glen Elder has done in the present volume, and the accomplishment deserves comment.

This volume testifies at once to the value of long-range longitudinal research, to the dedication and foresight of those who established the Oakland Growth Study more than forty years ago, and to the extraordinary ingenuity and persistence of Glen Elder, who took data collected for totally different purposes, reconceptualized them, and brought them to bear on a set of significant sociological questions.

The Oakland Growth Study was established in 1931–32 by Herbert Stolz and Harold E. Jones as a means of examining the physiological, psychological, and social aspects of the pubertal transition. Hence its original name, the Adolescent Growth Study. From the time the study members entered Junior High School (at an average age of eleven or twelve) until they graduated from Senior High School some six years later, they were observed, questioned, measured, and tested on more than a hundred different occasions. Many of the techniques used, the best available at the time, seem quite primitive now. But they were applied with care—one might even say loving care. The predominant orientation of the early staff was that of child psychology. The development of the individual child was broadly viewed in its physical, cognitive, and social aspects, but relatively little attention was given to the conceptualization and measurement of socialization experiences. Yet there was certainly a recognition that parental behaviors and life circumstances made a difference. Harold Jones, in particular, was interested in the new developments in American social science relating to the measurement of social class. He saw to it that detailed data were collected on the characteristics of the home, the father's occupation, and other facets of level of living.

It was my privilege to succeed Harold Jones as Director of the Institute of Human Development in 1960. As a newcomer to the institute, coming from a different discipline, I found the magnitude of the data archive there somewhat overwhelming. A major follow-up study of the subjects as they neared age 40 was approaching completion, under a grant from the Ford Foundation. Coding and rating of the new data were well under way, but analysis plans were fragmentary. The successive deaths of Else Frenkel-Brunswik and of Harold Jones, the two persons who had planned the follow-up study, left the project without a senior supervisor. An enormously complex project had come very close to chaos.

When Glen Elder joined the staff in 1962, fresh from a post-doctoral year at the University of North Carolina, he had already been engaged in a large-scale study of adolescents and their families. He brought to the program a solid knowledge of sociological and social psychological research and theory on adolescent development along with a seemingly insatiable curiosity and a prodigious amount of energy. He was an ideal choice to work with me in bringing a sociological perspective to bear on the longitudinal data. It gradually became apparent, however, that our originally planned collaboration on a monograph on the family relations and career development of the subjects was to be a casualty of my inability to find sufficient time and energy after meeting my administrative commitments. This must have been an extremely frustrating experience for my associate, but he coped with it by undertaking a series of analyses of career development and marital histories that resulted in important contributions to knowledge. Subsequently, he conceived of viewing the data in historical perspective and of explicitly examining the ways in which the Great Depression modified the lives of the families and influenced the development of the children who were subjects in the research.

The story that unfolds in the present volume has high intrinsic interest and significance. It is a seminal contribution to the sociology of the life course. We know that "life chances" depend on historical circumstances and on one's location in the social structure. But we are only beginning to formulate the nature of the linkages between particular kinds of experiences located in time and place, adaptive responses to these experiences, and long-term outcomes. Indeed, the great bulk of research on socialization influences simply assumes that particular patterns of relationship, guidance, or activity will influence later outcomes. The researcher is seldom able to follow the subjects whom he studied in childhood and adolescence into their adult years. If there is an attempt to check on specific linkages between early experience and later personality characteristics or career lines, it usually entails starting from known outcomes and working backwards, using retrospective reports. But since the past is almost inevitably revised in retrospective reconstructions to accord with present perspectives, the cloak of evidence is of insubstantial fabric. Longitudinal studies or personal documents maintained over long periods of time afford the only adequate bases for tracing the linkages by which change comes about in the life course. Only through the use of such data can one delineate the sequence of events, relationships, and interpretations that underlie the individual's commitments to career, family, and other spheres.

Even in longitudinal research there are inevitably gaps in one's knowledge. One could not possibly monitor or review all of the salient experiences of a single individual, even if one knew how to ask all of the relevant questions. Under such circumstances, the richer and more diverse the data collected by earlier investigators, the greater the likelihood that their successors will be able to address research questions not previously formulated. By the same token, however, the task of winnowing the data will be more complex and time-consuming.

If available longitudinal data afforded a basis for this particular study, the explicit framework of cohort analysis here utilized goes a long step beyond most longitudinal research. Cohort analysis has been an honored technique in demographic research. It has been used less in sociological research and hardly at all in social psychological inquiries. In cohort analysis, the investigator explicitly recognizes that human behavior must be viewed in its historical context. Ideally, he compares experiences in different cohorts, and this is a task in which Glen Elder is currently engaged. The current volume examines the experience of a single cohort, but by ingenious subgroup analysis the researcher is able to show that the historical era impinged upon different families in significantly different ways.

This volume represents the product of nearly a decade of painstaking research effort, although its author has carried out and published many other, more limited, studies in the same period. To watch this research reach fruition has been a highly rewarding experience for me, and I believe that the reader who retraces the developmental steps of the Oakland study cohort will be similarly rewarded.

John A. Clausen

Acknowledgments

The story of this project began more than forty years ago in the pioneering vision of Harold E. Jones and Herbert R. Stolz, then research director and director of the Institute of Child Welfare (now the Institute of Human Development), University of California at Berkeley. In 1932, they launched and directed a longitudinal study of growth and development with a sample of eleven-year-old children from the northeastern sector of Oakland, and later extended the project to the full life span. Without financial resources that are now customary, Jones and Stolz managed to establish and maintain a broad program of data collection during the 30s. This program and periodic adult follow-ups provided materials that were well suited for a study of the Oakland children as "children of the Great Depression." My debt is great indeed to these men and other staff members of the institute who labored so long and well in developing this valuable data archive on human development (supported by the Laura Spelman Rockefeller Foundation, Ford Foundation, and USPHS Grant MH 06238) and to the Oakland children whose lives span an unparalleled era of social-historical change.

The initial stage of data preparation and analysis was completed at the Institute of Human Development during my tenure as research sociologist (1962–67). Work on the project continued at Chapel Hill after I accepted an appointment (1967) to the sociology faculty of the University of North Carolina. Final revisions in the manuscript were made during a sabbatical year (1972–73) at the Institute of Human Development supported by Grant GS–35253 from the National Science Foundation. In all stages of this study of the Depression experience, from its inception to the final manuscript, I have benefited from John Clausen's encouragement, perceptive criticism, and wise counsel. I was first exposed to the opportunities of longitudinal research on the life course through his project at the Institute, and my initial work on socioeconomic change in family and life patterns was made possible by funds from this program of research (Grant MH 05300, NIMH). If this influence and more generally that of the Chicago school (dating back to W. I. Thomas) is as evident to my readers as to me, I shall be very pleased.

I owe a special debt to the staff of the Institute of Human Development and that of the Institute for Research in Social Science at Chapel Hill for assistance in data preparation and analysis; and to Ella Barney, Christine Godet, Natalie Lucchese, Linda Anderson, and Patricia Sanford for their expert care in preparing drafts of the manuscript. M. Brewster Smith, Mary Jones, and John Clausen made valuable criticisms and comments on an early version of the manuscript. An expanded draft was read and criticized by Neil Smelser, Reuben Hill, John Clausen, Mary Jones, Dorothy Eichorn, and Robert Jackson. These evaluations and related discussion prompted many improvements in the book.

Chapters 7 and 8 draw upon material in three articles that are based on the Oakland Growth Study sample: "Intelligence and Achievement Motivation in Occupational Mobility," *Sociometry* 31 (December 1968): 327–54; "Appearance and Education in Marriage Mobility," *American Sociological Review* 34 (August 1969): 519–33; and "Role Orientations, Marital Age, and Life Patterns in Adulthood," *Merrill-Palmer Quarterly* 18 (January 1972): 3–24. Permission of the publishers is acknowledged for quotations from Robert S. Lynd and Helen Merritt Lynd, *Middletown in Transition: A Study in Cultural Conflict*, Harcourt, Brace, 1937; Studs Terkel, *Hard Times*, Random House, 1970; C. Wright Mills, *The Sociological Imagination*, Oxford University Press, 1959; Joseph Adelson, "Is Women's Lib a Passing Fad?" *The New York Times Magazine*, 19 March, 1972; Mirra Komarovsky, *Blue-Collar Marriage*, Random House, 1962; Helena Z. Lopata, *Occupation: Housewife*, Oxford University Press, 1971; and Reuben Hill, *Family Development in Three Generations*, Schenkman, 1970.

Throughout the course of this work, its ups and downs, my wife, Karen, has been a constant source of encouragement and understanding. Her good humor and vibrant outlook were more than a match for a preoccupied husband. With grateful appreciation, this book is dedicated to her.

Crisis and Adaptation: An Introduction

I

The city had been shaken for nearly six years by a catastrophe involving not only people's values but, in the case of many, their very existence. Unlike most socially generated catastrophes, in this case virtually nobody in the community had been cushioned against the blow; the great knife of the depression had cut down impartially through the entire population, cleaving open the lives and hopes of rich as well as poor. The experience had been more nearly universal than any prolonged recent emotional experience in the city's history; it had approached in its elemental shock the primary experiences of birth and death.

Middletown itself believes, not without some justification, that many families have been drawn together and "found" themselves in the depression. It is just as certainly true that in yet other families, the depression has precipitated a permanent sediment of disillusionment and bitterness, shown in part by the rapidity with which the divorce rate was climbing back toward its old level in 1935. Where the balance lies as between these two tendencies no one as yet knows.

[Newspaper Editorial] This Depression Has Its Points. Great spiritual values have come out of the depression. . . . Many a family that has lost its car has found its soul. . . . Nerves are not so jaded. Bodies are better rested, and though fine foods are not so plentiful, digestion is better. . . . Churches have been gaining . . . because some who were once members of golf clubs can no longer afford to play.

From Robert S. Lynd
and Helen M. Lynd,
*Middletown
in Transition.*

1

1   The Depression Experience

*It was the best of times,
it was the worst of times,
it was the age of
wisdom, it was the epoch
of incredulity, it was
the season of Light, it
was the season of
Darkness, it was the
spring of hope, it was
the winter of despair.*
Charles Dickens
A Tale of Two Cities

From various quarters we are reminded of the "greatness" of the Great Depression, as seen in its costs to human lives and social institutions. But there is evidence on the other side which shows that much was learned, that the Depression was an instructive experience which produced novel social adaptations. Polarities of this sort have long been noted in the study of social change and crises (Sorokin 1942). Nevertheless, our theories and studies tend to slight the contrasting elements and consequences of historical events. To some historians, for example, the Great Depression is a watershed in the evolution of American society, while others stress the degree of continuity between institutional change in the post-1929 era and social reform during the late nineteenth and twentieth centuries. (For a critical analysis of the "discontinuity" thesis, see Kirkendall 1964.) In any specific analysis, crisis situations are seldom viewed in terms of their potential for adaptive change and pathology.

These diverse outcomes arise in part from variations in exposure to the historical event (not all Americans suffered heavy economic losses or unemployment in the 30s) and from the different resources of individuals and their interpretations of the situation. Economic stagnation and hardship visited all sections of the country as unemployment approached one-third of the work force in 1933 and a much larger percentage of Americans were placed on shortened hours and reduced paychecks, but these conditions varied across segments of the population, defined by age and sex, occupation, race, and residence.[1] Evidence assembled by an economist suggests that this period was not a time of great economic deprivation for at least half of the population.[2] Severe physical want and poverty were concentrated among the urban and rural lower classes, in particular, while status or reputation loss and related anxieties were especially common in the middle classes. In view of these variations and the diverse backgrounds of writers in the 30s, it is not surprising that we have markedly different interpretations of what America was like in the Depression. "In a vast country,

3

contradictory impressions were inevitable in the observations of journalists, novelists, and storytellers of vastly different backgrounds and predilections; contradictory viewpoints were often expressed by the same writer."[3]

Questions of validity naturally arise from these contradictory reports, but this is more of a problem in reports that rely solely on the memories of persons, a relatively common source of data in recent books on this historical period (for example, Terkel 1970). The past is often reconstructed to fit the present. While the "good old days" are an enjoyable topic of conversation and improve with the telling, there is little reward in remembering the "bad days," unless they reflect favorably on one's present situation and successful ascent. In either case, memories yield an inaccurate picture of life experience in the Depression. Noting that many Americans who lived through the Depression are unwilling to talk about it, one writer observes that the passage of time has had an anesthetic effect on memories of the painful and unpleasant. "This may be nature's way of maintaining the emotional stability of the human race, but it does not make for accurate history—we remember only what we want to remember."[4] As one critic exclaimed, "It's strange, but everyone who writes about the thirties, writes about them defensively."[5]

Reliable knowledge of social realities and life experiences in the Great Depression thus depends on the availability of archival data. The problem here is that such data are both limited and fixed. One does not have the option of collecting additional information to fill in the lacunae, which unfortunately are all too common. At most points in the Depression, for instance, the country did not have accurate nationwide statistics on the unemployment rate. Archival data from agency files have proved to be an invaluable source of information for community studies, but they offer very limited information on the subjective situation and experiences of families and individuals, especially in the lower strata.

Since the 1930s we have gained little reliable knowledge on family life during the Depression, and this is even more true of the experience of children under varying conditions of economic hardship. We also lack evidence on a question which has aroused much interest and speculation—the psychosocial effects of growing up in the 1930s. An example of this speculation is Herbert Gans's assumption that the "low threshold for excitement" among Levittowners is due to their childhood experience in the Depression: "Excitement is identified with conflict, crisis, and deprivation. Most Levittowners grew up in the Depression, and, remembering the hard times of their childhood, they want to protect themselves and their children from stress."[6] Other explanations, which apply to the aging process, are equally plausible.

The Research
Problem and
Approach

This book is based on a study of the Depression experience in the lives of some Americans who were born in 1920–21 and in the lives of their parents, but it is more broadly concerned with the implications of drastic socioeconomic change for family change and intergenerational relations. We follow these children of the Depression from the early 30s in Oakland (California) through World War II, the postwar era of the 40s and 50s, and the early 60s.

Archival data in the Oakland Growth Study, located at the University of California (Institute of Human Development), offered a unique opportunity to identify economic change in family life and its consequences for persons born before the Great Depression. The project was launched in 1931 to study the physical, intellectual, and social development of boys and girls, and commenced data collection in 1932. The 167 children who were intensively studied from 1932 to 1939 were initially selected from the fifth and sixth grades of five elementary schools in the northeastern section of Oakland, California. According to the family background of enrolled students, two of the schools were largely working-class, one was lower-middle-class, and the other two were middle-class.

These children are representatives of only one of the age groups which passed through the Depression, but the 1916–25 cohort has historical significance as a major source of World War II veterans, the postwar "baby boom," and the presumed generational gap (see Cain 1970, and Easterlin 1961). With few exceptions, the males served an average of three years in the armed forces during the war, and the females were occupied in the "familistic" postwar years with child rearing. Most of the men and women married during the war and had their first child shortly thereafter in a period of relative affluence. A large proportion of their children who entered colleges were enrolled during the student protests of the 1960s.

In a literal sense, these two generations are offspring of contrasting childhoods, one marked by scarcity and the other by affluence. A sharp contrast in childhoods also appears between the subjects and their parents, who were born before the turn of the century and entered the Depression in the prime years of life, their late 30s and early 40s. The nonmanual fathers were generally self-employed merchants and professionals in the "old middle class." Through marriage or occupational achievement, most of the offspring of these men established careers that are related to bureaucracies in the organizational society which evolved from the Depression era.

I start with the fact of differential economic loss among families and investigate its social and psychological effects; very little attention is given to factors which account for variations in the breadwinner's economic and job loss. The first half of the book centers on variations in economic deprivation among families in the middle and working classes, as expressed in the family structure, social experience, and personality of the children; these effects are then traced in the later chapters to careers, values, and psychological functioning in adulthood. With socioeconomic change as the focal point, the study necessarily leads to various outcomes in the life span, as I conceptually specify its effects in family organization and life situations, and pursue their implications for adult experience. The analysis thus resembles a funnel, narrow or focused at the outset and broad in the adult years. It is important to make special note of this feature since the analytic requirements differ markedly from those of studies which center on a single outcome or dependent variable, for example, "What are the conditions under which rationalized economic behavior makes its appearance?"[7]

When we are interested in the primary sources of variation in a dependent variable, we tend to select independent variables for the analysis which will enable us (according to theory) to account for a creditable portion of this variation. What social factors, for example, are likely to account for variation in egalitarian sex-role orientation among women? for variation in the balance of marital power? In studies of such questions, the amount of explained variance is a reasonable criterion, among others, for evaluating both theory and results, but it has less value when the analyst focuses upon the effects of an independent variable or antecedent factor, as in the present study. Economic deprivation was selected for study on theoretical and historical grounds, not in terms of its presumed efficiency in predicting one or more dependent variables. In this regard, two kinds of outcomes will be of interest as we pose questions on the effect of economic deprivation in the life course: Does economic deprivation have an effect on a particular aspect of adult experience, and how does this effect compare with that of other relevant variables, such as family social class?—the question of *relative effect*; and, How is the effect *linked* to this aspect of adult life?—a question which centers on the interpretative task.

An Approach to
Family Change

In the realm of social change, the study is defined by its focus on actual families and individuals in concrete situations, as compared with the analysis of abstract social systems and structures. The socioeconomic change of families (with parents and children) is a strategic point at which to investigate the dynamics of generational change, of change between old and young in the succession of generations. If family adaptations to change are constructed from customary lines of action and features of the new situation, its perceived requirements and options, we are led to expect some restructuring of the child's world—in relation to others, and in tasks within the household and extrafamilial settings. Whether intended or not, the actions of parents in response to situations of family change inevitably pattern or impinge on their children's upbringing. Mothers who sought jobs in the Depression presumably did so in order to supplement family income, but their actions may have had a host of other consequences for the upbringing of their daughters. For example, the working mother would establish a behavioral model for her daughter and was likely to gain influence in family affairs, while the daughter was drawn more fully into household operations. Each of these conditions has implications for the learning or reinforcement of values.

This approach enables the analyst to gain some insight into the process by which change occurs,[8] an admittedly neglected feature of prominent macrotheories on social change, for example, theories of class conflict and sociocultural evolution. The problem before us is not simply whether economic change produced family and generational change, or the nature of that change; it includes questions concerning the process by which such change occurred. What are the conceptual linkages between economic change and the adult careers of men and women who were children in the 30s? It may be clear from what has been said that basic features of this approach are indebted to the early work of William I. Thomas, and especially to his classic study (with F. Znaniecki) *The Polish Peasant in Europe and America* (1918–20).[9] Thomas trained his analytic eye on linkages between social structure and personality and made a convincing case for studying such linkages at points of discontinuity or incongruence between person and environment, as seen in his theory of crisis situations, of adaptations to new situations. From the vantage point of the present study, we also appreciate Thomas's emphasis on developmental concepts of life experience, on the use of life records and histories.

The study of families in concrete situations of change meshes well with the analytic requirements of research on historical events in family change. A number of major events in the present century directly affected millions of family units—especially mass emigration (Europe to America, rural to urban), World Wars I and II (which at least temporarily removed fathers and sons through military service, and drew women into the labor force), and the Great Depression—but events of this sort rarely enter accounts of family change. From the typical text on family systems in America, one would never grasp the implications of these event-structured conditions for the organization, adaptations, and change of families. Some relevant studies are available in the literature, from research on families in crisis to longitudinal studies of family units, but the findings have not brought much progress toward an understanding of family and intergenerational change (cf. Goode 1968). While the present study is severely limited as a study of family change, owing to archival resources, it does make a preliminary venture in this direction by tracing the impact of socioeconomic change to the family and life course.

Concepts in the Analytic Framework

The study relies most heavily upon five concepts: economic deprivation, crisis or problem situation, adaptation, linkage, and cohort. Our comparison of birth cohorts (mainly parents and children in the Oakland study) will utilize the concepts of crisis, adaptation, and linkage in an effort to assess and interpret the effects of economic deprivation. Such comparisons rest on the assumption that social change has differential consequences for persons of unlike age, which suggests that age variations are related to variations in the meaning of a situation, in adaptive potential or options, and thus in linkages between the event and the life course. We assume that children experienced the effects of economic deprivation primarily through family adaptations, for example, change in consumption and production activities.

Economic deprivation as decremental change. Economic deprivation refers to a decremental mode of economic change, not to persistent deprivation in chronic unemployment, public assistance, or poverty. By decremental change, we mean a loss in the economic status of a family between two points in time, between 1929 and the year most economic indicators reached their lowest point in time, the year of 1933. For most families, the lowest point did not remain a stable condition; as the economy improved in the last half of the 30s and the nation mobilized for war, family status generally improved accordingly.

However drastic, economic declines of a temporary nature present different implications for family and child than does a chronic state of deprivation. During the 1960s, the concept of deprivation drew attention to lower-class populations of children and, with few exceptions, tended to link social and economic forms of deprivation with pathological outcomes in personality development. If conditions in the lower strata are an extreme form of deprivation, their effects on the development of children are by no means uniformly negative (U.S. Dept. of HEW 1968). The association between these environmental factors and psychological impairment is well known, but deprivation may under some conditions eventuate in resourcefulness, adaptive skills, and mature responsibility. This outcome is more likely in the case of decremental change, which is not restricted to families in which parents and children generally rank low on adaptive resources—cultural, educational or intellectual, etc. The study of adaptive potential is enhanced when the field of investigation is broadened to include families from the middle class, and especially when their economic decline is due mainly to structural dislocations in the economy (as against deficiencies of the breadwinner). Such downward movement has occurred since 1950 through plant closings, the curtailment of divisions within large corporations, and general reductions in the employment of skilled men, but the most dramatic example is seen in the Great Depression. For the middle class, in particular, deprivational conditions were novel events which called for new adaptations in economic maintenance, family organization, and child socialization. The present study includes a large proportion of deprived families which were located in the middle class before the onset of hard times.

Crisis and adaptation. At first thought, crisis situations would seem to require little clarification; most of us have a rather clear idea of what the term refers to—social dislocation, disruption, strain. Crises are a continuing source of fascination to students of human society, and with good reason; they reveal the inner workings of group life, its unquestioned premises and problematic features, and arouse the adaptive impulse in social transformations. As Nesbit observes, "no substantial change in social group or organization, or in the structure of any form of social behavior, takes place except under the impact of events that cause crises" (1970, p. 328). And it is generally agreed that the Great Depression was a crisis of this magnitude in American life, or more generally in industrialized, Western societies; to study crises of this sort is to explore the incipient process of adaptation and change.[10] But what are the elements that make a crisis?

As applied in this study, crisis refers to a problematic disparity between the claims of a family in a situation and its control of outcomes or, more specifically, to a gap between socioeconomic needs and the ability to satisfy them.[11] Crises may thus arise when claims are elevated well beyond control potential and realities, or when changes in the situation markedly diminish control of outcomes. The former condition is likely to emerge in periods of growth and affluence, the latter in economic depressions. Assuming an initial stability in expectation, the breadwinner's loss of income would diminish his family's control options while increasing its economic needs.

Crisis situations are a fruitful point at which to study change since they challenge customary interpretations of reality and undermine established routines. The disruption of habitual ways of life produce new stimuli which elicit attention and arouse consciousness of self and others. Control over events becomes problematic when old ways are found lacking as means for dealing with social demands and satisfying basic needs or standards. Situations enter the crisis stage when they are interpreted or defined as such by a group or individual, and thus constitute a problem which calls for novel solutions and lines of adaptation. For the child in a family which has suddenly lost income and status, adaptation may involve redefinition of self and others, the restructuring or clarifications of goals, and the assumption of a new status or role.

Crises do not reside within the individual or situation but rather arise from interaction between an individual and a particular situation; they emerge at the interface of individual and social situation, of group and its social environment. A crisis situation thus refers to a type of *asynchrony* in the relationship between person or group and the environment. Adaptations to crisis situations are ways of dealing with resources and options that are employed in order to achieve control over the environment or life situation, to solve problems that arise from the disparity between claims and control of outcomes. For the economically deprived family, lines of adaptation would include a reduction in consumption of material goods, reliance on more labor intensive methods in securing goods and services, the employment of mother and older children.

Just as crises emerge from the interaction of individual or group and situation, so also do lines of adaptation. In terms of the individual, a problematic disparity between claims and control activates consciousness, attentional capacities, and methods of problem solving in the construction of new forms of adaptation. Environmental factors influence this process through social options (perceived and objective), adaptive requirements or situational demands, and support from others in shared resources and social reinforcement. The degree of choice or volition in the adaptational process is an empirical question. Under what conditions do actors have a particular choice among lines of action? These distinctions are discussed at greater length in chapter 2.

Two sets of individual characteristics bear upon the adaptational process: claims or expectations with respect to outcomes, and modes of adaptive potential. For parents and children in the present study, this potential refers mainly to resources, to their mobilization and coordination. Some years ago, Thomas observed that the mind operates through knowledge, which is based on "memory and the ability to compare a present situation with similar situations in the past and to revise our judgement and actions in view of the past experiences" (Volkhart 1951, p. 218). Life organization, in Thomas's analytic scheme, represents the totality of intellectual methods of controlling reality, as formulated within the individual's career. Life organization is thus constructed and reconstructed in the course of self-reflection at crisis points "when new experiences cannot be practically assimilated to the old ones" (Volkhart 1951, p. 157). In modern psychology, these methods of control would include the array of coping mechanisms, i.e., concentration, tolerance of ambiguity, empathy, objectivity, etc.[12]

Resilience and resourcefulness come to mind when we think of personal attributes that make a difference in a person's ability to cope with unusual problems and setbacks in life. From a developmental perspective, we could trace these attributes to past experiences in surmounting hardships. Experience of this sort is a major element of preparation for the demands of problem situations, and various studies have linked preparedness to effective adaptation. However, the crucial factor in such experience is whether it is marked by failure or growth through successful management (see Levine and Scotch 1970, esp. chap. 10). Success experiences across different situations develop a repertoire of adaptive acts, an array of skills enabling resourcefulness and flexibility. Resilience connotes an image of the competent self, consisting of personal worth, of self-confidence, inner security, and self-control (Smith, in Clausen 1968). In chapter 2 we shall view the mental ability and class position of parents and children as two general indicators of their adaptive potential in situations of family change.

In this study we are interested in the responses of both individuals and groups to socioeconomic change in the Depression; in the adaptation of parents and children, on the one hand, and of the family unit, on the other. Over the years, research has identified two general dimensions of a family's adaptive potential in a crisis situation: adaptability and integration. An example is Robert Angell's study (1936) of middle-class families in the Depression.[13] Selected components of family adaptability, outlined in Reuben Hill's pioneering *Families under Stress* (1949) roughly correspond to elements of adaptive potential

11

that we specified on the individual level. These include flexibility of commitment to physical standards of living, flexibility of role relationships, and success in meeting prior crises. The picture becomes more complex when we note that nuclear families with children are composed of three units or subsystems: conjugal, parent-child, and sibling. Each unit has its own requirements, even though interdependent, which suggests that adaptations to economic hardship may vary widely in effectiveness across these domains within the same family. As Hill observes, "there is no guarantee that pairs which have worked out a satisfactory marital relationship are competent to assume the responsibilities of parenthood with its challenging troubles and sicknesses, its jealousies and competitions, and its heavy obligations" (Hill 1949, p. 321). We shall give special attention to adaptations in marriage and parent-child relations.

When we speak of the consequences of adaptation we refer to outcomes that are evaluated according to criteria which pertain to the welfare of a group or individual. Since any line of action impinges on the welfare of the actor *and* various others, these evaluative frameworks can lead to markedly different assessments of consequences. Consider the effects of a mother's employment. How does this activity bear upon the family's economic welfare, the harmony or stability of the marriage, child rearing, the psychological well-being of the mother herself? In a value climate which did not favor the employment of mothers, the benefits of earnings could be offset by greater marital turmoil and the aggravated emotional state of the unemployed husband. Economic benefits can be viewed as the *intended* consequence of a mother's entry into the labor market; she seeks work in order to help meet family needs, not to gain greater influence in marital or family affairs or to disparage her husband as a breadwinner.

Under the compelling requirements of economic survival, rationales for adaptation are apt to be highly restricted in scope and time perspective.[14] Scope refers to the breadth of considerations at a point in time, such as a narrow interpretation of the effects of aid from relatives and public assistance. An emergency situation implies that short-run considerations outweigh the potential consequences of action for the future welfare of the family or individual. This characterization of adaptations to change (in which the intended effects are narrowly defined within the present) broadens the field of unintended outcomes and takes issue with a prominent interpretation of social change in child socialization: at points of change, the socialization of children is altered through parental adaptations to the anticipated future of their offspring.

Inkeles argues that "parents who have experienced extreme social change seek to raise their children differently from the way in which they were brought up, purposively adapting their child rearing practices to train children better suited to meet life in the changed world as the parents see it."[15] This perspective assumes a high degree of future awareness, rationality, and choice in parental behavior, and thus seems most applicable to situations in which family survival is not at stake. In a survival context, the unintended consequences of family responses to immediate needs play an important part in structuring a child's experience. Change in the division of labor and authority pattern may be adaptive for the family as a whole in the Depression, in terms of survival, and yet ultimately handicap the life prospects of children; what is adaptive for the social unit in a crisis situation may not be so for the lives of individual members. As we shall see, the socialization environment and the response of parents to children in deprived situations during the 30s had much less to do with their anticipation of life in the future than with the immediacy of survival requirements.

Linking socioeconomic change to life experience and personality. In this study, we shall formulate analytic models which specify linkages between socioeconomic change in the Depression and its psychosocial effects within the life course. On the theoretical level, linkages provide answers to the question of why economic change has particular effects; they offer an interpretation of the relationship, an account of the process or mechanisms through which social change influences personality and behavior.[16]

To illustrate the construction of theoretical linkages, let us consider the hypothetical relation between the economic deprivation of a family unit in the Depression and the marital orientation of daughters. We assume that economic deprivation fosters a relatively early interest in marriage among girls through interpersonal strains in the family and domestic socialization. Two questions are posed by this analytic model; does family deprivation have such an effect on marital orientation, and is it mediated by the specified intervening variables? Another question concerns the relative importance of the two proposed linkages; does economic deprivation affect marital interest mainly through family strains or through domestic influences in the household? To identify the particular relevance of these global constructs for orientation to marriage, we convert each to more specific and concrete manifestations. Family strain is thus phrased as marital conflict and emotional estrangement from father; domestic socialization as mother's centrality in the family, the daughter's role in the household, and lack of parental support for the daughter's higher education. This procedure in formu-

The Depression
Experience

lating conceptual bridges between antecedent and consequent variables will be employed repeatedly in the analysis, as we draw upon extant theories and move beyond them.

There is little evidence of these bridges in conceptualizations of the Depression experience in human lives. In the case of a hypothesized association between family deprivation in the 30s and adult psychological health, we are left with questions of why and how, of theoretical specification and empirical test. To interpret this relationship, we need to specify and investigate the intervening linkages, which undoubtedly include aspects of adult experience. Deficiencies of this sort are especially common in speculation which links the work values of men to early experiences in the Depression.[17] A proponent of this "theory" might argue that economic hardship and unemployment increased the value of work and job security in the minds of young boys through exposure to parental hardships and generalized deprivation in the community. Even if data in the 30s show value differences along this line, can we assume that they will persist into the adult years? If some boys in a deprived group enter white collar careers and others end up in manual jobs, is it likely that these differences in worklife will make *no* difference in the relation between family background and adult values?

We have organized the analysis along the lines of a multistage approach, beginning with an assessment of the most immediate effects of economic deprivation, in terms of family adaptations, and concluding with adult outcomes of the Depression experience and their linkages to economic change. Outcomes of the first part of the analysis thus become potential linkages in the model as we move to the adult years.

The most general analytic model defines family adaptation and conditions as linkages between economic deprivation and the child. These linkages, which are discussed more fully in chapter 2, include: change in the division of labor—the necessity for new forms of economic maintenance alters the domestic and economic roles of family members, shifting responsibilities to mother and the older children; change in family relationships—father's loss of economic status and resulting adaptations in family maintenance increase the relative power of mother, reduce the level and effectiveness of parental control, and lessen the attractiveness of father as a model; and social strains in the family—status ambiguity, conflicts, and emotional distress are a consequence of diminished resources, loss or impairment of parents, and inconsistency in the status of the family and its members.

This approach will generate complex networks as we trace out the effects of socioeconomic change to aspects of family life and beyond; multiple lines of analysis branch out in different directions. Consider the implications of a change in the division of labor in which the mother seeks employment, the daughter assumes a major role in the household, and the eldest son acquires part-time work. Each of these emergent activities presents an array of implications for parents, children, and the family unit as a whole. Mother's entry into the labor force has potential consequences for the household responsibilities of other family members, for the balance of power in marriage, and the parental role model. To manage such complexity, we shall break networks of relationships into analytic segments and employ multivariate procedures.

In the course of this study, the concept of linkage will serve a useful purpose if it but reminds us that an association between variables at T_1 and T_2 is little more than a point of departure in the research process; that we are still faced with the problem of accounting for the relationship. In some cases, alternative interpretations will not have the benefit of an empirical test, owing to data limitations. Or the data may permit only a rough indication of intervening conditions. Even so, there is a discipline in linking constructs, conceptually and empirically, which alerts us to an essential dimension of the research task.

Cohort and subgroup comparisons. Three group distinctions enter into our assessment of economic change in family adaptations and life outcomes: birth cohorts, status groups within a particular cohort, and economic sectors of status groups. Cohorts and their components are associated with particular life experiences, opportunities, and resources which bear upon the deprivational experience of individuals in the Depression.[18]

As members of the same family unit, parents and children in the Oakland sample would obviously share many situations in the Depression, though not from the same vantage point, owing to generational differences in childhood environment, career, and life stage in 1930. Each generation is distinguished by the historical logic and shared experience of growing up in a different time period, and by the correlated activities, resources, and obligations of their life stage. Particularly in times of rapid change, individuals are thought to acquire a distinct outlook and philosophy from the historical world, defined by their birthdate, an outlook that reflects lives lived interdependently in a particular historical context.

In times of drastic change, the history and career stage of a cohort shape situational interpretations and lines of adaptation. As each cohort encounters an historical event, whether depression or prosperity, it "is distinctively marked by the career stage it occupies" (Ryder 1965, p. 846). While the Oakland parents were directly implicated in the responsibilities and shame of family hardships, their children were too young to experience personal failure in economic roles, or to assume major obligations in this area. For the latter group, adaptive options and vulnerability to family deprivation were structured by its age status, social and developmental. At the time of maximum hardship in the early 30s, the Oakland children were well beyond the dependency stage of early childhood, with its consequences for intellectual and emotional development, and they reached the age of majority after opportunities had improved through nationwide mobilization for war. Persons born ten years before the Oakland children would have entered the labor force during the worst phase of the economic collapse, while the welfare of persons in the 1929 cohort would have been entirely dependent on conditions in their families. These differences clearly suggest the risk of generalizing across cohorts on the Depression experience.

In cohort analysis, it is recognized that a specific stimulus condition in an historical period tends to vary in its effect across different subsets of the age group, defined by class, sex, ethnicity, etc. Karl Mannheim has referred to these subsets as generation units (1952, pp. 276–322). On class variation, we know that middle-class families which have never encountered hard times are especially susceptible to the psychic trauma of joblessness and loss of property. They are most likely to define unemployment and income losses as stressful, and "to overestimate the hardships which they define as threats to their social position and aspirations of their children" (Hansen and Hill 1964, p. 803). But one cannot assume that a particular stimulus has similar intensity and duration among even a majority of the members of a specific status group. Available records show a wide range of deprivational experiences among middle-class families in the Depression and even among the families of unemployed men. Since behavior is a function of both group or individual and situation, their properties must be included in any assessment of adaptations to economic deprivation.

This study focuses on intragroup variation, in contrast to the traditional intercohort model; on deprivational categories of families and individuals within class groups of a specific birth cohort. The analysis is structured around four groups of parents and children, defined by social class in 1929 and relative income loss between 1929 and 1933. Within the middle and working class, we shall compare the life experience and personality of persons who were brought up in relatively nondeprived and deprived families. The income loss of nondeprived families averaged slightly less than 20 percent, which is roughly equivalent to the decline in cost of living up to 1932. Most deprived families in both social classes suffered economic losses which exceeded half of their 1929 income.

The children selected for the study were born during the first two years of the twenties, were preadolescents and adolescents during the Depression decade, and graduated from high school just before World War II. All of the children selected for the study were white, most were Protestant, and approximately three-fifths came from middle-class homes. The group of nonmanual families was almost entirely working class (as against lower class). Three-fourths of the families were intact throughout the Depression and were headed by native-born parents. The median IQ of the children, based on an average of scores on the 1933 and 1938 Stanford-Binet, was approximately 113.

Willingness of parents to cooperate and their stated intention to remain in the city in the foreseeable future were the primary criteria used in selecting the subjects and their families for the study. While these procedures are likely to produce some bias toward the selection of middle-class families, a comparison of the Oakland Growth Study sample with cross-section samples of children in the junior and senior high schools attended by the subjects showed no significant percentage difference in this direction (see table A–33; note that all tables numbered with the prefix "A" are to be found in Appendix A). Approximately 53 to 63 percent of the children in these schools were middle-class. All of the children attended the same junior high school and with few exceptions they also entered the same high school. In the early thirties, the junior high school served approximately 1,000 children and was staffed by 38 teachers. The larger high school, with some 1,900 students and 92 staff members, was primarily geared to college preparatory studies.

During the 1930s, data on the children were obtained from staff observations and ratings of social and emotional behavior, from self-report questionnaires and teachers, and from interviews with mothers.[19] One hundred and forty-five members of the adolescent sample were contacted in at least one of three adult follow-ups. The first follow-up (1953–54) entailed a series of interviews, personality inventories, and a psychiatric assessment. The second (1957–58) involved primarily a series of lengthy interviews, averaging twelve hours. The third (1964) included interviews and a mailed questionnaire. From these data, a life history protocol was constructed up to 1958 for each member of the study. No differences were found between the adolescent and the adult samples in IQ, family social class in 1929, ethnicity, and household structure. A more complete description of the sample and major sources of data are presented in the appendix.

Socioeconomic Conditions in Oakland and the Nation

Interpretations of the analysis must take into account the degree to which socioeconomic conditions in Oakland were comparable to conditions in other urban centers and areas of the country. Even though children in the Oakland study closely resembled their schoolmates in family characteristics, results from the analysis would have very limited generality if socioeconomic conditions in Oakland and the surrounding Bay area were substantially less severe than in other cities. Given the systemic character of the economy, it is not surprising that economic declines in major industries were interdependent and extended across state boundaries. Thus we find that New York and California were among those states with the highest rate of unemployment. However, the full brunt of the Depression was felt approximately six months later in California than among the industrial states of the Northeast (Huntington 1939, p. 7).

Oakland is situated on the east shore of San Francisco Bay and is part of a densely populated area composed of Berkeley on the north and a number of smaller communities on the south. In 1929, the city was a rapidly growing metropolis with a population of 284,000, serving as a major transportation and distribution center for the Bay Area and the West. The civilian labor force was equally divided among service, distribution, and conversion industries. A total of 126 national industries in the city had 48,000 employees on the payroll in 1929. Shipbuilding, utilities, rail and air transportation facilities were prominent employers. Just prior to the Depression, the vice-president of the American Trust Company in the city observed that "industrially, Oakland has ranked among the three fastest growing cities of this country." This picture of economic health changed dramatically in the Depression.

On most indicators of the national economy, the lowest point in the first half of the thirties was reached during the first months of 1933, and this was true of California and Oakland as well. Thereafter a steady rise occurred in employment, commerce, and industrial activity up to the sudden but less prolonged decline of 1937–38. For the nation as a whole, employment in manufacturing industries had dropped to 55 percent by 1933 (1926 = 100); in California the comparable figure was 54 percent (Huntington 1939).

Using available unemployment data, a study sponsored by a research group in social economics at the University of California estimated that approximately one-third of the normally employed in the United States were unemployed in 1933. By the latter part of 1934, nearly a fourth of this group was still unemployed. The unemployed category included persons out of a job, able to work, and looking for a job on the day preceding the enumerator's call, and persons who were temporarily laid off from their job. In California and Oakland, approximately 30 percent of the normally employed were out of work in 1932. And between 1928 and 1933, the average number of families receiving publicly funded relief in Alameda county, of which Oakland is a part, increased sevenfold. Comparable increases were reported for Los Angeles and San Francisco.

Another indication of the relative status of Oakland in the Depression was obtained by comparing the city with selected metropolitan centers on three indicators of economic conditions: the number of building permits issued, as a measure of construction activity; net sales in retail trade, an index of commercial activity; and employment in retail trade. The six cities included in the comparison were San Francisco, Los Angeles, Detroit, Cleveland, Atlanta, and Philadelphia. On all three indexes, the economic decline between 1929 and 1933 in Oakland was comparable to the average decline in the other cities (see table A–1). In 1933, the number of building permits issued was only 40 percent in the city of Oakland. The decline was greater in Detroit, Cleveland, and Philadelphia, but the average loss for all of the comparison cities was very close to the Oakland figure (42 percent).

An upswing in construction activity between 1933 and 1937 was more pronounced in Oakland than in the other major cities, although no differences in recovery appear in retail sales and employment. Net sales in retail trade averaged 50 percent for the six comparison cities in 1933, as compared to 51 percent for Oakland. Employment in retail trade reached a low point of 70 percent in 1933 for the comparison cities, and did not differ appreciably from the decline in Oakland. Overall it appears that Oakland is within the middle range on these measures of economic conditions. Economic decline was more severe in Detroit and Cleveland, and less so in San Francisco and Atlanta.

The most appropriate index for comparing the economic loss of families in the longitudinal study, in Oakland and in the country as a whole, is median family income. As noted earlier, economic deprivation in the Oakland study is based on relative loss in reported family income from 1929 through 1933, the low point on economic indicators. In 1929, the median income of families in the sample was $3,179, in comparison to $1,911 in 1933—a decline of slightly less than 40 percent. We were unable to obtain data on family income for Oakland, and precise data for the country were not available before 1935.

The Depression
Experience

According to rough estimates, the average family income for American families in 1929 was $2,300; this figure dropped by nearly 40 percent to approximately $1,500 in 1933. A similar decline was found by comparing national income data from unaudited taxpayer returns in 1929 and 1933, although the average figures for each year ($3,156 and $1,989) are substantially inflated by the exclusion of individuals who reported no net income in these years.[20] If the percentage loss of income shown in these data is reliable, economic decline in the Oakland sample does not appear to be out of line with the average loss among families in the country as a whole.

Some evidence of citizen attitudes and reactions concerning economic conditions in Oakland is found in the more popular views expressed in letters to the local newspaper. One such viewpoint expressed the belief that city employees should receive substantial cuts in wages and salaries to bring them in line with the economic status of the average resident: civil service employees were living high off public funds, teachers' salaries were too high, and firemen and policemen should voluntarily take reductions in their wages. On the other side of the issue, City Hall was a frequent target of abuse for its efforts to economize through the reduction of funds for schools and public services.

In view of these conditions, the attitudes and perceptions of some high officials in City Hall strangely reflect an entirely different world. Concerning the economic health of the city in 1933, the mayor observed that "Oakland is one of the few American cities to have remained completely solvent throughout this period of economic strife." Congruent with this image is a local history of Oakland during the Depression which presents a more positive description of socio-economic conditions than is warranted by statistics collected by state and federal agencies.[21] Given the investment of city officials in a prosperous community and optimistic future, it would not be surprising if they selectively used observations and statistics to construct this image. Denial of economic realities and human suffering was one of the more common political responses during the early years of the Depression. In their classic study of a Midwestern community, *Middletown in Transition* (1937), the Lynds describe the tenacious commitment of business and political leaders to an optimistic future and their insensitivity to the physical want and suffering of severely deprived residents. Though statistics on Oakland and other cities in the Depression are both scarce and unsatisfactory on a number of counts, there is no evidence that economic conditions in Oakland were out of line with those in other major cities.

Researching the
Past:
A Cautionary Note

A study based on archival data inevitably faces a certain disparity and degree of tension between ideal models and possibilities in the research process. The problem at hand establishes a set of requirements for suitable data and features of the research design, but the investigator's options are constrained by decisions and actions in the past. Archival data are givens which have a tendency to be not quite what the researcher would like. To be sure, history, as well as longitudinal research, could be more adequate or accurate than it is *if* "people would only take more care and leave appropriate records of their conduct,"[22] though appropriateness itself is historically bounded. Criteria change with intellectual cycles and social problems, along with methodological preferences. Given these circumstances, there is virtue in data collection whose scope leaves open a wide range of possibilities for research.

The Oakland Growth Study was not designed in any explicit sense for research on the effects of economic deprivation in the Great Depression, though staff members were very much aware of these effects in the lives of parents and their offspring. The most crucial and fortunate aspect of the data archive, in terms of the present study, was the availability of socioeconomic information for 1929 and 1933. Of all years in the Depression, these two were the most important for a comparative assessment of economic change.

From its inception, the Oakland study focused more on the biological and psychological aspects of human development than on sociocultural phenomena, and yet the files contained substantial information on family life, school and social experiences, and on the larger milieu of the 30s. As of 1962, most of this information had not been coded or processed for statistical analysis. From the standpoint of family life in the Depression, the archive's major deficiency is the lack of information on fathers. They were not regarded by behavioral scientists in the 30s as a key figure in socialization, and they appear in the present study only as perceived by other family members; no data were directly obtained from them.

Overall, the primary sources of information include staff observers, the subjects themselves, and their mothers, classmates, and teachers. As one might expect, research procedures in the study provide a historical portrait of the "state of the art" at the time. Study participants were not recruited from a probability sampling frame, and the sample size is modest at best; little attention was given to sampling and the problems associated with generalization. On the positive side, repeated use of identical instruments permitted the construction of relatively stable measurements of a number of key variables for the first and latter half of the Depression decade. These instruments are described in detail in Appendix B, along with an evaluation of sources of error and modes of statistical analysis.

Other sample problems are inherent in the design of long-term longitudinal studies. These include sample attrition, and effects of study participation. We have noted that attrition between the adolescent and adult years did not produce a difference between the family characteristics and intelligence of the study sample at these two points in time. However, continued participation in the study may well have had some effect on the subjects, and there is no satisfactory way to assess this impact. Despite these various limitations, the Oakland study offers greater resources and options than other sources of data on children of the Depression and their lives in adulthood.

At first thought, there appears to be no reason why information which is missing in the data archive of a longitudinal study could not be obtained from the adult subjects through either retrospective or contemporaneous reports. This option is frequently not available, however, and for a number of important reasons. The researcher in a long-term project, such as the Oakland study, does not have the privilege to collect the data he needs when he needs it, unless his plans coincide with the overall plan for data collection. Unregulated requests for data would thoroughly disrupt orderly data collection and exhaust the goodwill of the subjects. The interests of the individual researcher should be subordinated to the long-term interests of the project. This necessary limitation is clearly illustrated by the following conflict of interests. In the present study, a comparative analysis of persons from the Depression and postwar generations would have been possible with appropriate data on the subjects' offspring. However, such contact was in direct conflict with a major follow-up that was scheduled in the near future.

If we could return to the 1920s and design a study of families and children in the light of current knowledge and resources, we would employ probability procedures in sampling and a panel design which extends from the pre-Depression era through the 1930s and follows the children into their adult years. A panel design would enable both pre- and postmeasurements, relative to conditions in the Depression, and thereby facilitate causal analyses of family and individual change resulting from economic deprivation. Despite valiant efforts to promote well-designed studies of families and children in the Depression, the

Crisis and Adaptation

best-known studies are small in scale, were launched after 1929, and used selective, unrepresentative samples. Research from the Depression era does not include a single study which satisfactorily incorporates the above features, and even the available demographic data on socioeconomic conditions are deficient by contemporary standards. Nevertheless, an investigation of human lives and experiences in this extraordinary period of history has no satisfactory alternative to the adaptation of existing records for research purposes, however limited, using ingenuity and proper caution. The moral for the secondary analyst is "to make the best of what we have" (Hyman 1972, p. 281).[23]

Historical accounts of human adaptations to crisis situations are generally distinguished by their emphasis on either a narrative chronology of events and action or analysis within a conceptual framework. Both strategies have made substantial contributions toward understanding the past, and each generates knowledge or data which is invaluable for the other, though it is difficult to satisfy both aims in a single work. The flow of events is interrupted, for example, when the author steps back to "take stock" and then proceeds with the narrative. Indeed, the sacrifice may be such that neither aim is adequately met. First priority in the following account is given to a comparative analysis of children who grew up in relatively nondeprived and deprived families within the middle and working classes; and especially to conditions which link their social experience, personality, and life course to economic deprivation and class origin in the 30s. But we also intend to place the analysis within the historical context and the sequential pattern of events in the life course of the Oakland cohort. Hopefully, this approach will tell a story of how the lives of these Americans were shaped by the Depression experience.

Human adaptations in crisis situations have been researched in a large number of studies which suggest hypotheses that are directly relevant to the life situation of the Depression children (see chapter 2). But we are less concerned with the test of key hypotheses than with the overall pattern of results, with their direction, size, consistency, and overall configuration. In small longitudinal samples, the meaningfulness of results is especially dependent on this overview. Statistical tests will be used at points, but only as one criterion, among others, for evaluating differences and relationships. Even findings of borderline significance in small samples may yield challenging clues and problems for future study.

The value of this research can be assessed from at least two vantage points: as a contribution to our understanding of social change, expressed through family change and intergenerational relations generally, and as a source of insight into family life and individual adaptations in the Great Depression and the life consequences of such adaptations for veterans of this historic epoch. Given the best of all possible worlds, the results will make contributions to our knowledge in both areas, though failure to break new ground on the human effects of economic deprivation would not be fatal as long as we gained some understanding of these effects in the Depression experience. The Depression generations have been a major force in the profound changes that have occurred in American society since the 1930s; yet their varied experiences in the 1930s are largely unknown, and no study has related these experiences to personality formation and adult careers. Continuities and contrasts between parents and their Depression-reared offspring in family relations and values may be an important factor in understanding contemporary intergenerational relations and family change.

More generally, we find that most research on the psychosocial effects of economic deprivation is based on cross-sectional samples of lower-class populations. By focusing on extreme, persistent deprivation and its correlation with disability, we have ignored the social-psychological problem of downward mobility from the upper classes, whether temporary or not. The present study of decremental change in the Depression includes a sizable proportion of children from families which were located in the middle class before the Depression, and directs attention to adaptive resources in the relation between deprivation and human development, as indexed by class position and intelligence. Downward mobility, unemployment, and economic loss are experienced by significant numbers of high-status families in contemporary society and have become serious problems in some areas during the economic recession of the late 60s and early 70s.[24] Even voluntary career changes among the highly skilled occasionally entail substantial economic loss and stringent austerity. Results from this longitudinal investigation should be of value in broadening present knowledge concerning the psychosocial effects of parental career change on children, and the conditions associated with specific deprivational effects in childhood and the adult years, whether pathogenic or growth-promoting.[25]

A valuable outcome of any research is its heuristic contribution, and this is especially true of studies in relatively uncharted domains. In these contexts, longitudinal projects become a valuable source of hypotheses and are uniquely suited, as Kessen has noted,[26] for posing fresh perspectives and opening up new areas for fruitful study. These outcomes are perhaps the most appropriate measure of the present study's contribution to an understanding of human adaptation to socioeconomic change.

2

Adaptations to Economic Deprivation

A crisis is a crisis precisely because men cannot act effectively together. . . . Some emergency action is required.
Tamotsu Shibutani
Improvised News

Economic change in the Depression produced a crisis for many families, and called out a wide range of adaptive responses. According to available records, deprived families generally followed a course of adjustment from crisis to disorientation or disorganization and then to partial recovery through new modes of action and eventual stabilization (see Bakke 1940; Hansen and Hill 1964). The lines of adaptation worked out by parents in turn impinged upon the experiences of their children.

As a point of departure for the current research, we shall first examine theory and findings from other studies which have focused on the adaptation of families to depression and deprivation. Particular attention is given to the division of labor in economic maintenance, to marital power and parent-child relations, and to their implications for the family experience of children. The latter half of the chapter relates status change to personality and achievement, and explores the role of adaptive potential in mediating the effects of economic hardship on psychological well-being.

Deprivation and Adaptations in the Family

Economic deprivation tends to generate pressures for change in three areas: in family maintenance, in the perceived status or position of the family, and in the breadwinner's status within the family. The story of family maintenance in the Depression can be expressed as three modes of adaptation: family needs or claims, consumption (the purchase of goods and services), and economic resources (earnings, savings, property, financial aid, etc.). The initial problem of economic deprivation concerned the disparity between income on the one hand, and family needs and its customary level of consumption on the other. Some families could maintain their financial status, despite loss of the breadwinner's earnings, by relying upon savings, loans, and the new earnings of other family members. But as the economic situation worsened, pressure increased to bring needs and consumption in line with financial realities. One consequence of this accommodation is reflected in change toward a more labor-intensive household economy; more goods and services were provided through the labor of family members—family gardens, canning, making clothes, laundering, etc.

Status interests in expenditures were generally subordinated to the material needs of the family as economic hardships became more severe. In a New England community, the adjustments of unemployed workers and their families were found to be correlated with a reality orientation toward the present and diminished comparisons between the former way of life and immediate possibilities (Bakke 1940, chap. 7). During the initial phase of unemployment, these families generally looked to the past and defined their situation in terms of it. Only minor recreational costs and luxuries were pared. As supplementary earnings and other sources of income proved insufficient for family needs, the past receded before the emergencies of the present. Basic needs were redefined, and expenditures were structured accordingly.

The higher the status of the family before economic decline, the more status considerations entered into decisions on the allocation of resources: the "higher the climb," the harder it was for families to accept the reality of status loss. Even among blue-collar families, studies show that "families whose previous standard of living had been relatively high, who had a concept of themselves as a 'high-class family—maintaining standards, codes, and responsibilities appropriate to that status,' fought most energetically to postpone any departure from that status" (Bakke 1940, p. 237).[1] This was attempted in part by withholding information from friends and neighbors, and by maintaining a social front through status expenditures, for example, painting the house, buying shutters, heating all rooms when friends were expected.

Social defenses are symptomatic of an attachment to "the way things were." Comparisons with past gratifications and standards only served to intensify discontent in deprived families and made readjustments more difficult and prolonged. Readjustments among workers' families were "attended by real frustration" as present possibilities were compared with the way things used to be. Discontent became less acute with the passage of time as the urgency of present problems directed attention toward "today's opportunities rather than yesterday's achievements" (Bakke 1940, p. 175).

Income and occupational change produced various forms of inconsistency in the status of families; of the three major sources of family prestige—the husband's income, occupation, and education—only the latter (along with the wife's education) was not subject to downward shifts in the Depression. Loss of both income and occupational position thus produced discrepancies between past and present, and with level of education.[2] Not infrequently, college-educated men were forced to take jobs that were well below their qualifications in order to support the family. If income and occupation are viewed as rewards for the investment required in obtaining an education, we might expect some degree of anger and frustration among men when rewards fall well below common expectations on outcomes. However, widespread deprivation in the 30s may have lowered expectations as men and their families became aware that their misfortune was shared by countless other families and as they attributed this state to external circumstances.

Another implication of status inconsistency is the ambiguity of the family's social position. Education, income, and occupation all yielded varied impressions of status relative to other families. Economic misfortune could be used by neighbors to evaluate a family's position, in lieu of the higher educational and occupational level of the father which formed the self-evaluation of family members. In view of the relatively greater status investments of middle-class families, we expect feelings of dissatisfaction and frustration to be more strongly associated with economic deprivation in this stratum than in the working class (see chapter 3).

While some degree of inconsistency in the status of families represents a common structural feature of industrial societies, we do not as yet fully understand its implications for family life. Recent empirical assessments have led some analysts to regard status inconsistency in contemporary American society as a "trivial" factor in preferences on social change; inconsistency adds little to the explanation beyond the main effects of status factors.[3] If this judgment applies to the present age, it is surely less applicable to periods of drastic change, such as the Great Depression. Status inconsistency is an outstanding characteristic of drastic socioeconomic change, and the nature of this change is likely to make this state a conscious matter. Sudden dislocations generally heighten consciousness; they are likely to become a problem with personal and social significance. This is an important consideration if we assume that status incongruence makes a difference in family life when it is perceived as a problem.

Economic deprivation and related changes in father's status had direct consequences for two areas of family life in the Depression: the division of labor in family maintenance; and family relationships, including relative power in husband-wife and parent-child relationships. A heavy loss of income increased dependence on alternative

Adaptations to
Economic Deprivation

forms of family support and reinforced labor-intensive aspects of the household economy. Both of these developments are conducive to the greater involvement of mothers and children in economic and domestic activities.

The Division of
Labor in Family
Maintenance

Role failure on the part of the husband and father tends to shift economic responsibilities to other family members. As economic conditions worsened in the 30s, employment became more compelling to women and acceptable to their husbands, despite hostile sentiment in the community (Bakke 1940, p. 184).[4] In the working class, women's place was in the home, except in extreme emergencies, and prolonged unemployment of the male breadwinner created such an emergency. Wives of laboring men sought employment when savings were nearly depleted and credit extended beyond acceptable limits, though few did so with small children in the home.

If economic conditions led to maternal employment and a curtailment of paid services, they would also favor the involvement of children in domestic roles, in addition to economic resourcefulness outside the home. We suspect that contributions to the family welfare were structured along sex-role lines, with boys specializing in economic roles and girls carrying domestic chores. Available evidence suggests that challenging demands were placed upon older children in the Depression and that they frequently responded with unusual effort and competence. From studies of crisis situations, we find that role change on the part of the parents sometimes initiates a compensatory change of roles among children which serves to maintain the family (see Perry et al. 1956). Children are known to have assumed major responsibilities that were formerly handled by a parent who was incapacitated or who had regressed to a childlike state. In chapter 4 we shall compare the roles of children in the household economy of nondeprived and deprived families within the middle and working class.

Conditions in the Depression denied some young people the protected, nonresponsible experience of adolescence by extending adultlike tasks downward to childhood. As Albert Cohen recalls, there were no "teenagers" in the Depression.[5] In more affluent times, adolescence is vulnerable to an entirely different encroachment, the upward extension of childlike submission and dependence to the adult years. As surplus labor in a consumption-oriented society, contemporary youth are excluded from productive roles during a prolonged stage of preadult dependency. Both an extended adulthood and childhood have their costs, but the former condition did at least involve the young in valued tasks and a cause beyond the self. Children from economically deprived families were an important factor in the household economy, according to available evidence; their labor and monetary contributions were needed. Moreover, juvenile delinquency was not more prevalent in the Depression, but less so than in subsequent, more affluent decades (see Glaser and Rice 1959). In some respects at least, it is perhaps true that "affluence can destroy the young as easily as poverty."[6]

Beyond their contribution to family welfare, domestic tasks and work experience are commonly regarded as valuable for developing favored habits and attitudes, including resourcefulness, responsibility, and self-reliance. Implied by the practice of assigning household duties to a child is the assumption that important lessons are gained from this experience; "habits of industry, order, and regard for the rights and ideas of others, and the fundamental habit of subordinating his activities to the general interest of the household."[7] In the scientific literature on child rearing, participation in domestic tasks is described as responsibility training,[8] while folk theories tend to compare the liabilities of idleness to the virtues of work—self-reliance, practice in managing money, and social responsibility. Reliable empirical support for these benefits is exceedingly scarce,[9] and this is partly due to the variable nature of task experience. If industry and responsibility are a product of tasks that are both demanding and meaningful, we would expect these qualities to be relatively common among children from deprived families, especially in the middle class. Moreover, work experience outside the home requires some measure of independence from parental control.

*Marital Decision-
Making and Family
Relations*

In normal times and crises, the occupational success of men is generally related to their power and status in the family. Wife dominance is most prevalent in the lower class, where the economic status of men is precarious and unrewarding, and such conditions were common in the Depression (see, e.g., Scanzoni 1970). When father's authority in the family derived mainly from cultural traditions or affection among family members, it was most likely to survive economic failure. In the only study which systematically explored the causal effects of unem-

Adaptations to
Economic Deprivation

ployment, the wife's attitude was a determining factor in status change (Komarovsky 1940).[10] Male authority based on affection or tradition was distinguished from authority supported by economic productivity and fear (utilitarian) in a sample of forty-nine families in the New York area. Where authority was based on affection, the husband's influence was upheld by personal qualities and harmonious relations. Tradition as a basis of authority referred to the wife's belief that family leadership is the husband's right and responsibility. Unemployment proved to be a significant cause of authority loss among husbands only in families in which the wife, prior to the Depression, held utilitarian attitudes. This result corresponds with differences in male authority in the lower-class families of two minority groups. Male authority in the Mexican-American household is supported by cultural tradition; it is the right of the husband and father to exercise authority. Male authority lacks traditional normative support in the black, lower-class family and is consequently highly vulnerable to economic circumstances.[11]

Given the interdependence of family roles, change in conjugal relations tends to have corresponding effects on parent-child interaction. This is shown by findings obtained in two studies of families in the Depression (Komarovsky 1940, and Bakke 1940).[12] In both cases, father's loss of power and status in the marital relationship was found to be related to a corresponding loss in relations with children. Fathers in wife-dominant families seldom maintained their authority over children. The upgrading of mother's position in deprived families generally increased her salience in the attitudes of children.

In previewing two major lines of family adaptation for the subsequent analysis, we have emphasized the potential role of these adjustments in mediating the effects of economic conditions on children in the Oakland study. We linked the involvement of girls in domestic tasks and of boys in gainful employment to the requirements of economic deprivation for family maintenance and then to personal characteristics which have been attributed to these task experiences. Likewise, power relations between husband and wife were related to conditions of family support on the one hand, and to parent-child relations on the other.

There is yet another general link between deprivation and the experience of children which is formed by the social strains of family change, by the resource costs, inconsistencies, and conflicts associated with economic loss and status adjustments. Social change alters routine relations in which the self is anchored and defined, making both interaction and social bonds problematic.

Status Change in Personality and Achievement

Since children are assigned the status of their family, any change in this position affects their status and identity relative to peers and other adults. Along with achievements and future prospects, family status is clearly a major determinant of their life situations and rewards. As noted earlier, economic deprivation in the Depression created disparities among factors which position families in the social structure, and these differences were inconsistent with normative expectations.

The most obvious discrepancies occurred between economic status before and after income loss, between income and occupational status of father, and between income and the educational status of father and mother. Conditions of this sort may have impinged on children in at least three ways: in the resulting status ambiguity and tension between and within families; in status frustration or discontent among parents; and in change in the relative attractiveness of parents as role models. In the world of peers, economic decline produced a highly visible clash between the past and present status of children by curtailing expenditures for clothing and recreation.

Status inconsistency fosters consciousness of self and other by undermining expectations and evaluations that structure interaction and define the self. Behavior becomes self-conscious in situations of conflict which arouse attitudes in the self that are activated in others.[13] In order to appreciate the consequences of status incongruence for coordinated action, it is best to start with the occupant of a single status. The actor's position structures the expectations that others have of him, that he has of himself, and that he has regarding the appropriate behavior of others toward him. A relatively stable position, uncomplicated by conflicting statuses, defines an expectable, routine situation. Interaction is nonproblematic, and self-identity reflects the integration and coherence of the environment.

Multiple statuses do not adversely affect the orientational function of expectations as long as they are congruent, but when change places the individual in a position of status incongruence, he presents conflicting stimuli to others and to himself. Role complementarity breaks down in this context and "feeds back into the awareness of the participants in the form of tension, anxiety or hostility, and self-consciousness" (Speigel 1960, p. 365; see also Zollschan 1964, pp. 258–80). Failure of complementarity was a common source of misunderstandings, disappointments, and conflict between husband and wife in the cycle

Adaptations to
Economic Deprivation

of readjustment among families of the unemployed in the Depression. This failure and fearful anticipation of it are recorded in transactions between families and in relationships between children from deprived families and their peers.[14]

Uncertainty and conflicting expectations about appropriate behavior in the roles of parent, spouse, and breadwinner define an unpredictable environment for parents and children. Kasl and Cobb suggest that stress resulting from the status incongruence of parents is expressed in an unstable self-image, frustration, unsatisfactory marital and parent-child relations, and arbitrary parental authority (Kasl and Cobb 1967). The hypothesized effects of these conditions on children include inconsistent or unfavorable attitudes toward the self, poor identification with parents, and feelings of rejection. These self-attitudes may also arise from the effects of status change on the child's relation to peers, such as a decline in the quality of clothing.

Self-consciousness and imaginal role taking represent an adaptation to threatening, novel, or fluid situations in which the actions and attitudes of others are unknown or unpredictable. Tensions associated with uncertainty and conflict "intensify the discrimination between stimuli which are felt to be 'internal' and those felt to be 'external.' The self increasingly becomes an object to itself when its impulses are not reflexively in keeping with other's expectations, and then it receives responses not completely in keeping with its own. The self grows in self-consciousness when it does not view itself exactly as others do" (Gouldner and Peterson 1961, p. 43).

The emergence of self-consciousness among children in deprived families would thus sensitize them to the emotional stress and attitudes of parents and others. Self-consciousness implies a state of acute sensitivity to social cues. By heightening social sensitivity, crisis situations in the family are likely to augment the influence of significant others and foster self-assessments, with their implications for personal change. Accordingly we expect self-consciousness, emotionality, and feelings of insecurity to be most characteristic of children from deprived families in the middle and working class (chapter 6). These proposed effects of deprivation closely correspond with clinical descriptions of persons in situations of social and cultural marginality. According to the classic description, marginal persons who stand on the borders of diverse worlds are excessively self-conscious, hypersensitive, moody, and nervous.[15]

Economic conditions which severely limit options and resources are known to foster apathy, restricted needs and goals, and identity fore-closure.[16] This may describe the life situation and adaptations of some working-class children in the Oakland sample, but it has much less relevance in the late 1930s to the situation of middle-class children from deprived families. By and large, hope and a general commitment to the future are likely to have remained strong among these families during hard times, or at least were restored by improved economic conditions toward the end of the decade. In this context, family hardship may have increased the importance of future achievements as a basis of status and self-definition among the young. This outlook is derived from the assumption that status incongruence is a source of cognitive strain and emotional stress, that individuals strive to minimize these states and maximize their social position, and that young people derive status beyond the family from their projected status, defined by potential and goals. While family status is not subject to change by dependents, anticipated status can be so adjusted and may have gained significance as a basis of self-definition through family losses.

If economic deprivation increased the importance of future status among middle-class youth, it also made this goal more problematic through loss of family resources and gave them more responsibility for status attainment. The Depression "made work seem not only precious but problematic—precious because problematic" (Riesman 1950, p. 344). As family support for achievement declines, personal resources gain significance in determining status prospects and attainment. When a goal acquires importance and its achievement depends largely on personal resources, both goal and means are likely to receive considerable thought among capable youth. Experimental research indicates that both the importance of a goal and the expectation that one can achieve it leads to thought about the means, to selective interest in aspects of the environment that are relevant to goal striving, and to overt action (see Stotland 1971, p. 17).

In relation to the Oakland sample, these correlates of goal orientation suggest that boys from deprived families will show earlier certainty about what they want to do in adulthood than youth in nondeprived families, and that this orientation will be most characteristic of boys who rank high on personal efficacy and expectations of goal attainment, i.e., those of middle-class or high intellectual status. In this hypothesis, we assume that crystallization of goal orientation is fostered by thinking about a future status and the steps leading to it (chapter 7). One might also view this orientation as an outgrowth of inconsistency of family status and the need to reduce status ambiguity. Some reduction is achievable through the determination of status destination.

A key factor in the adult achievement of the Oakland children is opportunity. The increased importance of a future status, crystallized goals, and determination count for little if structural conditions do not afford the opportunity for education and desired employment. Per-

Adaptations to
Economic Deprivation

ceived opportunity is also a basis of hope and future orientation. Increased financial need and status change in the deprived family would limit its role in status placement and may have pushed the young into full-time work roles at a relatively early age.[17] Moreover, both early entry into work roles and marriage acquire value as a source of independent status under conditions of restricted opportunity. Life opportunity is greater in the middle class than in the working class, and the cultural environment of the middle-class family is more supportive of achievement. For these reasons, we expect the most adverse effects of economic deprivation on life achievement among persons from the working class, and particularly among those of low ability.

Life achievement and especially psychological health in adulthood hinge on the amount of emotional stress associated with family deprivation and its image on the developing personality. Hyperconsciousness of self may be adaptive as a response to the demands of a problematic environment, but it may also result in excessive vigilance and fearfulness. For a given situation or context, we need to know the conditions which increase the level of emotional distress and the probability of psychological disorders. This problem leads us to a consideration of adaptive potential and its role in determining the psychological effects of economic deprivation in the Depression and their persistence into the adult years. The concluding section of this chapter is devoted to a discussion of these issues.

Adaptive Potential and Personality

If we constructed estimates of adult psychological health, based solely on the deprived life-situations of persons in the Depression, they would be extraordinarily low. In the 30s such estimates were informed by assumptions which viewed the human organism as vulnerable to environmental pressures and constraints. This image of man is found in psychoanalytic theory and is expressed in the prognosis of a psychoanalyst during the early years of the Depression decade: fear, loss of confidence, continued submission and masochism and discouragement were seen as the psychological heritage of children who experienced the "devastating effects of the breakdown of morale in parents."[18] Some conditions resulting from severe deprivation are thought to have etiological significance for psychiatric disorders, including situations which block striving sentiments associated with physical security, orientations to self and society, and recognition.[19] But the relation between these conditions and psychological functioning depends on many factors, including individual differences in adaptive potential.

Even in the records of extreme deprivation during the Depression, such as the classic study of Marienthal (Austria), the health of children is not adequately explained by socioeconomic conditions in the family (Jahoda et al. 1970). Marienthal, a village of some 1,500 inhabitants, became an unemployed community when its only employer —a large textile plant—closed down. With the exception of eighty persons, the entire village had been out of work for a period of three years at the time of a sociographic report. The population was living on an average of five pence a day; meat served at meals consisted mainly of horseflesh, while a little bread and coffee was common fare at suppertime. Under these extraordinary conditions, the investigators found that the wants and desires of parents and children had contracted or narrowed, thus reducing the full impact of poverty. Impairment of physical health among the children decreased with the employment of family members, but even in the healthy group most family members were unemployed. To explain variations in health, more information would be needed on the adaptive resources of both parents and children.

To understand why some persons successfully adapt to challenging situations and others do not requires knowledge of their resources and motivation, the support provided by the family and larger environment,[20] and characteristics of the event or situation itself. The alchemy of a crisis situation involves all three elements which together determine how a person defines and responds to events. In the Oakland sample, class position bears directly upon personal resources and environmental support for coping, while intellectual skills in problem solving, resourcefulness, and mastery are assets in meeting the demands of problem situations. In what follows, we shall relate these factors to adaptive potential and explore their implications for the enduring effects of economic deprivation on psychological health in adulthood.

Variations in
Adaptive Potential
by Class and
Intelligence

Social support for individual adaptation includes both preparation and reinforcement. The former refers to socialization and the mechanisms by which persons are prepared for life situations. A positive image of self, problem-solving skills, and a sense of competence are key aspects

Adaptations to
Economic Deprivation

of this preparation within the family. Reinforcement includes incentives for engaging in productive behavior and modes of evaluation, both approval and disapproval. Reinforcement affects "not only what the person wants to do, but perhaps even more important, the means he can use in dealing with particular challenges" (Mechanic 1968, p. 310). Social support through preparation and reinforcement are thus social complements to the individual's coping abilities and motivation.

Middle-class families cannot match the firsthand experience of lower-class families with economic hardships and the lessons they provide, but they offer their children a wider range of problem-solving experience and skills and provide greater emotional support.[21] In addition to their economic advantage, middle-class parents tend to know more about the workings of their community than do lower-status parents, and are more familiar with available avenues for solving problems.

Conceptions of reality that arise out of life situations in the lower classes reduce the value of prior hardship experience in promoting adaptive responses to economic change. Orientations in the lower class are more often distinguished by feelings of distrust and fearfulness, by a rigid and oversimple conception of reality, and by a fatalistic belief that one's life is subject to the whim of external forces. Born of capricious circumstances, restricted job experience, and limited education, these beliefs handicap the ability to cope with ambiguity, uncertainty, and change.[22]

Similar differences in adaptive assets appear in social-class comparisons of children. Middle-class children are less prepared for economic adversity and family strains, with respect to prior experience, but they are better equipped in resources and orientation to work out adaptive responses to the complexities and challenge of change (see Elder 1971, esp. pp. 29–113). Given reasonable prospects to exercise control through ability and effort, motivation to cope is likely to result from the status changes associated with economic deprivation. As an index of adaptive potential, we expect class position to make a significant difference in the psychological effects of deprivation among members of the Oakland sample: psychological health will be more adversely affected by economic deprivation in the working class than in the middle class.

Frustration and extreme discomfort in a crisis situation arise when a person is highly motivated to act but lacks skills appropriate to the problem at hand. According to research on natural disasters, individual adaptation varies by motivation, familiarity with relationships, and knowledge of what to do (Barton 1969, p. 68). Improvised activities and nonadaptive responses are most probable under conditions of strong motivation and limited competence. In one disaster, emotional stress and nonadaptive responses were found to be concentrated among persons in the impact area who lacked disaster-relevant experience (military experience, professional training, etc.). In a prolonged crisis, such as the Depression, an inability to act and its emotional effects may be only a temporary stage in the learning or adaptive process for parents and children, or it may result in more permanent forms of withdrawal and immobilization. The latter response is especially prevalent in situations of extraordinary deprivation and physical want.

Since emotional stress interferes with coping, control of inner states represents an important component of adaptive potential, in addition to resources and motivation. However, strong defensive reactions may be self-defeating, such as false or selective perceptions of the situation which lead to inappropriate actions. Occasionally defenses become an end in themselves, reducing motivational investment in active coping through progressive avoidance (Mechanic 1968, p. 308). Heavy drinking and social isolation among unemployed men in the Depression, and their cumulative, deteriorating effects on employability, illustrate this response and its consequences.

Both individual characteristics and degree of family support for coping influence how a situation is defined, but the interpretation itself must be worked out collectively if individual responses are to have social validity and become part of a common enterprise. Ideas and feelings are tested and validated through observing and interacting with other family members. Thus the emotional and behavioral reactions of parents to crisis situations serve as a potential model for the response of children.[23] By regarding class position as an index of adaptive potential among children in the Oakland study, we assume a degree of interrelationship in conceptions of reality and problem-solving resources among parents and children in coping with social change and economic deprivation.

Childhood
Experience and
Adult Health

There is considerable support in the research literature for the position that stressful experiences in childhood increase proneness to psychological disorders or illness in adulthood (see Rahe 1969). Less evidence is available on the developmental effects of stress situations, although it is widely recognized that "frustration and misfortune may lead to and perhaps be essential to the growth and strengthening of a

Adaptations to
Economic Deprivation

person, just as they also lead to maladjustive reactions."[24] In fact, there has been a tendency to focus only on the maladjustive outcomes, thereby neglecting the full picture of psychological functioning. Empirical studies show that psychological well-being is not a function of positive or negative sentiments alone, but of their relationship or ratio (see Bradburn 1969).

The "proneness" thesis finds relatively strong support in a series of retrospective studies of adults conducted by Hinkle and Wolff.[25] Life changes were found to evoke psychophysiologic reactions which have causal significance in the natural history of many diseases. The more severe or demanding the life change, the greater the likelihood of adverse change in health status. Illness-prone adults were generally persons who reported they had been reared in families broken by divorce and characterized by parental conflict, hostile and rejecting attitudes toward offspring, emotional deprivation, and unusual demands or restrictions placed on children. Relatively few of the healthy adults had experienced any of these conditions to a significant degree. In the adult years, divorces, separations, marital conflict, and unrewarding occupational experience were mainly concentrated in the illness-prone group.

Results compatible with the above findings are reported by Kasl and Cobb in a retrospective study of the childhood antecedents of adult health (1967). Adults coming from families in which the occupational status and education of parents were highly discrepant tended to report more physical symptoms indicative of low energy, anxiety, and poor physical health, and described themselves as more depressed, angry, and less self-confident. In these families, the parental marriage was portrayed as relatively affectionless, the same-sex parent was not seen as an attractive role model, and male offspring recalled their childhood as unhappy and insecure. As in any retrospective study, the validity of these reports on childhood must be regarded as uncertain.

The stress-pathology relationship also receives support from a cross-sectional survey of adults in New York City, although the results did vary in relation to class origin (Langner and Michael 1963). The number of stress factors in childhood and adolescence which were reported by the respondents proved to be a highly significant predictor of their mental health rating in adulthood. As the number of deprivational conditions in the preadult years increased, the degree of psychiatric impairment also increased. However, stress factors did not have the same effect on psychological functioning among persons from different social strata. Adults in the lower class ranked higher on mental health risk at any given level of stress than persons from the middle class. In these and related findings, class position in childhood emerges as an important factor in adaptive potential.

Studies by Gregory suggest that deprivation in childhood may have developmental value under certain conditions.[26] Using data obtained from all students admitted to Carlton College over a five-year period, Gregory found that loss of parent did not adversely affect achievement or health. Students of each sex who had lost a parent were grouped according to type of parental loss, sex of parent lost, age at parental loss, and whether the remaining parent remarried. None of these factors adversely affected graduation status or academic achievement or were correlated with visits to the Health Service and known psychiatric consultation. On the contrary, the evidence suggests that loss of a parent through divorce or separation actually promoted achievement striving and increased psychological health among some bright students.

Lastly, the age of the child at the time of a stressful event in the family seems to make a difference in the psychological effect. Although Gregory found no differences by age at parental loss, studies generally show an inverse relationship between the effect of family stress and the age or maturity of the child. (For a review of studies which show the age effect, see Wolff 1969.) In the New York survey cited above, a broken family followed by parental remarriage was more strongly related to mental health risk in adulthood if it occurred before rather than after the age of six. And in a longitudinal study, men who encountered a high level of family conflict during adolescence were rated substantially higher in adulthood on their effectiveness in coping with impulses and external conflict than were men reared in a more tranquil, supportive home (Weinstock 1967). This relationship did not obtain when family conflicts occurred earlier in life. Such conflicts were associated with regressive and maladaptive behavior in adulthood. These findings have considerable significance for the Oakland sample, since the subjects were preadolescents in 1930.

Despite some obvious weaknesses in studies which rely upon retro-spective data, two general conclusions are warranted which have implications for the Oakland analysis. First, family crisis or strains generally increase the risk of personality disorders or unfavorable health in adulthood, although the degree of this relationship is uncer-tain. Other things being equal, the more drastic or severe the crisis and its demands, the greater the risk. Secondly, the psychological effect of change or stress situations varies according to the individual's adaptive potential—his personal resources and motivation as well as environ-mental support. The lower the potential for adapting to challenging situations, the higher the mental health risk. This potential is relatively high among older children, those well above average in cognitive functioning, and among children in the middle class. It is limited among young children who are low in intelligence and family status.

Crisis and Adaptation

Coming of Age   II
in the Depression

*One of the most common things—and it certainly
happened to me—was this feeling of your
father's failure. That somehow he hadn't beaten
the rap. Sure things were tough, but why should
I be the kid who had to put a piece of cardboard
into the sole of my shoe to go to school? It was
not a thing coupled with resentment against my
father. It was simply this feeling of regret, that
somehow he hadn't done better, that he hadn't
gotten the breaks. Also a feeling of uneasiness
about my father's rage against the way things are.*

*He would get jobs he considered beneath his
status during this period. Something would
happen: he'd quarrel with the foreman, he'd have
a fight with the boss. He was a carpenter. He
couldn't be happy fixing a roadbed or driving a
cab or something like that.*

*My father led a rough life: he drank. During the
Depression, he drank more. There was conflict in
the home. A lot of fathers—mine, among them
—had a habit of taking off. They'd go to Chicago
to look for work. To Topeka. This left the
family at home, waiting and hoping that the old
man would find something.*

*I don't think most children escape this. The
oldest son, like me—it had the effect of getting
me out of the home earlier. It's not a question of
disowning your family. Any great economic upheaval, I think, alters patterns. Children develop
doubts about their parents. They leave home
early, out of necessity. They must find jobs
quicker and quicker. Different from the current
generation.*

*I remember coming back home, many years
afterward. Things were better. It was after the
Depression, after the war. To me, it was hardly*

the same house. My father turned into an angel.
They weren't wealthy, but they were making it.
They didn't have the acid and the recriminations
and the bitterness that I had felt as a child.

Labor organizer, son
of skilled craftsman.
In Studs Terkel,
Hard Times.

3

Economic Deprivation and Family Status

We had been quite well off, but after the Depression came in '29, then we were the opposite—quite poor. My dad lost his job as a broker and his money during the fall months, and went to driving a truck for $15.00 a week.
Member of the Oakland cohort

As the economy plummeted to its lowest point in 1933, severe financial hardship became a new reality for many Oakland parents and their children. Family income at the end of the twenties averaged slightly more than three thousand dollars among families in the sample. Three years later this figure had dropped below two thousand. The objective of this chapter is to explore the antecedent conditions and the consequences of this drastic loss for the family, with primary emphasis on change in family position, strategies of economic maintenance, and the psychological response of parents.

A number of options and issues were considered in constructing a suitable measure of economic deprivation. In the first part of the chapter I discuss these matters, describe the index of economic deprivation, and investigate some correlates of family hardship in the worklife of the Oakland fathers. Two lines of inquiry are posed by the uneven hand of economic misfortune; not all families were economically deprived. Are there pre-Depression differences between fathers who lost heavily in the 30s and those who did not? How did economic loss affect family life, the parents and children? Answers to the first question bear upon the context of economic hardship, but we are more concerned with the consequences of this condition. Two areas of impact (taken up in this chapter) have particular significance for the life situation of the Oakland children: modes of family maintenance under deprivational conditions; and the psychosocial response, adaptations, and perceived status of parents. Parental adaptations, objective and perceived, offer a potential link between economic change and the social roles, self-attitudes, and life prospects of children in the study.

Economic Deprivation and Father's Worklife

At least two factors are involved in the determination of economic deprivation and its impact: the degree of loss or change, and the context in which it occurs. Degree of loss is deceptively straightforward as an objective measure of economic deprivation. By standard measurement criteria, percentage loss is at least an ordinal measure of deprivation, but little more can be claimed for it. The difference between a 10 and a 20 percent loss is not likely to be comparable in psychophysical or social properties to an identical percentage difference at a higher level of deprivation.[1] In fact, one could make a convincing case for giving greater weight to identical change at either end of the continuum.

More generally we are faced with the problem of determining what a meaningful percentage loss might be in terms of social change. Is a 10, a 15, or a 20 percent loss meaningful in this sense, or does it depend on initial status? In terms of its effect on resources for family support, a one-fifth cut in family income is likely to have more serious consequences for low- than for high-status families, but the latter are generally more sensitive to change which threatens their reputation or image (Hansen and Hill 1964, p. 803.[2]) The assumption that an economic change of this sort is meaningful only in the lower classes can thus be challenged by evidence showing the stronger subjective reactions of middle-class families to unemployment and economic decline.

If economic change is determined within specific contexts, the effect of variations in loss poses an empirical question for analysis. In line with our expectation regarding deprivation effects by class, we shall view economic change within the middle and working class defined by father's occupation and education in 1929.[3] Since income is moderately related to both education and occupation, class position specifies the relative economic and sociocultural position of families in the sample before the Depression. Approximately three-fifths of the Oakland families were positioned in the middle class at this time. A fourth of the families were upper-middle class (levels I and II on the Hollingshead index), 36 percent were lower-middle class (level III), and a similar percentage were located in the working-class (level IV). The sample includes very few families that were severely deprived before the Depression. Only 5 percent were in the lower class.[4] In terms of residential area, most of the middle-class families were living in or near the prestigious Oakland Hills in the northwestern corner of the city, while the working-class families were generally located in "the Flats," an ecological mosaic of neighborhoods which varied more in economic status than in social rank.

Degree of deprivation was measured by calculating the percentage loss of family income between 1929 and 1933. According to qualitative information on socioeconomic status obtained from interviews in 1932 and 1934, families lost or were forced to dispose of assets with some

Coming of Age
in the Depression

frequency only when income losses exceeded 40 percent. This evidence, coupled with change in the cost of living, indicates that a 35 percent loss in family income is a meaningful division between relatively nondeprived and deprived families. Estimates made by the U.S. Bureau of Labor Statistics show that the cost of living in the Oakland area declined by 18 percent between 1929 and 1932.[5] This decline continued through March, 1933, and thus significantly minimized the loss of purchasing power among families in the nondeprived category.

In the following analysis, nondeprived status will refer to families that received less than a 35 percent decrease in family income between 1929 and 1933; as a group, these families did not experience a significant loss of capital assets. The economically deprived category includes families with heavier losses. At various points in the analysis we shall subdivide this category according to whether economic loss was accompanied by unemployment of the father. Table 1 shows the median income of deprived and nondeprived families in 1929 and 1933 within each social class, and the percentage decline for each group. As one would expect, the average amount of loss is greater in the middle class, but the degree of relative change is comparable across the two classes within categories of deprivation.

Table 1   Median Family Income and Income Change (1929 to 1933) among Nondeprived and Deprived Families in the Middle and Working Classes

Social Class (1929) and Economic Deprivation	Median Family Income and Income Change			
	Income 1929	Income 1933	Income Loss 1929–33	Relative Income Change 1929–33
Middle Class				
Nondeprived (N = 40)	$4,068.00	$3,198.00	$ 850.00	−20%
Deprived (N = 49)	$3,600.00	$1,487.00	$2,220.00	−64%
Working Class				
Nondeprived (N = 21)	$2,400.00	$2,040.00	$ 360.00	−15%
Deprived (N = 46)	$2,780.00	$1,118.00	$1,560.00	−58%

In terms of percentage loss, economic change is three to four times greater among deprived families than among nondeprived families, and the former outnumber the latter in both classes but especially in the working class. Economic inequality between the social classes is virtually nonexistent among deprived families in 1933. The economic position of middle-class families in the deprived category is substantially lower in 1933 than that of nondeprived families in both social classes. By any standard, the amount of economic change among deprived families is drastic and carries profound implications for family maintenance and the psychology of family members.

An important aspect of economic change is expressed by the degree of inconsistency it produced among dimensions of family status. In 1929, the relative economic standing of families generally corresponded with their class position, as indexed by father's occupational and educational status ($tau_c = .43$). By 1933, this same measure of class status bore little relation to the reported income of families in the deprived group (.09). Father's education remained constant throughout the Depression and failed to predict family income in 1933 only among the economically deprived (.06). This last is also the only group of families in which the association between father's occupation and education decreased between 1929 and 1933 (from .60 to .45). These coefficients (Kendall's tau_c, an ordinal measure of association) indicate the degree to which pairs of values in the proper order (such as high social class and income) exceed in number those pairs in the reverse order, i.e., high class, low income. Numerical values range from -1.0 to $+1.0$. In subsequent analyses, we shall use the Pearson r correlation as an index of association (an interval measure) wherever warranted by analytic requirements or the frequency distribution.

Income change among the Oakland families reflects a combination of factors that are usually associated with depressed economic conditions: cutbacks in wages, salaries, or sales; a reduction in work hours resulting in underemployment; a temporary or permanent layoff which results in full unemployment; and father absence. A complete record of these conditions and their distribution in the sample is not available since worklife histories and appropriate data were not collected in the thirties. However, we were able to determine whether the fathers were *ever* unemployed between 1929 and 1934, using information from the 1934 home interview. In the middle class, unemployment was almost entirely limited to families in the deprived group (52% vs. 9%). A larger percentage of working-class fathers were out of a job at some point in this period, owing to the greater prevalence of joblessness among fathers in the deprived and nondeprived groups (59% vs. 33%). Within the middle and working class, fathers who experienced some unemployment were most likely to lose occupational status between 1929 and 1934; a third of the unemployed fathers moved down one or more levels during this period, in contrast to only 7 percent of the employed.

Beyond 1933, which was the low point of the Depression in Oakland, we do not have income data on families in the sample. This means that we are unable to chart the extent to which deprived families recovered or surpassed their economic position in 1929. However, it is necessary to make some determination of this matter since it has direct implications for the upbringing and future prospects of children in the sample, especially for those in deprived middle-class families. Status loss is most clearly evident in this group of families. To determine the long-term effects of economic change, we assembled all available evidence on the social class position of families at the end of the 30s. Adequate data were obtained on social class in 1941 for 105 families in the sample, and they were compared with the 1929 index. Both measures of social class were based on the five-level Hollingshead index.

The comparison shows a high degree of stability between the two time periods. Most deprived and nondeprived families were located on the same status level in 1929 and 1941: 67 percent of the former and 76 percent of the latter. Only 8 percent of the families in each category had dropped one or more levels, while the remainder had advanced at least one level. Within the middle class, downwardly mobile families were generally located on the lowest level in 1929. An example of this decline is seen in the case of a lower-middle-class family which dropped to the bottom rung of the class structure after father's loss of job and remained at this level through 1941. The father was a salesman for a small furniture company during the twenties, lost his job during the first year of the Depression, and remained out of work for three years. By 1934, he was driving a delivery truck part-time; this was followed by work as a janitor and then as a service station attendant. This dramatic change is rare in the Oakland sample, and so are relatively minor declines between 1929 and 1941. As a rule, deprived families recovered their former status by the end of the Depression decade.

Social Factors in Economic Change

The degree of variation in economic loss among families in the Oakland sample disputes a popular assumption that economic hardship in the Depression was a pervasive experience which placed American families in a common situation of shared misfortune. While most of the Oakland families were placed in a deprivational situation, some did not experience the additional burden of unemployment, and there were enough families in the "well-off" category to increase feelings of deprivation among the less fortunate. This variation in economic misfortune inevitably leads to the following question: What conditions or factors differentiated families which suffered heavy losses from those of nondeprived status? In this section, we shall examine four characteristics of the Oakland fathers which bear upon economic security and employability: occupational status and type of work in 1929, birthplace, age, and education.[6]

Overall we find that economic loss and unemployment varied more by work status and father's birthplace than by either father's education or age. The likelihood of economic deprivation was greatest among the self-employed in the middle class, with foreign parentage largely concentrated among deprived fathers in the working class. The former is indicative of the high risks in small business operations during economic depressions, while the latter may reflect differential treatment by ethnic status.

The likelihood of income and job loss was lowest among the professionals in the Depression and greatest among the unskilled, with self-employed men tending to lose their money but not their employment.[7] Four-fifths of the self-employed fathers were economically deprived compared to two-thirds of the unskilled, half of the white-collar and skilled men, and a third of the professionals. The unskilled and white-collar workers ranked highest on unemployment (40%), followed by the self-employed and skilled (30%), and the professional-managerial group (14%). From these comparisons, it is clear that evidence of unemployment consistently underestimates the extent of economic hardship, especially in the middle class. This point warrants consideration in view of the common tendency to rely upon unemployment data for estimates of deprivation in the 30s.

The self-employed occupied a relatively unique position in relation to depressed conditions. Despite the insecurity of their situation, these representatives of the "old middle class" had the advantage of flexibility and autonomy in working out solutions to their financial problems. Shaky businesses were kept afloat by cutting overhead, by replacing nonfamily employees with family members, and by extending business hours. A long work day and week were prominent features of the social world of men who were able to save their businesses in the Depression.

Foreign birth increased the likelihood of economic loss among fathers. This status was most common in the working class (25% vs. 14%), and is linked to hardship primarily in this stratum. Four-fifths of the foreign-born in the working class were economically deprived, in contrast to a little more than three-fifths of the native-born. The same comparison in the middle class produced a difference of only eight percent on deprived status. Overall, the foreign-born tended to rank higher on economic misfortune across occupational categories and, in keeping with this picture, were more apt to experience an unstable worklife during the 30s, as indicated by periods of unemployment and fluctuations in occupational status. This pattern may reflect discrimination by financial institutions and employers, though we have no direct evidence of such practices among families in the sample.

Apart from discrimination, we might expect the foreign-born to be especially disadvantaged by their worklife if they were older and less skilled than native-born fathers. In the jobless category, older men are generally less attractive to employers than younger workers. However, age was not a factor in the deprived status of men; this status was *not* more common among older or younger fathers in the middle and working class. As might be expected, fathers who had emigrated to America were less educated on the whole than the native-born, but this difference cannot account for the sizable ethnic differential among deprived and nondeprived men in the working class. In this class, formal education beyond the eighth grade was only slightly more common among the nondeprived (38% vs. 28%). In the middle class, half of the nondeprived fathers had achieved at least some college education, as against 41 percent of the deprived men. An important factor in this difference is the relatively low education of the self-employed. Historically, this type of worklife has provided access to economic achievement for men who lacked the educational requisites of high-status jobs. Across all occupational categories above the semi-skilled, the likelihood of stable employment and income during the Depression is only slightly related to formal education.

Father's work status, education, and birthplace shed some light on the social context of family deprivation and will be taken into account at appropriate points in the subsequent analysis. Father's occupational status and education, as components of family social class (1929), define the two socioeconomic contexts of family hardship—middle and working class. Parental nationality will enter the analysis as an index of values on family roles. However, we are mainly concerned with the *effects* of economic deprivation. Variation in economic loss thus represents a *given*, a point of departure rather than a fact to be explained.

Family
Adaptations
in Economic
Maintenance

Two general lines of adaptation were available to deprived families as they attempted to work out solutions to problems of economic maintenance: to reduce expenditures and to generate alternative or supplementary sources of income. New sources of income became a necessity in the face of prolonged deprivation—the entry of mother into the labor market, money from relatives and boarders, and the last resort, public assistance. As might be expected, each type of support was most common among working-class families in the sample, but even in this group they were concentrated among the economically deprived.[8]

*Family Options
in Economic
Support*

In contrast to public assistance, these options refer to support derived from family labor and kin resources, to mother's employment and funds from relatives or boarders. An interview with mothers (1934) obtained information on their work status at the time and on whether the family had received any money from kin or boarders between 1929 and 1934. The work hours and status of mother's job are unknown, and so is the amount of support received from these sources. Nevertheless, the data do provide a general account of two important options in family maintenance.

The climate of opinion in economically depressed Oakland offered no encouragement to women who felt that they had to supplement or earn the family income; "They were said to be taking work from jobless men who had families to support." In some cases, employment policy ruled out married women (school districts in the area), though jobs (generally low-wage, part-time) were available to women, and economic need prevailed over adverse sentiment in a number of families. Twenty-nine percent of the working-class mothers in the sample were employed, compared to 19 percent in the middle class. A smaller percentage of families in each class received income from boarders and relatives (16% vs. 21%). As expected, each type of support was more frequent among the deprived in both social classes.

To identify degrees of economic need, we assigned each family to one of three groups, defined by economic loss and father's unemployment: the nondeprived, the deprived with father employed, and the deprived with father unemployed. As shown in table A–2, economic loss is the principal source of variation in both family options. Father's work status adds little to the picture except in the middle class; in this group, the percentage of families that received some income from relatives or boarders increased directly by level of deprivation, but working mothers were most common among deprived families in which father remained employed. The primary explanation for this outcome

Coming of Age
in the Depression

is found in the adaptation of self-employed men to economic conditions. Despite heavy losses of income, a large percentage of these men were able to avoid bankruptcy or loss of the business, and the merchants did so in part by cutting payroll costs through the employment of family members. Forty percent of the wives of the self-employed held jobs, in contrast to 25 percent of the wives of unskilled and skilled men.

The number of working women in the nondeprived group brings up an important consideration. As measured in the study, relative economic loss indicates the degree of change in the *total income of families*, and thus includes the financial gains of women. Women's earnings, though unknown, were very likely a major factor in the economy of deprived families and, in some cases, may have made the difference between deprived and nondeprived status. Among the full array of family adaptations to economic change, only mother's employment is incorporated in our measure of deprivation. The decline in total family income is clearly the most appropriate measure of economic change as we move into the realm of social adaptations—parental interpretations of the changed situation, social involvement and withdrawal, family roles and relationships.

Public Assistance

Lack of community support for working mothers was paralleled by attitudes toward public assistance or "relief" which implied that "something is wrong with a man who can't support his family." The notion that family dependence on relief funds reflected personal deficiencies stubbornly persisted in Oakland as the number of relief cases climbed dramatically to over six times the 1929 figure and became increasingly associated with unemployment.

A third of the families in the Oakland sample sought assistance from some public agency between 1929 and 1941. These data were obtained from a county charities commission which served as a coordinating agency in the city for public assistance. Relief allowances seldom exceeded forty-five dollars per month in the city, a figure which is well below the minimum cost of living at that time for a laborer with children.[9]

The 108 contacts with agencies between 1929 and 1941 included direct economic aid (38%), medical assistance (44%), and assistance for older children (14%). Most families with single contacts obtained direct economic aid, while multiple contacts generally included economic and other types of assistance. Twenty families had three or more contacts with public agencies, and a majority were in the working class.

The relation between deprivation (with and without parental unemployment) and receipt of public assistance is shown in table A–3 for two time periods: 1929–33, a period before federal funds became available on a large scale in the city, and 1934–41. In both periods, public dependence was mainly a "last resort" of families in which the father was unemployed.

Middle-class families were less likely to have received public assistance than families in the working class, a difference which is considerably larger after 1934 than before. Welfare was mainly a source of economic support for families of jobless men in both social classes and increased in prevalence after 1933 due in part to the increasing availability of federal funds in Oakland and the progressive exhaustion of family resources. Between 1929 and 1933, twenty-three families contacted relief agencies at least once, a figure which doubled in the following years. Sixteen families received assistance in both time periods. Throughout the 30s, less deprived families were more likely to utilize family options than public assistance, and it is among these families that alternative modes of economic support are most clearly seen. Maternal employment and support from relatives markedly reduced the likelihood of social dependence.

Especially in the working class, persistent dependence on public aid reflected extreme hardships and some family disorganization. In one such family with a total of six contacts, the father had been unemployed for over three years. The children became the target of his sense of failure and frustration; they were nagged, belittled, and closely watched. Nothing the children did merited their father's approval. The continuous quarreling frequently exploded into shouting matches and threats between husband and wife. Other deprived parents were simply resigned to their situation. In one case, the father appeared to the interviewer as very "easy-going" and the mother "as having learned not to worry."

In summary, both supplementary forms of family maintenance and public assistance were most frequent among deprived families in the middle and working class. However, it is clear that problems of economic maintenance were appreciably more acute for working-class families at all levels of deprivation. In the nondeprived category, aid from relatives, material employment, and public assistance were all more common among working-class families. Four-fifths of these families earned less than $2,500 in 1933, as compared to a third of the middle-class families on this level. In the total sample, working-class families were twice as likely to have earned less than $2,500 in 1933. Economic hardship was a reality to most working-class families in the Depression, but especially when unemployment was coupled with economic loss. It is in this situation that we find the greatest dependence on relief payments.

Some Effects of Status Loss on Parents

Status loss in the Depression entailed change in both economic position and social prestige. Expectations established in the 20s exceeded attainments and rewards as families suffered income losses and unemployment. The higher the climb before the Depression, the greater the investment in the way things were at that time, and the more intense the frustration of downward mobility. If a comparable percentage loss in income brought the most severe economic hardship to families that were barely above subsistence, high-status families were distinguished by what they had to lose in social standing.

To avoid or lessen the social and psychic costs of "coming down in the world," families made attempts to disguise poverty and hardships by maintaining a front—"the brave social front that local canons of respectable competence require a family to present to its neighbors" (Lynd and Lynd 1937, p. 145). In Oakland and elsewhere, social workers were sometimes faced with difficulties in persuading middle-class clients to spend their money for basic needs instead of on prestige symbols that seemed so important to them. "Folks don't see what you eat," one client protested, "but they know where you live" (Bird 1965, p. 276). In the Oakland sample, a daughter of deprived middle-class parents recalled that her father was extremely stingy in providing her mother with food and clothing money, and yet spent what seemed at the time to be a huge sum of money painting the house because "everybody could see that."

The social investment of middle-class parents, punitive contrasts in status loss, and attitudes which blame individuals for their misfortunes lead to the prediction of high emotional stress among economically deprived parents in the middle class. Dissatisfaction with living conditions and status, depressed feelings, and doubts about personal worth are all likely to be correlated with the economic misfortunes of middle-class parents. Though loss of prestige may not have been as much an issue in the working class, especially when compared to the daily problem of economic survival, low-status persons are at a disadvantage relative to the middle class, and the resulting social comparisons foster discontent. Numerous surveys have found unhappiness, dissatisfaction, and other expressions of dysphoria to be more common in the lower strata.[10] These considerations make uncertain the psycho-

Economic Deprivation
and Family Status

logical effects of economic loss and unemployment in the working class.

In what follows, we shall use both interview data from mothers and the reports of children in determining the psychological impact of economic deprivation on parents. Related to this impact is the problem of defending the self from negative evaluations and aversive experiences. The social front and isolation are examples of defensive efforts to avoid anticipated "failures of complimentarity" in status recognition. Social withdrawal and heavy drinking are viewed in the following analysis as strategies which may serve to minimize aversive social stimuli. Most of the analysis will be focused on the mothers, owing to the availability of data.

Perceptions
of Mothers'
Emotional State

Interviewers evaluated the mothers' emotional state and functioning on seven-point ratings after home visits in 1932, 1934, and 1936. To increase the stability of these measurements, scores on each rating scale were averaged across the three years. Five of the ratings, in particular, were appropriate as indicators of the predicted psychological effects of deprivation. A high score on each rating is described by the following titles: (1) dissatisfaction with lot—conditions in home fail to measure up to expectations; (2) feelings of inadequacy—feels inferior, self-conscious; (3) fatigued—tired-looking, worn-out, shows lack of rest; (4) feels secure—light-hearted, no worries, carefree; and (5) an unkempt appearance—clothes and shoes ill-fitting and worn, poor grooming and hygiene. As judgments, the ratings may well differ from the actual perspectives of mothers in the sample. No self-reports were obtained from the mothers on their subjective reactions to deprivation. For the purpose of this analysis, we compared the nondeprived with that portion of the deprived group in which father was unemployed at some time.

Symptoms of emotional distress are generally more prevalent among working-class mothers, and show little variation by level of economic deprivation in this subgroup (table A–4). Even mothers from severely deprived families, which were lowest on income and most dependent on relief payments, do not differ appreciably in psychological well-being from mothers in nondeprived households. The former were judged only slightly less secure and dissatisfied.

Substantial differences do appear in the middle class, however, and these are mainly associated with unemployment and its consequences for loss of social position. As noted earlier, downward mobility was primarily associated with unemployment among middle-class families. The mothers with unemployed husbands were rated higher on dissatisfaction, fatigue, sense of inadequacy, and lack of security. They were also characterized as more unkempt in appearance than mothers from less deprived families. Overall the degree of emotional distress evident among these mothers closely resembles descriptions of mothers in the working class at all levels of deprivation. On a broader scale, this subgroup in the middle class may be largely responsible for research findings in the Depression which show a high degree of similarity between the dissatisfaction of middle- and low-status groups.[11]

Though we did not expect status loss to have a strong effect on the emotional state of working-class parents in comparison to middle-class parents, the virtual absence of any discernible effect does not square with the substantial differences in objective life situations by level of deprivation. One factor which may have contributed to this result is a relative insensitivity of the interviewer to variations among working-class households and persons. Middle-class standards may well have biased their judgments. Since children's reports on parents are not subject to the cultural bias of an outside observer, and are more informed by the realities of family stress, we compared them with the interviewer rating on dissatisfaction with lot. The perception of children was measured by the statement, "I wish my mother were happier," an item obtained from a list of wishes on a questionnaire that was administered when the subjects were in high school. The children were instructed to check only those wishes that reflected their true feelings.

In the total sample, there is a modest level of agreement between the two evaluations of mother. Boys and girls who expressed the wish that "mother were happier" were likely to have mothers who were rated above average on dissatisfaction with lot by the interviewer (tau$_c$ = .36), and this relation was slightly stronger in the middle class. However, the perceptions of working-class children did vary more by deprivational conditions than the interviewer's rating. The wish for a happier mother increased from 49 percent in nondeprived families among working-class children to 68 percent in deprived households, and a larger difference was found among middle-class children (38% vs. 70%). Despite differences in the characterization of working-class mothers, interviewers' and children's perceptions are generally consistent with our original expectation of stronger psychological effects in the middle class.

We have suggested that the psychological costs of deprivation in the middle class derived more from prestige loss than from economic loss, with the reverse pattern most likely in the working class. When social standing is low before economic hardship, status commitments are less

Economic Deprivation
and Family Status

apt to draw attention away from basic needs. One procedure for testing this proposed difference is to compare the effects of prestige and economic factors on the attitudes of mothers in each social class. For an indicator of social standing or prestige, we chose neighborhood status in 1934. The socioeconomic status of a family's neighborhood was a highly visible symbol of its status in Oakland. The "Hill," "the downtown section," and "the Flats" referred to significantly different status areas in the city, but the important prestige distinction is between the Oakland Hills and the low- to moderate-income neighborhoods in the Flats. To the extent that economic deprivation resulted in a loss of status through residential change, low residential status would be a potent source of dissatisfaction in the middle class.

Economic need and pressures are partially a function of the number of children in the family. The larger the family, the greater the economic demand, and the smaller proportion of family income which is available for each child. Family size provides an indication of objective economic pressures which is largely divorced from status considerations. The number of children in the family was neither a cause nor a consequence of relative income loss, but rather defined a context which mediated the effects of economic loss. The average working-class family had more children to feed, clothe, and shelter than the average family in the middle class, and this characteristic may have partially accounted for the generalized prevalence of discontent among low-status mothers.

To analyze the effects of neighborhood status (1934) and family size on mothers' dissatisfaction in both social classes, we dichotomized the former index at the median and family size between two and three children. The main effects of these factors on the percentage of dissatisfied mothers (scores above the median) were assessed in each social class through a multiple classification analysis which made adjustments for variations in economic loss and employment.[12] The data show that neighborhood status made a difference in mothers' discontent only in the middle class (51% of the mothers in low-status areas were dissatisfied in comparison with 26% in high-status areas), while three or more children increased discontent only in the working class (from 56% to 80%).

One explanation for the effect of low residential status on middle-class mothers is that it represents a visible prestige casualty of economic loss and unemployment. There is a moderate relation between economic deprivation and a low-status neighborhood among middle-class families ($tau_c = .24$), but we cannot conclude that deprivation actually caused downward mobility in residence which in turn aroused feelings of discontent. Precise information on residential change is simply not available. Nevertheless, two considerations make this interpretation credible. First, neighborhood status and economic deprivation are not related in the working class, and neither factor influenced the degree of dissatisfaction among low-status mothers. Second, residential status made a difference in the attitudes of middle-class mothers primarily among mothers who were members of families which lost a sizable proportion of their income. It is low residential status, coupled with and presumably resulting from economic loss, which appears to be the main source of frustration. Mothers in this situation were more highly dissatisfied than deprived mothers living in more prestigeful areas, while discontent was lowest among nondeprived mothers in high-status neighborhoods ($\overline{X}s = 4.5$ vs. 3.8, $p < .05$; the mean rating on nondeprived mothers in high-status areas is 3.0).

Up to this point, we have viewed mothers' attitudes within the context of their class and family situation in marriage. This framework neglects two sets of experiences that also bear upon such attitudes—relations with contemporaries (with siblings, friends, coworkers) and parents. From scattered qualitative data, we find suggestive evidence on the significance of the grandparental generation in the lives of the Oakland parents and children, especially under deprived conditions. Economic interdependence and shared residential quarters gave added force to the reality of grandparental figures as evaluators and standard-bearers.

If grandparents were significant elements in the life situation of deprived families, they were unfortunately overlooked in the process of data collection. No data were obtained from them or indirectly from their children, with the exception of the parental birthplace and date. Judging from these data, we estimate that most of the grandparents were born between 1855 and 1870, and were emigrants from Europe or from eastern sections of the United States. The collective experience of this cohort spans an extraordinary phase of the nation-building enterprise in America—rural to urban migration and settlement of the West, rapid industrialization, economic and social dislocations through a series of depressions and wars. This experience, as mediated by family status and upbringing, bears upon the parents' situation in the Depression in at least three ways. As hypotheses for future research, we suggest that the parents' interpretation of the situation and response, both social and psychological, were conditioned by socioeconomic expectations that are rooted in family upbringing; by the extent to which early experience prepared them for coping with the realities of economic uncertainty and hardship; and by intergenerational comparisons (e.g., the tendency of a wife to evaluate her husband by her father's achievement).

Economic Deprivation
and Family Status

Only one view of the Oakland fathers is available in this study; their characterization in the perceptions of offspring. The fathers were not interviewed about their relations to parents, in-laws, or wife, and the mothers were not asked questions about their attitudes toward the behavior of their husbands. This deficiency generally reflects an assumption which was widely shared in the 30s, that father was relatively unimportant in the total picture of upbringing. Nevertheless, the Oakland children were old enough in the early 30s to be aware of economic conditions in the larger community, and the meaning of these circumstances, as they impinged upon the family, was formed in part by parental interpretations. (On awareness of poverty among ten- and eleven-year-olds, see Estvan 1952.)

The children were asked questions in a senior-high questionnaire which provided information on their perception of father's morale and social standing in the community. Low morale and a sudden change of this mood from a more buoyant, optimistic attitude are suggested by children who wished that their fathers were happier. Changes in mood are more likely to elicit attention than stable emotional states. The wish statement on father was included, along with a comparable item on mother, in a list of desires or wishes. The children were less likely to check this wish for father than for mother (only 20 percent did so), perhaps because of their greater contact with mother, but fully 90 percent of those who did were members of economically deprived families. The desire for a happier father was expressed most often by children whose fathers had suffered unemployment and a heavy economic loss, and it did not vary by social class or sex of child.

In line with our assumptions regarding prestige loss in the middle class, we expected economic loss to make the greatest difference in children's perceptions of father's social prestige in this stratum. Residential change to a lower-status neighborhood and unemployment were more visible indicators of status loss in the middle class. An extreme example of this change is the unemployed middle-class father who eventually lands a blue-collar job and acquires symbols of the working class through associations on the job and clothing style. A nine-point scale on perception of father "as a respected man in the community" was used as an index of perceived social standing. Scores on this scale represent the average of ratings made by three judges who read self-report and observational materials on each subject for the senior-high period.

Despite the status changes which occurred in the Depression, middle-class children placed their fathers significantly higher on community standing than did children from the working class ($p < .01$), and there were no differences in this perception between boys and girls. Within the middle class, the perceived status of father was considerably higher in nondeprived families than in deprived households ($\overline{X}$s = 6.8 vs. 5.6, $p < .01$). This difference remained even when fathers in the two groups were matched on occupational and educational status in 1929. Among deprived families, the data show a slight tendency for lower evaluations among fathers who were unemployed. Turning to the working class, we find that economic deprivation made very little difference in children's perceptions; nondeprived fathers were not appreciably higher on perceived status than fathers in the economically deprived category. Deprived families in both social classes were relatively similar in 1933 on economic position, but their differences in background, education, and style of life are reflected in the significantly higher status attributed to the middle-class father ($p < .05$). In all of these comparisons, the influence of family status in 1929 is clearly seen in the children's perceptions.

Children's evaluations of father are known to be influenced by mother's attitude toward him. In this respect, mothers who openly attributed blame for status loss to their husband's inadequacies would markedly increase the sensitivity of children to his social failure. Such attitudes were not obtained from the mothers, but qualitative materials from interviews do suggest the effect of mother's shame concerning the father on chiidren's attitudes. An example is provided by the case of a merchant who lost his business and capital investments in 1931. One setback followed another from that point on, and most of his jobs were very low in social prestige—for example, janitorial work, night watchman. As an adult, the son recalled that his mother was crushed by the rapid descent in style of life. Through words, gestures, and deeds, his mother expressed a deep sense of shame concerning the father's status and work. "It was a very difficult thing for mother— someone who had always had something—to have to go down to Goodwill to get clothes for the kids." Eventually these attitudes were acquired by the son. He could remember being asked, on forms in school, what his father did, and having to ask his mother what "he did." Throughout adolescence he attempted to avoid situations which required acknowledgement of father's status and the family's social position. "It's a terrible thing to have done so, but I just didn't know what he did." This family is not typical of severely deprived families who were positioned in the middle class before 1930, since very few permanently lost status. Nevertheless the case does illustrate the strategic position of mothers in creating emotional climates in which children's attitudes are formed.

Withdrawal as a
Defensive Response
to Status Loss

Withdrawal from stressful situations is most likely to occur when events or conditions seem overwhelming or unsolvable. Withdrawal from aversive stimuli is one function of social isolation and heavy drinking, and both conditions are associated with the economic failures of men.[13] A reduction in associational life and contacts outside the family is one of the costs of unemployment, an effect which does not involve defensive interests in the initial stage. With prolonged deprivation, however, isolation may acquire secondary value as a mechanism for avoiding the negative judgments of others. According to Bakke's research, this seems to have been the response of some families to the anticipated "failure of complementarity" in relations with neighbors. Heavy drinking extends this function of social isolation by temporarily moderating aversive internal states (depressed feelings, etc.) and also reduces social sensitivity.

Among parents in the Oakland sample, both restricted social interaction outside the family and heavy drinking were primarily associated with unemployment in middle-class families. A three-category index of parental involvement outside the family (high, moderate, and low) was constructed from qualitative materials on family visiting and associational memberships in the 1934 interview. It was not possible to distinguish between family and nonfamily participation. Sixty percent of the middle-class parents were classified as moderate on participation, with 15 percent in the high category. No working-class families were judged high on participation, and only 44 percent were classified as moderately active.

In the middle class, unemployment made a substantial difference in parental participation; half of the parents in middle-class families where unemployment existed were judged at least moderately active in comparison to 85 percent of the families with employment. Apart from unemployment, economic loss did not affect social participation. Neither economic loss nor unemployment made a difference in the relatively low participation of working-class parents, perhaps because of continuing involvement in kin activity. While cause-effect relations cannot be determined in these data, the substantial effect of unemployment in the middle class is consistent with the psychological impact of status loss in this stratum.

Most fathers who were perceived by their offspring as having "a drinking problem" lost their job at least once during the Depression: two-fifths of the unemployed fathers were so described in comparison to 8 percent of the fathers in other families. The prevalence of drinking problems among the unemployed was slightly greater in the working class. Since these data were obtained from the retrospective reports of the children in the 1964 follow-up, their validity is uncertain. Nevertheless, interview materials in the 30s provide numerous examples of heavy drinking as both cause and consequence of unemployment. Fathers who increased their consumption of alcohol after losing their job also increased their prospects of becoming unemployable even when economic conditions improved. In both the middle and working class unemployed fathers who drank heavily were disproportionately represented among families that failed to recover the social status they lost in the Depression.

Review

Depressed economic conditions in the 1930s were neither uniform nor completely random in their impact on families in the Oakland sample. Income loss for a majority of families averaged more than 50 percent between 1929 and 1934, but a number of families suffered losses that barely exceeded the decline in cost of living. Unemployment of father was a major factor in heavy economic loss among both middle- and working-class families. In the middle class, fathers with entrepreneurial jobs were most likely to lose their income, but unemployment was more common among white-collar workers. Economic loss in the working class was most prevalent among fathers who were born in a foreign country. Fathers who remained employed ranked slightly higher on education in both social strata, but they did not differ in age from other men.

We defined economic deprivation by relative income loss between 1929 and 1934 within social-class contexts measured in 1929. The class position of families in 1929 indicates both resources for adapting to economic change and delineates frames of reference in which such change is defined. Using qualitative information on economic adjustments in the family and change in cost of living as guidelines, we defined two categories of income loss: relatively nondeprived (below 35 percent) and deprived (a greater loss). The average percentage loss among deprived families was three to four times greater than among families in the nondeprived category. Deprived status was most prevalent in the working class, but the average loss of families in this category is comparable in both social classes.

Economic loss and unemployment brought adverse changes in the social position, economy, and climate of the family. Instability of family status and downward mobility in the 1930s were mainly associated with unemployment and economic loss. While most of the Oakland families occupied the same class position in 1941 which they held in 1929, families which failed to at least recoup their loss in status were generally headed by fathers with a history of unemployment. Heavy drinking among these men contributed to this permanent loss. One of the most visible symbols of status, the prestige and quality of neighborhood, was a casualty of economic misfortune among some families in the middle class.

Parental adaptations to problems of economic maintenance involved reliance on both family and public sources of income. Working mothers, money from relatives and boarders, and dependence on public assistance were correlated with family deprivation in both social classes, and were most prevalent in the working class. Public welfare represented a "last resort" of families in situations of prolonged unemployment. One consequence of financial need and parental adaptations to this problem is an expansion of labor-intensive activities which offer children meaningful roles. The employment of mother, in particular, is likely to have had this effect. The following chapter on children's roles in the household economy and their relation to economic conditions completes our coverage of adaptations in family maintenance.

The meaning of economic deprivation and unemployment depends in part on the relative importance and consequence of prestige loss and financial strain. These costs were not limited to families in any one class, but prestige considerations appeared to be more prominent in the discontent and perceived status of middle-class parents. On interviewer ratings, dissatisfaction, insecurity, and fatigue were significantly correlated with economic loss and unemployment among mothers in the middle class. Economic deprivation most strongly influenced feelings of dissatisfaction when it was coupled with residence in a low-status neighborhood, a finding which points to downward mobility in residence as a source of frustration. Parental unhappiness, as a matter of concern to children, increased in perceptions of mother and father by level of deprivation. Middle-class fathers in deprived families were also attributed lower prestige by their offspring than were fathers in nondeprived homes. The psychic costs of status loss are suggested by restricted social activities outside the home and heavy drinking among fathers; both were most common in severely deprived families.

Perceptions of parental distress did not vary as strongly by economic deprivation in the working class. Intense economic need among all working-class families, the lower visibility of status decline, and social comparisons with the middle class may account for this result. In any case, the rating of mother's dissatisfaction was more strongly related to family size than to economic loss, unemployment, or low neighborhood status. As in the middle class, parental unhappiness was more of a problem among children from deprived families, but economic conditions had less effect in this subgroup than among children from higher-status families. In addition, deprivational status made no significant difference in children's perception of father's social standing in the community. On the basis of these class differences, one might expect economic loss and unemployment to be more pronounced in their effect on family relation in the middle class. The desire of boys to emulate their father is known to be contingent on his perceived prestige in the community. This and other consequences of status loss are explored in chapter 5.

The preceding summary of family change and adaptation provides an empirical foundation which largely corresponds with the assumptions that underlie our expectations relating to children in deprived and nondeprived families. The substantial degree of status change associated with economic loss and unemployment clearly has implications for the role of children in family maintenance, for conjugal and parent-child relations in the family, and for the children's self-image and social activities. These data also raise some doubts about the life accomplishments and psychological health of children from deprived middle-class families.

4

Children in the
Household
Economy

*It was an enormously
hard life. . . . But there
was also a sense of great
satisfaction in being a
child with valuable
work to do and, being
able to do it well, [able]
to function in this world.*
Margot Hentoff
*New York Review
of Books*

The roles that children assumed in the economy of deprived families
are an integral aspect of two adaptive strategies. As noted in the
preceding chapter, deprived families both curtailed expenditures and
developed alternative sources of income. The first strategy orients the
family unit toward a more labor-intensive economy in which some
goods and services formerly purchased in the marketplace are acquired
through family labor. Food preparation, making clothing, and home
repairs are examples. These activities and particular sources of income,
such as boarders, generally increase the utility of children's labor. This
applies to girls in particular, since most household tasks are traditional
aspects of the homemaker's role.

Family efforts to supplement income include activities in which
children earn money on jobs in the community. Apart from parental
demand or encouragement, this activity is a logical response to personal
needs and an awareness of family requirements. However, economic
options were limited for the Oakland children. They were still enrolled
in school and were too young during the early years of the Depression
to obtain permits enabling full-time employment. Part-time jobs for
children offered low wages, but they were relatively plentiful in
Oakland during the 1930s. Examples include newspaper carrier, baby
sitter, janitorial assistant, store clerk, and delivery agent. According to
cultural prescription, boys are more likely than girls to have taken
economic roles.

The involvement of children in the household economy is not by
itself an indication of accelerated entry into the adult world, though it
would imply a downward extension of adultlike responsibilities in the
Great Depression. The act of managing substantial tasks in the home
and community is more compatible with the work orientation of the
young adult than with the "irresponsible" theme of youth culture,[1] a
mass phenomenon that emerged after the depressed 30s. In the latter
half of this chapter, we shall compare children from nondeprived and
deprived families on behavior patterns that reflect an orientation toward

the realities of adult life, as expressed in the sex-differentiated world of the 30s: mature judgment in the handling of money; dependability; social independence among boys and domestic concerns among girls; an interest in the company of adults and a desire for adult status.[2]

Children's Economic and Domestic Roles

Children's roles in the household economy were explored in a series of questions that were asked of mothers in the 1936 interview. The most severe phase of economic hardship had passed at this point, although deprivational conditions persisted well into the second half of the 30s. The interview was timely in relation to the children's capacity to make significant contributions to family maintenance. They were old enough in the mid-30s to handle demanding jobs away from home and parental supervision.

Two-fifths of the children were employed in part-time jobs, according to their mothers. Over half of the boys held at least one paid job compared to a fourth of the girls. In measuring the performance of household tasks, we included selected chores and questions dealing with the child's response to them. Unlike employment, which includes some measure of quality control, the quality of household assistance is not necessarily indicated by assigned chores. In the data, however, measures of assistance and quality of response were sufficiently related to warrant including both in a single index. Five items were used: three dealt with the performance of chores (cares for room, helps with cooking, and helps with odd jobs around the house), and two indicated the child's response (helps without being reminded and grumbling). An affirmative response by mothers to at least three of the items was defined as a measure of involvement in household chores. Though most children in the sample were involved, this pattern of activity was especially common among girls (82% vs. 56% among boys).

Employment and domestic tasks were related to economic deprivation in both the middle and working class, with boys tending to specialize in the former and girls in the latter. Since class differences were negligible, only the effects of economic loss and father's work status are shown in table 2. The one point where social class made a difference in these results appears in the prevalence of employed girls among deprived families in the working class (44% vs. 16% of all other girls in the sample). Variations in task specialization by economic conditions are most pronounced among boys. Forty percent of the boys from deprived families were engaged in a paid job, and did not have responsibilities in the home. By contrast, most working girls also managed tasks in the home, and over 90 percent of the girls from deprived families made some contribution to the family economy—domestic, economic, or both. At the other extreme were girls from non-deprived homes, a large number of whom lacked any obligation to household operations or employment. Forty-two percent were not engaged in either activity.

| Table 2 | Children with Economic and Domestic Roles, by Sex of Child, Economic Deprivation, and Father's Work Status |

Economic Deprivation and Father's Work Status	Percentage of Boys and Girls with Work and Domestic Roles[a]			
	Employment		Domestic Chores	
	Boys	Girls	Boys	Girls
Nondeprived	42 (37)	16 (26)	69 (37)	56 (26)
Deprived				
Employed	57 (21)	19 (20)	46 (21)	92 (20)
Unemployed	72 (25)	43 (27)	43 (25)	89 (27)

Note. Percentages were statistically adjusted for the effects of social class (1929) in a multiple classification analysis. The correlation of employment and chores with social class was less than .08 in parametric and nonparametric measures of association (r, Kendall's tau_c). A comparison of nondeprived and deprived groups in each sex and task group yielded the following results: work role—boys ($\chi^2 = 5.0$, 1 df. $< .05$) and girls ($\chi^2 = 1.5$, ns.); chores—boys ($\chi^2 = 5.3$, 1 df. $< .05$) and girls ($\chi^2 = 12.4$, 1 df. $< .01$).

[a] The parenthetical figure beside each percentage represents the number of cases on which the percentage was computed.

One consequence of a decremental change in family status and resources is to heighten children's awareness of parental investments which made possible the goods and services they had formerly taken for granted. These include the effort and skills which provide income for the family unit, as well as the labor involved in homemaking and child care. Economic scarcity brought out the reciprocal aspects of consumption which entail obligations to others. Especially in middle-class families, deprivation generally changed one-sided dependency regimes, in which parents indulged their offspring's desires, to an arrangement where children were expected to demonstrate more self-reliance in caring for themselves and family needs. From qualitative data on the

Oakland families, we find that change in parental roles typically preceded a shift in responsibilities to the children. Examples of this change are suggested by parental preoccupation with financial problems and alternative sources of income, by father's unemployment and departure from the family in order to find a job outside the community, by parental illness resulting from the emotional stress of family hardships, and by the inability of parents to provide money for the children's school expenses, clothes, and social activities. These conditions often placed children in responsible positions within the home and challenged them to take on some of the burdens in family maintenance.

While most working boys held only one job, some were involved in two or more enterprises. As an example, one boy from a hard-pressed, middle-class home delivered newspapers, made ashtrays which he peddled on the street, and helped his mother around the house while his father was searching for a job in Los Angeles. Another youngster washed dishes in the school cafeteria and supervised the work of six delivery boys after school. Six of the Oakland children coupled work in their father's business with occasional paid jobs in the community. A common pattern among working girls entailed baby-sitting for neighbors and employment in local stores or businesses.[3] Particularly in severely deprived families, a portion of the children's earnings was used for basic expenditures.

We have interpreted the relation of children's activities to economic deprivation as a consequence of labor and economic needs in the deprived family. An important element in household needs is whether mother was employed. Maternal employment tends to increase both opportunities and the need for children's assistance in household operations.[4] Since working mothers were most prevalent in deprived families, this adaptation may account in part for the domestic activities of girls in these households. In fact, boys and girls with employed mothers were more likely to have domestic responsibilities than other youth (an average percentage difference of 13, with deprivation controlled). Though boys from deprived families were more apt to have a job than domestic tasks, working boys were not more prevalent in the families of working mothers. As a supplementary source of income, the employment of mother may have lessened the economic incentive of children to get a job. In any case, the data show no positive effect of mother's work on the work status of boys and girls.

Economic loss occurred in the context of cultural and social factors which have different implications for the role of children. Family culture, for instance, may advocate responsible roles for children or express no position on this matter. Two value standpoints on children's roles are suggested by the entrepreneurial ethic of self-employed fathers

Children in the
Household Economy

and the traditional family beliefs of foreign-born parents. As likely subscribers to the Protestant ethic, fathers in entrepreneurial occupations should be in favor of hard work and economic activity on the part of their sons. Other aspects of this value orientation include individual responsibility, thrift, and self-denial. In traditional family cultures, work experience and domestic tasks are generally regarded as virtuous activity for children, and tasks are assigned according to sex role—employment for boys and household chores for girls.

More than any other social attribute of the family, number of children has direct consequences for labor and economic needs in the household. As the number of children increases, household operations must expand, caretaking and parenting become more demanding and less available for each child, and financial resources per member are reduced. In the large family, older children commonly assume adult tasks which are usually managed by parents in small families.[5] The labor-intensive economy of large families thus resembles that of deprived households. In terms of children's roles, the large deprived family should differ markedly from the small nondeprived family.

Children in entrepreneurial families were more likely than any other youth to have sex-typed roles, but this effect is entirely due to economic conditions in these families. Foreign parentage and family size do have some effect on children's roles which is independent of economic conditions, and both of these factors are related to deprived status. However, they do not account for the effects of deprivation on children's activities.

The belief that children are obliged to carry their share of responsibilities in the home was a common theme in interviews with foreign-born mothers. In a Swedish family the children were described as "having borne their share of responsibility in a capable manner," despite very trying circumstances. The mother made a special point of assigning tasks to even the youngest child, a five-year-old. A similar attitude was expressed by a first-generation mother from Eastern Europe. Each of her four children had some task in the home, and all were expected to help each other. These attitudes generally correspond with the household role of girls in the families of foreign-born parents. Even with economic deprivation controlled, these girls were more likely to have domestic responsibilities than girls with native-born parents (a difference of 14 percent). Other than this result, foreign parentage had a weak negative effect on the work status of girls and was only slightly related to the roles of boys, both economic and domestic.

The most significant effect of family size is seen in the work role of boys. Two-thirds of the boys with three or more siblings were employed, in comparison to 44 percent in smaller families. The proportion of girls with tasks in the home also increased from small to large families, but the difference is not as large (17 percent). Neither social class nor economic deprivation had an appreciable effect on these results, though differences in activity were most striking between children in large deprived and small nondeprived families. Over three-fourths of the boys in the former group were employed, compared to one-fourth in the latter group. The contrast in domestic involvement among girls is equally pronounced (from 88 to 47 percent).

In deprived families we find no evidence that the eldest child was more likely to earn money or help in the home than younger siblings, and this result did not vary between two-child and larger families. Available evidence does suggest, however, that the eldest child generally had greater responsibility in the household. In fact, some mothers explicitly noted that they expected their eldest daughters to assume a supervisory role with respect to housework and the younger children. One of these girls, with three younger brothers, was described by her mother as carrying much of the responsibility for running the household. That younger siblings make a difference in responsibility is most clearly seen in the special case of the only child. Even in the most deprived circumstances, only children were less frequently employed and involved in the home than members of larger families.

In review, two conditions are particularly noteworthy as determinants of the roles children played in both household and work setting: economic deprivation and a large family. Economic loss generated labor and financial needs which favored the involvement of girls in home operations and of boys in work roles, and led to parental adaptations (such as mother's employment) which enhanced the value of children's efforts in the household economy. Since maternal employment was not a potent source of children's domestic roles ($r = .12$), it is a relatively weak link between this activity and deprivation, but it is theoretically important as an example of interdependence in the family. Change in the mother's role initiates change in the household role of children. We should note that information on the work status of mother was available in 1934 and not two years later when data were collected on children's roles. While the 1934 data may provide a reasonable estimate of mother's employment in 1936, any error would necessarily attenuate the effect of this adaptation on household operations and children's responsibilities therein.

Next to economic deprivation, a family of three or more children is the most significant predictor of sex-typed roles among boys and girls. On the work experience of boys, the main effect of family deprivation is stronger than that of family size (betas of .29 and .22) and is even more pronounced on the domestic roles of girls (betas of .32 and .13).[6] The pressures and needs of a large family would seem to be greatest under deprived circumstances, and yet we find little evidence of such variation. Number of children had no appreciable effect on children's roles under deprived conditions, and economic loss did not have a stronger effect on children's activities in large families.

Throughout this analysis we have used the family system as a frame of reference for interpreting the economic roles of children in deprived families. According to this perspective, children sought jobs in response to economic needs and pressures in the family. Their perception of family circumstances is the untested link in this account since we do not have direct evidence on how or whether objective economic loss was expressed in the subjective world of the Oakland children. In some cases, the actual extent of family hardship may not have been recognized. A disparity of this sort could explain why a number of boys did not have jobs in the most severely deprived families.

Under deprived conditions, we would expect the personal needs or desires of children to be associated with their perception of the family situation. Awareness of family hardship is implied in the outlook of children who felt deprived of spending money and desired greater control over their life situation. For boys, in particular, gainful employment is a logical outlet for these motivational orientations in situations of economic hardship, and the data generally show this connection between family deprivation and economic activity. Very briefly, we find that aspirations on spending money that exceeded the perceived economic status of age-mates were most common among boys from deprived homes in the middle and working classes, and clearly distinguished the gainfully employed from boys who did not have jobs, regardless of family deprivation. Likewise, boys with a deprived background and those with a job were most likely to be described as ambitious in social aspirations during the high school years; trained clinicians rated them highest on the desire to control their environment by suggestion, persuasion, or command. Even among the economically deprived, this desire was most characteristic of boys with jobs.[7]

From the data at hand, we do not know for certain whether economic or mastery aspirations led to or developed out of work experience. There is sufficient reason to claim that employment was prompted by a sense of financial deprivation, but one could argue that money-making endeavors increased economic desires. Both outcomes are likely. Also, the developmental experience of work supports the assumption that jobs both expressed and reinforced the mastery desires of boys from hard-pressed families.

Children's Tasks as a Developmental Experience

A common folk belief in rearing children defines household tasks and jobs as a valuable apprenticeship for the realities of adult life. The presumed benefits of this experience include sound work habits, reliability, judgment, and, in the case of household obligations, an awareness of the needs of others (see chapter 2). Work roles in the community also entail independence from family, and provide experience in self-direction. As applied to children from deprived families, this interpretation describes an adult-oriented form of upbringing. The other side of these activities points to the interpersonal costs of children's contributions, to the restriction of social experiences, playful leisure, and experimentation which are normally characteristic of modern adolescence. In addition to these social costs, the following outcomes of task experience have particular relevance for personality and adult values: judgment and values concerning the use of money; dependability and industry; and social independence, with emphasis on freedom from parental control.

Paid employment away from home generally offers experience in learning the value of money and skills in managing income. There is some evidence that children who are made aware of economic problems in the family and earn their own money are likely to act responsibly in financial matters.[8] Though involvement in household operations should increase awareness of family hardships, judgment on economic matters may be more contingent on how spending money is obtained. Are children paid for doing chores or do they receive money as needed? The latter offers minimal experience in handling money.

Conditions in deprived families presented children with a moral challenge that called for their best effort, reliable and energetic. Though most studies of children in affluent times have not found support for the developmental value of tasks in the home, economic and labor needs in deprived families created urgent, realistic, and meaningful demands which were not in any sense contrived. In this respect there is a suggestive resemblance between the role of children in deprived families and farm households. Labor needs are real and meaningful on the family farm, the jobs are demanding and adultlike, and children seem to take their responsibilities seriously. (For a suggestive comparative study of children's roles in farm and urban families, see Straus 1962.) In both types of families the labor of children has value and consequence for the family unit as a whole.

Most paid jobs in our study placed children in a situation that required independence from the family and self-direction, while domestic obligations drew them more completely within the family circle. In the context of economic hardships, the emancipating influence of a job should be most evident among boys, since they were more often employed than girls, especially in jobs requiring some measure of independence. In addition to their consequence for family dependence and parental supervision, household activities are a significant mode of domestic upbringing for girls, an apprenticeship in homemaking. Compared to the daughters of nondeprived parents, girls from deprived homes can be expected to rank higher on family dependence and domestic interests.

An empirical test of these relations is presented below, beginning with sources of financial judgment.

Financial Judgment

Apart from family need and values, wisdom in spending and saving money is dependent on practical experience with financial matters. When a child has his own sum of money to manage, an ill-considered expenditure has direct consequences for him and, especially in deprived households, for the family as a whole. Personal funds may be acquired by paid jobs, whether in the work setting or home, or by a regularly scheduled allowance. Unlike these sources of money, the practice of giving money to children according to need (as determined by parents) fosters economic dependence. As shown below, economic dependence was more characteristic of girls than of boys, owing partly to the roles they assumed in the household economy. But more noteworthy is the negative effect of economic dependence on financial judgment.

For the total sample, economic support which offered some measure of autonomy on financial matters was more common in the experience of boys than of girls. Two sources of data were used in the analysis: the 1936 interview with mothers and a self-report questionnaire completed in 1937. Mothers were asked whether they gave their off-spring an allowance and paid them for doing chores. Information on whether money was received according to need was obtained from the questionnaire. Forty-six percent of the boys were given an allowance, 20 percent were paid for doing chores, and 25 percent received money according to need. A smaller proportion of girls received an allowance and were paid for helping in the home (40% vs. 10%), while a majority were given money upon a determination of their need (61%). As might be expected, middle-class parents were more apt to give their offspring spending money than were lower-status parents, an average difference of 16 percent.

Parental support was highly contingent on whether the child held a job, and thus varied by deprivational conditions mainly among boys. This result reflects conditions which motivated employment—economic need and the inability or unwillingness of parents to provide spending money. Boys from deprived families in both social classes received less support from parents—as an allowance, pay for chores, or when needed—than members of nondeprived homes, but the difference is largely explained by their work status. An allowance and economic support by need were less common among working than among unemployed youth (30% vs. 66% and 15% vs. 39%). Most boys in nondeprived families were engaged in household chores, and slightly more than a third were paid for their labor.[9]

If economic dependence on parents restricts practical experience in the use of money, this deficit should be most evident in the financial responsibility of girls. Only a small proportion were employed, and those who only helped their parents were seldom paid for their efforts. Especially in deprived families, girls with domestic responsibilities were more often given money when needed than an allowance, and very few working girls received any money from their parents.

In the 1936 interview, mothers were less likely to attribute responsibility in the use of money to daughters than to sons. Seventy-six percent of the boys were described as both saving their money and spending it wisely, in comparison to 64 percent of the girls. Good judgment in the use of money is correlated with deprived status among boys (a difference of 21 percent between nondeprived and deprived groups), but does not vary by either class or deprivation among girls (differences of less than 7 percent). Neither class background nor economic loss proved to be as influential as an allowance and job in determining the mothers' evaluation.

To assess the main effects of an allowance and task experience, we included these factors in a multiple classification analysis which statistically controlled both social class and deprivation.[10] Three factors (characteristically present = 1, not present = 0) were constructed from patterns of employment and domestic chores: employed, only chores in the home, and neither role. Boys and girls were combined in the analysis since the results did not vary by sex of child. Children who received an allowance were more often perceived by their mothers as financially responsible than other children (82% vs. 60%), but this effect is less than that of employment and domestic chores. Eighty-seven percent of the employed were viewed as financially responsible, in comparison to 38 percent of the children who lacked

73

obligations. Between these extremes were youth who only carried responsibilities in the household (66%).

Do these variations in financial judgment have any significance beyond the adolescent world of the study children? in their economic behavior as adults? Unfortunately, we do not have adequate *prospective* evidence of such effects. Available data is restricted to the practice of saving money. From data collected in the 1958 interview, we were able to identify variations in the regularity of savings. Approximately 70 percent of the respondents saved money on a regular basis. Class origin, family deprivation, employment status in 1936, and mother's evaluation of financial judgment were all analyzed in relation to the above index of economic behavior, with adult status controlled. While none of these factors were predictive among women, men who saved their money were most likely to have been reared in a deprived family, to have had a job, and to have been judged responsible in the use of money as an adolescent. Of these three factors, the most significant predictor was employment. Eighty percent of the men who earned money in the 30s reported a saving program, compared to 54 percent of those who did not have a job.

However fragile the evidence, a large number of the study members are convinced that hardship in the Depression has made a difference in their financial outlook. They tend to use the Depression as an explanation for their behavior. In the words of a young white-collar worker, hardships in the 30s made him "realize that money doesn't always come so easy. It makes you just a little conservative in spending money, especially in spending it beyond your means." Such explanations are of little value as a guide to the formative origins of economic attitudes, but they do provide a rationale for conduct and may have social significance for the young as object lessons. A survey of 171 undergraduates at the University of California, Berkeley, during the fall of 1965 indicates that parental memories of the Depression's impact are frequently communicated to children as moral lessons.[11]

Dependability and Industry

The tasks children performed in the Depression can be viewed in terms of the behavior they required. In varying degree, paid jobs call for punctuality, courtesy, thoroughness, and obedience to superiors. If jobs in the household or work setting entailed some measure of dependability and industry, were these patterns of behavior generalized to other situations? Were children who engaged in these activities perceived by adults outside the family as relatively dependable and energetic?

Coming of Age
in the Depression

As measures of this behavior, we selected three scales from the 1937 Situation Ratings (see Appendix B). Each scale was constructed from the averaged and standardized ratings of staff members at the Institute of Child Welfare who observed the children in social activities and school affairs. As described by their characteristic behavior, the three scales are: dependable—"assumes responsibilities and performs them reliably, is conscious of the rights of others"; resists authority— "deliberately breaks rules, refuses to comply with requests of person in charge, resists authority"; industrious—"energetic, concentrated effort displayed in activity."

Boys in domestic or work roles were not distinguished by their dependability or resistance to authority, and neither of these ratings were correlated with economic deprivation or class position. However, industry was attributed most often to working boys, and was also related to deprived status ($p < .01$). The effect of deprivation is largely due to its relation to employment, and diminished to insignificance with the latter controlled.[12] Economic hardship is a plausible stimulus of energetic behavior, as suggested by Bakke's research on children in deprived families (see chapter 2), but it is also likely that jobs were more often found by the industrious. Furthermore, the time required by the job, coupled with the usual requirements of school, family, and friends, would place a premium on energetic activity.

Girls in deprived families were judged slightly higher on dependability and industry than members of nondeprived households, but neither this difference nor the effects of social class were statistically reliable. An explanation for this outcome is seen in the observed behavior of girls in domestic and work roles. Those who only helped out in the home were most prevalent in deprived families, and their observed behavior closely resembled that of girls who lacked obligations. The main contrast occurs in relation to girls who were doubly committed, those with domestic responsibilities and a paid job (table A–5). They were rated substantially higher on both dependability and industry.

A work-oriented life style is most evident in the behavior of girls who assumed roles in both household and work setting. Are their social characteristics more a consequence of factors related to economic loss or of socialization in a lower-status family? Employment was mainly restricted to girls from deprived families, and two-thirds of the working girls were members of working-class families. However, dependability and industry were equally characteristic of employed girls in both social classes.

Another way of looking at the behavioral effects of task experience in the Depression is to take the respondent's viewpoint. Did responsibilities enhance the importance of dependability and industry? To

Children in the
                                          Household Economy

explore this question, we must turn to the adult years for data on behavioral preferences. A questionnaire administered to members of the study (1964) included a list of sixteen attributes of children's behavior, including that of dependability. They were asked to check the three attributes which they considered most desirable in a teen-age boy and girl. In line with our expectation, men who valued dependability were most likely to have grown up in a deprived family, and a majority earned their own money as teen-agers. Even with adjustments made for family and adult status, 52 percent of the men from deprived families favored dependable behavior in a boy and girl, compared to 26 percent of the nondeprived. This effect proved to be much greater than that of employment during the Depression. Neither economic loss nor roles in the household economy were prominent in the behavioral preference of women.

In retrospect, the premise that task experience selectively conditions behavior and values rests on assumptions which may not be valid for the social roles assumed by some members of the Oakland study. One of these assumptions concerns the duration and demand character of tasks in the home and work setting, neither of which were directly measured. As in the case of occupational roles, the behavioral impact of tasks in the preadult years is likely to vary directly with both of these conditions. Without empirical support, we have also treated the domestic and work activities of children in 1936 as if they were characteristic of their adaptations to economic hardship throughout most of the Depression decade. A detailed history of these activities is clearly needed to provide a developmental measure of task experience.

Social Independence and Domestic Values

As adaptive responses to economic deprivation, gainful employment and domestic involvement differ in their apparent consequence for social independence. The former response implies some measure of autonomy and responsibility outside the family, especially for boys, while the latter function among girls entails activity in the home and domestic constraints.

There are two aspects of social independence in the preadolescent and adolescent years which need to be distinguished: the freedom to select same-sex friends, places, and times for social activity; and the freedom to associate with members of the opposite sex, as in dating, socializing with boys and girls in the evening, and attendance at unchaperoned parties. Since boys lag behind girls in heterosexual interests and development, the most appropriate index of social independence for sex-group comparisons is one which is not restricted to interaction with the opposite sex. In the 1936 interview with mothers, this form of independence was indexed by answers to a question on participation in social activities on school nights. Degree of independence in heterosexual activities was measured by replies to whether the child associated with boys and girls on weekend evenings. Affirmative responses to each question were defined as an indication of social independence. Girls were most likely to associate with groups of boys and girls on weekend evenings, while boys were more often involved in activities on school nights.

As shown in table A–6, social independence is related to deprived status among boys in the middle and working classes. This relationship is strongest for school-night activities, and is partly a function of employment and its liberating influence. Boys from deprived families were likely to have a job ($r = .33$), and both family deprivation and a job are similarly related to involvement in extrafamilial activities on school nights ($r = .21$). In a regression analysis (which defined deprivation and family status as givens), the direct effect of deprived status proved to be stronger than its indirect effect through unemployment (betas $= .20$ vs. $.15$). Even though low-status parents generally supervise their offspring less closely than parents in the middle class, class background did not make a difference in the social liberties of boys.

In size and consistency, deprivational conditions had less of an effect on the social independence of girls. Within the middle class, girls from deprived families were more rather than less likely to associate with peers in the evening, but the only meaningful difference occurs in heterosexual activities. This result is contrary to our expectation, cannot be attributed to economic or domestic roles, and differs from the effect of deprivation among the working-class girls. In their group, social independence is most prevalent among the nondeprived, and especially among those who had no obligation in the family or work setting. Approximately half of the girls who did not have role obligations engaged in social activities on school nights, compared to a fourth of the girls who earned money and assisted their parents in the household. The size of this difference, which accounts for the effect of deprivation, most likely reflects the burden assumed by girls who performed both economic and domestic roles.

This difference in the working class also shows up in the leisure time and social experience of girls, according to the reports of mothers (1936). Girls and even boys from the deprived working class ranked lower on free time and social experience than other groups in the

Children in the
Household Economy

sample—the nondeprived working class and both deprivational groups in the middle class. While most children were described as having adequate opportunities for social contacts and hobbies, this was least true for members of deprived families in the working class (68% vs. 86%). Similar differences appear on the interviewer's rating of free or play time and of the variety and suitability of friends. These variations are at least consistent with the constraints and pressures of life in the most deprived sector of the working class, but they do not emerge in staff observations of the study children in social situations. Neither economic hardship nor responsibilities produced differences in the observed popularity of boys and girls. These data do not support the assumption that family deprivation and children's responsibilities imposed severe limitations on social experience, but we intend to look more closely in chapter 6 at sources of acceptance and popularity, such as grooming and clothes, and to explore their relation to economic hardship.

Up to this point we have defined employment as a causal link between family hardship and the social independence of boys. There is an alternative interpretation, however, which has not been ruled out. As an outgrowth of economic burdens in the family, social independence may have preceded and increased the likelihood of employment. According to this perspective, the boys who found jobs were more self-reliant and liberated from traditional family constraints than other youth. The important question, then, is whether differences in social independence preceded or followed the point at which they were hired for the first time. If we assume that this point occurred no earlier than the seventh or eighth grade, we can test this question by using data from questionnaires which were administered in junior and senior high school.

In each time period, identical questions were asked on whether the respondent resembled a young person who is allowed by his parents to stay out late at night, is able to go places without permission, and is permitted to associate with friends in the absence of adult supervision. Since the items were interrelated, scores on the five-point scales (ranging from one "low" to five "high") were summed to provide a single indicator for each period. As one might expect, degree of independence increased sharply between the two time periods among boys in the sample ($\overline{X}$s = 6.8 vs. 11.4). Girls reported less social freedom than boys, but they also acquired more liberties during these years ($\overline{X}$s = 5.8 vs. 10.1).

In junior high, economic conditions did not make a significant difference in the social freedom of either boys or girls, and there is no evidence that boys who later obtained jobs were more liberated from parental constraints at this time than other youth. On the contrary, the former group reported slightly less independence than the latter, and similar results were obtained among girls (an average difference of .53). In high school, however, boys who reported the greatest amount of social freedom were generally members of deprived families, and a majority held jobs. Of these two factors, employment most strongly influenced degree of independence and accounted for the influence of economic deprivation. On the average, boys who earned money on jobs reported more independence ($p < .05$), and showed much lower stability in this respect from early adolescence than the unemployed. This difference in stability and its relation to work experience is shown by correlations between the two measures of social independence among the employed and unemployed ($r = .25$ vs. .52). The largest gains in social freedom were experienced by boys who obtained jobs.

In high school, girls who reported a high degree of independence were not distinguished by deprived status, class position, or role in the household economy. As in table A–6, economic deprivation did have a slight negative effect on reported independence among working-class girls, and parental limitations were correlated with domestic involvement. These variations were too small, however, to be statistically reliable.

Up to this point, the data on social independence are mainly consistent with our expectations on boys in the Depression. All of the evidence suggests that economic loss and work roles tended to free boys from the traditional restraints of parental control. While most girls responded to family hardship by assuming household responsibilities, this adaptation had little consequence for their dependence on the family or parental control, with the possible exception of girls from working-class homes. But apart from the issue of parental control, involvement in household operations has implications for social learning in the role of homemaker. These implications include exposure to domestic models and values. Were girls from deprived families more inclined to favor domestic interests and the role of homemaker than members of nondeprived homes?

To investigate this question we used measures of domestic interests which were based on a vocational questionnaire in the high school period (the Strong Vocational Interest Inventory). From this inventory we obtained two measures of domestic interests: a single item which asked whether the respondent favored only marriage and the home-maker role, a career, or both lines of activity; and a clinical assessment of the relative strength of domestic and career interests, based on profiles in the inventory.[13] Since very few girls were characterized by a predominant career orientation, the main comparison is between those

Children in the
Household Economy

who preferred domestic activity and those who showed a combination of career and family interests.

Domestic interests were associated with economic deprivation and household obligations, but only among girls from middle-class families, a subgroup which is less conservative on sex-role behavior than the working class. Both indicators of role preference showed this result. Two out of three girls from deprived families in the middle class preferred domestic activities to a career (the single item), a preference level which is well above that of girls in nondeprived households (38 percent). In this social class, girls who favored the domestic role were more likely to be involved in household operations than other girls, but the difference (21 percent) is not large enough to account for the effects of economic deprivation. Sixty-eight percent of the working-class girls in both deprivation categories chose family over career interests, and domestic obligations made relatively little difference in this preference.

As seen in these findings, the context in which economic conditions influenced the girls' values and social freedom is specified by their social class. Traditional family values are less prevalent in the middle class than among families of lower status, and the reinforcing effect of family hardship in domestic socialization occurred only among girls from the middle class. Economic deprivation tended to increase the resemblance of middle- and working-class girls on family interests. If the responsibilities of working-class girls were heavier and more time-consuming than tasks managed by girls in the middle class, this would help explain the results on social independence. Economic hardship and domestic activity restricted the social freedom of girls only in the working class.

The Downward Extension of Adultlike Experience

Roles in the household economy of deprived families are not by themselves an indication of accelerated entry into the adult world, but in the Depression they were performed in a sex-differentiated context which placed unusual responsibilities on the young. Early emancipation from family constraints, a preference for dependability, and maturity in the management of money are at least consistent with this interpretation of Depression influences among boys; and so are the dependability and domestic inclination of girls. But we need more direct evidence of this orientation toward adult life, such as an indication that children from deprived households were most likely to seek out and associate with adults and to show an interest in growing up rapidly. Traditionally, the apprenticed young display this mode of social development, and we discern basic elements of apprenticeship in the life situation of the Depression children.

If the years between childhood and adult status take the form of preparation, they represent a developmental phase in which experience has direct consequences for subsequent activity. The young learn by doing as they engage in the occupational ways and constraints of adult life. For the Oakland children, economic deprivation in the 30s increased the common involvement of mother and daughter in household operations, and encouraged economic activity which often placed boys in a responsible position to nonfamily employers. To a considerable extent, adolescents from deprived families were engaged with adults in conjoint activities of mutual significance. From the standpoint of adult orientation, economic roles in the community have special significance as a mode of exposure to nonfamily adults. In an important sense, the transference of attachment from parents to nonfamily adults represents a step toward adulthood, a movement away from the particularistic world of family and kin.

As a general measure of adult orientation, we used a staff rating of adult-oriented behavior in school-related situations (drawn from the Situation Ratings, 1937; see Appendix B): seeks adult company— "seeks out adults in preference to children in a group. Hangs around adults making frequent bids for attention. Identifies with adults and is very cordial to them." In the various settings where the behavior observations were made, adults included teachers, playground supervisors, visitors, and the staff observers.

Children from deprived families and the working class were most likely to be described as adult-oriented, as were those who held jobs. But the most significant factor is gainful employment. Boys and girls who were employed showed much greater interest in adults and spent more time with them in school-related activities than other children ($p < .01$).[14] Even within the deprived group, working youth were rated higher on affiliation with adults than the unemployed. Interest in adults was neither more nor less prevalent among children who were committed to responsibilities in the home.

A variety of factors may lead children to seek the company and attention of adults outside the family, apart from shared activity. These include the need for a parent-surrogate (resulting from family turmoil, rejection) and a desire to be recognized as an adult. One might expect this desire to be characteristic of youth who favored the company of adults—and some evidence of this relation does appear in the data.

Children in the
Household Economy

Boys and girls from economically deprived families were most likely to aspire to grown-up status.[15] This aspiration is related to low family status, but it was most prevalent among deprived children within each social class. In these data, at least, the goal of adult status is very much a function of family hardship. The greater the hardship, the more prevalent the goal.

According to our analysis, the roles children performed in the economy of deprived families paralleled traditional sex differences in the division of labor, and oriented them toward adult ways. Economic hardship and jobs increased their desire to associate with adults, to "grow up" and become an adult. This adult orientation is congruent with other behavioral correlates of roles in the household economy, including the responsible use of money (as perceived by mothers), energetic or industrious behavior, dependability and domesticity among girls, and the social independence of boys.

If "coming of age" was accelerated by economic hardships, did this developmental course entail a premature closure of identity and role preference? In what ways, if any, did the adultlike experience of children shape their options, decisions, and life course as they moved into the early and middle years of adulthood? Two additional types of adaptation in the Depression bear upon these questions: adjustments in family relations, including roles in decision making, and the psychological response of children to family change, status ambiguity, and stress. Economic loss required new adaptations in family maintenance that involved both parents and children. How did these adaptations affect the relative power and emotional status of father? In the next chapter we examine data relevant to this question and identify family conditions that have consequences for the emotional state of children in the Oakland study.

5

Family
Relations

Mother expected everyone to love her because she did so much, because she worked so hard—we were obligated to her.
Daughter's view,
Oakland Cohort

Economic failure and new modes of household support favored a series of adjustments in father's position within the family. Three areas of adjustment are of special interest in this chapter: the exchange between parents in terms of power and emotional support; affective ties and control in parent-child relations; and the degree of correspondence between marital and parent-child interaction. Our point of departure is family leadership—a sensitive barometer of adaptation and strain in crisis situations and a determinant of intrafamilial relations. Under what conditions did economic loss augment the power and significance of mother in the eyes of her offspring?

A durable principle in the politics of crisis assumes that continuity of leadership varies with perceived success in resolving crucial problems or conflicts; in crisis situations, groups tend to replace leaders who display an inability to come up with effective solutions. Reciprocity is an integral feature of this adaptational view of leadership. In democratic groups, the consent to be governed is exchanged for the expectation that a leader will act effectively in meeting the needs of members. Failure in this respect creates an imbalance in the relationship and shifts support to other options. Empirical evidence on crisis resolution in leadership stability is found in a wide variety of groups, ranging from political regimes (e.g., the transition from Hoover to Roosevelt) to the nuclear family.[1]

Economic conditions in the Depression put adaptive skills to the test and set the stage for adjustments in the relative power of husband and wife (the demonstrated ability to control or direct the other). New adaptive responses were required to meet the pressing needs of family support under conditions of severe income reductions and persistent unemployment, for example, a shift in responsibilities to women, children, and outside agencies. Adaptations of this sort, which occurred in deprived households at all status levels in the Oakland sample, established situations that favored wife dominance. Studies of the unemployed show a moderate degree of correspondence between the structure of family leadership and economic support. We have previously noted Bakke's study, which found a negative relation between father's unemployment and power in the family. A similar result has been reported by Ginsburg (1942). More generally wife dominance and father absence are common structural characteristics of families in chronic poverty.[2]

The adaptational perspective on leadership includes assumptions on social exchange and applies to situations where power is derived from consent rather than coercion. Some theoretical and empirical work on the family suggests that failure in crisis management is least likely to produce role change when power relations in the precrisis stage are characterized by extreme unilateral dominance and physical coercion.[3] Under more voluntary circumstances, the likelihood of a loss in father's power is maximized during prolonged crises when his primary contribution to marital exchange is defined in financial terms (see Komarovsky 1940, chap. 3; Heer 1963). An extreme example is the material exchange of money and sex in the lower class.

Love, understanding, and respect in marital relations, fostered by life success and a sense of well-being (see Scanzoni 1970, chaps. 2–4) sustains the husband's status in economic setbacks. There is some evidence that unemployed workers in the Depression maintained their power and esteem among family members when love and understanding were prominent in marital relations (Komarovsky 1940, chap. 3). Since these sources of husband's power increase by social class, at the expense of economic factors, deprivation should be most strongly correlated with wife dominance in the working class.

Two other resources in marital relations also support this prediction: comparative work status and education. Mothers in the Oakland sample were most likely to be employed under conditions of hardship, especially in the working class, and most studies have shown that the working wife exercises greater influence in decision making than the nonworking wife.[4] As a symbol of status and expertise, education is a valuable resource in marital relations. The spouse with superior education enters family decision making with greater leverage and exerts greater influence.[5] In the Oakland sample, this advantage was least often held by men in the working class. Given a situation of economic hardship, wife dominance seems most likely in families where the wife worked and possessed superior education.

The meaning of economic loss for power relations in the family also depends on cultural prescriptions regarding manhood and a male's rights in the family. According to traditional ideology, a man's right to final authority in the family is inherent in his status as father and husband, regardless of performance in problem situations or personal

84

resources; this right does not depend on proven ability to meet family needs. In the Depression, unemployed men whose authority was supported by these beliefs were less vulnerable to status loss than other men.[6] We shall use foreign birth as an index of these beliefs in economically deprived families.

A counterpoint to ideological support for male dominance is the utilitarian premise which judges men according to their work and family provision. Contrary to the structural roots of economic failure in the Depression, it was commonly believed that men could find work and support their family if they really wanted to. By this logic and evaluative framework, unemployment was cast as moral failure, and a large percentage of the jobless accepted this definition of themselves. As Jane Addams observed in the winter of '32, "One of the most unfortunate consequences of the Depression is the tendency to call a man a failure because he is out of work." In times of economic hardship, "the stage is set for one of the most cruel and futile of all our undertakings—one human being punishing another in order to reform his character."[7] Shame, ridicule, and hostile outbursts were elements of this marital drama.

Both economic hardship and related marital structures have potential consequences for conflict and hostility in the deprived family, for the relative status of mother and father as sources of affection and values, and for parental control. Financial problems, a leading cause of marital disputes even in affluent times, are endemic to families of the unemployed and deprived (see, e.g., Komarovsky 1962, pp. 290–91), while conflicts are generally more prevalent in wife-dominant households than in families with other power structures.[8] The latter condition is partly a reflection of the problematic status of wife dominance; few husbands or wives regard this arrangement as desirable or legitimate. While shared authority is a popular ideal in contemporary society, most Americans acknowledge that "the husband should be the head of the home" (Scanzoni 1970, p. 152). Economic hardship also frequently sets in motion a cumulative, circular process which lessens joint problem solving and harmony by diminishing mutuality of expressions of love, sharing, and respect. As emotional distance increases, hostile feelings are aroused which further aggravate relations.

Loss of family status and wife dominance symbolize two related changes in the family which bear upon attitudes toward parents; the increasing prominence of mother in family affairs and a decline in father's position. As shown in chapter 3, boys and girls from middle-class families assigned greater social prestige to nondeprived than to deprived fathers. The community status of mothers, however, was not influenced by economic loss. Are these differences reflected in feelings of closeness and attraction to each parent? While economic loss and wife dominance would increase the centrality of mother from an instrumental standpoint, did she occupy a similar position in the affection and value preferences of her daughter in particular? This seems likely, since power is known to be an important factor in parent emulation, and girls are generally closer to mother than to father. Hostile and withdrawn behavior on the part of father, urgent household needs, and a vacuum in leadership would also add a sense of legitimacy to mother's dominance in family affairs.

Lastly, family structure in deprived families has implications for the social independence of boys and girls which parallel the effects of their roles in the household economy. Given the usual pattern of parental specialization by sex of child, the form of parental control would depend on the type of family power structure.[9] As father's influence increased in marriage, so also would his control over sons, while traditional constraints over daughter are intensified in mother-dominated families. In the Depression, for instance, the unemployed father who suffered a decline in marital power often experienced similar fate in the sentiments of his offspring (Komarovsky 1940, p. 114). In particular, financial problems handicapped the bargaining position of parents in securing compliance from adolescent sons, especially in relation to educational and occupational matters. Economic hardships and status loss made passage to traditional adult roles more discontinuous and problematic for boys than for girls.

Our first objective in the following analysis will be to test the effects of deprivation on marital power, and the conditions associated with wife dominance in deprived families, for example, prolonged failure to resolve economic problems, relative education, and traditional family values. At this point we shall turn to the hypothesized consequences of deprivation and marital power, namely, family conflict, differential preference for each parent, and parental control. The enduring significance and legitimacy of these family patterns cannot be determined by limiting our focus to the Depression years. To achieve a broader canvass for this appraisal, we shall compare perspectives from two stages in the life cycle of the Oakland respondents: from adolescence in the 1930s and from middle age. These perspectives include evaluations of mother and father as parents, relative closeness to each parent, and the emotional significance of kin. Did mothers and fathers who were "important" figures to children in deprived families maintain this status in the attitudes of their grown-up offspring? Are the roles assumed by each parent in situations of economic hardship just as acceptable in adulthood to the Oakland children as they were in the Depression?

Economic Deprivation and Marital Power

Economic problems in the Depression overshadowed other family issues, especially in deprived households, and were seldom far below the surface in most areas of marital interaction. This pervasive concern appears repeatedly in interviews with the Oakland mothers. Many problems with offspring, kin, friends, and community roles were consciously attributed to lack of money and its side effects. On this basis alone, one might assume that marital power in the Depression is satisfactorily measured by decision making on financial matters. By following this approach, however, we might overlook significant variations across families on problematic issues and their relative importance. Sensitivity to these variations is incorporated in "generalized questions" on family structure, which asks the respondent to report who usually decides or has the final say when an important problem or disagreement arises. The advantage of this method is also its disadvantage; it rules out family comparisons in specific areas of decision making. The relative power of husband and wife on budgetary issues is not necessarily the same in other areas.

A generalized question was used in the present analysis to index the structure of marital power, along with qualitative data in family protocols that were constructed from interviews with mothers and family observations in the 1930s. Since we did not have direct reports on marital power from parents or children in the Depression, we asked the following question of study members in an adult survey: "During your adolescence, which parent decided major issues that affected your family?" Responses for intact families were coded father-dominant, equalitarian, or mother-dominant.[10] The qualitative information on family structure was not obtained systematically from all families, and for this reason it was used mainly to validate the above perceptions. In terms of these data, selective distortion and faulty memory do not appear to be an important source of error in the retrospective measure. The two sets of data showed a high degree of correspondence on the direction of power, whether father- or mother-dominant. The few disparities mainly occurred between the dominance structures and equalitarian relations. By viewing marital power from the children's perceptions, we are taking a perspective that is generally consistent with our focus on the psychosocial effects of economic deprivation. Just as economic hardships do not have the same meaning for all members of a family, the reality of marital power for children is largely a function of how they perceive it. This perception has direct consequences for their attitudes toward parents.

Though economic levels in the Depression favored dominance by the wife and mother, this mode of family leadership was reported less often by sons and daughters in the Oakland sample than father dominance (28% vs. 39%) and shared decision making (33%). However, the dominant mother is largely a product of low economic status; the lower the family standing before the Depression and the lower the relative economic status (1933 vs. 1929), the greater the likelihood of leadership by the mother, as perceived by the children. *But economic deprivation is by far the more important factor.* In the perceptions of sons and daughters, economic loss is more strongly correlated with the relative power of mother than is family status ($r = .39$ vs. $-.12$).[11]

The main difference by social class occurred on father dominance, a role pattern reported most often by the offspring of middle-class families (45% vs. 27%). Both equalitarian relations and mother dominance were slightly more common in the working class (an average difference of 9%). Contrary to our initial expectations, the relative power of mother was not most strongly associated with economic deprivation in the working class. In both social strata, this structure showed the same increase by level of deprivation (approximately 30%) and was more prevalent than any other role pattern among deprived families, as shown below.

Since class origin did not modify the relation between deprivation and dominance, we eliminated this factor from the analysis and compared forms of marital power on three levels of deprivation: nondeprived, deprived with father employed, and deprived with father unemployed. Families dominated by mother increased markedly across these levels, from 12 percent in the nondeprived group to 33 percent and then to 49 percent in the most deprived category. This trend directly parallels a decline in the percentage of families in which father was described as holding the upper hand in decision making; slightly more than half of the nondeprived families were headed by father, in comparison to 16 percent of the severely deprived households. On each level of deprivation, approximately one-third of the families were characterized by equalitarian relations between father and mother.

The most extreme examples of unilateral dominance by the mother appear among deprived families with unemployed fathers. Some women made and carried out decisions on major financial and household matters without consulting or even notifying the spouse. In one unusual case, the father was first informed of his mate's decision to rent another house when he returned one evening to find that all of the furniture had been moved. In other cases, wives generally prevailed in conflicts over property disposal and expenditures. The interviewer's summary assessment of power relations in one of these families applies more generally to other households of the unemployed: "Mother has complete charge of everything." According to interview data, some of these women continued to dominate family decision making even after economic conditions improved and their husbands were again able to support the family.

Following the adaptational perspective on leadership, we have assumed that income loss and unemployment produced a crisis in family maintenance which undermined the instrumental base of father's power. Failure to resolve the crisis, which was assured in some degree by structural conditions, initiated role change in which the mother acquired greater influence on family matters. While the data show this relationship, the causal sequence is uncertain. In what sense can men with dominant wives be regarded as more vulnerable to economic and job losses than other husbands? One answer might be that both wife dominance before the Depression and economic loss during hard times are explained by the same set of factors, such as lower education vis-à-vis the wife, heavy drinking, etc. According to this interpretation, both of these conditions weaken the power position of men in family affairs, increase prospects for layoffs and persistent unemployment in the Depression, and account for the relation between economic deprivation and wife dominance. As such, the latter association is noncausal and spurious.

The most satisfying test of the causal path between economic loss in the Depression and wife or mother dominance would entail a comparison of family structure before and after the economic crisis. Change in marital power could then be directly related to variations in economic loss between 1929 and 1933. This design permits the identification of conditions under which women were most likely to gain power in family decision making. Up to the present, studies of families in the Depression, including the Oakland research, have lacked the before/after measurements to make this a viable research option. Nevertheless, there is no evidence that pre-Depression characteristics, such as the relative education of each parent (see below), account for the relation between deprivation and mother dominance.

On theoretical grounds and previous research, there is reason to expect the following social factors to predict both economic status and marital power in the Depression: father's education and its relation to the educational status of mother; the age of husband; and foreign birth. From chapter 3 it will be recalled that fathers in the deprived group were slightly lower on education than men of nondeprived status; that economic loss was unrelated to the relative education of parents and to father's age; and that foreign birth was associated with economic deprivation in the working class. None of these factors explain a significant amount of the variation in economic loss, and they are not likely to show the same relationship to mother dominance, in terms of direction. Consider place of birth. As an index of traditional ideology, birth in a foreign country should be negatively related to mother dominance in marital decision making, even though foreign-born parents were most prevalent among deprived families. On relative education, the wife's advantage may have been a source of power in decision making, as other studies suggest, but it is not correlated with economic loss.

Turning to the data, we find that fathers of foreign birth were not perceived as more powerful than the native-born in either social class. However, foreign birth did make a slight difference in the balance of power among deprived families. Under conditions of economic hardship, an arrangement in which father was perceived as equal to or more powerful than mother was more common in families with foreign parentage, when compared to the families of native-born parents, but the difference is worth noting only in the working class (13%).

Though unrelated to economic deprivation, both father's age and relative status on education produced some differences in the structure of marital power. In the middle class, the likelihood of mother dominance was moderately related to the age and educational disadvantage of the father (average $r = .16$). That is, older men and those who were not superior to their wives in education were most likely to be perceived as less powerful than mother. These results are congruent with a resource interpretation of marital power: a wife's dependence on her husband decreases by age (older women are less obligated to home and child-rearing tasks) and by her equality or superiority in education (see Heer 1963).

Father's age did not affect perceptions of marital power in the working class, and father's advantage in education did not correspond with his influence in family affairs. On the contrary, the more powerful fathers tended to have less education generally and even less than their wives ($r = -.32$ and $-.23$). Personal factors, which support male dominance in the lower classes, may account for this reversal. These factors include physical strength and a willingness to use it in marital conflicts, decisiveness, and initiative. As one study concludes, the husband in the less-educated group "is more likely to excel in personal resources for the exercise of influence," an advantage which narrows considerably as one moves up the educational ladder (Komarovsky 1962, p. 114). Similar class differences in age and education effects are shown for *deprived* families in table A–7. This table compares the relative effects of three sets of factors on marital power in deprived middle- and working-class families: indicators of parental competence and resources (relative education and father's age); traditional values (foreign birth); and role performance (downward mobility, unstable worklife, and employment of mother). The performance measures are a more direct indication of effectiveness in a crisis situation than education or age, and are generally more predictive of mother dominance. Especially in the middle class, the perception of mother as more powerful than father was highly related to loss of family status during the Depression years. Corresponding evidence on mother's power in downwardly mobile families has been reported in other longitudinal research.[12] Loss of family status subsumes joblessness as well as employment on a lower status level, and is more predictive of mother dominance than simply unemployment of the father ($r = .29$). Downward mobility is not a major option for low-status families and is less predictive of mother's power than a disorderly worklife.

Conditions which reflect the father's inability to meet standards of acceptable support in the Depression are more predictive of mother's leadership than her own characteristics, such as education, age, or work status. Working mothers were more likely to dominate marital decisions than the full-time housewife, but the effect of work status is relatively minor. Other characteristics of women and more adequate measures of employment might alter some details in this picture, but not the primacy of role failure in deprived families.

Loss of earning power and a job are most disruptive of family relations when they result in maladaptive reactions—apathy, depression and self-pity, and forms of social retreat or withdrawal, such as heavy drinking. The latter is a potential cause and consequence of economic loss and unemployment. The heavy drinker is subject to layoffs and dismissal owing to irregular and ineffective work habits, and, once jobless, becomes increasingly more unemployable. Alcohol temporarily screens out the harsh realities of economic problems and blocks effective action. Most of the fathers with a "drinking problem" were members of deprived families (see chapter 3), and were also perceived by their offspring as relatively weak in family affairs.

*Economic
Hardships and
Family Conflicts*

Unemployment and a sudden loss of income disrupt accustomed reciprocities in marriage, including the relative contributions and expectations of each partner, and necessitate hard choices among restricted expenditures. In these respects, the stage is set for destructive criticism, interminable quarrels, and hostile outbursts. Even among the more considerate and empathic wives, deprivations and a wearing imbalance in family contributions inevitably foster greater awareness of the husband's faults. This point is lucidly expressed in a recent study of low-income families.

A barely perceptible weakness, one which might be tolerated in a good provider, tends to be seized upon as a possible cause of the husband's failure. This excessive sensitivity to the husband's faults unhappily feeds into another typical tendency: fault-finding is easy because economic failure is likely to magnify shortcomings. The poor providers are, themselves, frustrated and anxious. Not many men can handle these destructive emotions without painful consequences, such as drinking, violence, irritability, increased sensitivity to criticism, and withdrawal. . . . [Furthermore], poor providers offer their wives too obvious a weapon to not be used in a fit of anger. Thus, a wife insisted that her child finish the food on her plate and her husband took the daughter's part, saying that he sympathized with his daughter's dislike of this particular dish. "The wife hollered at me at the table and said that if I'd make enough money she could get the food they liked." [Komarovsky 1962, p. 291.]

Economic hardship entails sacrifice, and choices on expenditure force the question of who is to sacrifice or give up what. Marriage and family life may thus become an arena of competing interests for scarce resources. Agreement on priorities is hampered by restricted marital communication when topics are "too sore" to discuss. Among the low-income marriages, quarrels occurred on even minor differences of opinion concerning economic priorities: "over the order in which bills are to be paid—the milk bill first, so that the children can be fed properly—or the electric bill, so that the light is not turned off. They quarrel over the few discretionary expenditures that do remain—beer, cigarettes, or clothes" (Komarovsky 1962, p. 291).

Economic problems and conflicts are a way of life among low-income families, but were they as prevalent among downwardly mobile families in the Depression? The contrast here is between persistent and decremental deprivation. In the Oakland sample, deprivation often represented a drastic loss of family income, ranging above one-half of the 1929 figure. This change ensured conflict between customary standards of living and experienced outcomes, a disparity which is not likely to be as great among chronically impoverished families with a comparable level of income. Attachment to high standards not only hampers adaptive change in expenditures but also maintains frustration. These and other correlates of economic loss are conducive to family conflicts.

As we did with marital power, we shall view family quarrels or disputes from the children's perspective. Using interview and self-report data collected in the 1930s (senior high period), three judges rated members of the Oakland sample on their perceptions of family conflict (see Appendix B). The nine-point scale ranged from no conflict (score of 1) to high conflict (score of 9). No distinction was made on the relational context of interpersonal conflicts. That is, potential sources of conflict included both mother-father and parent-child interaction. The salience of relations with parents for the family experiences of children necessarily distinguishes their interpretation of conflict from the perceptions of parents who are likely to be more sensitive to and aware of the quality of marital relations.

In the family experiences of boys and girls, conflicted relations generally increased by economic deprivation in both social classes, but deprivational effects were significant only among the girls. Girls from deprived families experienced more conflict than the nondeprived ($p < .05$); no class differences were found on either level of deprivation.[13] On the whole, boys were just as likely to experience conflict in deprived families as girls, but they perceived a much higher level in nondeprived families, a difference shown by means of 4.9 and 3.9.

To a considerable extent these differences reflect the contrasting roles of boys and girls in deprived families. Economic hardships encouraged boys' activity outside the household, while girls more often encountered family obligations, especially in the working class. Consequently, conflict over independence is most likely among boys in the nondeprived group, which would effectively obscure any association between marital quarrels and deprivation, and in the deprived families of girls. In fact, boys whose mothers were relatively low on marital power were most likely to report conflicted relations, while conflict directly increased with mother's power among girls.[14] The latter association anticipates a consistent theme in our subsequent analysis of parent-child relations: *the prominence of social distance and conflict between father and daughter in deprived households.*

Some evidence on deprivational factors in marital dissension was obtained from parent interviews and observations in the 1930s, and from retrospective descriptions of family relations in the 1958 interview. Among deprived families, conflict over expenditures, criticism of the husband's faults as a provider, and attempts by the more powerful parent to enforce his will were common elements in most battles. Disparagement of the father was most evident with mother as the dominant figure. Adults from these families vividly recalled father's drinking bouts, prolonged "silent treatments," mother's nagging, name-calling, and ridicule: "Father was generally silent as mother criticized him"; "they'd argue about anything and mother was always beating him down"; "they barked at each other all the time—I can remember bickering, fear, and quarreling."

Among conflicted families in which father ruled the household, arguments and hostile outbursts were occasioned by challenges to his authority on the expenditure of family income. Conflict situations in one family were precipitated by the mother's tendency to run up bills without consulting her husband. In another case, father's criticism of "unwise" expenditures provoked retaliation in the form of personal attacks on his stature as a husband, father, and provider. Father's unwillingness to allocate a reasonable portion of his income to food and clothing led to shouting matches in a third family. His daughter remembered him as being "tighter than a tick, so tight he squeaked— he wouldn't buy my mother a new dress unless she didn't have a stitch on her back," but he seemed quite willing to spend his money on "status" commodities.

By focusing on hardships in social conflicts, we have failed to acknowledge the large number of families in all class and deprivational groupings which were relatively free of dissension, at least on the basis of our data. From the children's perspective, there is no evidence of marital feuds or severe parent-child conflicts in at least half of the deprived homes. Over two-fifths of the girls from deprived families reported little if any friction among family members, a proportion which is slightly larger among the boys. Harmony and conflict are thus two contrasting family patterns under conditions of economic hardship. What accounts for the difference? What conditions, social and psychological, distinguished harmonious from conflicted families in the deprived group? These are important questions which bear directly upon an understanding of family adaptations in the Depression. But they are exceedingly difficult to research without information on family functioning before the 30s. An appropriate analysis also requires more adequate data on marital relations than we possess. However, some progress in this direction can be made by enlarging our analysis of family structure to the relation between parent and child.

Up to this point the analysis of deprivational effects in family relations has been restricted to marital interaction. This is a major sphere of family life, but its primary significance for our purposes hinges on its consequences for attachment, preference, and control in the parent-child relationship. Economic hardship may directly influence these relations, or indirectly influence them through patterns of marital power. Did economic conditions in the Depression weaken parent-child attachment, shift preferences from one parent to another, or produce both outcomes? In what areas did forms of marital power impinge on relations with parents? These and related issues are taken up in the remainder of the chapter, beginning with perceived relations in the Depression and concluding with adult evaluations of family and parents.

Parents as Significant Others

In children's sentiments, the significance of parents is not solely a consequence of status in the larger social structure, nor can it be adequately explained by knowing only the internal structure of the family. These aspects of the family are related and jointly structure emotional ties, interaction, and judgments. Deprived families lost both resources and status in the community, and were characterized by a "deviant" family structure—wife or mother dominance. In both community and family, father occupied relatively low status. How did this condition affect attitudes toward both parents, the significance of other adults and peers, and parental control?

The implications of status loss for relations between father and child are well-documented in the research literature, especially for sons. The attractiveness of father, as a model and source of values, is related to his occupational status: the higher the status, the stronger the attraction.[15] Though mother's social prestige is derived in part from family status, the association is generally not as strong in children's perceptions. These relationships suggest two main outcomes of economic deprivation in both social classes: compared to fathers in non-deprived families, the deprived father is regarded less favorably by children and is ranked lower than mother by girls and boys.

Variations in marital power have similar consequences for children's evaluations of parents, according to modeling theory,[16] and may partially account for the effects of economic deprivation. Fathers who lost heavily in the Depression were generally perceived as less powerful in family affairs than mother, and neither condition—low prestige or power—defines father as an example to follow in adult roles, particularly in a hostile or nonsupportive context.

This sequence is less clear, however, in crisis situations. While effective problem solving tends to strengthen a leader's base of respect and support, the parent who dominated affairs in deprived families through default or tradition is a vulnerable target for blame and hostility. Default was a factor in the dominant position of mothers in deprived families, and there is no evidence of a generalized belief in the Depression which defined this marital structure as more acceptable than male dominance. If mother is a dominant figure in the respect and affection of children from deprived families, this position may derive more from a decline in father's salience than from her power and personal qualities.

The problematic status of deprived fathers in the sentiments of their offspring has direct consequences for the emotional and normative significance of age-mates. This significance increases, relative to parent preference, when emotional needs are not met within the family. Children who receive little emotional support, encouragement, and direction from their parents generally turn toward peers for need satisfaction and, with age, increasingly favor their friends over parents as sources of affection and guidance.[17] By contrast, an equally, positive attitude toward parents and peers is most characteristic of children from homes which are supportive and democratically structured.

On these points, it will be recalled that boys and girls from deprived families were more oriented toward adults outside the family than the nondeprived, and that boys, in particular, were highly involved in social activities with friends. But what about the relative status of mother, father, and peers? Were friends more salient than father in providing companionship and advice? In time of need, were children from deprived families more likely than the nondeprived to rely upon significant others outside the family—peers, teachers, other adults, etc.? Lastly, how did marital structures affect the relative independence of boys and girls? Were boys liberated and girls more constrained by a family situation in which mother prevailed in decision making?

Companionship and Guidance

Companionship and guidance describe two functions of social referents, or significant others in the lives of children. From the child's standpoint, other people may acquire significance as a source of company or of normative direction and values. In the first case, the child may seek out or prefer the company of peers to that of mother or father, an initial developmental pattern in the transition to social maturity. Given family changes associated with economic deprivation, this orientation should be most pronounced among children from deprived families. While preference for peers as a source of values also generally increases by age, the shift from parents to peers is more gradual and selective than the shift in preferences regarding companionship. For this reason, value preferences are likely to be a more discriminating measure of the relative status of mother, father, and peers. In the subsequent analysis we shall first examine children's evaluations of parents and peers during the early years of the Depression, beginning with associational preferences. The following section includes an appraisal of the relative status of mother and father in the high school years.

Shortly after economic conditions reached their lowest point in the Depression, the Oakland children completed a questionnaire on family relations and social experiences (1933–34). In one question, they were presented with a hypothetical situation—a trip to the local circus—and were asked whether they would prefer the company of father, mother, a group of friends, or their best friend. Three options were provided on each referent—first, second, and third choice. This activity clearly favored a preference for age mates, and friends did rank high among the choices of boys and girls. Boys were most partial to father, followed by their best friend, mother, and the peer group. As might be expected, girls expressed less interest in the company of father and were slightly more positive toward mother. Overall, girls showed less differentiation in their preferences and ranked friends relatively higher than parents when compared to the preferences of boys.

Average preferences for each social referent were first compared by level of deprivation and then by social class. Among boys, deprivational effects on preferences are consistently larger than variations by class position (table A–8). Preference for father is relatively low in the working class, but is lowest in each class among the deprived. Thirty percent of the boys from deprived families made father their first choice, in comparison to nearly half of the nondeprived. Mother's status in the attitudes of boys from deprived households does not compensate for the relatively low salience of father, but it is slightly higher than among the nondeprived. If both the peer group and best friend are considered, *the attractiveness of age-mates stands as the most significant effect of economic hardship.* In both cases, orientation toward friends is strongest among boys from deprived homes. A similar effect is shown for girls.

The peer interests of youth from deprived families reflect aspirations and needs even more than social involvement. In fact, close friends were just as common among children in both deprivational groups according to their report (not shown in the table); slightly more than half claimed that they had many close friends. But the desire for many friends, in contrast to a few, was more prevalent among children from deprived families in both social classes, an average difference of 13 percent.

Aspiration and social reality differed most strikingly among girls from deprived families in both social classes; 89 percent desired many friends, while only 52 percent claimed this achievement. No other subgroup approached the size of this difference. Among boys, for instance, aspirations exceeded reality by only 15 percent. The social aspirations of deprived girls generally corresponds with their distinctive preference for the company of many peers, as against that of a close friend. There is some evidence that children who favor group experiences over the company of a good friend are more peer-dependent, insecure, and emotionally deprived in the family (Hartup, in Mussen 1970, p. 434). In this case, the group compensates for the emotional sustenance ordinarily provided by rewarding achievements and family experiences.

Apart from a common interest in age-mates, there is a high degree of similarity among boys and girls in preference for the company of parents. As economic well-being improved on class position and deprivation, father's popularity increased while mother's declined. These small differences are congruent with the predicted effect of economic factors in attitudes toward each parent.

Associational preferences identify persons who were also favored as confidants, counselors, or problem solvers, although some differences occurred on relative significance. When asked to identify the person or persons they relied upon in time of need, more of the children mentioned mother than any other person on a list which also included father, siblings, teachers and peers. More than one person could be chosen. As might be expected, mother was more popular in the preferences of daughters than of sons (82% vs. 65%), while boys more often turned to father (49% vs. 36%). Considered individually, siblings, teachers, and friends were far down the list of significant others; each referent was mentioned by less than 18 percent. In combination, however, they do constitute a major alternative to dependence on parents. Approximately half of the boys nominated at least one of these reference figures, as did 39 percent of the girls.

Consistent with social preferences, mother was more important than father as a source of guidance among children from deprived families (table A–9). And within each social class, siblings, teachers, and peers were also more frequently chosen by members of these families.

On both companionship and guidance, reference orientations show two general changes by economic loss in the Depression. With increasing hardship in both social classes, mother gained significance relative to father both as company and as a person to rely upon in time of need. The centrality of mother is most apparent among girls, but it is also present among boys. Father's position generally declined on an absolute basis with an increase in economic hardship, while mother's status increased. In combination, these modest differences show a noteworthy change in the relative position of each parent.

This shift acquires additional significance when viewed in relation to a second change in the hierarchy of important persons, the orientational trend toward nonparental figures as associates and counselors. Best friends and the larger circle of companions are only one type of significant other beyond parents, and may not be the most influential, particularly in the long run. Both older siblings and adults outside the family can serve as parent-surrogates in the experiences through which children come of age, and seem most likely to do so when conditions impair the contributions of parents in emotional support, rearing, and social placement. This impairment, whether through objective privation or crippling psychological reactions, is most evident among fathers in deprived families, and is not restricted in its social effect to sons. In the broader research literature there is some evidence that social referents and contacts beyond parents become increasingly more salient to children as one descends the class ladder. In one case, dependence on peer advice regarding the future was found to be most pronounced among boys from low-status, father-absent families.[18] Mother, teachers, and other educated adults are recurring significant others in the life histories of youth who have managed to climb above their lower-class origins. Economic conditions in the Depression generally favored this reference set.

Attraction to
Parents in Mid-
adolescence

Two questions arise as we extend the scope of our analysis to the latter half of the Depression decade, when the Oakland children were in high school. One concerns the issue of continuity and change in evaluations of parents. Did mother remain the more salient parent among the offspring of deprived parents throughout this decade? On the one hand, children's sentiments toward parents in the early years may have had a circular, reinforcing effect in which negative or ambivalent feelings toward the father aroused like sentiments that further polarized the relationship. On the other hand, one might expect some improvement in the relative status of father which paralleled a decline in economic hardship.

The second question is centered on the consequences of mother dominance for children's relations with each parent. How did the balance of power in marital interaction affect these relations? Is the centrality of mother in deprived families at least partially a result of her dominant position in family affairs? Mother dominance in the family is not a favored or most accepted arrangement in the family, and this was also true in the Depression. However, crisis situations often justify or legitimate adaptations that are labeled novel or deviant under normal circumstances.

Affectional and value orientations toward parents were measured by nine-point scales of relative and absolute status. Each scale represents the averaged ratings of three judges who reviewed both observational and self-report materials on the Oakland children during the latter half of the Depression decade (see Appendix B). The scale on relative status measured the degree to which the child felt closer to mother than to father. Scores below and above 5 indicated stronger feelings toward father and mother, respectively. Preference for either parent could occur on varying levels of affection. That is, a child might feel closer to his mother even though he had little affection for either parent. In order to obtain some measure of attitude intensity, we selected two nine-point scales which measured the degree to which the child perceived mother and father as attractive persons. On these scales, an attractive parent constitutes a potential model or example as well as a source of affection. The attribution of attractiveness to a parent is roughly equivalent to what is usually meant by the term "conscious identification."

We have seen in the previous analysis that father's attractiveness during the early years of the Depression was lowest in both deprived families and the working class. This status is also a product of family situations in which mother was perceived as most influential in family decision-making, as shown by zero-order correlations in table A–10. Economic deprivation and mother dominance are more strongly related to the relative status of each parent than to perceptions of each parent as an attractive adult figure.

In forming evaluations of parents, girls appear most responsive to family relations, while family status has a stronger effect on the attitudes of boys. Girls who reported a high level of family conflict held their fathers in relatively low esteem, and family standing made little difference in this assessment.[19] Boys' attitudes were shaped more by class position than by degree of family conflict. Mother's attractiveness also decreased slightly by level of family conflict among girls, while no meaningful variation was found among boys. These sex differences generally correspond with differences in the socialization of each sex. Compared to boys, girls are typically more sensitized to interpersonal relations, and were more exposed to family turmoil through involvement in household operations.

Economic loss and mother dominance increased positive evaluations of mother more than they diminished the perceived attractiveness of father. With or without a control on family status, negative evaluations of father were not significantly related to either deprivation or the perceived power of mother. It is important to note, however, that both of these conditions markedly lowered father's status relative to mother, especially among girls, and class position did not alter this outcome. As expected, the emotional centrality of mother in deprived families is partially a consequence of her perceived influence. For both boys and girls, one-third of the deprivational effect on closeness to mother occurred through the latter's power in the family.[20]

Mother's favored position in deprived families also appears in a preference for her side of the argument in family conflicts. Using retrospective data from an adult survey (1964), we find that both sons and daughters were more apt to align themselves with mother than to favor neither parent (51% vs. 40%) or to take the side of father (9%). The very few cases in which father was favored is a striking characterization of family patterns in the Depression, and so is the prevalence of alliances with mother in deprived families. Fifty-six percent of the children who grew up in deprived families reported that they usually sided with mother on occasions of parental disagreement, in comparison to a third of the offspring of nondeprived parents. Neither sex of child nor family status modified this result. As in the previous analysis, an alliance with mother was partly a function of her perceived power in the family; the greater the power, the more her position was favored in situations of conflict.[21]

Overall, the relative status of parents (not their individual status) stands out as most vulnerable to socioeconomic change. Fathers generally showed some adverse effect of family hardship in their salience to offspring when compared to mother but very little effect otherwise. Given the circumstances associated with family deprivation and the perceived social standing of deprived fathers in the community, it is surprising that they did not suffer greater loss of significance to their children. It is true of course that we are unable to appraise the full matrix of relationships and meanings that bears upon father's position in the family. To protect their social world, some mothers may have misrepresented or denied family conditions in the presence of children. In other cases, hardships may have increased the tendency for children to idealize their father, to exaggerate his good points and ignore his failings. We have no reliable estimate of these tendencies, though other studies do provide some impression of myth making and idealization in family life.

The second major finding concerns the relation between economic deprivation and an orientation toward persons outside the family among youth in high school (see also chapter 4). Compared to the nondeprived, boys and girls in situations of economic hardship were described by mothers (1936) as more interested in going places with friends than with the family, a difference which is most significant in the middle class. Also we found a relation between economic hardship and identification with nonfamilial adults. Members of deprived families in both social classes more often sought the attention and company of adults in mixed social situations and expressed stronger interest in becoming an adult. One explanation for this orientation may be found in the relatively low status of father in deprived families, with its implications for emotional and developmental needs, and another is posed by the economic roles assumed by children in deprived situations. As shown in chapter 4, boys and girls *with jobs* were more identified with adults outside the family than with other children. As a hypothesis, we suggest that family deprivation increased a need for adult support or attention outside the family and heightened desires for peer recognition, while employment reinforced adultlike interests through the apprenticeship experience of community settings.[22]

Family Structure
and Social
Independence

Economic deprivation had markedly different effects on the social independence of boys and girls, as shown in the previous chapter. Boys tended to gain independence through economic deprivation and the autonomy provided by work experience, while working-class girls in particular encountered less freedom in deprived families than in non-deprived situations. In both social classes, economic hardship increased the resistance of boys to parental authority, as well as their assertion of independence, while girls were most likely to accept parental judgment in deprived families.[23] Are these differences at least partially a consequence of mother dominance and its implications for the control of each sex? Did the ascendance of mother's influence in the family weaken parental control over sons through the withdrawal of father, and strengthen her presence in the lives of daughters?

The structure of power between mother and father is related to parental control, but in different ways among sons and daughters, according to information from an adult survey (1964). Retrospective data was available on the relative strictness of each parent in the Depression, and on parental strictness when compared to that of other parents. As mother's power increased, daughters were more likely to describe her as stricter than father.[24] By contrast, no differences in the strictness of each parent were noted by male offspring of families headed by either parent, although relatively weak control was most often recalled by the sons of dominant mothers. As father's power in the family decreased, so also did the strictness of parental control *relative to that in other families.* No variation of this sort was found in the perceptions of daughters.

With an increase in mother's power, boys were more likely to enjoy social freedoms, to participate in social activities on school nights, and to do things with a group of boys and girls, while girls were more constrained in mother-dominated families than in other households. Information on these forms of independence, reported by mothers in the 1936 interview, was used to measure autonomy in chapter 4. Forty-five percent of the boys from mother-dominant families were involved in both activities (general social functions and heterosexual associations), compared to a third of the youth from households in which father had greater power. In the latter situation, girls experienced greater independence than they did in families headed by mother, a difference of 14 percent.[25] The effect of mother dominance is not large enough in either sex group to account for the influence of economic deprivation on autonomy, although it is consistent in both social classes. Even among members of deprived families, family leadership made a difference in social independence.

Relatively weak controls in the family and a desire for adult status are conducive to an acceleration of social development and commitments, particularly in the field of heterosexual experience. In the absence of family restrictions, the first date is likely to occur at an early age, followed by more frequent contact, intimacy, and commitments that may lead to a relatively early marriage. This developmental course is more consistent with the life situation of boys than of girls in deprived families, and available data generally show this difference.

Up to the latter years of high school, girls in the sample were more active in heterosexual relationships than boys, but economic deprivation increased this activity only among boys.[26] In both social classes, the initiation of dating before high school, contacts with the opposite sex, and the amount of dating were all most prevalent in the deprived group among boys. These activities showed little consistent relationship to economic loss among girls, especially with class variations controlled, although dating appears to have been less common among girls from deprived families.

Premarital sexual experience is a logical consequence of early heterosexual involvement, as shown in a number of studies (see Moss 1964), and is consistently related to low socioeconomic status. In the Oakland sample, premarital coitus was most often reported by women and men who grew up in the working class, and to a lesser extent by those with deprived backgrounds in each stratum.[27] The influence of family status clearly overshadows the much smaller effect of economic deprivation. Since both heterosexual development and premarital coitus are known to have consequences for the timing of marriage, we shall explore these factors, and their relation to both class and deprivation, when we take up the formation of adult careers in chapter 8.

Parents and Others in the Depression: An Overview

Significant others among children in the Depression document a familiar theme on the interdependence of family and occupational systems in complex, industrial societies; the consequences of a man's work status and earnings for his social and emotional position in the family. Whether middle or working class, children from deprived families were most likely to perceive father as less powerful, supportive, and attractive than mother. This consequence does not apply to all or even most fathers who suffered economic losses, owing to other bases of role support and male dominance, although it is highly concentrated in the most deprived group of families.

The relation between economic hardship and father's subordinate status in the family evolved through a largely unexamined interpretive process. How was economic loss or unemployment interpreted by men, other family members, and the larger community? It is not surprising that male victims of the Depression were frequently blamed for setbacks over which they had little or no control, given a value system that extols individual responsibility and self-sufficiency. More important, however, is the generalized acceptance of this utilitarian self-evaluation among husbands and fathers who were deprived of the means to adequately support their families. Instead of attributing cause to deprivational conditions in society, to a force beyond the individual actor and his understanding, the record, such as it is, shows that the unemployed or hard-pressed workers were inclined to direct hostile feelings and frustrations toward the self,[28] punishing themselves for the consequences of an economic system. Actually we do not know how fathers in the Oakland sample interpreted economic failure; but it is certain that self-inflicted punishment, such as immobilizing guilt and defensive reactions (social withdrawal, drinking, etc.), would enhance the likelihood of status loss.

Within the family, we interpreted mother's social and emotional salience under conditions of economic hardship in terms of her power or resources; relative power and attractiveness are intercorrelated. Left unexplored in this view is the meaning of low-status to all members of the family and especially father's reaction to it. In the Depression, the most widely accepted structure of family life placed father at the helm, in a position of authority over his wife and children. This norm is the traditional counterpoint to a utilitarian standard for manhood, personal worth, and significance. In traditional ideology, male gender and subordination to wife are incompatible or incongruent statuses within the family, a structural contradiction and source of hostility.

Given the very limited information on the Oakland fathers, how they responded to contradictions of this sort largely remains an open question. Nevertheless, some withdrawal from family activity, both social and emotional, occurred in a majority of the cases which were adequately recorded in home interviews. Heavy drinking, physical isolation, and intense preoccupation with self, among other forms of withdrawal, temporarily reduced or minimized exposure to the punishing reality of a man who was not the head of his own household. The affective consequences of these adaptations are suggested by research on wife dominance. Using the perceptions of children, one study found that father's warmth and emotional support increased with his relative power on family matters; fathers in households headed by the wife were perceived as colder than men in a leadership position (Bowerman and Elder 1964, p. 563). In the Oakland sample, father's emotional distance or indifference may have been an important factor in the prominent affective status of dominant mothers in deprived families. Persons in a subjective position of disadvantage are less inclined to encourage or support others, to share or communicate.[29]

As we have seen, the centrality of mother among children in deprived families is coupled with an enlarged set of reference figures beyond the family, an extension which has the compensatory earmarks of an adjustment to decremental change within the family. Adults were more important to boys and girls from deprived families in both social classes, as were best friends and the peer group, and they more often sought the company and assistance of these persons. Though interest in adults is frequently placed in opposition to peer involvement, both serve to differentiate the young from the world of parents and provide complementary social experience for adult relationships, hierarchical and collegial.

The peer and heterosexual orientations of boys in deprived families paralleled their social independence, enhanced by work experience, and weakened control over sons in the mother-dominated home. The social independence of boys increased by level of deprivation in both social classes, as did their heterosexual experiences. Preference for the companionship of peers was equally pronounced among girls in deprived households, but they did not have the social liberties of boys, especially in the working class, and (in the deprived group) were not as likely as boys to be involved in dating. A disparity between strong social desires or needs on the one hand, and corresponding experience on the other, is most evident among girls from economically deprived families.

One of the more important questions on family life in the Depression pertains to the conditions under which families became more or less cohesive following economic loss and unemployment.[30] By centering our attention on selected effects of economic change for relationships in the family, we generally minimized the significance of deprived families in which father remained influential in family decision making and important to both sons and daughters. According to available data, *it is apparent that a sizable number of deprived families were father-dominant and emotionally stable.* The story told by these families is an essential part of any social analysis of the Great Depression, but it would be unwise to assume that they adapted more effectively to economic hardship than families in which mother gained influence at the expense of father and children became productive members of the household economy. Adaptation is a function of the interplay between individual or group and the social situation, and much more information is needed on all elements of this transaction, its alternatives and consequences, before appraisals are made.

The class position of the Oakland families before the Depression is an element which has considerable importance for interpreting our analysis. Nonmanual families in the sample are primarily members of the stable working class. Only a few families were located in the lower class, a subgroup which was most severely deprived by conditions in the Depression. In times of economic scarcity or affluence, the battle for survival from day to day is played out in the lives of parents and children within the lower strata of society. Unlike other studies of families in the Depression, the present research has very little to contribute to an understanding of crisis and adaptation in this subgroup.

The preceding analysis has viewed family relations within the immediate context of economic conditions in the Depression. Relations in deprived families established a relatively distinctive environment for processes of maturation and socialization, one with varying consequences for younger and older children. Selected variations may be noted by a brief comparison of three age groups, defined by the following birthdates: 1910–11, 1920–21 (Oakland sample), and 1928–29. Developmental vulnerability to family disruption, mother-dominance, and father-absence generally decreases with age of child; the older the child, the lower the probability of adverse psychological consequences from drastic change in the socioeconomic structure of the family. Accordingly, sex-role patterns, cognitive growth, and social

Coming of Age
in the Depression

competence in human development should be most negatively influenced by family crises among children in the youngest cohort who passed through the dependency phase during the early years of the Depression. At the other extreme is the oldest cohort, which reached the age of majority in 1932–33, a group which was more vulnerable to deprivational factors in establishing a life course than to the interior world of families in crisis. Situated between these groups are the Oakland children; they were beyond the dependency stage, but they were too young to experience the full brunt of lack of opportunity in jobs and education. However, they were old enough to participate in the economy of deprived families, as we have seen, and were subject to the deprivational effects in emotional states, orientations toward the future, and achievement.

Another legacy of family life in the Depression persists in the attitudes of adult offspring toward their parents. These attitudes should tell us much about the contemporary significance of childhood in the 1930s, the meaning of parental roles and effectiveness in crises. When members of the Oakland sample left home, did they remain as charitable or negative toward each parent, did they become more understanding and accepting as events backstage were disclosed, or did they take a more critical, judgmental attitude? To conclude our analysis of family relationships in the Depression, we shall test these alternative views of parents, and explore their implications for intergenerational relations.

Views of Family
and Parents from
Adulthood

The significance of family and parents to adult offspring was investigated from two angles. First, we compared the relative effects of economic deprivation, family structure, and class origin on attachment to kin, to relatives on either or both sides of the family. The emphasis here was on the importance or significance of these family ties. This was followed by an examination of adult attitudes toward mother and father as parents; their relation to family conditions in the Depression and correspondence to adolescent feelings toward parents in the 30s. Orientations toward family and parents in adulthood were indexed by responses to a series of open-ended questions on the 1958 interview.

One of the questions asked about the current significance of kin relationships and gatherings. Since no systematic distinction was made between attitudes toward the husband's or wife's side of the family, we constructed a single measure of sentiment toward kin in general.

Responses were assigned to one of three code categories: "very important, very close"; "important, but not extremely so"; and "family is of little or no importance." Women generally occupy the more central role in family and kin activities, "while men are the symbolic carriers of the temporal continuity of the family," of family name and prestige across the generations.[31] This functional difference is reflected in the feelings of Depression-reared adults. Women were more likely to regard family ties as important; 70 percent were assigned to one of the two affirmative categories, in comparison to 43 percent of the men.

As a matter of value, the family ties of women were influenced adversely neither by economic hardships in the Depression nor by class background. In fact, the daughters of deprived parents were more likely to view relatives as significant others than were the offspring of nondeprived homes, an average difference of 15 percent in both social classes (1929). Family structure largely accounts for this difference and brings to mind the notable strength of female ties among families mired in poverty. Close family ties were more often acknowledged by daughters of dominant mothers than by women who grew up in families in which father held greater power; 78 percent versus 66 percent regarded family as important. The causal sequence from deprivation to mother dominance and family ties is only suggestive, however, owing to the relatively small effect of both deprivation and mother's power.

The attitudes of men were also related to economic deprivation and dominance patterns, *but in the opposite direction*. Close family ties were reported most often by men from nondeprived homes which were not headed by mother, and class background made no difference in this result. Only a fourth of all men in the sample placed kin relationships in the "very important" category, but this attitude was more frequently expressed by the sons of nondeprived parents (43% vs. 13% of the deprived). Likewise, only 11 percent of the sons of dominant mothers claimed that kin were very important, in comparison to 41 percent of the sons of more powerful fathers. As an intervening variable, mother's perceived influence largely accounts for the effect of deprivation on subjective ties with kin.[32] The original difference of 30 percent was reduced by approximately two-thirds with dominance patterns controlled. For both sexes, then, *the importance of family ties is contingent on the relative power of the same-sex parent. Psychological distance from kin is most pronounced when a parent of the opposite sex was more influential.*

A plausible source of these sex differences is the type of kin associations established by families which were headed by either mother or father. Owing to father's withdrawal from the family, households headed by women may have specialized in associations through women

Coming of Age
in the Depression

in other units of the kin network, thereby developing relationships that appealed mainly to daughters. This assumes that initiative in the field of kin interaction is made by the dominant parent and that mother's initiative is most likely to favor contacts with female relatives. Children and family interests provide a common basis for contacts among women in the kin group, even when there are differences in economic and social status.[33]

In a culture which defines father as the legitimate head of household, and measures him in terms of individual achievement, status inequality and incongruence are bound to create psychological barriers to kin relations among men, a situation most characteristic of husbands in wife-dominated families during the Depression. It is known, for instance, that status dissimilarity has adverse effects on sentiment between brothers.[34] Assuming that male relatives are especially salient to boys, socialized attachments to kin should be most prevalent among the sons of fathers who maintained a position of strength in the Depression through economic and family roles, and the data show this association. The validity of this interpretation cannot be tested in the Oakland sample, owing to a lack of kinship information, and no study has explored the relation between marital power and the kin ties of offspring.[35]

Though most daughters of deprived parents felt close to kin in adulthood and were aligned with mother during the Depression, a large percentage do not remember either mother or father as a "good" parent. Adult attitudes toward parents in the 1958 interview were used to form two measures of evaluation. One indicated the degree to which each parent understood the respondent as a child in the 1930s: "very well," "fairly well," and "not at all or poorly." The second index measured the respondent's evaluation of mother and father as parents: Impressions of each parent were coded into four categories: "very favorable," "favorable," "negative and mixed feelings," and "strongly negative." The first two categories were defined as a generally positive or favorable impression. As shown in table A–11, a majority of the women rated both mother and father favorably, but this judgment is least positive among daughters of deprived parents.

At issue in attitudes toward mother is not her empathy or understanding but her status as a parent. Most women in the sample felt that mother understood them in adolescence, and neither economic hardship nor class background made a difference in this assessment. Mothers in deprived families did not fare as well as those in nondeprived families in their perceived stature as parents, and fathers in this group received the largest percentage of negative evaluations on understanding and parental qualities. By and large, the position of these men did not change appreciably in the sentiments of their daughters between the Depression and the late 1950s. By contrast, daughters' evaluations of mother in the deprived group were largely positive in the 30s, while over 40 percent, by the 50s, regarded her as an undesirable influence in at least some respects.

Like sentiments toward kin, a key factor in daughter's views on the parental behavior of mother and father is the structure of family power. As mother's influence increased, both her stature as a parent and that of father decreased in the recollections of daughters. Mother's power seemed to be an accepted adaptation to economic hardship in the Depression, at least in terms of adolescent regard, but it is clearly a major source of negative sentiment in the adult years. Only 44 percent of the daughters of dominant mothers held positive impressions of mother as a parent, in contrast to 86 percent of the women with fathers who were either equal to or superior to mother in the decision-making process. Evaluations of father showed similar variations across these types of family structure (50% vs. 77%).

As a correlate of both deprivation and adult evaluations, mother's power represents a significant intervening link in the chain of influence. In fact, the primary effect of economic loss occurs through mother's power and its negative implications to daughters in the 1950s. Economic deprivation did not make a significant difference in adult views of mother or father among women who were brought up in families which were headed by father or in which parents shared power. The mediational status of marital power does not of course explain why daughters' attitudes toward the dominant mother have changed over the years. Before we explore this matter, let us see whether similar change is evident in the attitudes of men.

Overall, men closely resembled women on evaluations of each parent; they were not more likely to have negative or positive impressions. However, men rated parents more positively on understanding, a difference which is most striking in perceptions of mother. Most of the men rated mother positively on understanding, compared to less than three-fifths of the women (89% vs. 59%). Father was less often a recipient of favorable judgments from sons (on understanding), and this was even more true among daughters (67 vs. 53 percent).

Class background played a more important role in the attitudes of men than economic deprivation, especially in relation to father. The perceived understanding and adequacy of father showed little consistent relation to the economic hardships experienced by men, apart from class origin. Surprisingly, men from the working class were more likely to remember father in a positive light than the sons of middle-class fathers, despite contrary differences in the severity of absolute deprivation. On both understanding and stature as a parent, approximately four-fifths of the men from working-class families gave father a favorable rating, in contrast to 56 percent of the men with origins in the middle class. Attitudes toward mother did not vary by either class background or deprivation.

Judgments of father appear to have taken extenuating circumstances into account, such as the burden of family support in the Depression. In some of the interviews, men from deprived families explained their positive opinion of father by referring to the fact that he "did the best he could," "was courageous," etc. Within each social class, such evaluations generally favored fathers in deprived situations.

Among adults who were closer to mother than father in adolescence, men appear to be more charitable toward father as a parent than women (table A–12); but this early preference is not an accurate index of how they now regard either parent. Sentiment toward parents tends to be more stable among women, especially on negative feelings toward father, though instability remains the principal theme. Even when we extend the analysis to specific ratings of each parent's attractiveness to adolescent offspring, the results closely parallel the pattern shown in table A–12.

Overall, we find that economic hardship in the 30s had less impact on the reported family ties of women than on assessments of their parents' understanding and adequacy as parents, while the reverse pattern appears in the attitudes of men; family misfortune had little to do with how men looked back on parents, though it frequently weakened their ties to family and kin. The important factor in their attenuated relations with family is the prominence of mother; relatively few men regarded family ties as important in their social world when mother was depicted as the power figure. We interpreted this outcome as evidence that the significance of family attachment is contingent on the relative power of the same-sex parent; kin generally mean more to men who are sons of dominant fathers. Some men may have been emotionally dependent on their mothers, though it is not clear how this attachment would affect relations to other members of the kin network.

A critical image of parents among women is linked with deprived status and is correlated with the perceived influence of mother in the family; negative judgments increased with her perceived dominance. Of particular interest, here, is the tendency for daughters to move toward a more critical image of the dominant mother between adolescence and the middle years of adult life. What aspects of the mother-dominated or deprived family account for this negative trend? There is little evidence, for example, that views of father have changed appreciably, in a positive or a negative direction, over this time period. As a group, fathers tend to remain the least attractive parent. One approach to this problem is to analyze accounts of or reasons for critical images of mother. What faults in mother's conduct were mentioned? From a review of qualitative materials, we identified a general complaint which appeared most often in critical assessments, *indebtedness and obligation to mother*.

In the typical characterization, mother consciously defined her labor or effort for the family as an extreme sacrifice, a contribution which could not be adequately repaid by the children without the sacrifice of their independence and integrity. Indeed, some mothers made every effort to avoid any semblance of full reciprocation in order to maintain the indebtedness of their children, a practice which frequently continued as the young left home and entered adult life. Indebtedness, a sense of obligation, and dependence all refer to an imbalance in parent-child exchange. To discharge one's obligation to parents is to restore balance to the relationship. The parental stimulus in activating obligations was expressed in various ways: "I didn't need to work hard and save money for your education, but I did"; "Remember what I gave up so that you could have good clothes and food?"; and "In view of the things I went through for you, you can at least do this for me."

One aim of sacrificial investments is to secure affection, gratitude, and praise—to feel needed, important, and respected. These responses represent the costs of receiving a sacrifice, whether desired or needed. When offspring reach adult status, the sacrificial investment of parents may be used to ensure some consideration in important decisions—on where to live, what job to take, where to spend a vacation or holiday. Sacrifices generate power and a sense of obligation when they are interpreted as such by the recipient, but this response is at least problematic. Indebtedness fosters resentment, which erodes the sense of obligation, especially when it is used to excess as a means of control.

Obligations to a possessive or controlling parent are by definition at odds with independence needs and particularly with the requirements of adult life. In the Oakland sample, the adult years generally marked the point at which the "martyr complex" of mother and the restraints of indebtedness became a conscious problem. It is also the point at which offspring became increasingly more resentful of the control tactics employed by their dominant mothers. In the words of one respondent: "Mother played the martyr like a veteran! Actually she's very selfish. I remember her as a very strong person with a lot of courage. But I don't think much of her."

Deprived situations in the Depression were made to order for the long-suffering, martyr role. Loss of income and social status made life much less rewarding, especially in the larger community, and much

Coming of Age
in the Depression

more difficult for mothers within the household. Whether families became more cohesive or not, these conditions increased the compensatory value of responsiveness and affection from children. Mothers with a martyr complex were remembered by their daughters as suffering from feelings of inferiority and insecurity; they felt victimized and ill treated. They augmented their visible plight at times by actively creating grievances and hardships. Overtures of assistance from members of the family were occasionally belittled and criticized, as if to say that no help could make up for the sacrifice.

Mother "made us feel obligated to her" aptly summarizes the daughter's sentiments. One mother was remembered as "expecting everyone to love her because she did so much, because she worked so hard—we were obligated to her." Another woman painfully recalled the times when her "mother would give us something," and then expect something in return. "The next thing you would wish that you had not gotten it because she would accuse you of not appreciating it or her." She added that "mother was always making us feel obligated, and this is still true. She gives with one hand and hits with the other. You want the affection but you fear what will follow."[36] One of the most common concerns of women in this family situation was the undesirable influence which they felt mother continued to exert over their lives. "I worry," said one, "about the shadow of my mother and its effect on me and my children. You think that your life is your own, but each life affects the next, and each generation affects the next."

Economic Change in Family Experience: A Summary View

We have taken a limited view of family experience in the Depression. Important topics were bypassed out of necessity; modes of exchange among members of the kin network, the expanding and contracting household through good and bad times, the relation between two or more generations of adults in the same residential unit, etc. There are many unknowns in the parental world owing to the restricted reports from mother and father. Only rarely do we grasp an outline of their inner and outer lives, and even then it leaves much to be desired. Nevertheless, some general themes have emerged which are worth noting at this point. These pertain to the interdependence of family life, the minimal effect of family status prior to 1930, sex differences in the Depression experience, and family linkages between economic change and the Oakland children.

It is apparent that no sector of family life is isolated or completely autonomous relative to other domains. Change in one area often ramifies to other areas. Modes of economic survival and social adaptation in the 30s played upon and were structured in some degree by the course of family relations and culture. To give only one example, mother's employment and father's economic disability shifted responsibilities to children in the household economy and increased the prominence of mothers in family affairs. Without knowing this impact of family hardship, we would have had difficulty in grasping the varied experience of children with their parents.

Family interdependence and response in the Depression crisis can be viewed in relation to three generalized feedback processes: control, adjustment, and adaptation. Loss of control, with its signal or call for recovery measures, is a distinguishing feature of crisis. In some families the reality of this message was denied or muted, out of allegiance to the way things were, with activities continuing as usual for the time being, while other families (according to the literature) responded with concerted action to the emergency norm, augmenting social coordination, interdependence, and efforts on behalf of the group. Perception of a substantial disparity between family income and needs frequently led to demands for a reordering of priorities or values on the allocation and consumption of resources; a general reduction in the level of consumption, a shift in consumption priorities to food, shelter, and safety needs, etc. Lastly, from an awareness of the persistent incapacity of father to meet family requirements emerged pressures for a restructuring of activities, responsibilities, and power among members of the family unit. With the onset and persistence of economic deprivation, families shifted to a more labor-intensive system which enlarged the roles of mother and offspring, accelerated adultlike experiences, and increased the importance of nonfamilial persons to the young. The casualties in this change begin with father's diminished position and may extend to the loss of family advantages in launching children on desired paths to adulthood.

Economic loss made a substantial difference in the household economy and relationships of families in the Oakland sample, *irrespective* of family status before 1930. As families entered the Depression epoch, their class position influenced parental interpretations of economic loss and subjective responses, as well as children's perception of father's social prestige, but it had little consequences for the household or economic roles of children in deprived situations (less among boys than among girls), or upon family relationships, marital and parent-child. Both in the middle and the working class, economic losses increased the involvement of children in household affairs, emphasized the centrality of mother in family matters and children's sentiments, and expanded the social world of children beyond the family in desire if not in activity. Economic conditions increased the significance of the family unit to children through its social demands, and diminished its resources for meeting their needs, material and social; children in deprived homes coupled involvement in household roles with an orientation to persons outside the family. Even though class position made little difference in these outcomes, its effect is most evident in the realm of values and developmental influences, for example, the domestic values of working-class girls and their traditional life in the household. The developmental implications of class origin will be more apparent as we explore the psychosocial adaptations of the Oakland subjects in adolescence (chapter 6) and the adult years.

We have gained some understanding of family deprivation in the lives of the Oakland children by tracing its impact through roles in the household economy and mother's dominance in the family, but these linkages are not the full story by any means. Neither factor completely accounts for deprivational effects, and yet they offer a rough estimate of the extent to which economic change influenced children through correlated family conditions. Figure 1 lists three general effects of deprivation which were partially mediated by family adaptations: attitudes and behavior, aspects of the nonfamilial world, and family relations. The chart sacrifices analytic qualifications and subtleties for the benefit of an overview which shows some important differences in the life situation and attitudes of boys and girls. To simplify the diagram, I included arrows indicating only the indirect lines of influence from economic deprivation; direct lines of influence are present in most cases and do not require additional emphasis.

Socioeconomic change in family life provides some insight on two general questions regarding child socialization and family structure. The first question pertains to change in the relation between age-graded expectations/activities and chronological age. Under what social conditions are adultlike expectations and experiences extended downward to persons of younger age, or are child expectations extended upward in the age hierarchy? Prolongation of the dependency stage is one correlate of societal complexity, of structural differentiation, role specialization, and an upgrading of skill requirements. But even in an advanced industrial society, children of the lower strata have least access to a lengthy period of social dependency; they enter adult roles at an earlier age than children of affluence and privilege. We find a comparable pattern among children of family misfortune in the Depression.

The second question focuses upon particular sources of change in family structure, specifically concrete, historical events—swings in the

Figure 1

Linkages between Family Deprivation and Child Characteristics

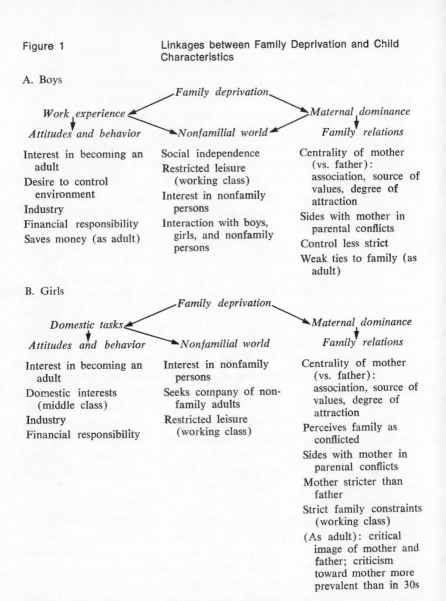

A. Boys

Family deprivation

Work experience / Maternal dominance

Attitudes and behavior / Nonfamilial world / Family relations

Interest in becoming an adult
Desire to control environment
Industry
Financial responsibility
Saves money (as adult)

Social independence
Restricted leisure (working class)
Interest in nonfamily persons
Interaction with boys, girls, and nonfamily persons

Centrality of mother (vs. father): association, source of values, degree of attraction
Sides with mother in parental conflicts
Control less strict
Weak ties to family (as adult)

B. Girls

Family deprivation

Domestic tasks / Maternal dominance

Attitudes and behavior / Nonfamilial world / Family relations

Interest in becoming an adult
Domestic interests (middle class)
Industry
Financial responsibility

Interest in nonfamily persons
Seeks company of non-family adults
Restricted leisure (working class)

Centrality of mother (vs. father): association, source of values, degree of attraction
Perceives family as conflicted
Sides with mother in parental conflicts
Mother stricter than father
Strict family constraints (working class)
(As adult): critical image of mother and father; criticism toward mother more prevalent than in 30s

business cycle, wars, mass migration, etc. No account of family change in the twentieth century would be complete without an assessment of such events. Maternal dominance among deprived families in the Oakland sample acquires significance from the structural basis of family deprivation in the 30s, in contrast to more individualized misfortunes, and in the long-term consequences of this family pattern for socialization, personality, and life styles across the generations. Deprivation was a generalized condition in the Depression, and countless American

Coming of Age
in the Depression

families brought up their children for some period of time in this type of environment.

Perspectives on the family serve us well by illuminating important aspects of the problem at hand, but they may also blind us to other properties or features. This point is illustrated by two views of families in the Depression: as a passive victim of conditions, and as an active, problem-solving unit. The latter concept views family and situation within a transactional framework, in contrast to the unidirectional, environmental bias of the former, and focuses attention on the process by which families worked out defensive and coping adaptations. Knowledge of the systemic causes of economic hardship is not sufficient to account for the variety and pattern of family adaptations.

The victim perspective stresses the pathogenic consequences of deprivation, the negative symptomatology of crisis situations—emotional stress and alcoholism, public relief and its social stigma, tensions and conflicts. A similar image of family life appears in American literature of the 30s; the family as a victim of the severe hardships imposed by an inefficient, exploitative, and humanly wasteful economic system.[37] From this vantage point, one is tempted to interpret responses to extreme situations as a pathological reflection of society, instead of probing their adaptive value in such contexts. Economic loss and unemployment might be seen as pulling the family out of shape, creating distorted images of its traditional form, such as wife dominance in the Oakland sample and the unusual importance of social referents outside the family to children in deprived situations.

In the problem-solving approach, both of these outcomes become potentially adaptive responses to conditions which diminished father's stature as provider, husband, and parent. This situation gave a distinct meaning and even legitimacy to mother's power in the Depression, apart from the countervailing judgment of traditional family norms. Mothers who were more powerful than father were also more salient to children (especially daughters) as reference figures, although their status declined with time and change of situation. In some cases, parents aggravated their plight through social withdrawal (heavy drinking, etc.), but there is considerable evidence of coping strategies as well: the working wife, the productive role of children in the household economy, etc. Lacking suitable data, we could not examine pre-Depression antecedents of these response patterns or explore their long-term consequences. Detailed family protocols from 1929 through the Depression decade would be needed for a thorough study of the interplay between family and crisis situation, the determinants, process, and consequences of adaptations, collective and individual, in this extraordinary crisis.

6

Status Change and Personality

Everyone is three persons: what he thinks he is, what others think he is, and what he thinks others think he is.
Frank Jones

Loss of family status required some adjustment in children's attitudes toward others, in others' attitudes toward them, and in their perceptions of these attitudes. The former outcome is shown in the preceding chapter by the response of children to mother, father, and peers, and its variation by socioeconomic change and marital power. In this chapter we shall turn our attention to the psychological effects of status change among children from deprived families, as expressed in self-orientations, relations with age-mates, and status striving.[1] Particular emphasis will be given to the social discontinuities and ambiguities occasioned by loss of family status. Since children's reputation is partially derived from the social position of their family, any change on this dimension has implications for their identity relative to adults and peers.

Children's Image of Self and Others

In a stable, homogeneous environment, children's images of self generally correspond to the images held by significant others. The family's position structures the expectations that others have of its offspring, that the children have of themselves, and that they have regarding the appropriate responses of others toward them. Social interaction is consequently nonproblematic, and personality reflects the integration and consistency of the environment. If indeed present before the Depression, this coherent world had little chance of surviving the social dislocation of heavy economic losses. Social inconsistencies emerged from comparisons between past and present, among dimensions of family position (income, education, and occupation), and between personal and public images of the family.[2] In this situation, children are likely to have presented conflicting stimuli to themselves and to others, thereby jeopardizing complementarity in social relationships.

118

In deprived families, the most likely source of status ambiguity for children is conflict between socialized conceptions of self and the perceived or uncertain view of others. This disparity should be manifested in their orientations toward self and others, especially peers, and in motivational responses to the devalued status which they believe others have assigned to them. Social ambiguity and conflict are especially conducive to self-consciousness or hypersensitivity. The self becomes highly self-conscious when it does not view itself precisely as others do. Sensitivity to others also tends to increase when relationships are unstructured or problematic, as reflected in feelings of "discomfort, doubt, and tension." Loss of family status made children acutely sensitive to any evidence which confirmed their suspicion of an unfavorable public image. Some evidence suggests that older children in the Depression frequently attempted to preserve their status by withholding information on family hardships from age-mates and adults.[3] Likewise, parental "social fronts" occasionally took the form of maintaining children's appearance in clothes, even at the expense of more basic necessities.

Feelings of unhappiness, moodiness, and anger tend to arise when one's perceived reputation falls short of a desired concept of self. As Cooley has noted, estimates of one's image and its evaluation among significant others elicit feelings of pride or shame, depending on its relation to the preferred image.[4] Conditions associated with economic deprivation favored expectations of a disparaging public. Whatever one's actual status, this expectation would define a social situation which has real consequences in emotional reactions and behavior. Accordingly, we expect unhappiness and emotionality to be most prevalent among boys and girls in deprived families.

Typically, depressed feelings, self-consciousness, and anxiety are correlated with social incompetence, school failure, and low esteem among adolescents (see Rosenberg 1965), but these relations do not take into account situational variations which are not linked to personal deficiencies. Social change and strains were major factors in the social world of deprived children, and are likely to have been a more important source of their emotional states than psychological deficits of an interpersonal or instrumental nature. In fact, self-consciousness can be viewed as an adaptive response to change and uncertainty, a sensitivity which enables adjustments and effective coping. If the interpersonal problems of deprived children were largely attributed to their environment, and not to the self, they should diminish as family circumstances improved. By contrast, personal deficiencies may well be the most important source of unhappiness and mood swings among the non-deprived, since they experienced less situational change.

Status Change and
Personality

Social discontinuities associated with economic deprivation favored individuation at the expense of a sense of relatedness, especially in children's relations to persons beyond the family circle, and are likely to have generated dependence on the evaluation of peers. This mode of dependence normally arises in adolescence as a response to the uncertainties in rapid biosocial change, but it also appears most evident among Depression children in deprived families; they were most likely to prefer the company of friends and to seek their advice. And boys from deprived families were much more involved with peers than the sons of nondeprived parents. While such activities are not a clear indication of social dependence on peers, theory suggests that conditions which break down relatedness intensify a willingness to subordinate self to group interests (a major theme in Fromm 1941). The important question, then, is whether social striving among deprived youth was predominantly self- or group-oriented, when compared to that of the nondeprived.

As a response to status ambiguity, dependence on peers is related to the last problem we shall take up in this chapter, the children's motivational adaptations to status loss. Subordination to group interests may take the form of passive acquiescence to social judgments or an aggressive striving for group recognition and acclaim.[5] The latter response is consistent with the presumed motivational effects of status withdrawal and displacement, under conditions of pride and competence. In relation to the Oakland children, this hypothesis defines perceived incongruity between past or preferred status among peers and current status as a stimulus to social striving which discredits contrary judgments based on family misfortune. Family origin is thus subordinated to status claims based on achievement. In the following analysis we shall give special attention to conditions that fostered socially aggressive and passive responses to status loss. Loss of status, for instance, was especially acute in the deprived middle class, and seems most likely to have spurred ambitions among youth who possessed qualities valued by peers, such as leadership skills, and intelligence.

Self-Orientations and Social Status

Our point of departure is the children's self-orientations and status among peers, as related to economic deprivation and social class. Self-orientations, which refer to self-definitions, self-evaluations, and feelings, were assessed in terms of mother's report within the family, the adolescent's self-report, and the perceptions of both adult observers and age-mates. In combination, these sources provide a characterization

Coming of Age
In the Depression

of the child's image of self and the image held by significant others, and enable comparison of their relationship among children in deprived and nondeprived families. The concluding part of the analysis is centered on motivational adaptations to status loss, on social strivings and their expression in leadership within the adolescents' high school setting.

A View from the Family

The Oakland mothers were interviewed in the home about their children's emotional well-being on three occasions during the Depression: shortly after the early stage of economic decline (1932), two years later, and then again in 1936. The latter interview is by far the most important source, although earlier reports shed some light on the cumulative impact of economic deprivation and status loss. Using information both from mothers and from offspring, we find that children's emotional responses to family deprivation were more evident between 1933 and 1936 than in preceding or subsequent years. As we shall see, situational factors emerge as a major source of variation in self definitions and feelings.

The first interview was mainly limited to behavioral indicators of psychological stress. Unfortunately, no information was obtained from mothers on their perception of the self-attitudes of their children. The mothers were asked a set of questions in three areas: sleeping behavior —frequency of disturbing dreams and night fears, restless nights, and sensitivity to noises; mood—cheerfulness, vacillation of mood, enthusiasm, and vitality; and food habits—appetite, attitude toward food, eating habits, and food problems. These types of behavior are several steps removed from self-adjustments to family change, and did not vary in relation to economic conditions. Such conditions made no reliable difference in sleeping behavior, eating habits, or mood in either social class among boys and girls. At this point in the Depression there is no evidence of adverse psychological effects resulting from family deprivation.

However, we do find some indication of this impact some two years later in the reports of mothers who were interviewed on the family situation. Nearly 55 percent of the mothers in deprived families felt that their children had been affected by change in family living conditions and status; and a majority emphasized negative consequences, such as the child's emotional response to family hardships and tensions and the disturbing influence of parental distress, withdrawal, etc. By comparison, a negative outcome was seldom reported on children in more fortunate circumstances. Little more than a fifth of the nondeprived mothers reported some effect. On the average, middle-class mothers were more inclined to perceive deprivational influences in their off-spring's behavior than were lower-status mothers, but this did not modify the above difference; variations by economic deprivation were comparable within each social class.

This general overview of psychological effects does not specify how the child responded to loss of family resources and status, or to emotional stress. Were feelings of self-consciousness, social sensitivity, and emotionality more often attributed by mothers to children in deprived situations? Useful information on these characteristics was obtained from a series of closed-end questions in the 1936 interview. For example, each mother was asked whether the child appeared self-conscious and whether his feelings were easily hurt. Responses were either yes (sometimes or more often) or no. Both questions tap hyper-sensitivity to the attitudes and actions of others, and assume some degree of psychological awareness on the mother's part.

We have argued that social change increases sensitivity by making social relations uncertain and threatening. The validity of knowledge regarding self and others is generally taken for granted by children until it is questioned by new problems, status change, and conflict. Economic deprivation created situations of this type and undermined stable anchorages for the self among a substantial number of children in deprived families. As shown in table 3, self-consciousness and emotional sensitivity were attributed most often by mothers to boys and girls in deprived families and are related to economic loss in both social

Table 3   Mothers' Description of Children's Social Sensitivity (1936) by Economic Depriva-tion, Social Class, and Sex of Child, in Percentages

Economic Deprivation by Social Class	Self-Conscious		Feelings Easily Hurt	
	Boys	Girls	Boys	Girls
Middle class				
Nondeprived (ND)	36 (28)	7 (16)	42 (26)	47 (16)
Deprived (D)	44 (27)	40 (21)	62 (24)	81 (21)
Working class				
Nondeprived (ND)	22 (9)	0 (9)	39 (8)	22 (9)
Deprived (D)	65 (17)	20 (24)	88 (17)	62 (26)
Comparisons by:				
Deprivation	nonsignif.	ND < D*	ND < D*	ND < D*
Class	nonsignif.	nonsignif.	nonsignif.	nonsignif.

* $p < .05$ (χ^2 test, 1 df.)

classes. Emotional sensitivity, reflecting more directly than self-consciousness a change that entails loss of status, is more prevalent among children in deprived families.

Though preoccupation with the opinions of others is commonly thought to be more characteristic of girls, this tendency varies by maturational stage and situational factors. In fact, boys were more often described as self-conscious by their mothers than were girls, regardless of family situation. This difference, which largely obscures deprivational effects among middle-class boys, is undoubtedly a consequence of the slower developmental rate of boys generally, especially in high-status families. Rapid growth could account for their social awkwardness and hypersensitivity. Boys in the sample were approximately fourteen years old in 1935, and this is generally the age at which the velocity of physical growth is greatest. The growth spurt generally comes about two years earlier among girls and is less pronounced (see Elder 1971, pp. 29–37).

The data suggest that sensitivity to others is more a consequence of status loss and uncertainty than of absolute deprivation. In the non-deprived group, working-class families were substantially lower on absolute income during the Depression than middle-class families, but offspring of the latter were more often characterized as self-conscious and emotionally sensitive. Likewise, psychological differences between the children of middle-class deprived parents and children of working-class nondeprived parents are more substantial than one would predict on the basis of differences in level of income. Across both measures of social sensitivity, variations by loss of economic status are greater than the effects of class origin.

If sensitivity to others is mainly an outgrowth of status loss, it should be most prevalent among children in families which were actually downwardly mobile in the Depression: those families in which father obtained lower-status employment after losing his job. Economic loss should be most threatening to the social image when it is expressed in public symbols of "coming down" in the world, such as the transition to a lower-status job. This impact is vividly expressed in qualitative materials on parent-child relations which depict the shame and embarrassment which some children felt when their fathers eventually acquired jobs that were well below their prior station in life (see chapter 3).

To test this expectation, we formed three groups of boys and girls and compared them on emotional sensitivity ("feelings easily hurt"). The first group was defined by nondeprived status; the second, by deprived status and stability or improvement in father's occupational status; and the third, by economic deprivation and downward mobility.

Status Change and
Personality

Emotional sensitivity increased from 40 percent in the first group to 63 and 78 percent in the other two groups. The primary effect is clearly that of economic deprivation and its implications for status loss, although downward mobility does identify an extreme group of children on emotional vulnerability.

A child whose feelings are easily hurt is dependent on the goodwill of others, on their friendship and support, and is consequently subject to mood fluctuations as situations, persons, and actions change. Social sensitivity also signifies a low threshold of emotional arousal and reactivity; experiences are likely to call out intense emotional responses, ranging from sullen anger or self-depreciation to euphoria. By and large, children in deprived families were more often described by mothers as emotional or easily aroused by disappointments, frustrations, and perceived insults; they were more often characterized as anxious, inclined to cry, and easily angered (table 4). In particular, economic deprivation markedly increased sex-typed emotional responses; boys were more likely to anger easily and girls to worry a lot. Though deprived youth generally ranked higher on emotionality, differences by economic loss are too small to be statistically reliable.

Table 4   Mothers' Description of Children's Emotionality (1936) by Economic Deprivation, Social Class, and Sex of Child, in Percentages

Economic Deprivation by Social Class	Worries[a]		Cries Easily[a]		Angers Easily[a]	
	Boys	Girls	Boys	Girls	Boys	Girls
Middle Class						
Nondeprived	38 (26)	33 (12)	23 (26)	16 (13)	28 (25)	42 (12)
Deprived	31 (23)	52 (21)	28 (25)	33 (21)	50 (24)	43 (21)
% diff.	7	−19	−5	−17	−22	−1
Working class						
Nondeprived	20 (10)	27 (11)	22 (9)	27 (11)	30 (10)	45 (11)
Deprived	45 (18)	48 (25)	35 (17)	34 (26)	50 (18)	56 (25)
% diff.	−25	−21	−13	−7	−20	−11

[a]   The effects of economic deprivation and social class are not significant.

In these reports from mothers, acute sensitivity to others with its attendant implications for emotional vulnerability stands out as the major psychological effect of family deprivation and especially status loss. Not all children in deprived families were characterized as self-conscious or emotionally sensitive, and this description was applied to some children in nondeprived homes. However, economic and status loss markedly increased the prevalence of these psychological states, and far exceeded the effect of class origin. Sex differences were less evident in emotional sensitivity than in emotional responses to aversive experiences.

These data provide an image of the Oakland children which is presumably based on a variety of interactional experiences within the relatively private world of the family. This inside view has special significance for understanding self-other relations in the context of status loss since the latter made social images and acceptance most uncertain outside the family. From available studies made during the Depression it is apparent that members of deprived families were inclined to present themselves to outsiders as they wished to be seen and regarded. Social fronts of this kind would be more difficult to maintain in the everyday, intimate contacts of family life and are less apt to be used in this context when social threats are mainly attributed to external relationships.

As observers of their own children, the mothers undoubtedly had certain vested interests which may have favored distortions on behalf of a positive report to the interviewer, especially when the truth reflected unfavorably upon their own qualities and the family as a whole. While this bias was noted in questions which dealt with the moral behavior of a son or daughter, and to a lesser extent on children's attitudes toward parents and family standing, it is much less probable in responses to questions presented in tables 3 and 4. These questions do not imply family or parental deficiencies and did not make reference to family hardships in the Depression. All indications suggest that the interviewer's inquiry was placed within a nonthreatening, developmental context.

Children's
Descriptions of
Self and Others

The interview with mothers did not specify the relational context of self-consciousness or emotional sensitivity. That is, we do not know whether these states were mainly a consequence of relations with parents, other adults, or peers. However, there is some evidence in the preceding chapters which suggests that loss of family status increased the importance and problematic nature of relations with other children and classmates. In attitude and behavior, the offspring of deprived parents were more strongly oriented to association with age-mates than were members of nondeprived families. Status loss placed children in a

Status Change and
Personality

strange situation which, in some respects, cast them as strangers among familiar acquaintances.

Th Oakland children were asked questions about their relations with peers in questionnaires administered in 1934–35 and 1937–38 (see Appendix B). One question asked whether they resembled an age-mate who is "unhappy a good deal of the time because he thinks no one likes him." A related question asked whether they resembled a youth who "seems to have a lot of fun." Answers to the first were reverse-scored and summed with values on the second item to form an index of social well-being.[6] Responses to both questions reflect the emotional effects of perceived distance or rejection in peer relations. In addition, the time span between the two administrations of the questionnaire permits an assessment of situational factors in social well-being. If perceived rejection is largely a function of family deprivation, one would expect this outlook to change as economic conditions improved through 1938.

One other set of self-descriptions was included in the analysis as a measure of more severe psychological distress. Emotionality was indexed by a summation of scores on fifteen items which comprised a checklist in the junior and senior high questionnaires. Examples include: "Do you often feel blue?" "Do you sometimes feel very happy and then suddenly very sad without knowing why?" "Do you think you are a rather nervous person?" This measure does not explicitly refer to social relations, unlike that of social well-being, and appears to index emotional states which are more resistant to situational change.

While economic conditions in the Depression made a difference in how children were perceived by their mothers, this difference is less evident in the children's own self-descriptions. During the early 30s, boys from nondeprived families neither reported a greater sense of social acceptance nor fewer symptoms of psychological distress, on the average, than the sons of deprived parents. As shown in table A–13, there is no consistent variation by economic loss in either social class. Compared to boys, girls were more adversely affected by family conditions in perceived relations with peers, but this is the only area in which their self-descriptions varied by economic hardship. Using the emotional index on boys and girls, we find that depressed feelings which are not explicitly limited to social rejection were more strongly influenced by family status in 1929 than by changes in status during the Depression.

Deprivational effects on the subjective status of girls were slightly greater when more visible indicators of status loss were included in the analysis, such as father's unemployment and downward mobility. In both social classes, members of families in which father was either unemployed or downwardly mobile rated themselves lower on social well-being than the offspring of nondeprived families, but the difference is statistically significant only among girls (an average difference between means of 2.1, $p < .01$). Emotionality, on the other hand, did not increase significantly under conditions of unemployment or status loss.

In these data at least, the emotional impact of family deprivation is mainly restricted to a strained relation between girls and other members of their age group. This outcome reflects the extraordinary significance of interpersonal relations for the self-image of girls, and is also consistent with the implications of an "appropriate" family background for their entry into prestigeful social circles. There are reasons for expecting economic loss to have less impact on boys' status among peers, in accordance with the data, such as the more severe effects of clothing restrictions for girls. Also boys may be reluctant to disclose inner feelings. It is clear, for instance, that boys scored somewhat lower on emotional symptoms than girls.

If strained relations with age-mates were mainly a consequence of status loss and family deprivation, this condition should be less prevalent among girls in the high school years owing to general economic improvements in the city of Oakland. A comparison of scores from identical measures of social well-being and emotionality in the two time periods (junior and senior high) showed no appreciable change in the emotional state of youth in the sample, although some relative improvement did occur among girls from deprived families; the latter became more similar to the daughters of nondeprived parents. Deprivational effects on social well-being were negligible for girls and boys in the high school years. As in the earlier time period, children of deprived families did not score higher on emotionality than children of nondeprived parents.[7]

The upward trend in social well-being among girls from deprived families could reflect growth in coping, as well as improvements in family conditions; they may have learned to be less sensitive to or bothered by evidence of social rejection on the part of their classmates. In this manner, awareness of rejection would become less closely related to personal feelings. In order to distinguish between perceived rejection and emotional responses, we selected another set of items which were included in a special section of the senior high questionnaire. Five of the statements expressed a critical stance toward social exclusion or elitism among students in the local high school: "one's classmates are snobbish and stuck-up"; "classmates who plan games or hikes or parties and then won't let others in on the fun"; "having certain pupils run everything"; "classmates you like who turn out to be so stuck-up they will play only with certain pupils"; and "groups or

Status Change and Personality

gangs that won't have anything to do with pupils outside of these groups." Each respondent was asked to check those statements which described things they disliked about school, and to double check those they disliked the most. Since responses to these items were interrelated, the statements were included in a single index.[8]

In the local high school, these signs of elitist behavior directly challenged the egalitarian ethos of the student community, "The Progress of All Through All," as promoted by student leaders and staff, and were severely criticized on numerous occasions by editorials in the student newspaper. This sanction is briefly illustrated by a broadside (published around 1940) entitled "Cliquish Student Doesn't Really Enjoy Life: Are You One?"

Mary is a member of a clique. You know what cliques are. Those things you can't break through unless you have "clothes," or "family prestige," or "personality," or live in the "right section of town," or have a father who's been lucky enough to provide you with a liberal allowance, or (if you haven't any other qualification) a superior attitude. Mary is not a very original person. She wouldn't dare do anything the crowd she travels around with doesn't approve of. . . . She goes out with a boy she doesn't like because he knows the right people. She affects a vacant stare whenever passing anyone who doesn't belong to the "elite." . . . Mary wouldn't even look at a girl or boy who doesn't dress the way she does, or if the girl or boy's father just makes a wage (instead of an income). . . . Most of Mary's friends aren't really friends. They go around with one another just to show they belong. There is little of the real loyalty and understanding which people have regardless of whether one has a boy friend with a Pontiac, a big house, or a "porkpie" to pass around. Mary thinks she is a good American— she knits for the R.A.F.—but she isn't living up to a certain clause in the Declaration of Independence which says, "All men are created equal." . . . When will Mary wake up? [9]

This editorial expressed sentiments which were shared by many girls. In particular, girls from deprived families were highly critical of elitist behavior on the part of their classmates, more so than the daughters of nondeprived parents, and the difference is statistically significant (table A–14). Trends in this direction also appear among boys, but they are too small to be reliable. As might be expected, working-class youth, both boys and girls, ranked slightly higher on social criticism than their middle-class counterparts.

As suggested, there is some evidence in these data that girls from deprived families were more critical of peer exclusiveness than depressed or unhappy over their relations with classmates, when compared to girls in nondeprived households. For example, this difference is suggested by correlations between the two sentiments, between social criticism, on the one hand, and social well-being, on the other. The latter was less negatively related to criticism of classmates among girls in deprived families than among those in more fortunate households, although the difference is too small to be reliable.

Up to this point, the psychological effects of economic hardship are mainly limited to the perceived relations of girls with their classmates. Though a majority of the children in deprived families were described by their mothers as emotionally sensitive, there is no evidence of this tendency in the boys' reported relations with peers. What social experiences might have accounted for this sex difference? Two factors, in particular, suggest themselves on the basis of our preceding analysis; deprivational family experiences and a disadvantage in social appearance (clothes, shoes, grooming, etc.). These conditions had particular significance for the daughters of deprived parents, as we shall see, and were most evident during the early years of the Depression.

As shown in chapter 4, girls were more involved in household affairs than boys, and their socialization is likely to have favored interpersonal sensitivities, which are in keeping with traditional concepts of feminine behavior. Sensitivity to the feelings of others would of course increase vulnerability to family climate and tensions, as would the tendency for daughters to share interests and activities with mother.[10] In previous chapters, stressful family experiences, such as mother's unhappiness and family conflict, were found to be correlated with economic conditions, especially among girls. Further analysis showed that both experiences were also more predictive of social unhappiness among girls in junior high school than among boys.

As discussed in chapter 3, perception of mother's feelings was measured by responses to the statement "I wish mother were happier" (checked or not checked). This statement combines both awareness of mother's emotional state and the desire for improvement. Perception of family conflict was measured by a nine-point scale (see chapter 5). In the junior high period, both perceptions were more negatively related to the social well-being of girls than to the self-reported feelings of boys (average $r = .31$ for girls and .14 for boys). In combination, these aspects of family stress represent a theoretically important link between economic loss and the self-feelings of girls, but they do not entirely account for this relation.

In the Depression, negative change in a child's appearance symbolized a loss in status, which had special significance for the social experience of girls,[11] and typically developed out of constraints on the purchase of clothes and shoes. In some cases, limitations also extended to hygienic practices; to the frequency of clothes washing, the availability of soap and heated water for baths, etc. Clothing constraints varied in degree across deprived families in the Oakland sample,

Status Change and Personality

according to available information, and led to a variety of adaptations, ranging from more extensive use of hand-me-downs and home-made garments to crude patchwork (for example, the use of cardboard to cover holes in shoes).

The most noteworthy effect of economic hardship is seen in the appearance of children who were members of middle-class families in 1929. By 1934, many deprived parents from this class had no more in the way of economic resources than impoverished families in the working class, and this dramatic misfortune was visible in the appearance of their offspring at the time. Using an adult rating of "well-groomed appearance," based on observations of the children in a playground setting at the institute, we find that members of deprived families ranked lower than the nondeprived on appearance in the junior high years (both groups were identical on measures of physical attractiveness). However, sizable differences occurred only in the middle class, and especially among girls (table A–15). These results generally matched the views of peers on ratings of appearance.[12] In the middle class, the relative disadvantage of deprived girls on social appearance helps explain their feelings of social rejection and unhappiness. Social well-being and an attractive appearance were more highly interrelated among girls than among boys.[13] Neither popularity nor leadership necessarily required a well-groomed appearance on the part of boys.

Observed differences in appearances by economic loss did not persist through the high school years. An adult rating of appearance, identical to the junior high measure, showed no consistent differences by economic deprivation among boys and girls in both social classes.[14] The social disadvantage of economic limitations on dress was countered to some extent by dress codes in the local high school. All girls, for instance, were required to wear a standard student uniform: a skirt and middy blouse.

This analysis from the children's viewpoint suggests the following conclusions on economic or status loss in self-attitudes and perceived social relations. First, the psychological impact of family deprivation was most evident from 1933 through 1936, a time period which roughly corresponds with the junior high years. By this stage in the Depression, the children were old enough to be aware of family deprivation and its social consequences. The absence of deprivational effects in the subsequent years of high school generally corresponds with known improvements in the economic life of Oakland. Secondly, psychological effects were expressed in self-consciousness and emotional sensitivity, as measured by mothers' reports, and in the girls' social unhappiness and perception of social rejection. Boys in deprived families were not distinguished by a greater sense of social rejection or unhappiness than members of nondeprived households. This sex difference occurred in part through a stronger effect of family stress and a relatively unattractive appearance on the self-feelings of girls.

Observed Status in a Social Setting

Self-consciousness and social unhappiness represent one aspect of a more general problem of interpersonal relations in situations marked by social ambiguity and stress, namely, the problem of working out new lines of action, shared definitions, and coordinated associations. A self-conscious sensitivity to others is symptomatic of a disparity between one's self-image and the image presumably held by others. An important question here is whether other adults and peers held views of the Oakland children which corresponded with their own self-definitions and evaluations.

The ambiguity of a changing situation is likely to have produced some error in the children's judgment of their social reputation, of their status in the eyes of other people outside the family, but what kind of error? When the attitudes of others are uncertain, personal feelings, which are unverified by the social facts of actual status, are likely to be attributed to others. Perceived rejection among girls, for example, may have been rooted more in traumatic family experiences than in actual relations with peers. Sullivan's observation that "one can find in others only that which is in the self" is perhaps most applicable to situations which make the responses and attitudes of others uncertain (Sullivan 1947, p. 22).

Though more unhappy and emotionally vulnerable, girls from deprived families fared surprisingly well in social competition with the daughters of nondeprived parents. According to adult observers, they were not significantly lower on social leadership or popularity, regardless of family status, and this was also true of boys (see table A–16). Neither family hardship and grooming disadvantages nor feelings of rejection are reflected in these observations. In high school, girls from deprived households were more critical of social elitism and snobbery among classmates than the nondeprived, but they were not less popular or lower in social leadership. Both types of characteristics (measured by scales which are identical to the junior high ratings) were equally represented among girls and boys from deprived and nondeprived families in the two social classes.

An adult's evaluation of status among adolescents may of course be less informed than peer judgments by subtle criteria that make a

Status Change and
Personality

difference in social acceptance, but there is little evidence of this. Peer evaluations were highly related to adult assessments and produced the same outcome. Using peer ratings of popularity and leadership in 1934, we compared members of nondeprived and deprived families in both social classes and found no reliable differences on either scale.

This degree of social equality, across varying levels of deprivation, is puzzling when one considers the pressing constraints of family hardships and emotional stress. Moreover, feelings of rejection frequently lead to alienating actions. For example, the reactions of adolescents with low self-esteem to classmates generally elicit responses that confirm their fears and feelings of rejection. They are inclined to reject overtures of friendliness, to respond with hostility and distrust, and to resist change (Rosenberg 1965). The fact that girls from deprived families were no less popular than other girls, despite stronger feelings of social unhappiness and emotional sensitivity, suggests that a different adaptational process is involved. What factors would encourage the outgoing orientation which is common among deprived children in the sample (see chapters 4 and 5)? What would lead them to invest more of themselves in relationships, as a response to feelings of social exclusion, instead of withdrawing into a private fantasy world? A majority of these children were not deprived of social options, and external conditions played an important role in their perceived social problems. The key factor may be the externality of family hardship, for we have no evidence that such conditions fostered self-blame among children in deprived families.

It is commonly thought that need satisfaction through fantasy acquires value in deprivational situations; fantasies of popularity arise when one feels disliked, of power when one feels powerless, etc. But such fantasies, though they may serve as compensation for an unsatisfying existence, may also serve as a directive for action and achievement, such as hope for the future. In the latter case, perceived social deprivation would increase social ambition in fantasy and efforts to enhance one's status. As a directive for action, social fantasy would be consistent with a coping response to the realities of a new situation and should find expression in *corresponding* behavior, with efforts to establish and maintain friendships. By contrast, compensatory social fantasy would be inversely related to social activity and status. Two questions, then, are of interest in probing the adaptational response of children to social ambiguity and felt deprivation. Were there differences, across family situations, in the strength of social fantasy? And did fantasy interests of this kind play a more directive role in the behavior of children from deprived families?

In the junior and senior high questionnaires, the adolescents were asked two questions concerning their interest in an imaginary world. The first question asked whether they resembled a young person who "has make-believe friends and a make-believe world which is nicer than the real world." The other question asked whether they resembled a boy or girl who "likes to sit by himself (herself) and imagine things and thinks it is much more fun than playing games." Responses to each question were made on a five-point, self-rating scale: "no" equaled a score of 1, and "yes" was equivalent to a score of 5. Since values on the two questions were intercorrelated ($r = .40$), they were summed to form an index for both time periods.

Despite social hardships, adolescents whose fathers lost heavily in the Depression did not express stronger interests in a fantasy world than members of nondeprived families. In fact, they rated themselves lower on this orientation in both time periods, and did so in both social classes. During the early years of economic hardship, boys and girls from deprived households scored significantly lower on social fantasy than the offspring of nondeprived families, and this difference was not modified by class background.[15] From this period to the high school years, deprivational differences persisted only in the preferences of boys.

From an adaptational perspective, the relation between economic deprivation and social fantasy is less important than the psychological function of fantasy, whether substitutive or compensatory, or an expression of directive tendencies in social behavior. The latter function is supported by the observed popularity of deprived adolescents and by their extraordinary interest in the companionship of their age-mates. Status changes in the Depression also provided a basis for attributing interpersonal problems to the larger environment, instead of to personal deficiencies which favor compensatory adjustments. As a substitute for satisfying relations with peers, social fantasy should be negatively correlated with measures of social popularity, and this is what we find among members of nondeprived families (table A–17). Correspondence between social interest in fantasy and behavior is more evident among members of deprived families, although empirical support is relatively weak. In the junior high period, social fantasy was negatively related to social well-being in both deprivational groups, and especially among boys, but it was more strongly correlated with evidence of emotional distress and unsatisfactory social relations among the nondeprived. Differences in class background did not alter these results.

There is some basis in these data for regarding social striving as a link between the status deprivation and self-characteristics of children from deprived families and their social acceptance or popularity among

Status Change and
Personality

peers. However, such efforts are not always conducive to social acceptance, as seen in strident attempts to gain attention which typically elicit hostility and rejection. Such behavior is a classic example of self-centeredness, of the pursuit of self-interests at the expense of others, and is diametrically opposed to the strong collective or group interests of adolescents from deprived families. Times of social upheaval or disruption are thought to intensify a willingness to subordinate personal desires for group interests as a path to social integration, and such interests were most visible to adult observers in the behavior of youth from deprived families.[16]

Since status changes in the Depression exposed members of deprived families to abrupt situational variation, it is not surprising that social factors were prominent sources of their emotional status. For the most part, emotional effects of deprivation in the early years of the Depression did not persist through the latter part of the decade. This trend can be interpreted as a change in the adaptational relationship between person and situation, and does not rule out the possibility of more lasting consequences for motivational tendencies, cognitive orientations, and psychological health, a problem taken up in the remainder of this chapter and in subsequent chapters. Personal deficiencies were more important elements in the relational problems experienced by the offspring of nondeprived parents; social fantasy was more of an escape from unsatisfactory social relations than a directive for action. And, as we shall see in the following section on status striving, these youth were more inclined than adolescents in deprived families to blame themselves or to depend on others in problem situations.

Social Status and Striving

Children in deprived situations coped effectively with the social disadvantages of family losses, as their popularity indicates, but the story of how they held their own with more affluent classmates is merely suggested by the reality orientation of their problem-solving efforts. An important feature of this response is the location of such problems in the larger environment, and not in the self, but there is also the matter of adaptive potential and social opportunity. Adaptive potential refers in part to resources for problem solving—the intelligence, social skills, and motivation which make a problem solvable—and lead to corresponding definitions of the situation. Resources would count for little, however, if social opportunities had been severely limited. For the most part, economic hardships had little consequence in this respect, although some evidence of social constraint is seen among girls from deprived families.

An understanding of social achievement in the deprived group requires knowledge of social support as well as opportunities. At the outset of this study we proposed that a clue to why some children successfully adapt to challenging situations and others do not would be found in their resources and motivation, in the support provided by family and the larger environment, and in characteristics of the event or situation. Though class background bears directly upon family support for individual problem solving and resources, such as intellectual skills, we found no evidence of a substantial class difference in the relative social achievement of children from deprived and nondeprived families. Deprivational effects in emotional state were frequently more pronounced among working-class children, but variations of this kind did not appear in the status perceptions of classmates or adult observers. Nevertheless, this outcome is highly consistent with, and may have been influenced by, the progressive philosophy and extracurricular policies of the local schools attended by the Oakland children.

Formal policies favored the social participation of students from all social and economic groupings. Codes enforced by students and staff affirmed the ideal that family background should not be a factor in determining student relationships, participation in extracurricular activities, and selection for leadership positions. Especially in the high school, regulations on dress were enforced by student boards, and costly social affairs were not encouraged. Counselors attempted to secure employment in the National Youth Administration and in other fields for students who needed funds to cover incidental expenses. In the local high school, more than 85 percent of the students were involved in extracurricular activity (see Jones 1958). School records also indicate that working-class students were elected for leadership posts but that a larger proportion of leaders came from the middle class. This difference is undoubtedly a reflection of class variations in social initiative, talent, and sophistication, as well as unequal opportunity. Faculty members in the junior and senior high school contended that relatively few overt acts of discrimination by family background occurred in student activities and relationships. As might be expected, this claim exaggerates the degree of equal opportunity in the two settings, although it does accurately reflect a high level of normative support for the equalitarian ideal, according to observations by staff members of the Institute. To an unusual degree, both schools encouraged the social prominence of students who lacked certain economic advantages and family prestige.

Within this framework of support and opportunity, social ambition is a more plausible source of accomplishment among deprived youth than intellectual skills or performance. In fact, conditions related to economic hardship lead to the expectation of lower intellectual performance among children from deprived families, especially in the school context. Studies consistently show a negative relationship between low economic status and academic performance, but low economic status is generally related to comparable status on parental education and occupation, a congruence not found among deprived families in the Oakland sample. By comparison, at least two conditions favored social ambition as an explanation of the social rewards achieved by members of deprived families: withdrawal of social regard, and family sources of status striving.

Withdrawal of social regard or respect is thought to arouse efforts to regain status, to prove or demonstrate personal worth, especially when the former position is highly valued and the loss is imposed rather than earned. Among members of deprived families, intellectual and social prominence is likely to have replaced family position as a preferred basis of social recognition and evaluation. Secondly, economic hardships produced some conditions which studies have identified as nurturant of a strong need for achievement among sons: freedom from interference and authoritarian control by father, training in independence behavior, achievement demands by mother in particular, and the presentation of high achievement standards within an emotionally supportive context. (For a review of studies, see Elder 1971, pp. 84–87.) We have no evidence on specific modes of achievement training, standards, or demands among families in the Oakland sample. Fathers who suffered losses did not present an attractive example for their sons, and deprived families were not generally distinguished by emotional support and integration. Nevertheless, sons were liberated from paternal control in deprived families, acquired experience in self-direction, and viewed mother as the most supportive parent. In some cases, mothers in hard-pressed families may have turned to the achievements of their sons for a vicarious sense of accomplishment.

Two strategies were employed in the comparison of intellectual competence and ambition as factors in the social achievement of adolescents from deprived families. First, subgroups defined by economic deprivation and social class were compared on indicators of each dimension of adaptive potential, with the entire sample used, and then the analysis was restricted to adolescents who were recognized as student leaders by their classmates. If an intense desire to achieve recognition was a factor in the social accomplishments of deprived youth, it should be especially characteristic of student leaders from this group.

Intellectual
Competence and
Ambition

Intellectual competence was measured by the Stanford-Binet test of intelligence and by teacher evaluations of academic aptitude. Stanford-Binets were administered to members of the sample in 1933 and then again in 1938. Scores on the two IQ tests were averaged to maximize reliability. As a group, girls were more likely than boys to come from working-class families, and their average IQ was lower (approximately 110 vs. 116). Three high school teachers who knew the adolescents well rated them on seven-point scales of academic interest and performance. Scores on the two scales were averaged to yield a single index of academic aptitude. This measure was highly predictive of the adolescents' grade-point average in high school ($r = .70$).

The intellectual competence of adolescents in deprived situations generally favored their status among peers in the sense that they did not score lower on IQ or academic aptitude than members of nondeprived families. The only exception appears among middle-class girls (table A–18). The primary source of variation is class origin, not economic loss. Even when the nondeprived were compared with adolescents in situations of unemployment and downward mobility, differences on intellectual functioning proved to be negligible among boys. Also, the income level of deprived middle-class families was considerably lower than that of nondeprived families in the working class, but this difference is not reflected in the mental ability or scholastic status of children in the two groups. The important contrast between these families is seen in the relative intellectual status of parents. Regardless of economic loss, middle-class mothers were rated significantly higher by interviewers on verbal fluency and intellectual skills than working-class mothers (see Elder 1968 and 1969a). Likewise, economic loss did not affect the educational status of parents, nor the cultural interests of the more educated. This educational advantage is not reflected in teachers' ratings, however, owing perhaps to school influence. In the middle-class climate of the high school, exposure to academic models and ambitious students may well have increased the school performance and ambitions of students from low-status families.

Since these data refer to intellectual competence at one point in time, they cannot answer questions about changes in test performance and

Status Change and
Personality

their relation to economic change, such as variations in performance during the most severe phase of the Depression—the years between 1931 and 1935. Some downward shifts of a temporary nature may have occurred in this period, even though deprivational effects on mental ability were negligible (1933).

Any interpretation of these results needs to take developmental age into account in adaptive responses to deprivation. Members of the Oakland sample were beyond the developmental stage in which children are most vulnerable to the adverse effects of family hardships on cognitive growth. Judging from other research on children who were born shortly before the Depression, age stands out as a potentially significant determinant of deprivational effects. The intellectual competence of younger boys, in particular, was negatively influenced by economic loss and downward mobility during the 1930s.[17]

On the behavioral level, the most striking theme up to this point is the extraordinary degree of similarity, both academic and social, among youth with widely diverse backgrounds in the Depression. According to the perceptions of teachers, classmates, and adult observers, members of deprived families in each social class were indistinguishable from the offspring of nondeprived families on scholastic standing and social status. Given this outcome, are there differences in motivational tendencies which underlie the accomplishments of each group? The same level of status can of course be achieved through different routes, through the expenditure of considerable effort, for example, or by means of special talents. An example of this difference is seen in a comparison of factors in the upward mobility of men from middle- and working-class families. Occupational attainment is more contingent on a strong need to achieve among men from the lower strata, while education plays a more important role in the social mobility of men from the middle class (Elder 1968). In a deprived group such as the lower class, a total concentration of energy and effort is needed to overcome obstacles which are seldom faced by persons of higher station. This drive is also likely to characterize youth from deprived families in the Depression, especially those who achieved recognition from their classmates.

Two types of achievement motivation defined by task and social orientation were included in the analysis, by the use of a set of psychodynamic ratings. These five-point ratings were constructed from extensive observational records of the adolescents' behavior in senior high school by three judges under the supervision of Else Frenkel-Brunswik (see Appendix B). Each rating was ultimately based on observed behavior, although the judges attempted to establish references to underlying motivational tendencies through a complex process of inference, using both subtle indirect cues and gross features of behavior. The psychological meaning of the ratings appears in terms of a cluster of divergent manifestations which cohere genotypically, though not often phenotypically. A desire for achievement on tasks was defined as "the desire to attain a high standard of objective accomplishments; to increase self-regard by the successful exercise of talent, to select hard tasks; high aspiration level." Two interrelated ratings were used as an index of desire for status and power: recognition—"the desire to excite praise and commendation, to demand respect, social approval and prestige, honor and fame; and control—"the desire to control one's human environment by suggestion, persuasion, or command."[18] Given the time period of these measurements, achievement motivation is uncertain as an intervening variable between deprivation and achieved status; it may both arise from and account for social success among classmates.

Needs for social recognition and control are most directly applicable to the deprived situation of children in the Depression. Economic deprivation made especially problematic a gratifying relation with more affluent peers, on the one hand, and a sense of control over one's human environment, on the other. Both measures index the desire to attain a high standard of accomplishment, as in the rating on need for task achievement, but more explicit reference is made to social comparison processes and status differentials. These motivational ratings were supplemented for boys by the prestige level of their occupational interests, as measured by the occupational level scale on the Strong Vocational Interest Blank.[19]

As predicted, a desire for status and power was more pronounced among boys whose families lost heavily in the Depression (table A–19). This difference shows up in both social classes and far exceeds variation by social class. Members of deprived households in the middle class experienced the greatest loss of status, and also ranked highest on status striving. This ambition was restricted in the social realm, however, to power and status relationships. It did not carry over to the more task-oriented form of achievement orientation, or to interests in prestigeful occupations, which more faithfully reflect class background. Within the deprived category, social ambition increased only slightly with downward mobility and father's unemployment.

Though girls were especially sensitive to the social consequences of family deprivation, there is little evidence of this concern in an assertive form of self-enhancement, expressed in power, status, or achievement motives. The three ratings did not vary meaningfully by economic loss in either social class, and differences by family background were insignificant. Upon reflection, it is apparent that we did not take into

Status Change and
                                         Personality

account the implications of sex differences in upbringing for motivational adaptations. For instance, an assertive response to status loss is most compatible with the conditioning of boys; to strive for accomplishments, social acclaim, and dominance is to respond in accordance with traditional male prescriptions. By comparison, interests in social acceptance, comfort, and protection are more consistent with the feminine role, as culturally defined. This sex difference has particular significance for the daughters of deprived families, in view of their domestic upbringing and interests. Neither achievement nor power goals are likely to have had much appeal to girls who were principally oriented to the role of homemaker and mother.

A broader inquiry into the motivational tendencies of girls in deprived families did not produce substantial clarity on this problem. Two additional ratings were used in this analysis: social ties—"the desire to join groups, to live socially, to conform to custom"; and succorance—"the desire for support from outside." Using these measures, we compared girls from deprived and nondeprived families in both social classes. The results showed no consistent or meaningful variation by economic loss, or by father's unemployment.

Motives linked to economic hardship do not indicate how they functioned in the adaptational process. If members of deprived families achieved popularity and leadership status among their classmates through a coping response in problem solving, this response should be expressed in congruent motivational adaptations to feelings of status loss and social unhappiness. In the case of boys, for instance, one would expect this response to take the form of aggressive social ambition rather than self-devaluation or a desire for social support. To explore this adaptation, we correlated the junior high index of social well-being with all motivational ratings within groups defined by sex and economic deprivation.

Support for our adaptational interpretation comes indirectly from the absence of self-blame and dependency as correlates of social unhappiness among the offspring of deprived families. The most noteworthy results occurred in the nondeprived group in the areas of self-abasement and desire for social support; reported social well-being was negatively related to self-depreciation among boys and to a dependency orientation among girls, as indexed by the rating on succorance ($r = -.46$ and $-.41$). These results generally match other characteristics of unhappy children in families that did not encounter severe hardships in the Depression, and differ sharply in this respect from the motivational correlates of social well-being in the deprived group (an average of only $-.06$ with the two ratings). By contrast, some evidence of aggressive tendencies appears only among socially unhappy boys from deprived families.[20] These boys, in particular, fit Jaffe and Sandler's observation that most unhappy children "have not capitulated, but rather show varying degrees of discontent and resentment, and their aggressive response is more directly manifest."[21]

Apart from the stimulus of family losses, is there any evidence of family influence in the status striving of boys? Since fathers, by and large, were less salient to sons than mothers in deprived circumstances, the influence of these families in achievement training, if any, would be heavily dependent on mother's role, attitudes, and actions. In contemporary research, mother is typically characterized as the most significant parent in the life success of sons from lower-status families, and all evidence points to a similar force among boys with origins in deprived families during the 30s. Ideally, one would like to know whether mothers who assumed family leadership expected a high standard of accomplishment from their sons and how they tried to implement their desires. We do know that mothers in this situation were generally perceived as the most supportive parent, and were not as restrictive as mothers who left final decisions to their husbands, but this tells us little about standards and demands. In view of these unknowns, it is not surprising that mother's power in the family was not significantly related to either need for recognition or social dominance among sons.

There is one other characteristic of mothers which has theoretical relevance as a source of status striving among sons; namely, the extent to which they responded to economic misfortune by expressing discontent in socially aggressive ways. Through words and example, highly dissatisfied mothers who channeled their frustrations toward the social order instead of the self may have spurred sons to greater achievement. These frustrations were common among mothers from deprived families, especially in the middle class (see chapter 3), but it is not clear whether discontent acknowledged defeat or a battle, except that "feelings of inadequacy" and "tiredness" were most prevalent in this group. In any case, there is some evidence that dissatisfied mothers were more likely to have socially ambitious sons than mothers who were relatively content, especially in the middle class.[22]

To specify an aggressive response to discontent which is directed toward the social order, we divided mothers who were at least moderately dissatisfied with their situation (a score of 4 or more on the seven-point scale) into two groups, defined by the interviewer's evaluation of their tendency to criticize things in general: not critical and critical. Critical attitudes were defined by scores of 5 through 7. The groups thus identify mothers who were not discontented; who were dissatisfied but not critical of things; and who were both dissatisfied and critical. Ratings of sons' desire for recognition and control or dominance increased significantly across these groups, more so than in relation to dissatisfaction alone. Using a summated index of the two motivational ratings, status striving proved to be moderately associated with the categorical index of maternal attitudes ($tau_c = .28$). These attitudes largely accounted for the relationship between economic deprivation and sons' ambition; economic conditions had no effect on the social motivation of boys whose mothers were both dissatisfied and critical of things in general.[23]

Social Ambition and Elite Status in High School

For boys from deprived households, the pathway to social achievement is mainly distinguished by status interests or desires, but the causal sequence remains uncertain. As we have noted, measures of ambition and perceived status among classmates were based on observational records collected during the high school years. It is possible, therefore, to interpret social ambition as an antecedent and consequence of social accomplishments. However, the latter interpretation is weakened by one fact: the similar status of boys across diverse economic circumstances. This similarity obviously cannot account for the stronger social motivation of boys from deprived families. Moreover, we have not shown that needs for recognition and control are related to status among fellow students.

If boys who made it to the top in social prestige did so through hard work or effort, this should be especially true of those from hard-pressed families, if only because their status was less secure. Even within the select circle of student leaders, one would expect a boy with a deprived background to have more to prove as a person of worth and promise than a member of a more affluent, stable home. Acclaim from peers would not alter the reality of family misfortune and its potential implications for social judgments. To assess the status correlates of social needs, we used the frequency and significance of mentions in the high school newspaper as an index of social prominence or elite status.

A total of 540 issues of the newspaper, spanning the tenth, eleventh, and twelfth grades, were read in order to construct a frequency distribution of adolescents in the sample who were mentioned in five major areas—student leadership, athletics, intellectual leadership, dramatic arts and music, interest clubs—and in miscellaneous contexts.[24] The total number of mentions per student ranged from 0 to 122. Since the social importance of recognition varied across news items, each mention was weighted on prestige level by the average judgment of staff members who were knowledgeable of the school during the 30s.[25] Within the most prominent group, the top 20 percent, three social types were identified: students in official leadership positions; talented performers in athletics, drama, or other modes of self-expression; and responsible workers on numerous committees. Student leaders were perceived by teachers as decisive in manner, energetic, and responsible. The performers included a wide variety of talents which were highly visible and valued in the student community. Students who were most active in committee work were distinguished by their industry, reliability, and competence.

Talents and high aspirations played more of a role in social prominence than family background. In fact, economic losses did not make a difference in the social prominence of youth from the middle or working classes. The most prominent group (upper one-fifth) included an equal number of boys and girls from deprived and nondeprived families. Low family status did not lessen prospects for social achievement among boys, despite the school's middle-class orientation, and was only a slight disadvantage for girls. Nevertheless, members of the elite group possessed qualities valued in youth culture, and they were distinguished by strong aspirations for recognition and power.

Adolescents in the top group were compared with eighteen who were not mentioned in the newspaper during the entire three years of high school, using measures of peer reputation, adult staff ratings, and motivational ratings. As one would expect, peer nominations as popular, leader, and friendly were heavily concentrated among the socially prominent, and adult observers rated them significantly higher on personal attractiveness. Boys in the active group were also rated higher on needs for recognition and power than the inactive ($p < .02$). Similar differences in social ambition were obtained for girls, although they were not as large ($p < .10$).

Within the prestige group, were social aspirations most pronounced among members of deprived families? Were leaders with deprived backgrounds characterized by more intense desires for recognition and power? In order to compare subgroups defined by economic deprivation, it was necessary to expand our definition of social prominence to include all adolescents in the upper two quintiles on the index. These 24 boys and 24 girls were then assigned to deprived and nondeprived categories: 13 versus 11 boys, and 14 versus 9 girls (one girl did not have information on economic loss). Three types of indicators were used in the comparison: the senior high index of social well-being; a measure of social aspiration specially constructed from items on the senior high questionnaire;[26] and the motivational ratings. A high score on the

Status Change and
Personality

index of social aspiration describes an adolescent whose ambitions regarding leadership and popularity greatly exceeded his self-assessed achievements in these areas.

Youth who rose to prominence in spite of family deprivation were more highly motivated than social leaders from nondeprived homes. The former were only slightly less happy and accepted by peers, according to self-perceptions, but they expressed stronger social aspirations; they were more likely to report social aspirations that exceeded their perceived achievements in high school ($p < .01$, boys and girls combined).[27] Active boys from deprived families were also rated slightly higher than leaders from more affluent homes on need for social recognition, while socially prominent girls from deprived homes were more oriented toward social acceptance than their counterparts from nondeprived families ($p < .01$). All other motivational ratings yielded insignificant differences.

For boys, in particular, the limitations of family hardships were overcome by a combination of valued talents, ambition, and opportunity. For example, Paul achieved social recognition in high school through his ability, in singing and dramatics, and was fifth among all boys in the sample in total number of mentions. He became known by students in other schools and by civic clubs for his talents as an entertainer, and was eventually paid for his performances. During the early years of the Depression, his father's earnings on a skilled, blue-collar job dropped by over 50 percent, a loss which eventually required the family to move in with relatives. This loss was very difficult for the family to accept, partly because of the good fortune of some relatives, and there is considerable evidence that Paul never accepted the social implications of this change. In a revealing self-portrait he made the following observations on his social ambitions: "To be a leader you have to have personality—to be able to talk to people and sell your talents, unless you are terrifically outstanding. . . . You have to have ambition—you just can't have ability and personality; you have to *work*."

The only boys from deprived families who were more prominent in high school than Paul were his friends Bill, Karl (the student body president), and Robert. Only Karl came from a working-class family. On self-reports and essays, these boys displayed a keen interest in achievement, in making a name for oneself. Bill, who was noted for his assertive manner, observed in an essay that "any boy who has the will or ability to get ahead in the world will certainly succeed." In high school he made a reputation for himself as an athlete, acquired friends easily, and was highly popular with both sexes. Student leadership and athletics were the primary activities of Karl. Attractive and energetic,

Robert was active in a wide variety of social activities in school. His mother described him as having "one driving interest after another, usually a practical one."

In contrast to the analysis of boys, we have been relatively unsuccessful in explaining the social accomplishments of girls from deprived households. Despite greater emotional distress, stronger feelings of social rejection, and a host of other social liabilities when compared to the nondeprived, these girls were not rated lower on popularity or social leadership by classmates and adult observers, and there is no evidence of differences in social ambition. The only clue to their social achievement appears in adaptations to discontent and unhappiness. As in the case of boys, unhappy girls in deprived families were less inclined than the nondeprived to withdraw from social reality through fantasies of friendship or to seek a dependent, protective relationship with others. This difference assumes special significance as a determining factor in view of the emotional correlates of family hardship.

Status Change and the Self: A Concluding Note

We have assumed that children from deprived and nondeprived families experienced themselves as a social object through their interpretation of the responses which others directed toward them. These interpretations frequently differ from the actual views of others, as we have seen in this chapter, and do not correspond in a simple one-to-one relation with established views of self, especially in situations of drastic change. Any change of this sort tends to alter the framework of meanings in which the self is anchored, creating a disparity between an acquired image of self, constructed from stable relations in the precrisis period, and interpretations of social judgments or evaluations in the new situation.

We were necessarily restricted to available information on children's self-orientations in the analysis, and the resulting measures do not adequately satisfy the requirements of our theoretical approach or of preferred methodological standards.[28] Accordingly, it is desirable to view the outcome of specific subgroup comparisons on a single indicator or measure within the context of other results. How consistent or coherent are the results? Using this standard, it is clear that family losses mainly influenced the way children interpreted their reputation or status among age-mates, with its attendant consequences for attitudes toward self and others, and not the actual views or evaluations of peers. Three issues, in particular, are posed by this conclusion: deprivational influences in children's subjective reality; definitions of the situation in their social strivings; and the equalitarian nature of the school environment.

Family Deprivation
in Subjective
Reality

Loss of family status sensitized children to the responses of others and led girls in particular to undervalue their status in the judgments of classmates. Self-consciousness and hypersensitivity were characteristic of both sexes in deprived families, according to the reports of mothers, but the emotional impact of family deprivation was concentrated among girls, owing partly to the stronger impact of family stress on their self-feelings and their greater social disadvantage in dress and grooming. In both social classes, girls from deprived families more often described themselves as unhappy with their social life and were highly critical of elitist behavior among classmates. Nevertheless, *neither staff observers nor classmates reported any reliable difference in the social leadership and popularity of children from nondeprived and deprived families in the two social classes.*

Subjective Reality in
Social Strivings

The disparity between how the Oakland children thought others viewed them and the actual views of others calls attention to the substance of their interpretations. If an actor's behavior in a situation is a function of how he defines it, definitions of the situation among children from deprived families would be a critical factor in any attempt to account for their social popularity. In this regard, we identified *external* causal attributions in perceptions as a plausible element in the social success of these boys and girls; their perceived social problems had less to do with personal deficiencies than with parental misfortunes and economic conditions. This outlook and the belief in one's ability to gain acceptance and recognition may be the reason why perceived social exclusion did not elicit like responses from girls in deprived families.

More generally, there is a notable difference between the presumed, modal response of parents to economic loss (as reported in the literature) and that of deprived children in the Oakland sample. It is claimed that many fathers responded to economic failure by blaming themselves, by turning frustration inward rather than focusing discontent on faults of the system, and their competence was of course more directly implicated in this problem than that of any other family member. Economic losses imposed hardships on children without regard for their own qualities, and a large percentage of older youth were not prepared to accept this judgment of their position or worth. While some children in deprived families undoubtedly turned frustrations inward, this response was not a modal adaptation in the Oakland sample, especially in the middle class, according to the evidence at hand. By and large, economic hardships spurred these boys and girls to greater efforts in the household economy and on their own behalf in relations with members of their own age group.

An Equalitarian
School
Environment? The
Objective Realities
of Public School

What kind of school environment would enable children from widely diverse backgrounds in the Depression to achieve the degree of social equality on popularity and leadership observed in this study? Considering the range of limitations and hardships in deprived families, one might expect to find related social disabilities in the school setting. Even if family deprivation prompted greater effort to win acceptance and recognition among classmates, it would amount to little if the school reinforced socioeconomic inequalities among students. The potential for rewarding social experience is likely to remain just that without suitable opportunity.

There is no lack of documentation regarding socioeconomic inequality in American public schools. However, available evidence indicates that the elimination of such inequality was a primary concern of staff members and student leaders in the junior and senior high schools attended by the Oakland children; both schools were heavily influenced by the progressive education movement. At various points in this chapter I have cited evidence of this concern in student editorials and policies on uniform dress. A journal published by the high school staff includes numerous accounts of faculty debates and strategies on widening the scope of social opportunities for all students, regardless of family background. While the effectiveness of this climate remains an open question, our data do correspond with a relatively equalitarian impact.

The Adult Years

III

The Depression affected people in two different ways. The great majority reacted by thinking money is the most important thing in the world. Get yours. And get it for your children. Nothing else matters.

And there is a small number of people who felt the whole system was lousy. You have to change it. The kids come along and they want to change it, too. But they don't seem to know what to put in its place.

A woman reformist
from an old Alabamian
family. In Studs
Terkel, *Hard Times.*

The "Depression experience" has become a familiar theme in folk accounts of adult behavior. Countless Americans who were born before 1929 are convinced, in retrospect, that experiences in the Depression have had an enduring impact either on their lives or on the lives of persons in their age group. And their children, now of college age or older, share this causal view when they assume that a childhood of scarcity accounts for outmoded parental conduct and priorities.

In their simplicity and exaggerated generality, characterizations of the Depression's continuing imprint ignore the extraordinary diversity of life situations in this historical period, as well as the differing resources with which people encountered hardships. The Depression was not the "worst of times" for all parents and children of the 30s, judging from our evidence, although few were in a position to regard it as the "best of times." As in any severe crisis, conditions in the 30s are likely to have produced extremes and even contradictory outcomes. In this respect we have assumed that economic hardships and related experiences had the most adverse effect on life patterns and adult personality among the offspring of working-class families.

Our objective in the next three chapters is to trace the effects of economic deprivation and class origin, through related experiences and adaptations, to life patterns and psychological health in adulthood. Life patterns are defined by the timing of major social transitions—the completion of formal education, entry into the labor force, marriage, and parenthood; by occupational status, attained in part through education, and worklife experience; and by social priorities among family, work, leisure, and community activities. Events in the life course have different meaning or implications for the careers of each sex. In the historical context of the Oakland cohort, men were expected to shape their life course through personal accomplishments in education and worklife, while marriage was the primary option and most fateful commitment for women. Since most of the Oakland girls eventually married and achieved adult status through the accomplishments of their husbands, important historical features of their life course are displayed in the lives of the Oakland men—the impact of World War II, change in the occupational structure. For this reason, we shall begin our analysis with the men, follow with the women, and then bring both sexes together in an assessment of their psychological health.

At a general level we shall employ a common analytic strategy in following the Oakland boys and girls into adult life. The diagram shown here outlines three sets of relationships: family background, as indexed by economic deprivation and class origin, to aspects of the life course; family background to values; and family background to values through aspects of the life course. In order to simplify the presentation, we have not specified adolescent adaptations to family hardship and their hypothetical status as linkages between economic deprivation and adult outcomes. For boys these adaptations include early work experience, vocational thinking, and ambition; for girls, domestic experience and interests.

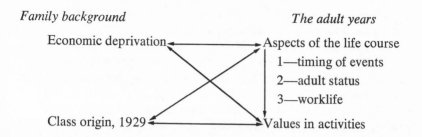

The analysis is organized around three basic tasks: a review of the life course from late adolescence to middle age; an assessment of the impact of family hardship on aspects of the life course; and specification of conditions under which adult values are linked to economic deprivation. There are two objectives in the overview: to describe the Oakland cohort in its historical context and to compare the age group with other cohorts. The long-term impact of economic conditions in the 30s depends in large part on the particular cohort's life stage at the time. In this respect we need to keep in mind the Oakland adolescents' entry into adult roles, and especially their point of departure from high school, 1938–39. By this date unemployment had declined appreciably in the Oakland area, and economic activity had surged above the 1929 level. Having passed through the most severe phase of economic privation, young members of deprived families had reason to be relatively optimistic about their future prospects. The nation was only two years away from official entry into World War II, an event which effectively closed the Depression decade and directly influenced the lives of men in the sample. By any standard, life opportunities were more favorable for the Oakland adolescents than for young Americans who came of age five or ten years earlier.

The second task focuses on the determinants of aspects of the life course. In the adult lives of the Oakland men, we shall give special attention to the process of status attainment, to the effect of economic deprivation relative to the influence of class origin, and to factors which link family background to occupational status. Did occupational fortunes generally favor men who did not experience family hardship in the Depression? If so, how can we account for this outcome? Were worklife disabilities related to deprivation or to barriers in the educational route to rewarding occupations? In the case of the Oakland women, we shall investigate two consequential events in their life course and their relation to a background of family hardship: when they married and the kind of men they married. The timing of marriage structures social options and the scheduling of subsequent events (parenthood, employment), while a married woman's career is dependent on her husband's occupational achievements.

The analysis to this point will have established a context in which to pose and evaluate questions on the relation between adult values and economic hardships in the Depression. Is there any basis for assuming that the Depression experience of adults makes a difference in their priorities or choices? Much evidence suggests that values are rooted more in the contemporary life situations of adults than in their childhood environments. Accordingly we must take these situations into account as we trace out the long-term effect of family deprivation on things that matter most to the Oakland adults. Under what conditions are specific adult values related to family deprivation in the 30s?

7

Earning a Living

Much of his ambition, drive, and energy comes from the Depression.... Son of a wealthy businessman

I mean, there's a conditioning here by the Depression. I'm what I call a security cat. I don't dare switch. 'Cause I got too much whiskers on it, seniority. Garbage worker

Growing up in the Depression, for boys who felt its impact, meant exposure to the uncertain aspects of earning a living. The search for employment, queuing for public relief, and rent strikes—these and other events dramatized the struggle to survive, to make a living. One might argue that boys became cautious or conservative men in their worklife as a result of this experience, favoring a steady job over the risks of job mobility, and vesting emotions in the more durable shelter of family relationships; or that hardship fostered work consciousness and commitments in aspirations, a determination to achieve greater material and social benefits, which enabled men to surmount handicaps (such as educational limitations) in their life course. Though seemingly in conflict, these interpretations are mainly distinguished by their reference to different aspects of adult life which have roots in childhood, to the meaning or relative value of activities and the process of status attainment. Our primary objective in this chapter is to determine whether and how these aspects of adult experience are linked in the lives of the Oakland men to family background in the Depression, defined by class origin and economic deprivation.

Any attempt to trace the values of men to experiences in the Depression must take their adult situations into account, since they determine the appropriateness or adaptive value of lessons from the past. Even if boys in the Depression were impressed by the importance of job security, security is unlikely to acquire priority among those who were most successful in their worklife. Men who advanced beyond their father's status tend to be more committed to the job and less attached to family life or leisure than the nonmobile (see Elder 1969*b*). Accordingly, we expect the association between family deprivation and adult values (job security, etc.) to increase with the degree of social continuity between the Depression and adult life. An examination of status attainment is thus a first step in identifying the adult contexts of predispositions acquired in the Depression.

Opportunities for social advancement were available in the late 30s to boys who did not pursue education beyond the high school years, but higher education was the most certain route to prestigious jobs, and it was also highly vulnerable to the limitations of family deprivation.[1] These limitations are mainly concentrated in the working class of the Oakland cohort, and should be most evident in the educational level of boys from this stratum. *Family resources in support for education are the only substantial difference between boys from deprived and non-deprived households; they were similar on ability, desire to excel (on tasks), and occupational goals in each social class.*

Educational opportunities relative to family hardships in the Depression are difficult to estimate for boys in the sample since they left home just prior to nationwide mobilization in World War II. In fact, the stirring of economic revival is generally dated from the outbreak of war in Europe in September 1939, just three months after the adolescents left high school. War spurred American markets and industries, generating opportunities and educational options for the young. "It was like watching blood drain back into the blanched face of a person who had fainted."[2] Shortly thereafter a majority of the male members of the 1915–25 cohort were called to serve in the military, and some eventually continued their education through the GI bill.[3]

These developments in the late 30s are reflected in a general mood of optimism among the Oakland boys when they were questioned at the end of 1938. Only half of the sample participated in the survey, and though all but a few respondents were members of middle-class families, their general outlook is at least suggestive of beliefs at the time. Regardless of family hardship, nearly three-fourths of the boys felt that the Depression, as they had experienced it, was over. The sons of deprived parents were not more discouraged about their future than members of more affluent families, but they displayed more awareness of potential disappointments in life. Exposure to family hardships and suffering in the community had not shaken their belief in the democratic system of government or in the formula of hard work and talent for getting ahead. On the contrary, these boys were more likely to subscribe to beliefs of this sort than relatively affluent youth.

The subsequent analysis is organized around the relation between economic deprivation and life achievement, sources of variation in this relation, and values. In the first section we shall provide an overview of the life course followed by the Oakland men—defined by marriage, initial employment, parenthood, education, and occupation—and then make comparisons according to family origin and economic loss. This is followed by an assessment of three potential sources of variation in the occupational attainment of men from deprived families: vocational crystallization and commitment, as expressed in worklife patterns; ambition in achievement striving and the utilization of ability; and education. If family deprivation reduced educational prospects for some boys, it also introduced them at a relatively early age to habits, attitudes, and responsibilities which may have proved beneficial in their worklife. Both involvement in productive roles and the insecurity of dependence on deprived parents are conducive to preoccupation with matters of economic support and occupational role, of focused goals and the utilization of skills. Having identified these elements in status attainment, we shall turn to adult values and their relation to experiences in the Depression. Particular emphasis will be given to the relative importance and meaning of work role and family life, the two dominant concerns of men in the Depression.

The sample for our analysis includes sixty-nine boys who participated as adults in at least one of three systematic follow-ups between 1941 and 1965.[4] Since the data collections (1953–54, 1958, and 1964) are described in chapter 1 and Appendix B, only two points warrant mention here. First, sample attrition over this time span is not related to class origin, household structure, ethnicity, economic loss in the 30s, or intelligence. Second, information collected in the adult follow-ups was organized in the form of occupational and marital histories through 1958. Since the Oakland sons in 1958 were approximately the same age as their fathers had been in 1929, intergenerational comparisons are based upon comparisons of adult status in these two years.

Adult Status in the Life Course of the Oakland Cohort

Three developments after the Depression decade left a distinct imprint on the career beginnings and life course of the Oakland boys: World War II, the expansion of higher education, and the growth of large-scale organizations and salaried positions in large corporations. Shortly after Pearl Harbor most of the boys were in uniform, and over 90 percent eventually served in some capacity. Organizational growth in the war economy and postwar years is manifested in their subsequent career lines and status achievements.

As a first step in the analysis we shall survey these developments in order to identify the average timing, sequence, and level of status achievement in the cohort as a whole. This overview will establish a context for assessing the relative impact of class position and deprivation on early events in the 40s and achieved status up to middle age.

A number of crucial transitions normally occur in the life course

Earning a Living

within a relatively short span of time: completion of education, entry into a full-time job, marriage, and the birth of the first child. No phase of the life cycle can match the rapidity of these multiple and often discontinuous transitions. To these events we must add induction into the military for the Oakland cohort. In a number of respects, the most fateful year was 1942, a year in which most of the boys reached the age of majority; 40 percent of the boys were called to serve by the end of the year. Only 20 percent were married at this time, and approximately 40 percent had terminated their education, by choice or circumstance, and would not return to their studies in the postwar years. Completion of education was followed by full-time employment, except for those who immediately entered the military. By the middle of 1943, three-fifths of the boys had at least entered the labor market on a full-time basis, and some experience in part-time work was shared by all members of the cohort. The contrast between this employment situation and that encountered by older youth in the Depression is worth noting. As one staff member of the Institute of Human Development recalls, "any lad who could breathe was able to find a decent job."

An equal proportion of the boys entered the military in 1942 and 1943 (see figure 2). Records show only two war-related deaths among members of the adolescent sample. Little is known about experiences in uniform, such as assignments to war theaters, front-line service, and career lines defined by rank and promotions. Most of the men were in uniform for either two or three years, and were discharged in 1945–46, a date of special significance in relation to the subsequent "baby boom."

Though some marriages were delayed during the Depression, the

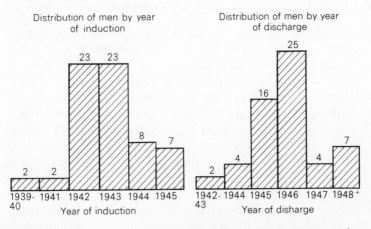

Figure 2   Years of Induction into and Discharge from Armed Forces (Oakland Men)

median age of American men at first marriage remained relatively constant across decennial censuses from 24.6 in 1920 to 24.3 in 1940 (Moss 1964). However, this age did drop significantly in the immediate postwar period, to 23.7 in 1947, a value which corresponds with the marital history of the Oakland men. By 1945–46, approximately two-thirds of the men ever married were wed for the first time (median age = 23.7). Figure 3 shows the percentage distribution of men ever married by age at first marriage and at birth of first child. Precise data on marital age were available for all but two of the men ever married; four men have never wed.

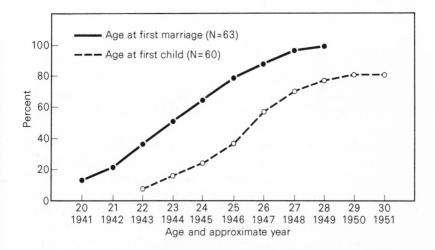

Figure 3   Percentage Distribution of Men Ever Married by Age at First Marriage and at Birth of First Child

Age at first marriage appears to have been influenced less by war absences than does the timing of parenthood. Nearly four-fifths of the men were married by the end of their twenty-fifth year, but only a third were parents at that age. Two years later, or by the latter months of 1948, the percentage of first births had doubled. This period corresponds to the initial stage of the "baby boom," which has been attributed in part to favorable economic conditions, the decline in age at first marriage, and an accelerated pattern of childbearing following the constraints of depression and war (Easterlin 1961). Number of children (median = 2.8 for ever married Ss, 1964) was moderately correlated with an early transition to marriage and fatherhood (average $r =$ −.28). A majority of the first marriages remained intact over the twenty-year period following World War II (85 percent), with half of the divorces occurring before 1950.

Most of the men entered the labor market as full-time workers in California and remained in the area thereafter, thus profiting from the state's "bullish" economy during the postwar years. According to a survey conducted by the Institute of Child Welfare in 1941, sixty percent were then enrolled in some form of education beyond high school. Records also show a third of the men employed full-time on the eve of Pearl Harbor. Educational status also changed very little for the cohort as a whole in the war years. Fifty-seven percent of the men had terminated their education by the end of 1943, a figure which increased by only 6 percent over the next three years. The war's disruptive impact, suggested by this plateau, was countered in some cases by the educational benefits of veteran status. Overall, 28 percent of the men eventually achieved a postgraduate education, and a similar proportion completed four years of college. In the subgroup which completed college after the war, six men are known to have received financial support through the GI bill.

Change in the organizational structure of American society since the beginning of World War II, a change some analysts have described as radical and even revolutionary, is reflected by career lines in the Oakland cohort. This change includes the growth of large-scale organizations or bureaucracies and of higher-salaried positions (Blau and Duncan 1967, p. 106). "Bureaucratic styles, language, culture, and personality have become the dominant matrix for life within the New Society" (Bensman and Vidich 1971, p. 5). A related development is the emergence of a new middle class which is largely college-educated: "It is a class of white-collar employees, managers, professionals, junior executives, and service workers in the higher-status services such as education, recreation, leisure, social work, psychiatry, and the other service occupations" (ibid., pp. 5–6). In contrast to the entrepreneurial style of the old middle class in the Depression, a style expressed by the small businessman and independent craftsman, self-employment is largely foreign to the worklife of men in the Oakland sample; 70 percent had no experience with self-employment up to the age of forty-three, and less than a fifth had spent as much as half of their worklife in an entrepreneurial capacity.

This change in work setting is most clearly seen in the occupational careers of boys who pursued advanced education and employment in the general fields of engineering and business. Approximately 15 percent were employed in each field at the end of the 50s. Despite a wide range of engineering specialties, including civil, electrical, and aeronautical, men in this occupational group generally occupied a similar work situation in at least one respect; a position of managerial responsibility in a large corporation or firm. By comparison, this status was rare among engineers in the paternal generation, especially in the supervision of more than ten employees. Discontinuity of this sort is also evident in the life histories of boys who became college-educated accountants and brokers. All but one have worked their way into high-level executive positions in banking, insurance, industry, or real estate. Some of their fathers were also engaged in similar lines of work, but they either were self-employed or held minor supervisory responsibilities.

The expansion of prestige occupations corresponds with the striking level of achievement among the Oakland men. A comparison of father's position in 1929 and son's in 1958, using the Hollingshead two-factor index of social position (occupation and education), shows considerable upward mobility. A fourth of the men were in the upper middle class as young boys in 1929 (strata I and II); 42 percent were lower middle class (III), and a third were located in the working class (IV and V). Some thirty years later, nearly half were positioned in the upper middle class; percentages for comparable strata are 49, 35, and 16. Much of this change occurred through expanding educational opportunities. As a group, the fathers achieved more than might be expected in higher education (17 percent were college graduates), according to college-going rates in the first quarter of the twentieth century, but their sons more than tripled this proportion.

Though experiences in the Depression varied from the relatively affluent world of some families to extreme deprivation, uncertainties and national obligations in World War II were more uniformly shared by the Oakland boys as they started out in life. In timing and duration, military service was invariant across diverse backgrounds in the Depression. If sons of working-class or deprived parents had greater reason to seek employment in the military, we have no evidence that they did so at an earlier date or remained in uniform for a longer time than the sons of relatively prosperous families. A major factor in this uniformity was the initiation of military conscription, the "draft," which became law on 16 September 1940.[5]

Economic losses in the Depression had surprisingly little consequence for the early adult events and accomplishments of boys in the sample.[6] The only adverse effect appears in the adult status of men with origins in the working class, and pertains especially to their education. The achieved status of men with deprived and nondeprived backgrounds is first shown by a comparison of subgroups (table 5) and then by a multivariate assessment of the relative effects of class and deprivation (table 6).

The early adult life of middle-class sons shows no adverse effect of deprivational experiences in the Depression. On the average, they married, had their first child, completed formal education, and obtained a full-time job (after leaving school) at the same time in both deprivational groups. Members of each group were equally successful in acquiring a college education, and there is no evidence that such achievement required greater sacrifice in parenthood from married men with deprived backgrounds. In both groups, the first child arrived some three years after marriage.

Table 5   Adult Status of Oakland Men by Economic Deprivation and Class Origin (1929)[a]

Indicators of Adult Status[b]	Middle Class		Working Class	
	Nondeprived N = 23	Deprived N = 20	Nondeprived N = 8	Deprived N = 14
Age at first marriage	23.8	23.3	24.5	23.5
Age at first child ·	26.5	26.2	26.0	26.3
Age at completion of education	22.3	22.1	24.0	20.3
College graduate (%)	61	60	50	43
Occupational status ($\bar{X}$ score: 1 = high, 7 = low)				
Following education	3.3	3.0	4.2	3.9
1958	2.5	2.2	2.8	3.1
Social Class, 1958 (% distribution)				
I	39	45	25	14
II & III	48	45	37	57
IV	13	10	38	29
	100	100	100	100

[a]   Information on economic loss was available for sixty-five of the subjects in the adult sample.

[b]   Average age refers to the median value. In each subgroup, one-half of the subjects married, had their first child, and completed their education prior to the reported ages.

    Though one might expect more of a delay in educational progress among the college-educated sons of deprived families in the middle class, this pattern is actually more characteristic of men from nondeprived households, even though they were no more likely to pursue postgraduate studies; 40 percent did not complete their education until after the war, compared to a fourth of the men with deprived backgrounds. This contrast effectively rules out financial assistance through the GI bill as an explanation for the educational attainment of men who grew up in deprived families. In fact, men who are known to have benefited from the GI bill in their college education show no consistent pattern in family background. As a group, men from deprived families in the middle class have achieved slightly higher status in the occupational world, both immediately after formal education and in middle age, than the sons of nondeprived parents.[7]

One of the more puzzling aspects of these life patterns is the lack of any discernible handicap resulting from the inability of deprived parents to support their son's education. Nevertheless, it seems likely that economic hardships strengthened dependence on financial sources outside the family of orientation for men who continued their education. This greater dependence does not show up on educational assistance via the GI bill or on scholarships, although this may be due to the inadequacy of our data. Other possibilities include self-support through employment and financial assistance from the wife's earnings. The latter source is suggested by the educational superiority of men from deprived families and the known tendency for women to terminate their education at marriage. These men were less apt to have college-educated wives than the nondeprived group (17% vs. 41%), and a majority surpassed their wives in education (66% vs. 40% for men in the nondeprived category). The data suggest that a substantial number of the women with husbands from deprived families sacrificed their education in order to put them through college; a larger number actually entered college and left before completing degree requirements (40% in the deprived group vs. 18% in the nondeprived).

Economic deprivation did leave its imprint on the educational attainment of men from working-class families, but only to a modest extent. Compared to other groups, the sons of deprived parents moved more rapidly into the labor force, and achieved less education on the average. Despite this educational difference, deprivational experiences in the Depression had little direct consequences for occupational attainment. A clearer picture of these background effects is shown in table 6, which presents the main effects of both class origin and deprivation on adult education and occupation.

This table clearly shows the more negative effect of family deprivation on the adult status of men from the working class. Variations in family hardship had no consequence for the educational attainment of men from middle-class families, and are even slightly related in a positive direction to occupational status. Deprivation was more of a career handicap for men of lower-status origin through its negative influence on educational attainment. This limitation most likely reflects conditions which discouraged or prevented entry into a program of higher education, as against financial barriers to the completion of college. Occupational ambitions and ability were relatively low among

Table 6   Socioeconomic Factors and Education in Adult Status Attainment: Partial Regression Coefficients in Standard Form (beta coefficient)

Socioeconomic Origins and Adult Education	Educational Status		Occupational Status (1958)	
	r	beta	r	beta
Total Sample (N = 65)				
Adult education	—	—	.71	.70
Economic deprivation	−.09	−.04	.01	.10
Social class (1929)	.22	.19	.23	.12
Middle class (N = 43)				
Adult education	—	—	.71	.71
Economic deprivation	.01	.11	.11	.11
Working class (N = 22)				
Adult education	—	—	.69	.70
Economic deprivation	−.20	−.20	−.10	.04

Note.   Scores on education, occupational status (1958), and family status in 1929 were reversed so that a high value indexed high status. Thus values on education range from "1" (low) to "7" (high); on occupational status, 1 to 7; and on family status, 1 to 5. Economic deprivation was treated as a dummy variable, with nondeprived status scored 0 and deprived status 1.

working-class youth in the Depression, and members of deprived families in this stratum entered the labor market at a younger age than other men in the sample. The more able boys in this group occupied a marginal situation vis-à-vis the future, in which aversive conditions weigh heavily on educational prospects. For those who entered college and married shortly thereafter, wife support may have been a key factor in the likelihood of their persistence through graduation, although the extent of wife support is difficult to estimate from available evidence. Only three men from the working class married college-educated women, and over half exceeded their wife's level of education.

Simply in terms of proximity to events in the Depression, one would expect educational prospects and attainment to be more strongly influenced by economic deprivation than occupational status in the middle years of adulthood. The dependence of status achievement on a preceding event generally varies according to their distance or separation in the life course; dependence increases as distance decreases. For the Oakland sample occupational status in 1958 is highly dependent on educational attainment some ten years earlier, but this relation is not sufficient to transfer an educational handicap intact to the occupational area. The weak chain of influence from economic deprivation through education adds little to our understanding of the occupational success attained by men with deprived origins in both social classes, a level which is at least equal to that of men from nondeprived households.

To what extent does the Oakland cohort's unique career stage in the Depression account for this result? Life cycle theory and observations underscore the belief that social change has differential consequences for persons of unlike age. In this regard I have suggested that the Oakland men were born at a favorable time relative to the Depression; they were too old to be highly vulnerable to family misfortune and too young to enter the adult marketplace of marriage and work when economic conditions were most depressed. In terms of future prospects, mobilization for war occurred at a critical point and undoubtedly neutralized or at least weakened the adverse effects of starting out life with a background of family privation.

By comparison, the Depression frequently had profound consequences for the worklives of older men, including some fathers of the Oakland men. This is shown, for example, in Stephan Thernstrom's historical analysis of Boston men across five birth cohorts: 1850–59, 1860–79, 1880–89, 1900–09, and 1930 (1973, chap. 4). The constraints of the 30s are most clearly seen in the worklives of men who were born in the first decade of the twentieth century, a group which had just entered lines of work and family roles prior to the economic collapse. Compared to the other cohorts, these men were less likely to achieve some upward mobility from first to last job. However, the long-term effects of the Depression varied according to occupational level at the onset of depressed conditions. White-collar workers and skilled craftsmen experienced economic losses, shifts to lower status jobs in the nonmanual category, and unemployment in some cases, but these reverses did not markedly reduce their chances for occupational advancement in later life. A darker side of the 30s shows up in the lives of laboring men, the unskilled and semiskilled. Compared to men with comparable first jobs in the other cohorts, they were least likely to move into the white-collar stratum by the end of their productive years. More than three-fourths of the men who had held semiskilled first jobs before the Depression were still in this stratum at the time of their last job, in contrast to fewer than half in the earlier birth cohorts.

According to both studies, the Depression's impact in the lower strata is linked to educational or skill deficiencies. With little in the way of formal education and acquired job skills, young laborers in Boston occupied a precarious and highly vulnerable position in the rapidly contracting labor market of the early 30s, and their marginal life situation may have impaired the educational prospects of their sons. In the Oakland sample, only the sons of working-class fathers were likely to experience some educational disadvantage as a result of family hardship. Given a widening array of opportunities at the end of the 30s, a temporary decline in family status and resources had less adverse implications for the life course of working-class boys than persistent economic deprivation and cultural limitations, as indexed by the class position of their families.

The differing implications of these two modes of deprivation (decremental and persistent) should be expressed in psychosocial experiences. What is it about the experience of decremental family change that would enable boys to take advantage of expanding job and educational options at the end of the Depression decade? Two factors, in particular, are suggested by our research to date: vocational development through the initial stage of full-time employment and motivation. Were there aspects of vocational development, such as an accelerated vocational focus and commitment, which enhanced the careers of men from hard-pressed families? In view of their early work history, one might expect boys from deprived homes to show an earlier resolution of vocational plans. The folk belief that Depression-reared men are especially reluctant to change jobs or fields is consistent with the working hypothesis that their childhood circumstances conditioned a vocational focus and commitment.

Related to this vocational pattern is the matter of ambition and the utilization of ability. Boys from deprived families in both social classes were more ambitious in social goals than more affluent youth, but it is not clear how this desire entered into their future occupational life, since they were not more achievement-oriented on tasks or goals. Perhaps they were more persistent in applying skills to a line of work in accord with crystallized vocational aims. The process of vocational development, taken up in the following section, establishes an appropriate context in which to assess intellectual ability and ambition in the adult careers of this Depression age group.

Vocational Development in Worklife Experience

Any approach to vocational development during the late 30s must be sensitive to the interplay between environmental conditions and personal resources. Occupational choice is neither a simple expression of personality nor a mirror image of social structure. For the Oakland cohort, our task is to determine how decremental change in family status, and related experience, influenced vocational thinking and commitments. An important element here is vocational identity, which develops from and is validated by relations to others and is therefore subject to modification as situations and associations change.[8]

The downward extension of adultlike pressures and obligations was manifested in the role of boys within the household economy, in their desire to be grown-up, and in their preference for the company of adults. Economic hardships exposed them to the realities of self-support. Family resources and prestige could no longer be taken for granted as a pathway to educational and job opportunities by youth in the deprived middle class. Accordingly, we suspect that occupational roles became more of a conscious problem to boys who grew up in deprived families, when compared to youth from more affluent middle-class households, and that vocational thinking accelerated commitments to occupational roles (cf. Super et al. 1963).

If economic losses increased preoccupation with vocational questions, prospects were influenced by perceived opportunity. Severe hardships are known to foster hopelessness by restricting options and resources, but these conditions were neither characteristic of Oakland in the late 30s nor of most low-status families in the study. In some cases, goals may have been lowered to accommodate family limitations,[9] but this adjustment, according to available evidence, was less a function of economic loss than of low-class origin. As noted in the preceding chapter, low occupational goals were related only to low family status before the Depression. Accordingly, we shall center our attention on dimensions of early vocational development, such as crystallization of interests and vocational commitment, and their consequences for worklife experiences in adulthood, the timing and orderliness of careers, and ultimate achievement.

Early Vocational Development

The boys' developmental stage in vocational crystallization was determined by clinical assessments of interest profiles on Strong Vocational Interest Blanks that were administered in 1938 and then again in 1941. These assessments were made by a single judge with many years of experience in clinical applications of the inventory.[10] Each set of interest profiles was coded without knowledge of the particular case or year, and then assigned to one of three levels of vocational development: transitional—interests are undeveloped, in process of developing; emerging—probable direction of interests can be discerned, but interests are not well formulated; and mature—well-developed, distinct area or areas of vocational preference. A comparison of these judgments between 1938 and 1941 shows considerable change toward greater maturity, as one would expect, although less than half of the boys were placed in the mature category. In 1938, 27 percent were assigned to the transitional category, 62 percent to the emerging category, and only 7 percent were considered mature. Three years later this distribution had shifted toward the mature stage with corresponding percentages of 13, 45, and 43. Rate of maturation in cognitive functioning as indexed by IQ was correlated with vocational maturity only during the high school period. Boys in the transitional stage scored significantly lower on IQ than members of the more advanced groups ($p < .05$). When they were tested again three years later, boys with transitional and emerging interests were not less able than the more mature.

Turning to the data on family conditions, we find that vocational maturity increased most sharply between these two time periods among boys from deprived families in both social classes. Neither social class nor economic deprivation made any difference in vocational development when the boys were in high school. By 1941, however, a majority of the boys in the deprived group were judged mature, compared to less than thirty percent of the nondeprived (59% vs. 29%, $p < .05$). With the transitional and emerging groups combined, vocational maturity was more strongly correlated with economic deprivation than with social class ($r = .28$ vs. .04), and did not vary in its relation to economic loss among boys from middle- and working-class families.

Though few boys had developed coherent interests in high school, commitments to a vocational preference were most common among the offspring of deprived families. On the 1938 inventory, a question on occupational choice was phrased to elicit general categorical preferences, such as engineer, carpenter, and salesman. Only two-thirds of the boys expressed a preference, and a majority were in the white-collar, managerial, and professional categories. The most frequently mentioned choices were engineer, doctor and lawyer, businessman, accountant, and skilled manual occupations. Engineering was preferred by the largest number (16 percent), with less than 10 percent stating each of the other choices. Prestige level of choice increased by family status, as noted earlier, while certainty of choice varied only by economic loss in the Depression. To evaluate the prevalence of vocational commitments in each deprivational group, we compared boys who were sure of their choice with those who were either unsure or did not know what they wanted to do. Approximately half of the respondents were defined as vocationally committed. This preference was most characteristic of the deprived group from the middle class (62% vs. 40%, ND), and the contrast was even greater in the working class (50% vs. 25%). On both maturity of interests and preference, economic deprivation is related to an accelerated pattern of vocational development.

The most influential figures in occupational choice varied by economic conditions in the Depression, as one might expect from knowledge of family relations and the importance of extrafamilial adults among members of deprived households. Mother and teachers were more popular reference figures in the lives of boys from deprived families when compared to the nondeprived, and they were cited more often some thirty years later (1964) as the major influence on the choice of their current occupation (29% vs. 13%). These men were also more likely to claim that no one influenced this choice (15% vs. 7%). Father was selected only by middle-class sons and by an equal proportion in both deprivational groups (20%). Adult influences, such as friends in an occupational field and wife, were more frequently cited by the offspring of nondeprived parents.

The impact of economic loss, through its relation to a more labor-intensive household economy, is more easily understood in the vocational development of boys from the middle class than of lower-status boys. As a group, the former were intelligent and resourceful and presumably benefited from the traditional aspirations and future-seeking attitudes of their stratum. Within this context, family losses can be interpreted as a precipitating or activating event with respect to economic maintenance and self-support, accelerating vocational thinking, judgments, and activity. It is apparent that such matters were a foremost concern in the deprived middle class, judging from parental preoccupations and the productive roles of children. In the lower strata, by comparison, one is more likely to find indecision and "don't know or care" responses as modal reactions to poverty situations and an unattractive future. The vocational stage of ninth-grade boys in a 1960 study illustrates this point; the less intelligent sons of low-status parents knew very little about the choices they would be required to make, were unaware of the implications of early choices for subsequent alternatives, and showed little understanding of the factors or conditions that should inform decision making.[11]

There are several considerations which may explain why this characterization bears so little resemblance to the vocational perspective of working-class males from deprived families. First of all, working class in the Oakland sample refers mainly to the upper-manual stratum, a category which includes the more stable, ambitious families in the lower strata. Second, boys from these families were not markedly disadvantaged in mental ability; whether economically deprived or not, their absolute standing on intelligence and achievement motivation was not a major limitation. Also we should note that all working-class boys in the study attended predominantly middle-class schools on the secondary level. On school resources, counseling, and occupational models they held an obvious advantage over age-mates who attended working-class schools in Oakland. Taken as a whole, these assets maximized life opportunities for the Oakland working class, and in doing so ensured considerable uniformity across social strata in cognitive aspects of vocational development.

Worklife
Experiences in
Adult Careers

In clarity of interests and commitment, the early occupational focus of men from deprived households offers a clue toward understanding the status they eventually achieved, although it rests on the untested assumption of continuity in vocational development from late adolescence through the formative years of adult worklife in the 1940s. Other things being equal, direction in career beginnings favors the establishment of an orderly worklife with minimal delay, a sequence in which changes are made between jobs that are functionally related and hierarchically ordered.[12] However, the benefits of such direction are also coupled with certain risks of premature specialization, such as a restricted breadth of perspective. These consequences are minimized when vocational options are left open for exploration into the adult years, although *prolonged* indecision leads to ambiguity of status and the potential disadvantage of a late start in life. In normative definition and opportunity, there is an appropriate age for the beginning of a worklife, for marriage, and for the birth of children.

If early vocational development was instrumental in the occupational status achieved by men from deprived families, its implications should be manifested in worklife experiences, as indexed by the timing of career establishment, number of employers and jobs in different phases of worklife, orderliness of worklife, degree of continuity between early vocational preferences and occupations some twenty years later, and a review of worklife experiences and accomplishments from the vantage point of middle age. The continuity thesis suggests that men from deprived families entered career lines at an earlier date than members of the nondeprived group, and were more likely to establish orderly careers. Since orderliness of career is related to education, this difference should be most pronounced among men from the middle class.

The timing of career establishment was defined by year of entry into a line of work which was followed for at least six years between 1940 and the late 50s. Line of work refers to a sequence of related jobs that are arranged in a hierarchical framework. As shown in table A–20, early career formation is related to economic loss, but the association is strongest for men of middle-class background, owing partly to the slower educational progress of the nondeprived group. Uncertain goals may have been a significant factor in this difference, since entry into a career line after 1948 is negatively correlated with vocational crystallization, as clinically assessed in 1941.[13]

This consequence of vocational indecision is most clearly seen in life history protocols, such as the following case of a middle-class boy who encountered no particular family hardship or restriction during the Depression. He was known among staff members at the Institute of Child Welfare as a bright, popular lad, a scholar of sorts, with vocational interests which ranged widely across teaching, personnel work, and engineering. He tended to favor the latter field in stated preferences because it was a "man's job," but felt uncertain about the opportunities it would provide for helping and working with people. Clinical judgments of vocational maturity placed him in the pre-maturity categories through 1941. From the point at which he entered a school of engineering in 1939 to 1948, his life was distinguished by considerable vacillation. Though disqualified for military service on medical grounds, he dropped out of school in 1942 and secured employment on local construction projects. After a year of practical experience, he returned to school, but dropped out again after a semester. This instability continued until he landed a job as an engineer with a large manufacturing firm in 1948, following marriage, a child, and a diploma from the university. Promotions soon followed in the company, and eventually opened up more promising opportunities in other firms. By 1958, he had advanced to partnership in a small company which used his talents in public relations and engineering. Despite this steady climb in prestige and income, neither engineering nor his work in public relations was wholly satisfying: "Things might be better if . . ." "If I had applied myself earlier I might have gone into something like medicine, something that would help people. I might have done something more important." He felt that his life would have been different and more rewarding if he had only "stood on his own two feet" sooner. However, he was not contemplating a more service-oriented line of work at the time he made these comments, since, as he put it, "I'm not convinced of what I'd do anyway."

It is commonly believed that exposure to economic loss and job uncertainty in the Depression conditioned a stubborn reluctance to change jobs and especially employers. For our purposes, the significance of this belief lies in its relation to a stable, if undistinguished, career line, although multiple employers and jobs do not, in themselves, provide a reliable indication of the orderliness of a worklife. These changes may entail transitions within the same occupational field or across functionally unrelated fields, from car salesman, for example, to psychiatric nurse. If men from deprived families acquired a conservative stance toward change in job and employer, there is no trace of it in their occupational histories. On the average, they moved through a larger number of jobs and employers over a twenty-year period than the offspring of nondeprived parents from the middle and working class (table A–21). However, this difference is restricted primarily to the unsettled years between high school and the postwar period.

In the postwar years, the most important worklife change, from the standpoint of social disruption and psychological strain, occurred in shifts between unrelated jobs. We identified this type of change for two time periods (1946–55 and 1956–64), using detailed work histories. Developmental variations by economic loss are reflected in job changes during the initial postwar period, but only among men with origins in the middle class; 28 percent of the nondeprived had made at least one change to another type of work, in contrast to 5 percent of the men from deprived families. Only two men of working-class origin had moved into an unrelated job. Occupational experience was a more important factor in job changes after 1955, relative to family deprivation. In fact, economic hardship made no difference in the likelihood of occupational discontinuity in this period; most of the changers grew up in working-class families (30% vs. 10% from the middle class) and all were classified as either stable or downwardly mobile in relation to father's occupation. These men generally changed their line of work in order to secure more rewarding employment.

Another test of career continuity is provided by a comparison of vocational preferences at the end of high school with occupations in 1958. This comparison is restricted primarily to the offspring of middle-class parents, since only two-thirds of the men reported a specific preference. The global nature of these choices necessitated a crude determination of similarity and difference. Thus all engineering positions, for instance, whether civil, electrical, industrial, or chemical, were considered a match for the adolescent preference of engineer. In line with our previous findings, career continuity or goal achievement was most common in the work histories of men from deprived families (66% vs. 29%). This difference was less pronounced among the small number of working-class sons who knew what they wanted to be in the late 30s.

Up to this point, we have viewed worklife experience according to objective measures from 1940 to the late 50s. The vantage point has been the socioeconomic context of "starting out life" prior to World War II and phases of the worklife itself, such as the timing of career establishment. Missing from this analysis is a subjective review of worklife events, successes and shortcomings. To conclude this section, we shall look back on work experiences, in the early 40s and in later life, through the middle-aged views of the Oakland men, and then proceed to an estimate of their consequences for occupational attainment.

During a lengthy interview conducted in 1958, the men were questioned about the age when they made a firm choice of an occupational role, the degree to which it was followed, and their feelings regarding worklife experiences to date. An overview of these retrospective materials is presented below through a comparison of men from nondeprived and deprived families. Class differences are noted wherever they appear.

By and large, memories of the past correspond with objective measures of early vocational development and worklife experience. When compared to the offspring of nondeprived parents, members of the deprived group more often reported an early choice of their current occupation (high school or shortly thereafter—57% vs. 33%), cited formal or informal preparation as a more influential basis for occupational decisions than external pressures or job opportunities (44% vs. 26%), and claimed that they followed their original occupational preference (46% vs. 33%). Though class background did not make a difference in these reports, it did influence evaluations of past events. Within the middle class, a larger percentage of men from deprived households were convinced that they had done better than their original expectations (55% vs. 31%), expressed satisfaction with the adequacy of their education (26% vs. 20%), and were not interested in changing past events if they had the chance (61% vs. 50%). These differences were reversed for working-class sons, and generally reflect the more difficult life situation of the deprived group. In particular the latter respondents were less apt to feel that they had surpassed their early goals (40% vs. 60%). Insufficient or inappropriate education was a salient factor in this appraisal; most of the men were not satisfied with this aspect of their preparation for work.

The work role is so intertwined with a man's social identity and esteem that one might expect some tendency to gloss over disappointments and failures in reviews of life accomplishments.[14] Nevertheless, it is noteworthy that most members of the sample expressed a preference for choosing their present occupation if given the hypothetical chance to begin their careers over again. Men from nondeprived families in the middle class are the major exceptions; only 43 percent preferred their present occupation, compared to over 70 percent in the other groups. For the most part, however, economic deprivation in the 30s had no appreciable consequence, direct or indirect, for attitudes toward the mobility and prestige aspects of jobs in the late 50s. Level of occupational attainment and differential mobility are more potent sources of these attitudes, and neither was significantly related to economic conditions in the Depression. This is shown by the degree of satisfaction with advancement opportunities, supervisory responsibilities, and job prestige, as expressed on five-category scales in the 1964 follow-up. Men from deprived families were higher on level of satisfaction, especially in the group with middle-class backgrounds, but the difference is too small to be statistically significant. More important is the experience of intergenerational mobility in occupational status, whether upward, stable, or downward relative to father's status. Regardless of past experience with economic hardship, the upwardly mobile ranked significantly higher on satisfaction with mobility opportunities and job prestige than the nonmobile, and the difference was greatest for men with origins in the working class (see Elder 1969*b*).

At the outset of this analysis we linked the significance of early vocational development in the Oakland cohort to its consequence for occupational attainment. Early involvement in productive activities and corresponding commitments restrict life prospects when they limit educational opportunities, and there is some evidence of this sacrifice among the sons of working-class parents. This cost was minimized for most of the men, however, by expanding opportunities during the late 30s and early 40s. In this context, the cultural aspects of family status and differential ability had greater consequence for educational attainment and occupational goals than economic loss or unemployment during the early 30s. Directly and indirectly through related experiences, economic deprivation in both social classes tended to accelerate vocational crystallization, commitments, and career establishment. Men from deprived households ranked higher on vocational maturity and certainty before World War II, on career establishment before 1948, and on continuity between early vocational preference and occupation some twenty years after high school.

The occupational life of men from deprived families has little in common with contemporary impressions of the Depression experience as "a limited life," and the narrow vision it presumably bestowed upon its offspring. Nevertheless, there are general considerations which point in this direction, such as the narrowing of interests and desires through defensive adaptations to severe poverty and the motivational consequences of need deprivation. One might expect basic gratifications associated with economic well-being and stable employment—food, safety, and acceptance—to acquire greater salience and priority in the motivational hierarchy of men who felt deprived in these respects during the Depression, although we do not know whether early desires would persist under very different conditions in adulthood.[15]

This issue is best examined after we have specified major sources of variation in occupational attainment (intelligence, ambition, vocational development, etc.) and their relation to economic deprivation in the 30s. From this analysis we should be able to identify more precisely the contexts in which values are formed within the life course.

Occupational Attainment in the Life Course

We have outlined two general paths to occupational attainment which were subject to the varied consequences of economic deprivation: the indirect path through higher education and a sequence defined by worklife orientations, events, and accomplishments. If only from an economic basis, we expected family deprivation to place boys at an educational disadvantage in occupational achievement. The data showed this effect, but only among the sons of working-class parents, and even in this group it had little impact on the occupational status they eventually achieved.

Ordinarily one might dismiss the negligible effect of family deprivation, and explore more substantial relationships, though in this case we are faced with the problem of explanation: *Why is there not a strong negative relation between economic loss and adult status, both educational and occupational?* We have suggested a number of factors which may have minimized the educational limitations of economic deprivation, especially the advantage of leaving high school shortly before economic mobilization in World War II, but education alone cannot account for the higher occupational attainment of men from deprived families in the middle class, when compared to the nondeprived. Do worklife orientations and skills account for this difference? Is the occupational success of boys from deprived families at least partly a consequence of their relatively early vocational focus and commitment, of their stronger desire for mastery and recognition, or of their application of skills in occupational achievement?

Clarity of goal would enable greater economy of effort and at least favors the persistent application of talents, with its cumulative impact on achievement. Well-defined objectives and disciplined ambition are familiar assets of men who have risen from lowly beginnings without benefit of advanced education: the ability to drive toward firmly held goals with a "total concentration of energy," as one study has depicted the life style of successful businessmen who were socialized in lower- or working-class families (Warner and Abegglen 1963). In a general review of research, McClelland concludes: "All the evidence supports the inference that boys with higher need for achievement are apt to be more upwardly mobile in society, especially if they are at a fairly low socioeconomic level to start with" (McClelland 1961, p. 322). As a hypothesis, we suggest that the slightly greater occupational attainment of men from deprived families in the middle class is mainly a consequence of their career advantage in vocational commitment, ambition, and utilization of skills. This advantage would also apply to the achievement of men from deprived working-class families.

As an initial step in evaluating these hypotheses, we shall view status attainment as a general function of class origin, the individual's capacity to achieve (intelligence and achievement motivation on tasks),[16] and educational level. Family status and capacity to achieve are defined as antecedent to educational achievement, which in turn precedes occupational status in middle age. The status men achieved in their worklife is hypothesized as a direct consequence of variations in family status, intelligence, and achievement motivation, as well as an indirect effect of these factors through educational level. After these causal relations are put to a test, we shall introduce economic deprivation and systematically trace its multiple effects on adult status through education, vocational development, and ambition.

Estimates of direct and indirect influences on occupational attainment in 1958 were obtained by using the path technique, a variant of multiple regression which assumes that relationships are linear, additive, and asymmetric.[17] A path diagram is a useful mode of presentation since it makes assumptions explicit about the sequence of variables and their indirect effects. In a diagram, the path connecting two variables whose relationship is asymmetric and linear is described by a one-way arrow and a beta coefficient. A curved two-way arrow is the conventional description for a correlation between variables that are given or, in other words, whose relationship is not to be explained. In the subsequent analysis, family status, intelligence, and achievement motivation were defined as given. Since path analysis requires that each dependent variable be completely determined by variables within the system, a residual factor—assumed to be uncorrelated with the antecedent variables or with other residuals—must be introduced to account for the unexplained variance. Figure 4 presents path coefficients relating occupational attainment to educational level, achievement motivation on tasks, intelligence, and family status in 1929. For the reader's convenience, a correlation coefficient for each relationship is presented within parentheses.

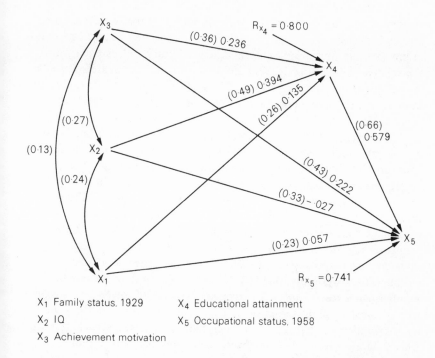

X₁ Family status, 1929
X₂ IQ
X₃ Achievement motivation

X₄ Educational attainment
X₅ Occupational status, 1958

Figure 4 Paths Relating Occupational and Educational Status in Adulthood to Achievement Motivation, IQ, and Class Origin (1929)

Men who achieved high status in their worklife ranked higher on intelligence and family status than the less successful, but their achievement is largely due to their greater access to higher education and its advantage for prestigious jobs. Apart from an indirect influence through education, neither mental ability nor family status are noteworthy as a source of high achieved status. The general pattern of these findings is highly consistent with the results of other studies, including a recent study of former college students which shows that the effects of academic ability on occupational attainment "operate wholly within the school system."[18]

Desire to excel is less restricted than IQ to achievement through education, as one would expect, and exerts a stronger direct effect on occupational attainment than either mental ability or family status. In terms of main effects, class origin is less consequential for adult status than either IQ or achievement motivation, although it is related to both. More important, however, are the diverse social contexts indexed by variations in class position, and their implications for sources of occupational success. When path models were constructed according to class origin (middle or working class), noteworthy differences emerged in the relative influence of IQ and ambition. Since these models are available in published form (see Elder 1968) and are only tangential to our interest in the status consequences of economic loss, we shall briefly summarize aspects which bear upon our analysis.

The role of intelligence and motivation in the accomplishments of men from middle- and working-class families generally reflects differences in their life situation, opportunities, and level of achievement. Higher education figured more prominently in the occupational attainment of men from middle-class families, and intellectual ability was more influential in this path to high status than a desire to excel—the most important source of achievement among men of lower-status origins. The more able men of working-class origin also generally made their way up the occupational ladder through higher education, although they were less likely to do so and were relatively few in number. As a result, only 22 percent of the men of lower-class origin were located in professional or managerial occupations in 1958, in comparison to 41 percent of the men with higher-status backgrounds. This difference in level of achieved status may partially explain the minimal effect of an educational disadvantage on the achieved status of men from deprived families, as well as the significance of motivation in their mobility. Advancement through middle-range jobs is less dependent on educational credentials, and relatively more open to the influence of motivation and resourcefulness.

Utilization of ability, in the sense of a strong relation between intellectual competence and the desire to excel, tends to gain significance for life prospects in a low-status environment. Without family support, what a boy wants to become and his occupational success is heavily dependent on his own resources. Intelligence generally provides access to rewards in all social strata, though it is most important as a social stimulus in the lower classes. Generally, middle-class parents expect their children to do well in school, even to the point where differences in ability are ignored. More attention from parents and teachers is likely to center on the bright working-class boy who is recognized as unusually competent when compared to children in his environment. The discrepancy between low family status and a high level of competence is another potential source of achievement striving, as we have suggested for members of deprived families. All of these considerations lead to the expectation that competent men from the working class were more highly motivated to excel than their counterparts of higher-class origin, and the data show this variation. Intelligence and achievement motivation were more highly correlated in the former group than in the latter ($r = .40$ vs. $.17$). An important question here is whether able men from deprived families in each social class were also more highly motivated than their counterparts in the nondeprived group.

From the preceding analysis and what we have discovered about the consequences of family deprivation, we would not expect economic loss markedly to alter the model of status attainment shown in figure 4. Neither IQ nor achievement motivation on tasks vary by economic deprivation. The only modification of any note is the negative effect of deprivation on the educational level of men from the working class. However, the model does not include aspects of worklife development which we have found most characteristic of the occupational life of men with deprived backgrounds, particularly focused vocational interest and goals. Did this vocational orientation enhance the worklife accomplishments of men from deprived homes? Is there any evidence that an early determination of vocational goals and minimal delay in career establishment at least partially countered educational limitations among the sons of deprived working-class families?

The model also fails to identify contextual influences on the relation between adult status and personal resources, such as achievement motivation and intelligence. By specifying contexts defined by class origin (1929), we found that, in the working class, occupational attainment was relatively more dependent on motivation to achieve than on IQ, as compared to that relation in the middle class. The contribution of motivation should also increase by family deprivation *within* classes if we assume that achievement is most dependent on personal resources in contexts of socioeconomic deprivation. The motivation/ability link between deprivation and adult status and that of vocational crystallization are put to an empirical test in the next two sections.

Vocational
Crystallization
as an Indirect
Influence

For this analysis we used the clinical measure of vocational crystallization (1941), and combined cases in the transitional and emerging categories (scored 0 versus a score of 1 for the mature group). The data show that boys with well-defined vocational interests before adulthood were likely to come from deprived families ($r = .28$) and to enter prestigious occupations by the late 50s ($r = .30$), but were not more likely to continue their education beyond high school. The significance of vocational maturity (X_2) as a positive link between deprivation

(X_1) and occupational attainment (X_3) is more clearly seen when its effect is controlled through partial correlation. This statistical measure provides an estimate of the extent to which the relation between X_1 and X_3 is due to their joint association with vocational maturity. The results show a modest increase in the negative effect of deprivation on occupational status from $r_{13} = .01$ to $r_{13.2} = -.08$.

Since economic deprivation proved to be more of a disadvantage in status attainment for men of working-class origin, we repeated the above analysis within groups defined by class origin. The results, presented in figure 5, show a vocational path to high status in both class categories, although it is slightly stronger among men from the working class. The status advantage of men from deprived families in the middle class is partly a consequence of their early determination of goals, as shown by a decline in the relation between X_1 and X_3 with this factor controlled. An additional control on educational level did not alter the result. The contrasting effects of the vocational and educational paths to occupational achievement among the offspring of deprived families are most evident in the lower-status group. The deprivational handicap in adult status would have been substantially stronger without the accompanying pattern of vocational crystallization. In fact, the association between family deprivation and occupational status is slightly positive when we partial out the educational disadvantage of economic hardship $(r = .06)$.

Vocational development leaves much to be explained in occupational achievement, but it fares well in comparison to more traditional background factors. Family status, for instance, is less predictive of occupational status, and so are intelligence and achievement motivation among working-class sons. The latter attributes played a more important role than vocational crystallization in the achievement of boys from the middle class (average r of .43 vs. .24), while achievement motivation and crystallized interests were more influential than IQ in the achieved status of working-class boys (as listed, $r = .38, .34, .07$). Successful men from this class are remarkably similar in these characteristics to descriptions of the upwardly mobile from blue-collar families in the research literature, i.e., a concentration of energy and interests in occupational advancement.

Ambition and
Intelligence as
Indirect Influences

In the life course, ambition and intelligence are commonly viewed as causal links between family background and adult status; family influ-

Middle class origin

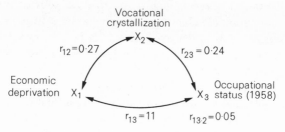

Working class origin

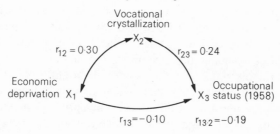

Figure 5   Zero Order and Partial Correlation Coefficients
Relating Economic Deprivation, Vocational Crystallization, and Occupational Status, by Class Origin

ences are traced through the achievement capacities of offspring. As we
have seen, this mediational model has only limited value for identifying
the long-term effects of family background, both sociocultural and
economic, in occupational attainment. To be sure, men from higher-
status families were more likely to enter prestige occupations than men
of lower-class origin, and they did so in part through their greater
ability and higher goals; but the adult consequences of these attributes
varied according to socioeconomic context. Owing partly to greater
educational opportunity, IQ was more predictive of adult status than
achievement motivation among the sons of middle-class parents, while
the reverse effects were found in the lives of men with backgrounds in
the working class.

Context is equally important for specifying the relation between
economic loss and capacity to achieve in the life course. Boys from
deprived families in each class were not less motivated or intelligent
than the nondeprived, but those with ability were most likely to be

ambitious and such effort played a more important role in their occupational attainment. Even though desire to excel showed little relation to ability among middle-class boys when compared to boys of lower status, intelligent sons of deprived parents in both classes were more likely to be achievement-oriented than bright youth from more affluent families (total sample, $r = .25$ vs. .01). Values for corresponding groups of middle-class boys were .26 and $-.10$.

In these data, the relation between motivation and ability increases as family status and resources decline, whether indicated by class origin or economic loss in the Depression. Greater effort is presumably required to get ahead without the benefit of family prestige or support, even with considerable talent, and this drive is a plausible response to a perceived disparity between personal competence and low family standing, an attempt to enhance one's social status by presenting self in the more favorable terms of individual competence and potential.

Boys who advanced beyond their father's occupational status from a background of economic deprivation were primarily distinguished by ambition in adolescence, but they were also brighter than youth who maintained or dropped below their father's status.[19] These differences are reversed for upward mobility from nondeprived households, as shown in table A–22. No comparisons were made for working-class boys owing to the small number of cases.

When two antecedent factors, such as IQ and achievement motivation, are interrelated, an effort to identify and compare their main effects is at best problematic. Depending on one's assumptions, the shared variance may be assigned to intelligence or to motivation. In order to obtain estimates of their relative effects in occupational attainment within deprivational groups, we assumed that family status preceded mental ability in time order, and that both factors were antecedent to achievement motivation. Results from the regression analysis are presented in table A–23 for sons of nondeprived and deprived families in the middle class and the total sample.

In all comparisons, intellectual ability is by far the more important source of high attainment for sons of nondeprived parents, and there is little variation in this effect by class origin. Ability is less consequential in the fortunes of men with deprived backgrounds, however, and is surpassed by the influence of achievement motivation, especially among men from the working class. These variations did not change with education included in the analysis. For both deprivational groups, the primary influence of intelligence and family status on adult status was mediated by educational level (compare with figure 4), while the effects of achievement motivation were evenly divided between a direct influence and the indirect path through advanced education.

The less prominent role of intelligence in the occupational attainment of men with lower-status backgrounds can be explained in part by their limited access to higher education, but this does not apply to deprivational variations in the effect of IQ, especially within the middle class. Even in the low-status group, educational variations by economic loss are not large enough to account for differences in the relative effect of intelligence and ambition.

The one factor which may have contributed to this difference is clarity of occupational goal or vocational crystallization, and its relation to ambition. Achievement motivation, as measured in this study, indicates a general or nonspecific desire which could be expressed in diverse areas or in relation to multiple goals. The achievement syndrome, as Rosen has pointed out,[20] includes the directional tendencies of achievement values and goals, as well as the generalized desire to excel. In some respects, however, vocational crystallization has even greater significance than values for the adult consequences of achievement motivation in adolescence, for, without clearly specified goals, ambition lacks direction and discipline. Other things being equal, early commitment to a well defined occupational goal should enhance continuity between adolescent ambition and occupational attainment.

To test this interpretation we formed two groups on degree of vocational crystallization: diffuse interests, which includes all cases in the transitional and emerging categories; and focused or mature interests. In each group, a partial correlation was computed for the relation between achievement motivation and occupational status (the variance in both measures was similar across groups), with family status statistically controlled. Ambitious boys were slightly more advanced in vocational crystallization than other youth, and they were also more likely to enter high-prestige jobs if their vocational interests were well defined. The relation between achievement motivation and occupational status increased from the group with a "diffuse" orientation to the vocationally mature ($r_s = .26$ vs. $.40$). Even with economic loss controlled, the achievement oriented were more likely to have attained high status if their vocational interests were well defined in late adolescence.[21]

According to the same logic, one might also expect the greatest correspondence between intellectual ability and occupational attainment in the more advanced group on vocational crystallization. The cumulative benefits of intellectual competence in worklife advancement should be more problematic when goals are uncertain, and yet the data do not support this expectation. One reason for the outcome is suggested by the relation between intelligence and adult status. The main effect of mental ability is mediated by educational attainment, and the likelihood of a college education did not vary by vocational development. The more able boys from diverse family backgrounds were most likely to pursue advanced education, which increased their prospects for prestige jobs, but this path did not vary by vocational certainty or crystalliza-tion. In some cases, delays in educational progress were associated with vocational uncertainty, though it had no permanent consequence in achievement through college and postgraduate studies. A second factor is suggested by a more detailed examination of the vocationally mature group. Well-defined goals increased the occupational attainment of less able men and thus minimized the effect of IQ on their adult status.

Two general conclusions on the Depression experience in occupa-tional attainment are supported by our data on the Oakland men. First, the process of educational achievement offers clues to why some men were thwarted in worklife advancement by the economic hardships they and their families experienced in the 30s. But to understand the occu-pational *success* of men from deprived families we must look to factors in their worklife experience. The Depression increased the contribution of these factors (vocational focus, early career establishment, concen-trated effort, etc.) relative to the influence of formal education. More generally this impact may be found (with some modification) in other Depression cohorts. For the young, family deprivation is likely to handicap progress in formal education through socialized constraints, conflicting demands, and diminished parental support, social and eco-nomic. A depressed economy also makes education a more problematic route to desired employment for the young worker or job seeker owing to the imbalance between supply and demand. Occupational placement and progress thus depend more heavily on personal factors that bear directly upon worklife experience.

Up to this point we have charted major events in the life course of the Oakland men, from the end of the Depression decade through World War II, the immediate postwar era, and into the late 1950s. At appropriate points we compared the timing and overall configuration of these events in the Oakland cohort with similar aspects in other age groups. This overview posed a number of questions on the long-term impact of family deprivation in the 30s on adult status and established a context in which to make this assessment. As we have seen, the impact was negligible overall and was only slightly negative among men from the working class. This outcome calls for an explanation even more than the expected negative impact, since the latter corresponds with a common image of the Depression in adult life. As a rule, we have tended to view the Depression experience primarily in terms of its disruptive, pathogenic effects in the course of human lives. Why did family deprivation not have a more adverse effect on adult occupational attainment?

Two answers are suggested by the analysis. One centers on cohort variations in the Depression's impact. According to life stage in 1930, the Oakland men occupied a position of advantage relative to other male cohorts; they were beyond the crucial developmental stage marked by total dependence on parents and they did not leave school and family until the end of the 30s during the economic upswing in war mobilization. By contrast, a large percentage of young blue-collar workers never overcame the adverse effects of the Depression in their worklife, as reported in Thernstrom's study of Boston men. A similar impact was experienced by some fathers of the Oakland men. The second answer concerns deprivation-related factors in worklife experience and the extent to which they *offset* educational handicaps associated with conditions of family hardship. While economic deprivation lessened prospects for advanced education among some offspring of working-class families, it also enhanced their worklife achievement through vocational development and an industrious application of talents.

Patterns of status attainment and their relation to economic conditions in the Depression shed some light on social contexts in which values and life styles are formed in the life course. These contexts will be kept in mind as we trace the effects of economic deprivation over a quarter-century to the adult values of the Oakland men.

Men's Values: A Legacy of the Depression?

Few issues have aroused more speculation than the presumed impact of the Depression on men's values—their standards of desirability or preference. The centrality of work, a reluctance to change jobs, and preoccupation with matters of job security are some of the more commonly cited legacies of this period. When applied to young people in the Depression, this interpretation suggests that certain values were acquired in deprived circumstances, that such preferences were maintained into the adult years, regardless of the particular life course, and are expressed in adult conduct. A strong version of this hypothesis claims that Depression-reared men are distinctly work-centered in life style because of the values they acquired in a time when jobs and income were hard to come by.

There is empirical support for a theory which regards values as a "bridge between position in the larger social structure and the behavior of the individual,"[22] but this perspective also argues against a position which automatically links the structural effects in one time period with corresponding behavior in a subsequent era, especially in a rapidly changing society. If values are shaped by life situations, social change and individual mobility should lessen cause-effect relations between T_1 and T_2. There is no basis for expecting occupational mobility in the postwar years, for example, to be less consequential for work values than hardship experiences in the Depression. In fact, the evidence at hand suggests that men's conceptions of the desirable in work and child rearing are explained more by their education and occupation than by aspects of their family background.[23]

Another weakness in the link between conditions in the Depression and adult values centers on the neglect of personal characteristics, such as intellectual competence, in the process by which objects or standards acquire value. What men experience in a situation is partly a function of what they bring to it. This has special significance for any consideration of work values, since awareness of personal competence influences interpretations of occupational demands and options. In line with our view of a problem situation, we assume that the meaning of an alternative is contingent on the perceived relation between situational demand and personal resources, which in turn generates expectations of rewards and costs.

Competence is an integral component of an *adaptational* perspective on value acquisition which asserts that particular activities or personal qualities acquire value in situations because they are adaptive; that is, they enable the individual to cope effectively. An example of this approach is seen in a study which found differences between the middle and working class in the qualities parents desire and emphasize in their children. The authors suggest that "parents of both social classes value for their children the characteristics that seem most appropriate to the conditions of the parents' lives. . . . Self-direction seems more possible and necessary in middle-class occupations; working class occupations allow much less room for, and in fact may penalize, anything other than obedience to rules and directives set down by others."[24]

Adaptive lines of action are based on assumptions concerning personal gratification. Especially pertinent in this respect is the effect of decremental change in status on the value attributed to objects. Social comparison and reinforcement theories suggest that an object which is positively regarded acquires value when one is deprived of it; that is, the motivational significance of a reward is likely to be greatest for persons who are deprived in this respect. When many desires are frustrated, adaptation centers on the fulfillment of the most basic needs, such as shelter, food, a secure home, etc.[25] An oversimplified version of the deprivation thesis is common in most folk accounts of the Depression's cultural legacy; to wit, Depression-reared men are distinguished by the value they attribute to money, a stable job, family comforts, and security because they were deprived of these objects or experiences as children in the 30s. In some cases, adaptational theory may lead to similar predictions, but it directs attention to situational change in the adaptive value of activities throughout the life course. The greater the continuity of situations in which particular lines of action acquired value in adaptation, the greater the continuity in values. Thus, a stable job and security should be most attractive to men who find themselves in situations which are not unlike their experience in deprived families. It is true of course that social continuity may be partly a consequence of lines of action which are based upon values acquired in childhood. Occupational values seem to have this effect in the selection of educational subfields in higher education.

We expect work and leisure to have special meaning among the sons of deprived families. Adaptation in the Depression entailed responsibilities in the household economy which are likely to have enhanced the value of employment as a source of independence, security, and identity. Through its fateful relation to family life, father's unemployment may have sensitized boys to the emotional significance of a secure home. To the extent that occupational success is dependent on intelligence, the more able men should favor the work role and prefer options which involve risks to gain greater rewards over the appeal of security in job protections. The less able and successful men, on the other hand, are apt to be most responsive to the security lessons of the Depression.

As commonly interpreted, work and the legitimacy of leisure were more tightly interwoven by conditions in the Depression. While joblessness increased time for avocational pursuits, it also reduced legitimate or culturally approved access to leisure or play for the unemployed. Just as "men must work in order to eat," according to the mandate of a scarcity culture, so too must they earn the right to play. Along this line, Riesman observes that we may have a large number of Americans "who more or less unconsciously feel some uneasiness in play—because by cultural definition the right to play belongs to those who work."[26] Is this uneasiness most characteristic of Depression-reared men?

If we asked men about the importance of work, family life, and leisure, we would undoubtedly find considerable variation in their relative importance. However, the essence of a value is manifested in the kinds of choices a person makes, in the priority assigned to each domain. The important question is not whether a man values his work, but whether he values it more highly than family life or leisure.

To obtain this hierarchy of preference, we asked men in the sample (1964 follow-up) to give their first and second preferences in four areas—work, family, leisure, and community (civic and social roles)—on three dimensions: the activity they enjoyed most, the one they would like to devote more time to, and the activity which provided the greatest sense of accomplishment. First, second, and no preference were scored 2, 1, and 0 respectively. Since the three items were highly intercorrelated (average $r = .52$), scores on each were summed to form a single index of activity preference, with values ranging from 0 to 6.

The men were questioned during the prime phase of their worklife, and their preferences reflect this fact. Worklife was valued more highly than family activity ($\overline{X}_s = 3.8$ vs. 2.5), and these preferences were followed at a distance by leisure and community roles ($\overline{X}_s = 1.8$ vs. 0.7). Though a majority of men were involved in at least one voluntary association, this activity is clearly less salient than other areas of life.

These spheres of activity differed in value to men from nondeprived and deprived families, but not entirely as we expected. Worklife is the major exception. Men from deprived families were not more committed to their worklife than the nondeprived, regardless of class origin, and both groups valued work more highly than family life, leisure, or community roles. What mattered for the significance of work is not class origin or family deprivation but the relative success of a man's worklife. Upwardly mobile and high-status men consistently assigned greater value to their occupational role, when compared to the less successful, and family background made little difference in this preference.[27]

Though not distinguished by interest in the work role, the deprived were less inclined to favor leisure, as popular imagery suggests, and they were also more family-centered than men from relatively affluent families (table 7). In both of these respects there is a suggestive parallel with the adaptations of deprived fathers. Despite tensions and conflict, we suspect that most households in the Depression became a haven or refuge in a hostile world for men who lost both job and income.[28] It was their private territory, a place where they could physically escape from the social embarrassment of their plight. The intergenerational connection between these experiences and the values of Depression-reared men depends in part on the meaning of their preferences for family life, an issue we shall explore shortly in greater detail, along with specific work values. For the moment, let us note that the family may be important for the interpersonal benefits in marriage (understanding, companionship, etc.), or for the security and gratification provided by home and children. The security benefits of home, both social and emotional, are consistent with a "refuge" image of the family.

Table 7   Activity Preferences (1964) of Oakland Men by Economic Deprivation and Class Origin, in Mean Scores

Economic Deprivation by Class Origin	Work	Family	Leisure	Community
Middle Class				
Nondeprived (N = 19)	3.9	1.8	2.1	1.0
Deprived (N = 16)	4.0	3.2	1.5	0.6
		ND < D*		
Total Sample				
Nondeprived (N = 22)	3.7	1.9	2.2	1.0
Deprived (N = 24)	3.7	3.1	1.5	0.5
		ND < D*		

*   < .05 (two-tailed t-test)

Any attempt to link adult values to economic hardship must eventually take competence and adult status into account, as we have noted on preference for the work role. Even in the high-status group, which is oriented toward work, this preference is likely to be most prevalent among the more capable men. More importantly, variations in adult status define contexts which specify the appropriateness of Depression experiences. For instance, even if economic failure heightened valuation of the family, we would not expect this value to be characteristic of *successful* men from deprived families. Their adult situation bears no correspondence to childhood experiences shaped by economic loss and unemployment, although it does apply to the life situation of low-status men and the downwardly mobile, especially to those who grew up in deprived households. The family-centered response of deprived men should therefore be strongest under conditions which approximate their situation in the 30s; in line with reinforcement principles, stability of response is contingent on environmental stability.

Work, family, and leisure preferences were first related to selected antecedent factors (adult social class, adolescent IQ, family deprivation, and class origin) in a series of regression analyses for the total sample of men, and then within two occupational contexts, defined by the upwardly mobile and the nonmobile. The measure of community preference was not included since very few men made this preference. Economic deprivation is not related to adult status or intelligence, and thus its main effect on the three adult values did not change in the analysis (table A–24). Work-centered men were just as likely to have experienced economic hardships as financial stability in the Depression, and they were not distinguished by more extensive work experience in adolescence. By and large, they are the more competent and successful men in the sample, although interest in the work role is not restricted to this group. Economic hardship is clearly the most important factor in family preference; men who favored this activity also tended to be relatively low in mental ability and adult status. Within the life course, the influence of intelligence is of course partly expressed through occupational attainment. The leisure-oriented were unlikely to come from deprived homes, although they were among the least able and occupationally successful in the sample.

Does occupational context make a difference in these results? Mobile men ($N = 26$) scored higher on work preference and lower on family and leisure interests when compared to the nonmobile ($N = 20$); the dispersion of scores on each index is generally comparable across the two groups. When due caution is exercised, this similarity permits a comparison of the relative effects of the antecedent variables in each group. Turning to work preference, we find that context does not alter the above results. In each mobility category, work-centeredness is *not* linked to family deprivation in the 30s. Occupational fortunes and competence are the influential factors.

Occupational context does modify the relevance of deprivation for family and leisure preferences, and much as we had predicted. Economic loss in the Depression is more predictive of family preference than any other factor (table A–24), but it is even more strongly associated with this value among the nonmobile (a beta of .63 in comparison to .16 for the upwardly mobile). Neither family status nor intelligence varied in their effects on this value across the two groups. Indifference toward leisure activity followed a similar pattern (a beta coefficient of −.77 versus −.09 for the upwardly mobile). It should be noted that this effect runs directly counter to the value which low-status men usually attribute to leisure activity. As shown in table A–24, men who ranked lowest on IQ and social class in adulthood were most likely to favor this activity, and the same is true of the nonmobile. But these men were least inclined to favor leisure activity if they grew up in deprived families. If we assume that hardship made leisure less acceptable or enjoyable in the Depression and enhanced the importance of family life, then value continuity is mainly found among men who have experienced relatively similar life situations in adulthood.

Equally noteworthy in social implication is the negligible consequence of economic deprivation for the values of men on the upper rungs of occupational achievement. Family hardships had greater significance for their accomplishments, for how they arrived at their present station in life, and this position offers some insight into their choice of life style. On work commitment and aversion to leisure activity, these men resemble a popular image of male character in a scarcity culture, yet neither of these value orientations have any notable link to economic hardships for the upwardly mobile.

Preference for work, family, or leisure does not tell us much about the nature of this activity nor of its features which are most highly appreciated or disliked. A rewarding activity or role generally offers intrinsic satisfactions; the activity is an end in itself rather than simply a means to an end. C. Wright Mills lists the criteria of craftsmanship as a measure of intrinsically satisfying roles: concern with the quality of the product, a work context permitting growth and development of personality, freedom to plan the activity, and an activity so satisfying that it blurs the distinction between play and work (Mills 1951, pp. 220–38). These conditions are most prevalent in high-status occupations, and men in these work settings are more oriented toward the intrinsic features of the job (suitability to interests, etc.) than blue-collar workers who must adjust to the realities of jobs that barely offer extrinsic benefits, such as money, leisure time, job protections. Among the latter, the significance of family is partly a function of their alienation from the job.[29] When the job is meaningful, it is likely to include a play component—"My job is my recreation"; when it lacks value, activities outside the work setting acquire importance. But there may be differences in the kinds of family activities which are favored by men who are alienated from the job, and these have relevance to learning in the Depression. Is it the security and comfort of a family, the chance to have children (also a source of security, for old age), or the companionship and understanding of wife and children? To achieve a more detailed picture of what men valued in work and family, we analyzed responses to a series of questions which were asked in the 1958 and 1964 follow-ups.

The Meaning of Work

Meanings assigned to aspects of the work role were indexed by evaluative questions ("How do you feel about the following aspects of your job?") and by a forced choice question on job security versus risk with the prospect of greater economic gain (1958 interview). Attitudes toward aspects of the job (1964 survey) formed three general clusters in a correlational analysis: extrinsic—satisfaction with income, work schedule, and free time; mobility and prestige—satisfaction with opportunity for advancement, supervision of others, and prestige; and intrinsic

—satisfaction with suitability of work to interests, use of skills, and freedom to develop ideas.[30]

Akin to Maslow's need hierarchy, the transition from economic scarcity to abundance channels concern away from extrinsic benefits to the intrinsic merits of a job. With strong labor demands and multiple options, the educated worker can bargain for more than simply a means to support his family. "Work calling urgently for workmen" in the abundant society contrasts with the world of scarcity in which the worker seeks "humbly any kind of toil."[31] If any mode of job dissatisfaction has roots in the Depression experience, it is likely to involve those extrinsic benefits that were so problematic for the worker of the 30s.

Economic deprivation in the 30s does in fact make a substantial difference in the degree to which men were content with the extrinsic features of their job. Economic loss is related to dissatisfaction ($r = -.23$), with achieved status, intellectual ability, and family status controlled. None of these status characteristics were as predictive of discontent as family hardship. However, the effects of deprivation did vary according to occupational experience; the more unrewarding the worklife, the stronger the relation between deprivation and discontent. This difference, which resembles our findings on family and leisure preference, is shown by a comparison of mobile and nonmobile men. The relation between negative feelings and economic deprivation increased across these groups, from an r of $-.11$ to a value of $-.39$, and the contrast was not reduced by controlling IQ and family status. In these and prior findings, deprivation in adult life appears to call out responses which are linked in social learning to past deprivations.

Issues in the standstill economy of the 30s had more to do with job opportunity than with intrinsic features, such as the compatibility of work and interests, but neither of these concerns were distinctive of men from deprived families. Satisfaction with mobility prospects and prestige was most strongly associated with upward mobility, and men in high-status jobs were most likely to appreciate the intrinsic qualities of their work. One might expect the mobile sons of deprived families to be especially gratified by the opportunities and prestige of their work, but there is no evidence of this in the data. A background of economic hardship did not influence feelings of either the mobile or the nonmobile toward these intrinsic aspects of the job.

Job security was not a focal concern during the late 50s or early 60s. This was a time of prosperity, if not peace, and a majority of the Oakland men with lower-status origins had worked their way into the white-collar or professional classes. When asked to cite three aspects of a job which are most important in making it satisfactory, only six mentioned job security. Suitability of work to interests was most salient (66 percent), followed by the amount of income (53 percent), use of skills and ability (32 percent), and freedom to develop ideas and use imagination (30 percent). This ordering of job priorities did not vary by family background or economic deprivation, although intrinsic features of the job (such as suitability of work) were most often mentioned by men who had little cause to be concerned with matters of economic survival—those of high status. It is noteworthy, however, that work schedule, stress of job, convenience for the family, and amount of leisure received no more support than job security.

To present the issue of job security as a potential choice, among other options, we posed the choice between a steady, secure job, on the one hand, and a less certain job with the possibility of greater reward, on the other. A job offer typically involves considerations of this sort, and the weighing of their costs and rewards. Any alternative includes more uncertainties than one's current job, and these must be balanced against its challenge and potential gain. The balance and its meaning depends in part upon the worker's age, occupational status, education, personal competence, and values. The risk of a job change, and especially a change of employer, increases with age and is greater among men with few salable skills.

The men were asked to choose between the alternatives of job security with a reasonable income and the risk of taking a new job with prospects of greater reward. Though age was not a major consideration at the time (median age = 38 years), nearly half of the men preferred job security to a less certain job with its greater reward. Resistance to change, in the form of security interests, was most pronounced among less able men who had encountered limited options and joblessness in the past. As shown in table A–25, both a deprived background and low adult status are related to the preference for job security, though neither factor is strongly predictive of this value. Limited ability is by far the most important factor in this choice. Security consciousness increased most sharply by economic loss in the Depression among men who failed to rise above their father's status. This outcome resembles other findings on values, but the mobility subgroups with job security information are too small to enable reliable comparison.

In response to worklife alternatives, security-oriented men frequently interpreted their present situation in the context of memories of the Depression, and this in turn provided an account for their choice of a steady, secure job. One of the men, a printer by trade whose father was unemployed through most of the 30s, claimed that he entered apprenticeship training at the urging of his mother, who wanted him to have a "steady and secure" job. His current job, as he put it, was the "sort of work where you're almost never out of work, providing that you are able to do the job well. The rate of pay isn't as high as lots of other things; however you don't do too badly. For example, the carpenters are out of work almost three months every year, and truck drivers are often on strike." Having been impressed with the importance of steady work, he was convinced that he "ended up ahead of people in those jobs," and enjoyed as much security "as any job offers today." In like manner, an accountant reflected on the losses of his father, "money, job, and all," and acknowledged that "I have been overly cautious rather than overly ambitious." Soon after completing college, he entered the personnel department of a large company, a job which offered little opportunity for advancement but much security. The "family" atmosphere of the company made him feel comfortable, and he felt no urge to leave. "If there was enough of an inducement I might take a gamble. But from a logical standpoint a steady job is the best." In both cases, there is some evidence that security interests from past hardship have led to the choice of jobs which are relatively free of risk, stress, and challenge; and the resulting work situations enhance the importance of this value orientation. In this respect, we see an example of a circular, reinforcing relationship, a sort of self-fulfilling prophecy, between preferred and actual courses of action. The more security is emphasized in occupational matters, and options are refused, the more a worker is locked into a system in which job protections become a focal concern.

From productive roles in the household economy to vocational commitment and occupational career, the experiences of men from deprived families identify work as a central element in their life style, dominating all other spheres of activity. As a group, they are found to value the work role more highly than family life, leisure, or community roles, but this is also true of men with relatively well-endowed backgrounds. The principal difference between these men resides not in the value but in its meanings, and then primarily among the sons who failed to rise above their father's status. In the latter group, men of deprived status most closely resembled their fathers in deprivational experience, and they evaluated their job on the basis of issues that were prevalent in the Depression. Compared to the nondeprived, they generally favored security over the risks of taking another job with the possibility of greater gain, and criticized their work for its deficient benefits.

From the days of the frontier and expanding economy, the American standard of success—whether a man could achieve a position higher than his father's—has proved costly for the nonmobile. Like many workers who lost both income and jobs in the 30s, Oakland men in the 50s with a nonmobile career felt victimized by life circumstances and sensed a lack of personal meaning in life, when compared with the more successful. (For more on this subject, see Elder 1969*b*.) They were also most likely to drink heavily in the adult years, as were unemployed fathers in the Depression. The nonmobile were less absolutely deprived than their unemployed fathers, but relative deprivation is a potent source of frustration in an affluent age.

Home, Children, and Marriage: Valued Aspects of Family Life

Knowing what men value in family life should bring us closer to an understanding of the connection between a family orientation and experiences in the Depression. There is the intrinsic value of marriage itself—companionship and mutual understanding in the most primary of relationships—and the extrinsic benefits derived through marriage, the chance to bear and rear children as well as the privilege of a comfortable home and security. If deficiencies in these areas of family life increase their value, home, children, and marriage should have special significance to the sons of deprived families. Home as a refuge, in the sense of the Depression era, seems strangely archaic in an affluent age, but perhaps not to men who have had troubles of their own in earning a living.

To assess the relative importance of home, children, and marriage itself, we asked the men (in the 1964 survey) to rank-order six aspects of marriage from the most to the least valued. The percentage of first or second choices is shown in table 8. Relations with spouse are consistently ranked first in studies of marriage (see Blood and Wolfe 1960), and we also find this priority. Companionship and mutual understanding are valued aspects of marriage for a majority of men, followed at a distance by "the chance to have and rear children" and the benefits of a home. For a Depression age group, it is noteworthy that so little emphasis is given to the material and security benefits of marriage.

The most distinctive value of men from deprived families is their orientation toward children, not the security of a home or the interpersonal benefits of marriage, and this contrasts with the centrality of marital relations among the offspring of nondeprived parents.[32] Apart from mutual understanding, which is a leading value in both groups, children rank with companionship as values in the marriages of men from deprived homes but are relatively unimportant to men of nondeprived background. Marital happiness is a potential element in these value differences, since children are apt to become a more important

193

Table 8   Most Valuable Aspects of Marriage as
          Rated by Men, by Economic Deprivation
          and Class Origin, in Percentages.

Aspects of Marriage	Middle-Class Origin		Total Sample		
	Nondeprived N = 16	Deprived N = 13	Nondeprived N = 19	Deprived N = 21	Total N = 40
Home					
The standard of living —kind of house, clothes, etc.	6	8	5	10	8
The security and comfort of a home	6	16	16	14	15
Children					
The chance to have and rear children	13	46	10	48	30
Relations with wife					
Sexual relations	30	15	30	19	26
Companionship in doing things	71	46	70	50	59
Mutual understanding of each other's problems and feelings	70	69	70	64	67

Note. These aspects of marriage are a modified and expanded version of categories used by Blood and Wolfe in their Detroit study of marriage: "Thinking of marriage in general, which one of the five things on the next card would you say is the most valuable part of marriage?" For the wife, these included childbearing and rearing, standard of living, husband's understanding, husband's expression of love, and companionship. See Robert O. Blood, Jr. and Donald M. Wolfe, "Husbands and Wives" (Glencoe, Ill.: The Free Press, 1960), p. 283.
  We asked the respondents to rank order the six aspects according to importance. Each percentage represents the number of men in the group who ranked the aspect in first or second place.

component of family life when marriage sours or provides little emotional gratification, but it does not account for them. Current status, not past deprivation, made a difference in the marital happiness reported by men in the sample; the higher the status, the more satisfying the marriage.

The marital values of men who have not risen above their father's status are similar to those associated with family deprivation, especially with respect to the significance of children. This applies to the sons of middle- as well as working-class parents, but in both mobility groups past deprivation tends to accentuate the preference. Even among the upwardly mobile, a third of the men with deprived backgrounds favored children as the most valuable aspect of marriage, in contrast to

8 percent of the men with more affluent parents, who were more likely to emphasize marital companionship (66% vs. 55%). The cumulative impact of deprivational experience on values is most clearly seen in the popularity of children across three groups: nondeprived mobile, deprived mobile, and deprived nonmobile—percentages of 8, 35, and 70. Children thus become a more important element of marriage as deprivation increases in childhood and the adult years.

The inverse association between occupational rewards or attainment and the value of children in marriage is consistent with the assumption that children become more important when marital relations and work are unrewarding. If we follow this interpretation, children would be a central value in the marriage of men who preferred family life over the work role, and the data do show this association. For the total sample, the two preferences are moderately related ($r = .31$). Though family values are influenced by religious preference, or more specifically by membership in the Catholic church, this factor does not account for the effects of either adult status or economic deprivation on the priority of children in marriage. Removal of all Catholics from the analysis did not alter the results. Number of children in the parental home also made no appreciable difference in the relation between deprivation and the importance of children in marriage.

If the Oakland men learned to value children from the experience in the Depression, they could, as adults, apply this preference in most cases without the economic constraints encountered by their parents; and those who regarded children as the most valuable aspect of marriage were also likely to have a large number of children. There is a moderate association between this value and the number of children born through 1964 ($r = .31$), and it is slightly stronger among the upwardly mobile. The ability to implement preferences may be a factor here as well as in the association between family size and economic deprivation among the sons of middle-class parents, from an average of 2.3 children in the nondeprived group to 3.4 among the deprived. Family size did not vary by economic loss in the Depression among men of working-class origin; their families averaged 2.7 children.

These fertility variations bear some correspondence with Easterlin's utility theory of cohort fertility in the postwar years.[33] The theory focuses on the relation between two variables, relative income in the life course and consumer preferences for material goods. An increase in fertility is favored when newly married cohorts, socialized in relatively low consumer tastes for material goods, experience a substantial gain in potential income. Easterlin regards this disparity as a major explanatory factor in the postwar "baby boom." These cohorts acquired consumer preferences during the depressed 30s and entered family roles during an era of full employment and prosperity. By contrast, birth cohorts in the 40s acquired consumer preferences in a more affluent context and experienced much less of an economic advantage at the time of childbearing; consumer demands increased more rapidly than relative economic status. Age-specific fertility should decline under these conditions, as it has.

Apart from other features of the utility model, in what ways does it correspond with the fertility of the Oakland men? The sons of deprived middle-class parents experienced the greatest relative gain in economic standing from the Depression to middle age, when compared to the other class-deprivation groups, and they also stand out on fertility—on their average number of children. We found little difference in absolute family income (1933) between deprived families in the two social classes; yet the sons of deprived middle-class families achieved a higher average rank in their occupational life than men from relatively affluent middle-class environments. If we assume that inexpensive material tastes were acquired under deprived conditions in the 30s, the utility model offers a plausible account of the markedly higher fertility of men from the deprived middle class. At the same time, we should note the lack of information on a crucial factor in this account—the deprivational background of wives and their consumer preferences. Any satisfactory explanation of fertility over the life course would have to take this information into account.

It is also clear that relative income and consumer preferences offer little insight into the origin of the importance of children among the Oakland men, even though this preference is moderately related to fertility. Children are more important in the marriages of men from deprived families, as utility theory would predict; yet they are not more important to men who have achieved occupational success or upward mobility when compared to the less successful. An improvement in occupational status had little effect on fertility (the upwardly mobile ranked slightly higher on average number of children than the non-mobile), but it did lessen the relative significance of children in marriage. Unlike desired family size, economic constraints do not restrict the value placed on children in marriage, at least in the Oakland sample. In fact, this value is related to conditions of relative deprivation in childhood and the adult years. Does this value have its origin in socialization at a time when children made valuable contributions to the family's welfare? To men impressed by the failure of economic security from the Depression to middle age, children (whether one, two, or more) might well be viewed as the most enduring and rewarding investment.[34]

The value of family life and children to sons of deprived families is at least consistent with a desire to satisfy needs which were unfulfilled in childhood. If some hard-pressed families "pulled together" and presented a model of emotional stability and effectiveness for the young to emulate, the Depression period more generally emphasized qualities which were elusive or scarce, such as tranquillity, security, and freedom from want and fear. That scarce experiences and possessions became focal concerns to offspring of the Depression is suggested by a psychologist's observations on the postwar generation of young adults.

We had as a nation emerged from a great war, itself following upon a long and protracted Depression. We thought, all of us, men and women alike, to replenish ourselves in goods and spirit, to undo, by an exercise of collective will, the psychic disruptions of the immediate past. We would achieve the serenity that had eluded the lives of our parents; the men would be secure in stable careers, the women in comfortable homes, and together they would raise perfect children. Time would come to a stop. Call it what you will—a mystique, an illusion, a myth —it was an ideology of sorts, often unspoken but, perhaps for that very reason, most deeply felt. It was the *Zeitgeist*, the spirit of the times.[35]

But experiences in the Depression did more than simply intensify the desire for a more rewarding family life, children and all; it provided examples of the family as an adaptive resource in times of economic trouble—a resource distinguished by the prominent role of women and children.

Values and Influence in Marriage

The importance of children to the sons of deprived parents corresponds with their role in the household economy, but is there any basis for expecting a degree of intergenerational continuity in marital relations, between mother dominance in deprived families and the wife's influence?[36] Assuming that initial concepts of marital roles are formed through interaction with and observation of parents, the offspring of deprived parents should be more accustomed to and accepting of the influence of wives in family decisions than other men. It is true that a number of men were critical of the dominant mother as they reflected upon parental roles in the Depression, but this criticism centered more on the martyr complex than on the legitimacy of mother's power or leadership.

More important as a limitation to intergenerational continuity is the extraordinary amount of change between the life situations of fathers and sons in the sample. Role patterns learned in a situation of family deprivation are ill-suited models for a state of economic and social well-being: self-other relationships are most likely to persist when a person "is locked into the kind of situation in which the pattern emerged."[37] Accordingly, continuity in wife influence should be most evident among men who have not advanced above their father's status or who have encountered economic deprivation in their own careers, that is, the nonmobile.

As measures of marital influence we used a series of questions which were asked in the 1964 survey. Two areas of decision making were selected for analysis: the sphere of economic issues, in which husbands are most likely to make the final decision; and child rearing, an area within the traditional province of the wife. By relying only upon the husband's report, we expected some degree of bias toward male influence; willingness to acknowledge the wife's influence is likely to depend on the perceived desirability of this family pattern.[38] Some reluctance in this respect would be expected among men who equate maleness with recognition as head of the household, and yet this response in itself reflects attitudes that may have roots in stable, male-oriented families in the Depression.

Some bias of this sort does appear on economic decisions; none of the men reported that their wives were more influential on how money was spent or on the selection and purchase of a car; 40 percent claimed that decisions on matters of this sort were shared, while the remainder assigned greater power to themselves. These patterns are reversed in child rearing; the majority of the men described their wives as having greater influence. Sixty-three percent claimed their wives more often had the final say on "how the children should be disciplined," on when the "children should date," and on religious training. A shared pattern on all three issues was reported by 23 percent, with the remainder attributing greater influence to their role. While this traditional structure of decision making may not correspond with the wife's perception in each case, the absence of wife dominance on economic matters offers no support for the thesis of a continuation of similar marital power from the older to the younger generation. It is still possible, however, that the sons of deprived parents are more inclined to acknowledge at least an equalitarian relationship with their wives in family decisions than are the sons of nondeprived parents. As we have seen, both groups are relatively similar in achieved status, and thus on conditions which directly affect the balance of marital power.

Since items in the two areas of decision making are intercorrelated, the scores were summed to form two indexes. Response categories on each item ranged from husband always (a score of 1) to wife always (a score of 5); thus the higher the score on each index, the greater the wife's reported influence.[39] The indexes were first correlated with economic deprivation, family status in 1929, and adult social class within the total sample, using an ordinal measure of association (Kendall's tau_c), and then related to family deprivation among the upwardly mobile and nonmobile.

Consistent with family relations in the Depression, the influence of wives on economic matters is negatively related to the achieved class of their husbands ($tau_c = -.16$), but the latter's economic well-being in childhood has a surprisingly strong effect, especially considering the time lapse of twenty-five years. Even with family status and adult class controlled, men from deprived families were more likely to report a shared pattern of decision making than the offspring of more affluent parents ($tau_c = .24$). Does this relationship vary according to male adequacy as a breadwinner in the adult years? If the appropriateness of wife influence is linked to male inadequacy in the childhood experience of men from deprived families, this association should be most pronounced among men in this group who have made little or no headway in their worklife, relative to father's occupational status.

The data do show this variation. Shared decision making on economic matters is most prevalent among the nonmobile and is more strongly related to a background of family hardship among these men than among the upwardly mobile ($tau_c = .35$ vs. $.15$). For the nonmobile, perception of maternal dominance in the 30s represents a significant link between their deprivational background and reported marital pattern; those who described mother as dominant in family affairs were also likely to report a shared arrangement on economic decisions in their own marriage ($tau_c = .25$). Similar results were obtained on the balance of power in child-rearing decision.

Given the available data, we have not been able to do justice to marriage as a relationship; only indirectly do the data take into account the perceptions, feelings, and activities of wives. The meaning of work and family, marital satisfaction and power, have all been assessed from the man's standpoint. Information from wives would have been most valuable in the area of employment and influence in family decisions. Women are likely to seek jobs under conditions of financial need, and employed status tends to increase their influence on economic matters in particular. This sequence is most applicable to the family situation of nonmobile men, but there is no unequivocal basis for expecting wife employment to alter the results we have obtained.

Another unknown is the extent to which men's values were modified by marriage to women who emphasized different aspects of marriage, family life, and work. Presumably, some wives were children of deprived parents in the 30s, while others were shielded by relative affluence from the hardships and suffering of the time. The principle of social homogamy in mate selection, of "like marrying like," suggests that value change through marriage would more likely take the form of convergence or accentuation than of qualitative modification. The only direct evidence of homogamy in the sample centers on educational similarity, but we can assume, following other studies, that the Oakland men married women who resembled them on a host of background characteristics and values. A more complete picture of the Depression's legacy in family roles and values should emerge from our subsequent analysis of the Oakland women, but in this case we must depend heavily on only one perspective—their view, which may or may not resemble that of their husbands.

A Résumé

The time at which the Oakland boys left high school (1939) stands out as a critical factor in their life opportunities and accomplishments. It was a hopeful time when compared to the preceding years; jobs were more plentiful and conditions more favorable for advanced education. Work, marital life, and education were interrupted by the call of military service, but this moratorium from civil pursuits offered benefits in maturity, breadth of experience, and subsidized education. Whether due to earnings in the war years, to the GI bill or specialized training in the military, or to the support of wives, it is clear that family hardships in the 30s had little overall consequence for the subjects' educational prospects. Only in the working class did economic loss adversely affect chances for higher education, and even here a substantial percentage of boys were able to acquire a college education. From the first job after formal education to the late 50s, we found no evidence of a substantial handicap in occupational status resulting from a background of economic deprivation, even among boys from the working class.

In one respect, the negligible effect of family deprivation on achieved status is not surprising, for it parallels the distribution of competence in the Depression. Except for family resources and structured opportunities, there would be no reason to expect a relation between economic deprivation and differential achievement in adulthood. Boys from deprived households in both social classes were not less able or motivated than the sons of nondeprived parents, but we had to move beyond these facts to explain their level of achievement; to their early vocational commitment, more crystallized vocational interests, and greater utilization of talents. In both the middle and working classes, boys from deprived families arrived at a firmer vocational commitment in late adolescence and were more likely to be judged mature in vocational interests than the offspring of nondeprived parents. In adulthood, they entered a stable career line at an earlier age, developed a more orderly career, and were more likely to have followed the occupation which they preferred in adolescence. Vocational maturity in crystallized interests established a positive link between family deprivation and occupational attainment, and at least partly offset the educational handicap of a deprived background. Desire to excel in adolescence proved to be the most important source of occupational achievement for boys from deprived families in both social classes, and was highly related to mental ability. As both framework and discipline for ambition, vocational commitment generally enhanced the occupational achievement of boys from deprived families.

By middle age the Depression was a distant memory for men in the sample, but it remained consequential for the things they valued. The contemporary relevance of past deprivations and acquired predispositions is especially pronounced among men who occupied situations in adulthood that most closely resembled the experience of economic deprivation in the 30s; these include downward mobility from the middle class, and status continuity or stability within the lower middle class and working class. Men from deprived families were not more or less committed to their work role than the nondeprived, but work did not have the same meaning to them, especially among the nonmobile; the former were more inclined to prefer job security and a reasonable income to the risk of pursuing more lucrative employment, and expressed more dissatisfaction with the extrinsic aspects of the job—income, work schedule, etc. Leisure activity meant little to these men when compared to its value among the sons of nondeprived parents, and they placed it well below both work role and family life in priority. The meaningfulness of marriage to men with deprived backgrounds centered in large part around "the chance to bear and rear children," in contrast to a singular emphasis on marital relations among the sons of more affluent parents, and the deprived attributed greater influence to their wives. These differences appear in the values and family relations of men who achieved a substantial measure of worldly success, but they are more striking among the nonmobile.

8

Leading a Contingent Life

Most women still lead contingent lives. . . . Great numbers of them prefer to work through another person and to find their own joys and compensations in the success of another.
Lorine Pruett

A life style dependent on marriage and the husband's career: these are features of a woman's contingent life. Depending on the man she marries, a young woman's occupational plans and preparation may be invalidated, modified, or receive the support needed for eventual fulfillment. Lacking advance control over this event, on which everything seems to hinge, most young women have been understandably reluctant "to take their future careers seriously" during the premarital years, or even until after the child-rearing phase of marriage (Bernard 1971, p. 172).[1]

An occupational life for women, apart from the family and its economic needs, was contrary to public opinion throughout the Depression decade; a woman's place was in the home, not in competition with men for scarce jobs.[2] While the percentage of married women in the labor force increased dramatically during the war, and has continued to climb in the 70s, prevailing ideology on the role of women is remarkably similar to attitudes in the 30s. Writing some thirty years after the Depression, a sociologist concludes that "the current view of the life cycle of the female in this society is outlined in very nonflexible stages. Her life is portrayed as a sequence of definite and irreversible states." "She is expected to move from birth and home-centered childhood into school attendance for a time sufficient to find a husband, but not so long as to waste valuable youth on knowledge used only for a short time. The next appropriate stages are work before and after marriage, giving birth to a limited number of children, rearing children, caring for the retired husband, widowhood, and death" (Lopata 1971, p. 363).[3] The contingent career, from its early development in the Depression up to middle age, is an essential point of departure for charting the life course of women in the Oakland sample; all but three women of those followed into adult roles have married, and most of the married women have at least two children.

Contingencies in a
Woman's Life

Three aspects of a woman's life have particular significance for the adult careers of the Oakland girls: the role preferences they acquired in childhood and adolescence, the timing of their marriage and first child, and the person they married. Domestic interests, for example, tend to favor an early marriage and a primary commitment to family roles. Their age at first marriage would condition prospects for higher education and structure the field of eligible husbands. As time passes, the field of eligibles narrows, increasing competitive pressures in mate selection and the prospects of marrying down. Lastly, their fulfillment, psychological health, and life style all depend, more or less, on the personal qualities and careers of the men they married.

All three aspects of a woman's career are implicated in the experience of the Oakland girls who were part of the labor-intensive economy of deprived households. Historically, such households in urban areas have fostered a traditional image of the woman's role, and we have seen this concept most often expressed in the value orientation of girls from deprived families. They were most likely to have come to maturity in a female-oriented household which required their labor in food preparation, clothes making, house cleaning, and child care. The roles of women expanded in situations of economic hardship, and their daughters were incorporated more fully, though not exclusively, into the traditional world of the homemaker. With this domestic background, and its orientation toward marriage and family, we expected the daughters of deprived families to marry earlier than girls from nondeprived homes, especially in the middle class, and to subscribe, as housewives, to the belief that "a woman's place is in the home."

Another tendency toward an early marriage is expressed in the emotional needs associated with economic hardship. It is in crisis situations, which undermine relatedness, that one becomes most needful and aware of others, even to the point of willingly sacrificing freedom for the security of social dependence. We have seen evidence of this psychological adaptation among girls in deprived families, in their consciousness of self and others, their emotionality and longing for peer acceptance; they were most willing, in fact, to sacrifice self-interests for the interests of peers. But more important, they were least likely to enjoy a close, supportive relationship with their father, a relationship which can affirm a sense of womanhood, desirability and personal worth. Emotional deprivations of this sort are known to add value and

Leading a Contingent
Life

urgency to early heterosexual commitments which culminate in an early marriage;[4] they also arouse romantic fantasies and subjectively lessen a girl's bargaining position in mate selection. In any relationship, the upper hand belongs to the person who is less interested in its continuation.

The plausibility of this early commitment to marriage is enhanced by the adverse effect of economic conditions and climate in the late 30s for the higher education of girls. Historically, American families have given first priority to the education of sons, following the traditional view of sex roles that boys must earn a living, while girls only become housewives. (For an analysis of this and other aspects of inequality, see Rossi 1964.) When asked in adulthood about parental aspirations, over two-thirds of the Oakland men claimed that mother very much wanted them to go on in higher education, in comparison to only a third of the women. If family hardship increased prospects for an early marriage by raising anticipated satisfactions in the marital role (domestic interests and emotional needs), it is likely to have done so in a context which lacked alternatives to marriage, such as college.

Beyond its relation to marital age, the education of a girl influences her prospects for marrying well. Selective mating opportunities increase with each level of educational attainment. Any barrier to higher education, resulting from economic hardships in the Depression, would thus handicap chances for achieving higher status through marriage. But apart from her education or field of eligibles, a girl's advantage in mate selection depends on physical assets, grooming, interpersonal skills, and "personality." Only grooming was negatively influenced by family hardships in the Oakland sample.

The near universality of marriage among the Oakland women, and the dependence of their life ways on this commitment, necessarily extends our interest to the men and careers they married. This extension, it should be noted, adds complexity to the analysis, when compared to the more straightforward influence of education and worklife experience in the accomplishments of men from deprived backgrounds. Even though personal achievement through education and employment may increase selective mating options for girls, some slippage is likely in the translation of this accomplishment to status in marriage. After marriage a woman has limited control over her life situation; in cases of the husband's occupational failure, she may work and even develop her own career, but she is seldom in a position to improve the status of her husband. As we follow the Oakland women into adulthood, we shall trace family deprivation to their *own* experiences in marriage, employment, and education, but we shall do so by taking into account the life situations they share with their husbands.

The contingent careers of married women are sufficient reason for surveying the background and worklife of their husbands. However justified, this approach would take us beyond available data resources and our principal interest in the adult lives of women who grew up in the Depression. We do not have systematic information on the childhood experiences of husbands in the 30s, and are thus unable to trace its effect on their values and subsequent careers. Nevertheless, major historical events experienced by the Oakland men were also generally encountered by the husbands of women in the sample, despite a slight age difference. From available evidence, the husband cohort also left high school in the latter 1930s, was favored by an upswing in economic activity, and benefited from educational opportunities during the war and postwar years. A large number were also called to military service. In these respects, our characterization of the Oakland men from World War II to middle age provides a general context for charting the life course of girls who married.

Seventy-six members of the Depression sample were contacted in at least one of the three adult follow-ups between 1954 and 1964. Using these data, adult histories were constructed up to 1958 for all women in the adult sample. A comparison of the adolescent and adult samples disclosed no differences in family status (1929), ethnicity, household structure, IQ, or economic loss. For comparisons of intergenerational change in status, we shall compare achieved status through marriage in 1958 with family status in 1929.

There are four general points to keep in mind as we move into the analysis: (1) family background, economic deprivation and class origin; (2) the adult life course, defined by the timing of marriage and parenthood, educational level, worklife and status achieved through marriage; (3) adult values and social roles—family, work, leisure, and community; and (4) adolescent experiences or adaptations that may link family hardship to adult outcomes—such as domestic roles and heterosexual experience. In the first part of the analysis we provide an overview of major events and patterns in the life course of all women, with emphasis on their historical context.[5]

The second part compares the effects of family deprivation and class origin on three critical events in the life course of women—the timing of marriage, educational attainment, and marital choice with its consequences for adult status. Linkages that help account for the outcomes are specified and tested. The last major part of the chapter takes up adult values and social roles, their relation to family deprivation in differing social contexts, and adolescent experiences which link deprivation to adult priorities. Childhood experience in deprived households has much in common with the "domestic" postwar decade, but it remains to be seen whether family-centered values in the life styles of the Oakland women have roots in these conditions.

Events and Patterns
in the Life Course

Marriage offered a variety of rewards to the Oakland girls in their passage to adulthood; it satisfies a generalized expectation of women in society; establishes a girl's right to residential separation from the family of origin, which in turn enables her to achieve independence from the claims of parents; and provides a legitimate context in which to satisfy needs for sexual relations, childbearing, status, and love. At the same time, marriage entails costs or sacrifices which may be defined as activities or opportunities foregone as a result of the primary, con-tractual bond to a man. These include a loss of autonomy through the interdependence of life aspirations and experiences, and opportunities which are more available to the single woman, such as advanced edu-cation, occupational careers, and travel.

From marriage to the arrival of a child, the family role of women is predominantly oriented toward the husband. This preference is most likely to persist through the childbearing and child-rearing years when the husband is successful in his career, according to income and social rewards, though emotional priorities generally shift toward children after the birth of the first child (see Lopata 1971, chap. 1). Role differentiation and segregation in marriage are especially pronounced at this point for middle-class families, as the husband spends long hours on his job and the wife centers her attention on the often lonely and restrictive activities of mother and homemaker. Marriage is coexistent with motherhood for most women in the Oakland sample, and thus represents the most appropriate point at which to begin an overview of their lives from high school to middle age.

During the peak years of economic distress, marriage and new addi-tions to the family were often postponed. The median age at first mar-riage in 1930 (21.3) increased during the 30s and remained slightly higher in 1940 (21.5) (Moss 1964). War mobilization brought greater support and urgency for early marriage as economic conditions im-proved and marriageable men were called to active duty in the military. By 1945, estimates show a remarkable decline of one full year in the matrimonial age of American girls, a change which exceeded the trend in marital age over the previous fifty years. The Oakland girls soon entered this milieu after leaving high school in 1939, and their marital behavior reflects pressures which were characteristic of this age. By late fall 1942, approximately two-thirds of the girls had married for the first time and a fifth were mothers. Only three members of the sample remained single through the 1950s.

Major events of life normally occur in rapid succession when girls enter the transitional years between dependency on parents and full adult status. For at least half of the sample, full-time employment, completion of formal education, and marriage occurred within the comparatively short span of two or so years after graduation from high school. As the girls turned twenty, a third were married, two-thirds had left school and were not to return, and a similar percentage were or had been employed full-time. Since the course of a woman's life depends on when and whom she marries, we shall order events according to marital age and its bearing on husband's status, and then relate types of career patterns (one role, two roles, etc.) to achieved status.

Marital Age in Life
Patterns

Marital age for the Oakland women (20.4 yrs.) is equivalent to the national average in 1945 (20.5 yrs.). The distribution on age of our sample at first marriage and first child is shown in figure 6. Approximately half of the women had become mothers for the first time by the age of 24, a date which corresponds with the last year of World War II.

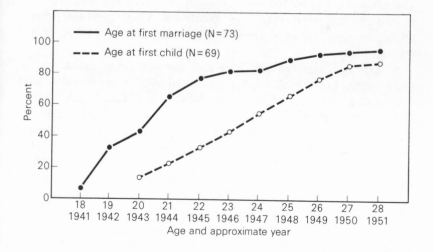

Figure 6   Percentage Distribution of Women Ever Married by
                  Age at First Marriage and at Birth of First Child

Leading a Contingent
Life

For purposes of analysis, we divided the women according to relative age at marriage, following the assumption that the expected time for a girl's entry into marriage is structured by norms and optimum social opportunities. In their respective settings, girls who marry at this age are on schedule, while those who deviate markedly are subject to liabilities or sanctions. Teenagers may be regarded as "much too young for marriage" and a social risk, with deviation on the other side producing greater pressures to marry.

Three groups of women were identified in relation to the usual age or time of marriage for the 1940s: early (before the age of 20)—32 percent; average (ages 20 through 22)—45 percent; and late (after the age of 22)—23 percent. The number of first marriages dropped sharply after the age of 22; all but three of the late marriers were wed after the age of 24. By 1964, three-fourths of the first marriages were still intact; seven out of ten of the broken marriages were dissolved by divorce or husband's death in the 1940s. Three husbands died in the Second World War and two in the Korean War.

Women who married before the age of 20 were least likely to have continued full-time employment during World War II and to have entered college. Over 85 percent had at least one year of full-time work in this period, but the likelihood of one to three or more years of employment is directly related to marital age (table 9); in the postwar decade, employment continued to be most common among women who married relatively late, corresponding with the onset of childbearing. The early marriers started their family at an earlier age than other women and had more children by middle age. Since the women were approximately 43 years of age in 1964, further growth in family size was not likely.

As expected, very few girls were able to enter and complete four years college (11%), although a substantial number completed at least some college. Level of education is related to both family status ($r = .37$) and marital age; the later the age, the higher the educational attainment. Though most of the early marriers came from working-class families, differences in class origin within this group were unrelated to their educational level. Among women who married later, some college was substantially more prevalent in the middle- than in the working-class group (88% vs. 30%). As marital age increased, so also did the likelihood of a college education among capable women. In the group which was above average on IQ, the percentage who achieved at least some college increased from 39 percent in the early-marriage group, to 62 percent in the average group, and to 90 percent for the late marriers. The role of intelligence in the personal achievement of these women was thus contingent on the timing of their marriage.

Table 9

Adult Status	Marital Age		
	Early	Average	Late
Years of Full-time work before 1946			
None	23%	6%	6%
One-two	41%	33%	19%
Three or more	36%	60%	75%
Years of full-time work, 1946–55			
None	45%	70%	27%
One-two	27%	10%	33%
Three or more	28%	20%	40%
Family patterns			
Median age at first child	22.3	24.1	27.9
Median no. of children	3.4	2.8	2.6
Education			
College (one or more years)	13%	50%	69%
High school/ vocational training	17%	29%	12%
High school only	70%	21%	19%
Marital history to 1964			
First marriage intact	52%	76%	94%
Death of first husband	13%	9%	—
One or more divorces	35%	15%	6%
Minimal number of cases in marital groups	22	30	15

Table 9 · Life Patterns of Women in Adulthood by Marital Age

Most girls who married early did not have the mating advantages of a college campus and bypassed the personal benefits of higher education, but they were not necessarily excluded from settings in which to meet well-educated, ambitious men. Secretarial jobs in white-collar settings may have offered such contact. Moreover, there were potential risks associated with delays in marriage: women who pursued a college education with an eye toward marriage during their late twenties risked a sharply reduced supply of eligible unmarried men. What they gained in personal development through higher education may have been countered by a handicap in meeting suitable men. In this respect, the modal age at first marriage resembles an "optimum" or "right time" for girls who were interested in maximizing both marital *and* educational prospects. Before we take up the matter of status prospects in early and late marriages, let us note the degree of intergenerational change in status.

Both change and continuity are expressed in the post or late adolescent situation of mother and daughter. Opportunity for women in higher education increased significantly between the early 1900s and the Second World War, and this change is reflected in the educational level of the Oakland girls and mothers; but little, if any, change occurred in the cultural image of marriage as the proper way for a woman to make a living. The coed's preoccupations during the war years were centered on finding a husband.

The priority of marriage and husband's career over a woman's own education or career interests, however latent, is a social fact of no small consequence in the lives of the Oakland women. Only 18 percent of their mothers entered college before the 1920s, but a majority of these completed their degree requirements. The daughters, by comparison, were about two times as likely to enroll in college, but only a fourth remained to complete their degree. In this and other comparisons, marriage and birth of the first child stand out as the critical determinants of the daughters' foreshortened educational career. The only gain in educational status from mother to daughter, on the group level, appears before the usual time for marriage. In a familiar tale, marriage during a girl's college career typically put an end to her education. As a consequence, the daughters were no more likely than their mothers to complete four years of college, despite greater opportunity to do so. In at least two cases, however, the daughter's college career ended abruptly when parents withdrew support (see table A–26). This sacrifice reflects priorities in marital exchange which assume that a wife's destiny is to derive satisfactions through her husband's accomplishments. Most of the husbands who entered college, for instance, completed their studies, in contrast to their wives, and a small proportion went on to postgraduate training. Some delays in higher education resulted from military service.

If we compare the generations in terms of a college education, the only significant increase appears between the fathers and the husbands of the Oakland women; the women tended to marry more highly educated men than their mothers, from high school through undergraduate and postgraduate studies. Only 27 percent of the mothers were less educated than their husbands, in comparison to 44 percent of the daughters. (For a picture of educational change across three generations, see Hill 1970, p. 35.)

This educational disparity is especially pronounced among girls who married men who achieved high status in their career, as one might expect. Most of the girls from working-class families achieved higher status through marriage without the mating advantage of a college campus, and over half were lower in education than their husbands. This compares to only 14 percent of the girls who married men in the working class. Higher education was more common among girls with middle-class backgrounds, but their husbands were even more highly educated. As a result, nearly three-fourths of the upwardly mobile were less educated than their mates, compared to slightly less than half of the girls who were less successful in marriage.

The principal change in occupational status between the girls' fathers and their husbands appears in a category which expanded significantly during the 1940s and 50s—the professional and salaried managerial group. Twenty-two percent of the fathers were located in this category (1929), in comparison to 40 percent of the husbands some thirty years later. The proportion of men in sales-clerical work increased by a third across the two generations, while the self-employed declined from a fourth to a fifth. According to the Hollingshead index of social position, based on the husband's education and occupation, 41 percent of the married girls were located in the upper middle class by 1958 (I and II), 29 percent were lower middle class (III), and 30 percent were positioned in the working class (all but one in IV). Percentages for comparable strata of fathers (1929) are 14, 35, and 41.

Girls who married occupationally successful men, in potential or in fact, frequently met them in college. In the total sample, the girls' educational level had greater consequence for husband's eventual status than their class origin (r = .51 vs. .27). But the marital advantage of college varied according to when they married. The late marriers ranked highest on educational attainment and were most likely to utilize their abilities in this respect, but a substantial number were not successful in exchanging their status for a comparable position in marriage. In fact, they were most likely to marry men who had less education (40 percent), compared to 15 percent of the younger brides.

The lack of valued qualities for exchange in marriage appears to have had an increasingly detrimental effect on matrimonial prospects as age increased. For instance, a third of the non-college-educated women who married before the age of 23 had professional or managerial husbands, in comparison to none of the late marriers in this educational category. Similar results were obtained on comparisons of women who were working-class in origin; the marital prospects of a working-class girl who did not go to college sharply diminished by age. One interpretation of this difference suggests that the age-related decline in eligible

Leading a Contingent
                                      Life

men (single and high-status) increases the bargaining position of men in mate selection. Their field of eligible mates includes younger women as well as those in their age bracket. Whether by choice or necessity, girls who delayed marriage entered a more competitive system of mate selection, which made their choices in marriage more dependent on personal assets.

*Women's Careers
and Husband's
Status*

The Oakland women are members of a cohort which tends to prize family roles (mother, wife, and homemaker) far more than any other activity. One study has found this priority even among married women who were gainfully employed or engaged in civic responsibilities. By and large, the collective opinion of these women affirms the view that "every woman should be married, that she should have children, and that none but family roles should be of even secondary importance to her before, during, or after the time that she is intensely involved in these relations by virtue of the life cycle" (Lopata 1971, p. 49). Even if these priorities seldom match the roles women actually perform, they do identify dominant themes in the lives of the Oakland women. Bona fide occupational careers, which have a measure of autonomy and equality relative to the husband's worklife, are practically nonexistent. From the day of high school graduation to middle age, all but 8 percent of the women registered at least one year of experience as a full-time employee, though less than 15 percent followed a relatively *orderly career* after marriage and children, with only brief interruptions. The latter category includes women who completed college or professional school—a landscape architect, a registered nurse, etc.—as well as women who achieved little more than a high-school education—an IBM operator, an insurance salesman, a draftsman, and a buyer for a department store. With few exceptions, there is little evidence in these work lives of a substantial increase in authority or status during the postwar years.[6]

Four employment patterns were identified in the life history proto-cols.[7] A fourth of the women followed a conventional pattern of employment; they were employed after leaving school, but soon left to marry or to have their first child, and did not return thereafter. A larger percentage of women in the sample (34 percent) established a double-track career, in which employment was only temporarily interrupted to have children or keep house. A third type of career line is best described as unstable (20 percent) and closely corresponds with the disorderly worklife of men. Women in this group alternated between employment and homemaking for reasons external to the job itself, such as financial need, health, and residential change associated with the husband's work. The fourth group (8 percent) delayed entry into the labor market until after marriage and homemaking.

Whether a woman continues working after children arrive depends on a host of factors beyond values, but especially on her economic situation, and this point is reaffirmed by the life course of women in the conventional category. As a group, women with conventional careers married exceedingly well, and have since cultivated interests in a wide range of activities beyond workplace and family. They were more likely to have achieved some college education than women in double-track or unstable careers, to have married men of high educational and occupational status, and to rank within the upper middle class by the late 50s. Seventy percent were upper middle class, in contrast to a third of the women who continued working, with interruptions, after marriage. There were no differences in these respects between women in the double-track and unstable groups. In 1964, the Oakland women who stopped working after marriage reported at least one major role outside the family (politics, artistic endeavors, community action, etc.), and four-fifths were active in at least two local or national associations, in contrast to a third of the women who continued working after marriage. It should be noted that some women in each career pattern are likely to change places as their children leave home and other concerns change. A third of the conventional group, in fact, reported plans (in 1964) to seek employment in the near future.

Economic Deprivation in the Life Course

From this brief overview we see three influential factors at work in the lives of the Oakland women, principally in mate selection, and all three were vulnerable to family circumstances in the Depression; their marital age, educational attainment, and choice of marital partner, with his subsequent occupational accomplishments. The important question for these women is not whether they married, but when and whom, since all but three eventually established a life pattern which was contingent on the career of a man. The timing of marriage is especially crucial in structuring life experience, as we have seen. If women from deprived families sought emotional fulfillment in marriage at an early age, this event would have restricted their own education beyond high school, quite apart from a lack of parental support, and hence restricted their

Leading a Contingent
Life

opportunities for meeting college-educated men. To relate these factors to economic deprivation in the 30s, we first compared women from nondeprived and deprived families in the middle and working class, and then identified the main effects of family deprivation and class origin. The analysis includes only women who were married in 1958 and classified according to deprivational status. Our point of departure is marital age since it has consequences for both educational level and achieved status through marriage.

Family Hardship in the Commitment to Marry

Early marriage (before the age of 20) is related to family deprivation, apart from its association with a working-class background. The main contrast is between early marriages and marriages at the average age; no variation occurred among the late marriers. A third of the girls from deprived families in the middle class married early, compared to only 8 percent of the daughters of nondeprived parents. Family deprivation made no reliable difference in marital age among girls from working-class homes; nearly half married before the age of twenty (46 percent), and in doing so may have emulated the marital pattern of their parents.

In some cases, objective deprivation may not be registered in the psychological strains which make early marriage attractive; objective hardship is not always defined as such, and definitions of the situation are a primary determinant of feelings and action. The girls' actual awareness of hardship was not directly measured in the Depression, but they were asked as adults about such experiences. In the 1958 interview, recollections of hardships were especially common among women who married early, regardless of class origin, and such memories were associated with adolescent perceptions of mother as an unhappy person. Half of these women recalled moderate to severe hardships, compared to only 10 percent of all other women in the sample.

Family deprivation increased the likelihood of early marriage through conditions which enhanced the attractiveness of this option. For girls from middle-class families, these include: (1) a family environment characterized by emotionally distant and nonsupportive relations with parents (especially with father), and considerable freedom to associate with boys away from parental supervision; (2) relatively early dating and intimate heterosexual experience; (3) a strong desire for social acceptance and emotional sensitivity; and (4) limited educational prospects through lack of parental support, low academic achievement, and a preference for the domestic role. The following summary of these linkages is based on analyses which are available in the research literature (see Elder 1972).

Girls who married relatively early were most likely to feel estranged from both parents, while both the early and late marriers were closer to mother than to father, when compared to the average group. The young brides ranked highest on the belief that parents were not interested in them. Both parental indifference and a preference for mother were associated with family deprivation in the middle class.

Distant relations with father in the extreme marriage groups also appeared in the girls' perceptions as adults. Only 11 percent of the women in the early and late groups (1964) singled out father as the easiest person to talk things over with, as against nearly 40 percent of the women who married at the average age. Comparable results were obtained on parental differences in offering praise and affection. When asked directly about their impressions of father as a parent, only a third of the women who married early expressed positive regard, compared to 50 percent of the women who married relatively late and 85 percent of those who married at the average time. Though some daughters from deprived families viewed the parental role of their mothers with disfavor in adulthood, estranged relations with father were the predictive factor in both early and late marriage. Impressions of mother did not vary by marital age.

Within the middle class, the socially independent tended to come from deprived households and were likely to marry at an early age. Girls in this marriage group often resisted parental authority by talking back and criticizing, as did the late marriers. Consistent with their social independence, the teenage brides differed from other girls in their accelerated pattern of heterosexual development: early dating, frequent interaction with boys, formation of a stable pair relationship, and increasing sexual intimacy. During the high school period, phone contacts and time spent with boys as well as a predisposition toward steady dating increased as marital age decreased, with the greatest difference occurring between the early and average groups. Premarital intercourse was most prevalent among the early marriers.

Emotionality and a desire for social status formed a substantial link between family deprivation and early marriage. In chapter 6, girls from deprived families were generally described as emotionally sensitive or self-conscious (feelings easily hurt, cries easily, etc.) by their mothers, and tended to underestimate their social standing among classmates. Both orientations distinguished girls who married early from those who married later. By contrast, the late marriers tended to overestimate their social popularity.

Leading a Contingent
Life

Lastly, economic conditions in the Depression minimized educational constraints to an early marriage by diminishing the attractiveness and possibility of higher education. Women who grew up in deprived households were more inclined toward domestic interests (especially in the middle class), when compared to the nondeprived, and such values were predictive of both an early marriage and termination of education at the high school level. Few women in the sample recalled parental encouragement for a college education, even in the middle class, though support was least common among the daughters of deprived families, and that lack of encouragement contributed to their tendency to marry at an early age. Women who married early were not less able on measured intelligence.

In this overview, four conditions emerge as noteworthy linkages between family deprivation and early marriage among women from the middle class: (1) estranged relations with father, (2) social independence and early heterosexual involvement, (3) emotionality and self-devaluation, and (4) a predominant orientation toward the domestic role and away from higher education. These linkages offer support for a deficiency theory of early marriage;[8] the process by which girls focus upon and commit themselves to marriage is accelerated by social and emotional deficiencies in the self or in self-other relations. Affirmation and fulfillment of self as a woman are sought through the presumed emotional security and rewards of dependency in marriage. Emotional deprivation vis-à-vis the most significant male figure in a young girl's life, her father, represents a key element in the motivational dynamics of this heterosexual orientation.

A deficiency interpretation of early marriage does not do justice to the evidence on social learning, on socialization for maturity in a domestic career. Whether from the deprived middle class or working class, the early marriers are distinguished by domestic interests as adolescents, by social independence and early heterosexual involvement, and by negligible support for education beyond high school. Emotional deprivation is not required to account for the predictable marital outcome of these factors, especially in the working class, where parents are likely to represent an early marriage norm in their own behavior. In relation to family hardship during the Depression, the domestic or marital socialization of middle-class girls corresponds in sex-typing to the vocational socialization of boys, to their vocational thinking and crystallized perspective.

It is clear that economic loss in the 30s and low family status are associated with elements of both interpretations of an early marriage; emotional deprivation, with emphasis on problematic relations with father, and domestic socialization. These factors are so interwoven in the life situation that they defy isolation. For example, social independence seems to imply a degree of social maturity, but it may also reflect indifference or lack of concern on the part of the parents, and thus contribute to the emotional rejection felt by some girls. In fact, a distant relationship with father was associated with the social liberty and heterosexual activities of girls. If we acknowledge the potential maturing experience of social independence and distinguish such freedom from evidence of social or emotional maturity, there is no essential conflict between the psychological-deficiency and socialization accounts of factors leading to an early marriage among the Oakland women.

For the sample as a whole, women who married early achieved less education, started their families at an earlier age, gave birth to more children, and were less likely to have stable marriages than other women. On the face of evidence presented thus far, we would expect this life pattern to be more characteristic of women from deprived families in the middle class. In fact, these women were less likely to enter college than the daughters of more well-to-do families, but other differences do not conform to predictions based on marital age. Regardless of class origin, women from deprived families gave birth to their first child approximately eight months *later*, on the average, than the nondeprived, did not give birth to more children up to middle age,[9] and were not less able to maintain their first marriages. In order to understand these results, we need to consider differences in marital achievement and their relation to family background.

Education and
Marital
Achievement

Women from deprived families in the middle class were more accomplished in marriage than in personal achievement; only 15 percent married men with less than a college education, and yet half never entered college themselves (table A–27). By contrast, women from nondeprived homes did not do as well in marriage. They advanced farther in higher education, but their husbands ranked lower on educational attainment than the husbands of women from deprived families, and they achieved lower status through husband's worklife by middle age. Thus family deprivation in the middle class lessened chances for higher education, but not for marital achievement.

Few women from the working class achieved more than a high school education, and a majority married men in this educational category. Nevertheless, their marital achievement clearly parallels that of women from the middle class in relation to family deprivation; the

Leading a Contingent
Life

daughters of economically deprived parents actually achieved higher status through marriage, on the average, than women from more fortunate homes. This unexpected difference, especially in the middle class, highlights the contingent or problematic aspects of marriage; education alone is not sufficient to ensure marriage to a man with equal or greater status. The important question is why this "slippage" in status is most characteristic of women who had every social and economic advantage in marriage—the nondeprived of middle-class origin. We know, for instance, that it is not due to the age at which they married, or more specifically to the risks of a relatively late marriage. They were no more likely to marry late than the daughters of deprived parents. Also unknown are the sources of marital achievement among women with a background of family hardship. Why do we find a high level of achievement through marriage among these women in both the middle and working classes?

The marital advantage of a middle-class home occurred in part through entry into college, but this advantage cannot account for the positive influence of family hardship on marital achievement.[10] Some noncollege women did meet men of high caliber in work settings, including their husbands, though we have no reason to believe that such contacts favored the daughters of hard-pressed families. Likewise, women from nondeprived and less fortunate homes were essentially identical on personal qualities that determine feminine appeal in the eyes of men, e.g., physical attractiveness, grooming, etc.

Beyond these group similarities, there may be differences in the extent to which personal assets were used or displayed to secure the attention and commitment of desirable men, just as we found motivational differences among able men from nondeprived homes. In a traditional upbringing, women are oriented toward self-presentations which are pleasing to men. And typically, "a woman is expected to use her attractiveness to gain certain legitimate ends such as recognition, status, and a husband."[11] This tactic is recorded in life histories of women (a New England sample) who were successful in marrying higher-status men; they "frequently combined social activity with the use of physical attraction, charm, and sex in the broadest sense to achieve mobility. . . . They flattered and charmed teachers in high school and college. Later on, they used the same techniques with the men they met in business."[12] Family deprivation is likely to have increased the value of this social technique for the Oakland women by making their future more dependent on what could be achieved through marriage by accepted or available means, including the appeal of a shapely figure and pretty face. In order to explore this proposed effect, we must first determine whether appearance and social ambition actually

Leading a Contingent
                                    Life

made a significant difference in the marital achievements of women in the sample.[13]

The most attractive women in physique and facial appearance, according to ratings made in the 30s, were likely to marry men who achieved rewarding careers as professionals, middle managers, and high-level executives.[14] As one might expect, physical assets made the greatest difference for women who had limited access to higher education, that is, the daughters of working-class parents. The relation between attractiveness and husband's status is considerably stronger in the lives of these women than among the offspring of middle-class families ($r = .46$ vs. $.28$). By implication, at least, this result supports our expectation of a strong relation between the appearance of women from deprived families in each class and the status they achieved through marriage.

A well-groomed appearance did not match the influence of physical attractiveness, except among women from the working class. Most women of middle-class origin were rated well above average on grooming, and those who married up were not distinguished by their appearance in this respect. However, women who married out of the working class seemed to anticipate their class of destination in both grooming and behavior. They were much better dressed and more attractively groomed during their high-school years than women who married into the working class, and were rated higher on self-confidence, peer acceptance, and leadership. They were also less likely to form steady relationships with boys in high school, and were generally more guarded and selective in social friendships.

Implicit in the above relations is the assumption that pretty girls were socially ambitious, attuned to ways of advancing themselves through physical appeal.[15] In fact, attractive women were among the socially ambitious in high school, as indicated by their desire to impress and control others ($r = .32$), but they were not more inclined to aspire to high status in adult life. In both respects, however, ambition was predictive of marriage to men who achieved positions of prestige and authority. Women from the middle and working classes resembled each other on social aspirations before marriage, and both orientations were associated with marital achievement. For all married women, husband's status was less highly related to social aspiration (as measured by the two indexes, both $r = .38$) than to physical appearance. Both ambition and appearance were most highly correlated with marital achievement among the daughters of working-class parents.

Physical attractiveness was relatively independent of educational attainment in the marital achievement of the Oakland women. Even those who did not continue their education beyond high school were more likely to marry men of high status or potential if physically attractive. These two sources of marital achievement are most clearly shown by the path diagram in figure 7. Academic aptitude (a seven-point rating by teachers) and the subject's educational level were defined as intervening between class origin and attractiveness, on the one hand, and husband's status, on the other. Both IQ and academic aptitude are interchangeable variables in the model and produced similar results. Separate analyses with each class group were not practical with education included in the model since very few women from the working class continued their education beyond high school. For the reader's convenience, correlation coefficients are presented in parentheses alongside the path coefficients.

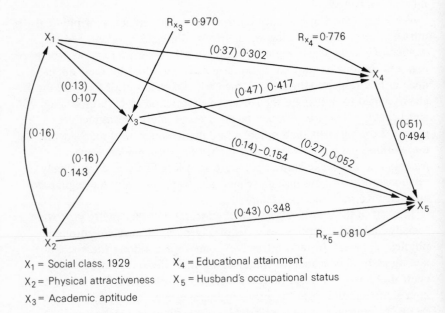

X_1 = Social class, 1929
X_2 = Physical attractiveness
X_3 = Academic aptitude
X_4 = Educational attainment
X_5 = Husband's occupational status

Figure 7   Paths Relating Woman's Educational Attainment and Husband's Occupational Status to Pre-adult Academic Aptitude, Appearance, and Class

The contribution of physical appearance in marital achievement, relative to that of education, suggests parallels between the careers of women from working-class and deprived families. In both groups, a domestic upbringing joined forces with restricted educational opportunity to emphasize the marital route to social achievement as well as the appeal of an early marriage. Does this correspondence also extend to the role of appearance in the marriages of women from deprived homes? Is attractiveness more influential in the marital achievements of these women than of women from nondeprived homes? The most appropriate test would be a systematic comparison of the relative effects of attractiveness and education within groups defined by economic deprivation. In view of the small number of women with a nondeprived background, we decided to compare the deprived group with all women in each social class. This design enabled us to make comparisons by deprivational background without obscuring previously noted class differences in life options.

Unlike its variation by social class, appearance did not play a more important role in the marital achievements of women from deprived families, regardless of class origin, although it was more influential relative to education. Attractive daughters of deprived parents were no more likely to marry high-status men than other women of similar endowment and class background. Our expectations were also not confirmed on the relation between appearance and social ambition; in each social class, family hardship made no difference in the relation between physical attraction and social aspirations.

In our effort to explain status variations by family deprivation, early events in the life course (such as marital age and education) have posed fewer problems than the status achieved by the Oakland women through marriage. The marital age and education of women from deprived families offer little help toward understanding their social accomplishments in marriage, and this conclusion also applies to variations in attractiveness. The analysis to this point, however, does provide a context in which to identify linkages between adult values and the childhood experiences of the Oakland women. Household adaptations to economic loss have relatively direct implications for women's attitudes on family roles. This domestic influence and the family activities of the Oakland women in the postwar decade coincide with a more general development in the lives of married women following World War II, a phenomenon which Slater describes as "ultradomestication": "While single middle-class women were becoming more and more liberated, married middle-class women were embracing a more totally domestic existence than ever before" (Slater 1970, p. 64). Is this life style most fully developed among the daughters of economically deprived parents, as it was in the family-centered values of the Oakland men, or does it reflect a more generalized desire, born of Depression and war, for the tranquillity of home life? Slater takes the latter position, arguing that the American females' domestic preoccupations were "part of a general postwar retreat from the world" (ibid., p. 65).

"A Woman's Place is in the Home"

There is little resemblance between the social world of women in deprived households of the 30s and that of middle-class women in the 70s, except in ideology concerning feminine roles. Now, as then, American women assign overwhelming priority to their family roles of mother, wife, and homemaker;[16] despite increasing higher education, civic participation, and employment among women, and a decline in the labor requirements of homemaking. In these developments we see the making of a cultural lag in which unequal rates of change produce strain on the interconnected social, economic, and cultural units of society.[17]

In their own life span, most women in the Oakland sample have belonged to households which varied greatly in labor demands on the homemaker—from the labor-intensive economy of deprived families which emphasized traditional sex roles, to the relatively affluent families of women who married into the middle or upper-middle classes. Their upbringing was fashioned by the maintenance requirements of households beset by heavy economic losses, not by a vision of future options for women, and consequently had little to offer a generation which would soon encounter radical change in the technology of homemaking. When they married and gave birth to their first child in the 40s, "home" was the unchallenged center of the woman's world. More women were working than ever before, but not in highly skilled occupations; more were going to college, though a smaller proportion entered the labor market with commensurate employment (see Knudsen 1969). Indeed, very few of the Oakland women with at least some college have applied their skills to appropriate careers, though most of those who married are involved in activities outside the household.

Abundant evidence of this domestic climate is found in a magazine which appeals to educated middle-class women, the *Ladies Home Journal*.[18] According to a content analysis, marriage was portrayed as a full-time job in the late 40s and early 50s, a career which entailed "training, sound preparation, and skills." Marital stability and family happiness received special emphasis as the presumed values of women who spent their days in household routines and lacked social outlets beyond the home. "Articles aimed at buoying up the spirits of this somewhat isolated but content housewife by confirming what she already knew: she was the mainstay of society and was indispensable in maintaining the stable happy family which, she was assured, was the central core of American life." As household demands lessened in the 50s and 60s, "free time" emerged as a problem; the idle or bored were

Leading a Contingent Life

counseled in ways of keeping busy through homecrafts, volunteer work, and gainful employment. The analysis shows a slight trend from the postwar, family-centered image in which women lived their lives through family members to greater self-orientation by the end of the 60s.

*The Value of Family
Life to the Oakland
Women*

In life style the Oakland women did their part in the postwar efflorescence of domesticity. Though less than a fifth reported no full-time employment up to 1945, this percentage trebled during the postwar decade, an active period of bearing and rearing children. If we had inquired at this time about priorities or values, the family would have faced no contest from employment, leisure, or community roles. After this stage, however, one might expect greater balance in preferences, assuming that priorities reflect activities. In the typical case, the eldest child was either an adolescent or a young adult at the time of our last follow-up (1964). Whatever the change in activities from early marriage to middle age, it did not alter the dominant value of family roles to most women (figure 8). Compared to men in the sample, their sentiments and gratifications were more committed to a single sphere of life; family activity ranked well above even the combined importance of work and leisure as a source of accomplishment, enjoyment, and interest.

There is some correspondence between values and behavior in the areas of family and work, though roles outside the home were consistently ranked below the family, even by the most active women and by wives who were dissatisfied with their marriages. The family-centered were not as well educated as other women, and were less likely to have worked in the postwar decade or in 1964.[19] A substantial number of family-oriented women were employed at the time, however, or were planning to work. Children were more prevalent in the households of women who preferred family roles, but the difference is too small to be reliable. Women who were most favorable toward work also had considerable experience in the labor market, and ranked slightly higher on education than other women. Their families were not smaller, however, than those of other women. Husband's status was not an important factor in either value orientation, family or work, though low status and small families were most common among women with a history of gainful employment.

These situational influences cast some doubt on the persistence of domestic values from the Depression to the middle years. Such commit-

Leading a Contingent
Life

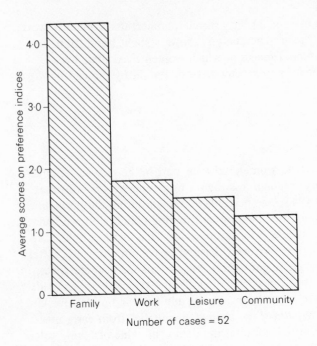

Figure 8   Activity Preferences of Women

ments were not favored by women with higher education and employment, and may have been weakened by these experiences. But it is also reasonable to assume that the domestically-inclined evolved a life course which excluded college, a career, and even gainful employment. In fact, women from deprived families did achieve less education, but were more likely than women from nondeprived homes to marry men for whom economic need was not a problem.

From data collected some twenty-five years after the Depression, we find no evidence that economic deprivation has become a less potent factor in the significance of family roles. Family life overshadows the combined importance of work, leisure, and community activities among women from deprived households, and is clearly more highly regarded by them than by women from nondeprived homes (table A–28). No other social factor in childhood or the adult years comes close to matching the effect of family hardship. Domestic values are generally prevalent in the lower classes, and this is true of women from the working class, but class origin does not approach the influence of economic loss in the Depression ($r = -.04$ vs. $.46$). Husband's occupational status, the subject's own education and employment, and family size were all less consequential for family preference than was economic deprivation.

Adult contexts also made little difference in the relation between economic loss and the importance of family life. The relation did not vary appreciably between the employed and the full-time homemakers, between those who had a high school and those who had a college education, or between women from the middle class and from the working class. Mobility through marriage also made no difference in this association. The consistency of the relation is most clearly seen in a comparison of the women with and without a college education. Daughters of deprived parents were less likely to enter college, and those who did were less inclined to prefer the family over other activities, but the effect of economic loss on this value was comparable in both educational categories. In the college group, 54 percent of the women from deprived families scored high on family preference (scores of 5 or 6), compared to 22 percent of the nondeprived group. The same comparison for women with less education produced values of 68 and 37 percent.

A plausible link between family deprivation and the significance of family activity is suggested by the adolescent environment of the Oakland women. For members of deprived households, this environment is distinguished by three factors that favored domesticity: domestic socialization, as indicated by involvement in household responsibilities; the social and emotional centrality of mother, which we shall index by perceptions of mother's influence in family affairs; and social contrasts, which are likely to have increased the attractiveness of family over work roles for young girls (a preference indicated by their domestic interests). Compared to the precarious and restricted economic position of men in deprived situations, the sphere of women's activities, influence, and responsibility enlarged under conditions of economic hardship.

All three factors—household tasks, perception of mother's influence, and domestic interests—are correlated with a preference for family activity in the middle years of adult life. Women who managed family obligations in the 30s, who perceived mother as the most influential parent in family decision making, and who preferred the domestic role as adolescents were most likely to prefer family life over work, leisure, and community roles. Of these factors, the first two define similar linkages between deprivation and family preference in each social class, and are thus shown for the total sample in figure 9. Approximately one-third of the relation between deprivation and family preference is due to the joint association of these factors with perceptions of mother's influence and household involvement.

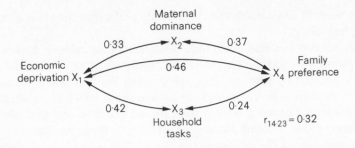

Figure 9   Correlation Coefficients Linking Family Preference to Maternal Dominance, Involvement in Household Tasks, and Economic Deprivation

One general conclusion can be drawn at this point from our results on the values of both men and women in the Oakland sample: family is most important to adults who grew up in deprived households during the Depression, regardless of class origin or current status. No other factor in the 30s or in adult life was more influential in accounting for differences in the strength of this value orientation. For both sexes, the data are consistent with the hypothesis that family life acquired value through exposure to conditions which made rewarding, secure relationships difficult to achieve and therefore scarce. Also, from an adaptational perspective, one would expect the family to acquire value as a means of coping with economic hardship—as an emotional haven, a production unit, and a source of alternative forms of economic support.

As we have seen, the relation between economic deprivation and family preference is clearly more general among women than among men. This difference may be due to the common relevance of the Depression experience to the family roles of women. Most of these women occupied similar marital, parental, and homemaking roles, even though they differed on educational level, work status, and class position. Work, not family, was the basic role for men, and their worklife experiences typically bore little resemblance to the experience of fathers in the Depression. Only in adult situations which closely resembled economic circumstances in the Depression did we find a substantial link between economic deprivation and their preference for family life.

Up to this point our attention has been limited to the predominant family orientation of the Oakland women and its relation to experiences in the Depression. But what is it about the family that matters most or least? When a woman subordinates all other activity to her roles in the family, she may do so for a variety of reasons, other than a sense of obligation. Uppermost in her mind may be the companionship, love, and understanding of her husband; the fulfillment in bearing and rearing children; the rewards of homemaking; or a combination of interests. These orientations are known to vary by stage in the family life cycle, from marriage to children to the "empty nest," but they may also be shaped by childhood experiences. Homemaking, for instance, closely parallels the household experiences of women who grew up in deprived families, and matches their adolescent interests.

Beyond the meaning of family activity, we have yet to explore the extrafamilial roles of women, both occupational and civic, and their interplay with family values and status in the life course. While family-centered women in our sample were less likely to have worked outside the home, a large number were either employed or involved in the organizational life of their community. An important question here is the extent to which outside activities are linked to family background and related values in the Depression, apart from the influence of adult education, husband's status, and family size. Other conditions being equal, are women with deprived backgrounds less involved in roles outside the home than the offspring of nondeprived families? Reasons for not working and the scheduling of employment around family demands should provide insight on the consequences of a family-centered value system. This priority is especially consistent with the conventional pattern of homemaking in which a woman works only up to marriage or the birth of her first child.

Three problems have thus been posed in rounding out our analysis of "a woman's place" in the values and actions of the Oakland women: the meaning of a basic commitment to the family, social roles outside the home and their relation to this commitment, and the scheduling of both family and work roles in the life course. Each problem is taken up in the remaining pages of this chapter.

The Social Roles of
Wife, Mother, and
Homemaker

Interests in family roles vary across life situations. The roles of mother and homemaker are known to be highly valued by women in lower-status families, while satisfactions in marriage generally increase with the wife's education and her husband's status (Lopata 1971, chaps. 1–4). These differences also appear in the Oakland sample, though we are mainly interested in general sources of gratification. Children were the primary attraction to the Oakland men who expressed strong family interests, and they were also most popular among the sons of deprived parents. Does commitment to the family have similar meaning to women in the sample?

We assessed the relative value of wife and mother roles by using a set of questions (in the 1964 survey) on basic aspects of marriage. Each married woman who had at least one child was asked to rank six aspects of marriage from the most to least valued. These include "mutual understanding," "companionship," and "sexual relations" in the marital relationship; "the chance to have and rear children—a measure of regard for the role of mother; and the material and security benefits of married life—the "standard of living" it provides and the "security and comforts of a home." Since specific duties of the home-maker were excluded from this list, we are unable to determine the importance of this role, in comparison to that of wife and mother. How-ever, we measured satisfaction with homemaking by a question which asked how each respondent felt about taking care of a home—"not taking care of children, but activities such as cooking, sewing, and keeping house."

Husband and children. The interpersonal benefits of marriage and children were by far the most valued aspects of marriage among all women. Two-thirds ranked "mutual understanding" in first or second place; followed in order by the "chance to have and rear children" (54%), companionship with husband (49%), and sexual relations (30%). Neither the material advantage of marriage nor the security of a home were salient features of marriage to women in the sample, as was true also of the men; less than 10 percent ranked these benefits in first or second place. This value hierarchy is relatively stable across adult statuses; the same rank order was found within categories of edu-cation, social class, religion, and family size. However, the valuing of children did decline slightly by adult status and was correlated with family size ($r = .14$). Mutual understanding was most widely valued among high-status women.

Women who preferred the family over work and leisure were likely to regard children as the most important aspect of their marriage ($r = .32$). Less central to this value orientation are features of the marital relationship, such as companionship and mutual understanding ($r = .22$ and $.15$). Marital happiness or discontent did not lessen the degree to which women preferred family life, or their regard for chil-dren, but it did affect their judgment on the importance of relations with husband. Among family-centered women, the value of companionship and understanding increased with their reported marital satisfaction.

The prominence of parenthood in the family preference of women is remarkably consistent with the value orientation of the Oakland men. As sons of deprived parents, they were most likely to value family life, and this value is correlated with the importance of fatherhood in their lives. Most of the men who valued children were offspring of deprived homes, and this value parallels the childhood roles of women in deprived households. However, we were unable to trace this value orientation to family hardship, owing to the small number of women in the nondeprived group.

There is another distinctive feature of deprived households, beyond the function of children, which may have conditioned expectations toward the role of wife: the dominance of mother in family affairs. Economic failure, with its domestic consequences, did not orient girls toward a life of independent achievement, though it did convey the uncertainty of dependence on a man's earnings and its implication for the homemaker's role. Out of this experience they may have learned to expect a measure of control over affairs in their own marriages, especially in situations of economic hardship. Some evidence of this relationship was found among men in the sample; the wife's influence on economic and child-rearing matters was most strongly related to family deprivation and mother's perceived influence among relatively unsuccessful men.

There is one unknown, however, which lessens prospects for generational continuity among women: the husband's attitude or ideology concerning a woman's role in the family. To a large extent, marriage patterns are dependent on this ideology and the husband's achieved status. A woman's desire for influence or equality in marriage has little chance of fulfillment if her husband is adamantly opposed to an arrangement of this sort, unless of course he withdraws from household affairs, as did some fathers in the Depression.

This reservation is at least consistent with the data. If women were oriented toward influence in marriage by their upbringing in deprived households, there is no evidence of this tendency. Using indices of decision making on economic and child-rearing matters constructed from items in the 1964 survey,[20] we found no reliable association between the marital influence of women and family deprivation in the 30s. Husbands were generally described as more influential on economic matters, while the final say on matters of child rearing was most often claimed by the women themselves; but neither marital pattern varied by maternal influence or economic hardship in the Depression. Similarity in life situation across the generations did not produce a connection between family deprivation and the wife's influence, as it did among the Oakland men.

Homemaking. No major function of women in the family is more stereotyped or devalued in the public mind than that of homemaking. Slater reflects this judgment in his reference to the "tedium and meaninglessness" of women's domestic chores (Slater 1970, p. 67). While labor-saving devices have lessened its demands, homemaking remains an attractive activity to most of the Oakland women; a majority, in fact, were more than simply content with this traditional role, even though we specifically excluded child care from the tasks. Fifty-six percent thoroughly enjoyed taking care of their home and rejected the notion that cooking, sewing, and cleaning are merely jobs that "have to be done." Another 20 percent reported some enjoyment in this role, while 15 percent did not have feelings either way, positive or negative. Only 10 percent of the women could be counted as antagonistic toward the duties of the homemaker.[21]

The committed homemaker experienced life situations which reinforced a domestic orientation. If from the working class, she terminated her education after high school, entered marriage and parenthood at an early age, and married a man who remained in the working class. Homemaking interests were commonplace among the daughters of working-class families, so common in fact that they ruled out any distinctive influence from a childhood of economic deprivation; most were domestically-inclined as adolescents, and close to 90 percent found satisfaction as middle-aged adults in the role of homemaker. Neither family deprivation nor even variations in adult status made a difference in this value. Women who married into the middle class were just as likely to favor homemaking as the wives of working-class men.

A domestic upbringing in deprived households is most evident in the homemaking attitudes of women who were exposed to settings which were least supportive of the traditional image of a woman's role. These include a middle-class background and higher education. Women from deprived homes in the middle class were more favorably disposed toward homemaking than other women (65% vs. 36%, $tau_c = .35$), and their attitude is related to family deprivation through social roles and interests in the Depression; household responsibilities, the prominence of mother in family affairs, and adolescent interest in the domestic role. All three factors were associated with an adult interest in homemaking (average $tau_c = .24$). Similar results were obtained in the social origin of homemaking sentiment among women who completed at least some college.

The importance of homemaking and children to women who prefer family roles has obvious implications for childbearing. Other conditions being equal, one would expect these women to have more children, on the average, than women who seek gratification in jobs or civic roles. A large family may be both consequence and source of motherhood or family values; yet neither function is visible in the sample. Women from deprived families did rank higher on their commitment to family roles in adolescence and middle age, but they did not have larger families, on the average, than other women. Whether family-oriented or not, most of the Oakland women had either two or three children. The connection between family values and fertility was stronger among the Oakland men, though in this case there is no way to determine whether children were a cause or consequence of values. From the evidence presented for men and women, family-centered values do not emerge as a significant link between economic loss in the Depression and subsequent fertility.

Social Roles beyond the Family

Work, leisure, and community activities—none matched the importance of family life to the Oakland women, and yet most were very much involved in these endeavors at one time or another. A large number worked after leaving high school and even after marriage, and have taken part in community life. They entered a labor market in which more women were working than ever before, though mainly in low-status jobs. With the arrival of children, outside commitments were put aside for an indefinite period; the postwar decade found most women in the sample occupied with child rearing and homemaking.

If family-centered women are mainly responsive to the needs of children and husband, these needs would be a logical starting point for explaining their involvement outside the home; they would seek employment to relieve economic pressures, but otherwise make family a full-time occupation. According to this line of reasoning, employment should be least common among women from deprived families, especially during the postwar decade. They did not have more children, but their values affirmed this course of action, and their economic situation in marriage was more favorable, according to husband's status, than that of women from nondeprived homes.

In view of these considerations it is surprising to find no appreciable variation by deprivational background on years of full-time employment, both during and after the war (table A–29). The differences, such as they are, show a higher rather than lower level of employment among women from deprived homes. Of greater consequence for employment are stages in the life cycle and husband's status. The proportion employed dropped sharply in the postwar decade of child rearing, though even here the working woman was more often the wife of a man in the lower-middle or working class. Economic need, inferred from husband's occupational status, was more strongly related to employment in the postwar decade than the number of children at home.[22]

Leading a Contingent Life

Family priorities emerge in the reasons women gave for not working as of 1964, and most were in this category: three-fourths of the women from middle-class homes were not working, in comparison to 38 percent of the daughters of working-class parents, and only a fourth of the "unemployed" expected to take a job in the near future. Beyond work status and expectations, which did not vary by childhood deprivation, the offspring of deprived parents were more inclined to explain their lack of a job by referring to family needs, even though such demands were not greater on objective measures than those encountered by other women. Sixty-two percent gave reasons of this sort ("My family needs me," etc.), regardless of class origin, compared to a third of the women from nondeprived homes. The latter more often cited lack of interest or of suitable jobs, a preference for volunteer work, or the apparent inability to locate work.

Despite their predominant interest in family roles, women from deprived homes were not more responsive to economic need as a precondition for their employment. With or without such need, they were just as willing to seek employment as other women, though family welfare was more of a consideration in their lives. For example, we asked each woman the following question in the 1964 survey: "If there is no economic need in your family, would you want to work if an appropriate job became available?" Women from deprived homes were not less interested under these conditions than other respondents, but their desires were unlikely to be implemented if they conflicted with the perceived interests of children and husband. We did not ask about the perceived legitimacy of a mother who works full-time when her children are still at home, though responses to date support the inference that women with a background of family deprivation would be least accepting of this arrangement, if not actually required by economic circumstances.

This family attitude is most fully expressed in the conventional pattern of employment in which a woman works up to marriage or the birth of her first child, and does not reenter the labor force. A fourth of the women followed this type of career line, and *all but one* grew up in deprived households; an equal proportion were offspring of middle- and working-class homes. After approximately twenty years of marriage, these women stand out in their attachment to family life, in their marital happiness, and in their organizational activities in the community. No other group of women expressed less interest in gainful employment, or assigned greater value to family activity and homemaking. Such values are consistent with their social origins in the Depression and correspond with their family situation from marriage to middle age.

The Adult Years

Compared to the sample as a whole, the conventional careerists achieved more education, and were more likely to marry college-educated men who were (by 1964) positioned in the upper middle class. Children and motherhood tell much about the adult lives of these women; each family included at least two children, and 44 percent had at least three. But children took second place to relations with husband as the most valued aspect of their marriage. In all cases, the first marriage had remained intact and a source of continuing happiness. These women were husband-oriented, economically dependent, and content in the lives they led. Neither values nor family situation and economic need were "push" factors on their participation in the labor force.

"Contingent living" is the most fitting description of the conventional career; those who followed this life course were brought up in the Depression to appreciate the virtues of family life, and their husbands made this option gratifying through their emotional and economic support. One might say that successful husbands made economic dependence a viable option for women who learned, as children, the value of a woman's role in the home. By customary standards, the college-educated in this group did not put their knowledge or skills to work, nor did they cultivate talents which would enable them to be self-supporting, should the need arise. The division of home and work along sex-role lines did not bode well for the continuing vitality of marriages among women in this career, especially after the children leave home,[23] though all were actively engaged in community activities of one sort or another.

On the basis of values alone, the conventional career is probably the life style most women in the sample would have wished for. In reality, however, a larger proportion interrupted their worklife only temporarily to have children or manage the home—a *double-track* pattern; while economic pressures and broken marriages led other women to adopt roles and values that are out of keeping with girlhood ambitions —the *unstable* pattern of employment and homemaking. The double-track career was more prevalent among women from nondeprived families (table 10), but only in the group with origins in the working class.

A review of the life course of women in the three major career patterns—conventional, double-track, and unstable—sheds some light on situational constraints in the expression of values. The conventional pattern is the purest expression of a family-centered value system, apart from the complete lack of work experience, but it was not a viable alternative for many women who preferred this way of life at an early age; for women who were not spared economic pressures by the earn-

Leading a Contingent Life

Table 10   Career Patterns of Married Women (up to 1964) by Economic Deprivation and Class Origin, in Percentages

| | Percentage of Married Women | | | | |
| | Economic Deprivation | | Class Origin | | Total |
Career Patterns[a]	Nondeprived	Deprived	Middle	Working	
1. Stable homemaking, with no work history. Married immediately after schooling or after a period of unemployment	9	7	9	6	8
2. Conventional pattern of employment: marriage, homemaking with no return to work. Employed after leaving school, but left to marry or before the birth of first child	4	36	24	25	25
3. Double-track: Interruptions to have children or homemake with return to work	44	29	21	47	34
4. Unstable: alternations between employment and homemaking due to poor health, financial needs, moving, etc.	22	19	21	19	20
5. Delayed employment: first employment followed marriage and homemaking	13	5	12	3	8
6. Other	9	5	12	0	6
	101 (23)	101 (42)	99 (33)	100 (32)	101 (65)

[a]   Adapted from M. C. McMulvey, "Psychological and Sociological Factors in Prediction of Career Patterns of Women," unpublished Ph.D. dissertation, Harvard University, 1961.

ings of their husbands and a stable marriage. A large number of women, who had little interest in employment, did not stop working at marriage or when their child was born, as we see in the group of women with an unstable worklife. These women were not less domestically-inclined or lower in class origin than women with a conventional career, but they tended to marry at a younger age, achieved lower status through marriage (on the average), and have had a more troubled marital history.

Economic pressures are also an important factor in the worklife of double-track women when compared to the conventional group. A larger percentage grew up in working-class families, married men in the lower middle or working class, and have had unstable marriages. In adolescence, these women were less interested in domestic activities than women in the conventional and unstable groups, and a substantial number recalled "wanting to pursue a career" at the time of the 1964 survey. This is the only group of women in the sample which expressed any serious interest in a career. On the basis of these comparisons, *events in the adult life course have more to do with the worklife of women than their family background in the Depression or related values.*

This conclusion also applies to the associational roles of women in the community. Membership in community organizations generally increased with the educational level and class position of women in the sample and was especially common among high-status women with conventional careers, while employment was most prevalent among low-status women. If we take adult status and work roles into account, a background of family deprivation makes no difference at all in community activity.

A note on class and deprivation in adult life. From the analysis to date, we have seen that economic loss in the 30s had a more consistent impact on the life course and values of women from the middle class than of women from the working class. This difference appears on marital age, educational attainment, and satisfaction with homemaking. The daughters of deprived parents in the middle class were more inclined to value domesticity as adolescents and the homemaking role as adults than were the nondeprived; they also tended to marry at an earlier age and were more likely to end their formal education with a high school diploma. These correlates of family deprivation are more generalized among women from the working class; they did not vary by degree of economic loss. In large part, this class difference reflects the corresponding effect of traditional prescriptions on a woman's role (working class) and the adaptational consequences of family hardship and strain (middle class). Early marriage, limited education and domesticity are more a part of a woman's life in the working class than in the upper strata. What we see in the lives of middle-class women are the domestic implications of family deprivation and adaptations in a context that would ordinarily provide some options beyond domesticity. In this group the Depression experience produced traditional outcomes

Leading a Contingent
LIfe

in the lives of a number of girls who were unlikely to have grown up in a highly traditional, sex-differentiated culture before 1930.

Early Family Life and Adult Careers in Marital Success

Marital success is not ensured by a wife's devotion to family members or by economic well-being, but one is hard-pressed to find any grounds for optimism in the early experience of women from deprived families. At the time of marriage these women seemed destined for more than their share of conjugal troubles. Severe economic hardship strained the emotional fiber of their families—at times to the breaking point—exposing them to a catalog of marital ills and failure; marital tension and conflicts, dissatisfaction with lot, heavy drinking, emotional exhaustion, and the physically broken home were all more prevalent in their family experience than in the lives of women who grew up in non-deprived homes. Relations with father were often strained and emotionally distant, and, though attitudes toward mother were generally positive in the 30s, a substantial number of the women remember their mothers in a negative light. Some of these conditions were linked to an early marriage and its high risk of impermanence.

The significance of these early experiences is brought out by the assumption that children are oriented toward marital roles in knowledge, motivation, and beliefs through the apprenticeship of family relations. Parents are thus models of conjugal roles, whether successful and attractive or not, and condition the probabilities of marital success in their children's lives. Provided one takes situational differences into account, this perspective is consistent with evidence on the transmission of authority patterns from one generation to the next, and finds support in data which suggest that "parental competence in marital relations tends to be transmitted to children to enhance their own prospects of marital success."[24] Correlations have been reported between the marital adjustment of parents and offspring in retrospective studies, though little is known about the mechanisms of this transmission process. In any case, some women in the study were very much aware of parental influence as an unwanted legacy.

This apprehension is not borne out in the quality of married life among women or men from deprived households. Their marriages were no less permanent or happy than those of other members of the sample. In fact, their first marriages were more likely to have survived up to 1960, although the difference is too small to be reliable. Marital happiness, according to reports in 1958 and 1964, also did not vary by family deprivation or class origin, even with adjustments for differences in adult status. These results do not rule out linkages between childhood deprivation and marital success in the Oakland sample, especially since we have not taken into account the early experiences of the spouses, but they do suggest the need for more intensive analysis of intergenerational patterns within a longitudinal design.

There is a paradox of sorts in the finding that women were happiest in marriage to men who were highly involved in successful careers, to college-educated men in higher managerial-professional occupations. No other group, according to our analysis of the Oakland men, is more likely to put occupational interests before all other considerations; to subordinate the companionship needs of wife ard children and community obligations to the discipline of a work-centered life style which consumes weekday evenings and weekends in activities that are separated from the life of family members. Work was largely a voluntary investment for most of these men in our sample, and they were not at all averse to devoting even more time to it. The implied loss of companionship is not without costs to the marriage. If we view married life over time, there is evidence from at least one longitudinal study that the external commitments of the husband, both occupational and organizational, are directly related to the probability of marital impermanence, dissension, and lessened gratification (Dizard 1968)—especially from the wife's viewpoint. Dizard found that the decline was less likely to occur if the wife shared some of her husband's experiences and priorities through a job of her own or by participating in community activities outside the home. However, the greatest increase in marital happiness from early marriage to middle age was found among couples who had minimal commitments beyond the family.

We are unable to determine whether change of this sort has occurred among the Oakland women who are married to successful men, since we lack information on marital life in the 40s. We do know, however, that they were most likely to be husband-oriented and happy with their marriage in 1958 and 1964.[25] They also expressed much greater satisfaction with the income and prestige associated with their husband's work than did lower-status women, and were not particularly critical of the job's demands.[26] In all of these respects, the rewards of husband's success, including his own sense of fulfillment, appear to have more than offset the loss of companionship. It remains to be seen whether this degree of satisfaction will continue into the latter years of married life.

In one sense, we might expect women whose life is focused on the family to expect more out of family activity than women with interests in a career of their own. By definition, they would be more dependent

Leading a Contingent
Life

on family members for their own sense of fulfillment and identity; and should be more vulnerable to occupational demands that reduce their husband's company and companionship with the children. From another perspective, however, we see that family-centered values are uniquely suited to an arrangement which sharply differentiates the activities of husband and wife—the former as breadwinner, the latter as wife, mother, and homemaker. By minimizing the priority of a woman's own career or employment, this value orientation maximizes dependence on the husband *and* augments the legitimacy of his occupational involvement, however onerous it may be. Of interest here are women who followed a conventional pattern of employment. Separation of work and family along sex-role lines is most fully expressed in the lives of the women who stopped working at marriage or shortly thereafter, and yet their marriages remained intact and emotionally satisfying. Both values and community roles may be factors in this marital picture. As acknowledged believers in the priority of a woman's role in the home, these women were nonetheless involved in a range of community activities, and frequently shared some of these interests with their husbands.

The Depression Experience in Women's Roles

Feminine domesticity in the postwar years coincides with the "baby boom" and represents ideals most favored by the daughters of parents (in the Oakland sample) who suffered heavy economic losses in the early 1930s. Their preference for family roles is partly an unintended consequence of family adaptations to economic loss, of their involvement in household operations and the centrality of mother in family affairs. Just as family survival often hinged on the contributions of mother and daughter, the latter generally defines her primary role in adulthood as service to her family. The centrality of family life to these "children of the Depression" may also express the wish to undo the "psychic disruptions" of Depression and war, as one member of this generation put it; "to achieve the serenity that has eluded the lives of our parents."[27]

Zeitgeist, mystique, withdrawal from the world—these and other sensitizing concepts have found their way into accounts of privatism and the domestic pulse among young women following the war, leaving the impression that we understand or have explained the phenomenon. Other "theories" of the postwar trend refer to the disruptions or trauma of family separation in the war, to the compensatory interest of returning servicemen for a "traditional" home life, and even to the Spockian doctrine on *Baby and Child Care*. In his essay "The Spockian Challenge," Philip Slater makes a broad inferential leap in arguing that the good doctor's handbook encouraged domestication of the American (middle-class) female through its emphasis on woman's family role and the challenging task of child rearing (Slater 1970, p. 64). Child care thus expanded to consume hours no longer required for household chores, in accord with Parkinson's Law for Women: "Work expands so as to fill time available for leisure."[28] "Underneath all the qualifications and demurrals, most middle-class, Spock-oriented mothers believe, deep in their hearts, that if they did their job well enough all of their children would be creative, intelligent, kind, generous, happy, brave, spontaneous, and good—each, of course, in his or her own special way" (Slater 1970, p. 64).

Whatever the domestic climate of the 40s, our data suggest that receptivity to traditional roles is concentrated among women who grew up in deprived households that depended heavily upon the involvement of female members. From adolescence and the late 30s to middle age, a domestic life style is more characteristic of these women than of women from nondeprived homes. They were more involved in household chores, expressed greater interest in domestic activities, and, in the middle class, were more likely to marry at an early age. A smaller proportion entered college, when compared to the nondeprived in each social class (1929), but a larger percentage married into the upper middle class. Many factors, other than values, entered into the decision to seek gainful employment, and no substantial difference was found in the total amount of work experience by deprivational background in the Depression. However, the daughters of deprived families were most likely to stop working at marriage or when they gave birth to their first child; and (if from the middle class) to enjoy the common tasks of homemaking. The meaning of family preference centered first on the value of children and secondarily on the interpersonal benefits of marriage.

There are suggestive parallels between the position and learning experience of girls in deprived families of the 30s and in father-absent homes during World War II. In both cases, loss or curtailment of father's contribution to family maintenance shifted responsibility to female members and stressed the importance of women's roles in the household. Female participation in wartime industries did not, to our knowledge, weaken the impact of male absence on women's commitment to the family. From our analysis of the Oakland sample, there is reason to expect some connection between the traditional aspirations of women who launched their families during the late 50s or early 60s and childhood experience in father-absent homes during World War II.

9

Personality in Adult Experience

Personal soundness is essentially a way of responding to the problems set by life. . . . Its marks are realism, adaptability, and the development of a sense of responsibility based on internally determined principles.

Frank Barron

Situations which call for new adaptations in adult life are generally associated with transition or change points, such as entry into marriage and parenthood, change in work situation, death of spouse or divorce, the departure of the youngest child. An ability to cope with these situations without undue harm to self and others is commonly regarded as one indication of psychological health or soundness. In this respect we think of the Oakland fathers who responded to job loss and privation in ways that seemed to keep "body and soul" together and enhanced family survival, as against men who withdrew from family responsibilities and drank heavily. Contrasts of this sort may be due to differences in adaptive resources, apart from variations in external support and the vicissitudes of opportunity.

Interest in psychological functioning has traditionally centered on illness or impairment, though we know that soundness or well-being is not merely the absence of pathological symptoms.[1] In this final analytic chapter on the Oakland cohort, we shall take a broad view of psychological health, its relation to family deprivation and adult situations, beginning with evidence of impairment and ending with problem orientations in politics and outlook. Illness, effective adaptation, and psychological growth will be assessed mainly by clinical judgments in the 1950s. Subjective impressions of health, competence, and life satisfactions enter the analysis in evaluations of the personal consequences of parenthood, an appealing state for many adults from deprived homes but also a potential crisis point in married life, and in a review of life experiences since the 1930s. The final section moves from specific aspects of health to problem definition and orientations in politics and views of the future.

Childhood Deprivation in Adult Health

There is modest support (as we have noted in chapter 2) for the hypothesis that family strains and emotional distress in childhood increase the risk of illness or impairment in later life. The other side of the continuity thesis is expressed in the widely acknowledged link between a secure childhood and adult health. By most indicators, stressful circumstances in the Depression were relatively common in the lives of children from deprived households, but their risk for adult health depends on many factors, including those which influenced the psychological impact of family deprivation and the persistence of health states from childhood. In both respects the evidence leads us to expect the most adverse effect in the health of adults from working-class families.

In the course of our literature review and analysis, we identified class differences in adaptive potential which link the more enduring psychological costs of economic deprivation with low family status. For members of the Oakland cohort, these include the objective severity of economic privation in the working class, and the more limited resources of parents and children in this stratum. Among objective deprivations, unemployed fathers, physically broken homes, and dependence on public assistance were all concentrated among families in the deprived working class. Class differences of this sort were less evident in perceptions of economic loss as a problem, owing partly to its status threat in the middle class, though middle-class families were better equipped to define this problem as one which could be met or solved. Whether because of education, opportunity, or resilience, episodes of joblessness among the Oakland fathers were not as long in the middle class. Class differences in adaptive potential are also suggested by the greater regard of middle-class children for their parents, regardless of economic loss; and by their higher rank on intellectual skills, peer acceptance, and self-assurance.

The adaptive implications of these class differences appear to be contradicted by the observed relation between symptoms of emotional distress and economic deprivation among children from both middle- and working-class families. Hypersensitivity, unhappiness, and emotionality were just as strongly correlated with family deprivation in both strata. Nevertheless, class differences in health outcomes are implied by conditions which influence the persistence of psychological symptoms (see Dohrenwend and Dohrenwend 1969, esp. chaps. 9–11). Persistence is most likely if situations which induced emotional distress in the Depression are also encountered in adult life; if emotional reactions to family situations acquired secondary value as ways of achieving support, care, love, etc.; and if economic hardships led to psychological deficiencies in the ability to cope with difficult situations. On the first condition, the offspring of working-class parents were more likely than members of higher-status families to experience deprivations in adult-

Personality in Adult
Experience

hood; their average level of occupational and marital achievement is considerably lower, and a large proportion remained in the working class. Secondly, socially induced symptoms of emotional distress that persist by their secondary value are thought to be most prevalent in the harsher environment of the lower classes. An example of persistence through secondary gain is seen in the self-pity of mothers who played the martyr role in the Depression and have continued to do so with their grown-up offspring. Lastly, the known consequence of limited income, education, and adaptive skills in psychological impairment, among young and old, would assign the greatest health risk to adults from hard-pressed families in the working class.[2]

If preadult experience is evaluated in terms of its preparation for life problems and strains, we see an important difference in the health risks of persons who grew up in nondeprived and deprived families, a difference which is most simply described by the relation between situational demand and adaptive capacity. Severe economic loss markedly increased the situational demands faced by children—demands sometimes too great to cope with. Whatever benefits they derived from hardship as preparation for adult life would depend on how well they were able to manage without harming themselves or others. Successful adaptation in the long run is not always apparent in responses to hardship at the time of its occurrence. Indeed, one could argue, with the literature on social movements, that discontent in situations of deprivation is a critical, if not sufficient, state for problem definition and concerted action. Dissatisfaction and anger are not inappropriate or necessarily maladaptive responses to a sudden reduction in family income (and some families experienced a reduction of more than 65 percent between 1929 and 1933). Handicaps arise when discontent is not channeled into constructive action, is turned in upon the self, or becomes an end in itself.

The risk for members of nondeprived families in the middle class centered on a life situation which failed to test or challenge their adaptive capacities. "Smooth sailing" in a protected childhood may not develop adaptive skills which are called upon in later life. This point is noted by Sanford in a critique of the adjustment interpretation of psychological health: "A person might be so well adjusted to his environment, or his environment might be so simple or so protective of the individual, that he was not called upon to manage any severe strains. He might have all the health he needed in the circumstances, or even all he would need for any foreseeable future, but still be relatively lacking in what it takes to deal with a variety of severe strains" (Sanford 1966, p. 30). This causal hypothesis is implied by Macfarlane's observations on the status of some adults in her longitudinal study who were thought to have had "confidence-inducing lives" in the preadult years. "As children and adolescents, they were free of severe strains, showed high abilities and/or talents, excelled at academic work and were the adulated images of success. . . . [But] one sees among them at age 30 a high proportion of brittle, discontented, and puzzled adults whose high potentialities have not been actualized, at least as of now" (Macfarlane 1964, pp. 121–22). In the Oakland sample we have no conclusive evidence of a deficiency of growth-promoting experiences among adults from relatively well-off families in the middle class. However, the risk is worth noting as a counterpoint to our emphasis on the psychological effects of family deprivation.

During the adult years, health data were collected primarily in two follow-ups: 1953–54 and 1958. The first entailed a thorough medical examination, a series of interviews, and personality inventories. From this mass of information, Louis Stewart, a clinical psychologist, constructed a psychiatric classification, with emphasis on specific types of impairment or illness.[3] We shall supplement this classification with more recent information on problem drinking. A more complete view of psychological functioning is provided by two sets of measurements which are based on typescripts of the 1958 interview: clinical ratings of ego functioning by a team of psychologists under the direction of the late Suzanne Reichard;[4] and personality types delineated from Q-sort descriptions of each subject by Jack Block.[5] Stewart's health groups, Reichard's ratings, and Block's personality types represent markedly different theoretical and methodological preferences, but they are valuable in combination, as indicators of both illness and positive health. The principal handicap in the following analysis is that no set of measurements is available on all adults in the sample. Any interpretation of our results is thus qualified by this potential bias.

Stewart's classification includes a group defined as relatively symptom-free and five illness categories. In assigning members of the sample to appropriate groups, priority was given to somatic illness among those who were characterized by physical and mental illness; otherwise, placement followed the predominant class of symptoms. An illness score was calculated for all subjects who were not placed in the behavior disorder and psychosomatic groups by summing the number of adult illnesses, chronic symptoms, and operations reported in health records. All subjects in the lower third on the index were assigned to the symptom-free group. *Anxiety and tension states* refer to reports of nervousness, emotional tension and anxiety, and physical complaints of a hypochondriacal nature; *psychosomatic illness*, to clearly discernible physical disorders of the type most commonly defined as psychosomatic, e.g., stomach ulcers, essential hypertension, migraine headaches, spastic colitis, asthma, etc.; *psychotic reaction* includes all subjects with a history of psychotic reactions; *behavior disorders*, all persons judged as having serious psychological difficulty in one or more important life areas, e.g., history of psychiatric treatment, alcoholism, exceptional difficulty in heterosexual relationships, poor vocational development manifested by authority conflicts, frequent dismissal, etc.; and *somatic illness*, cases with heart trouble, cancer, major operations, etc. In the total sample, nearly a fourth of the adults were considered outstanding in general health, and a similar number were assigned to the psychosomatic group; behavior disorders and somatic illness were next in order of prevalence (approximately one-fifth in each category). Other than in psychosomatic illness, which was slightly more prevalent among women, the distribution of cases did not vary by sex.

We compared the percentage of adults who ranked highest on health by class origin and then by family deprivation within each stratum. The first comparison yielded no surprise in view of the advantages of a middle-class background in family life and status attainment. Both sons and daughters from the middle class were more likely to be judged symptom-free than adults of working-class origin (27% vs. 15%); and the difference was substantially larger with somatic illness excluded from the comparison. While this difference suggests that we might find similar variations by economic loss in the Depression, especially in the working class, there is no evidence of this outcome in the total sample. To make sense of this result we must take class origin into account. Illness is slightly related to family deprivation in the lower strata, though not in the middle class. Compared to all other groups, men and women with deprived middle-class backgrounds are disproportionately represented among the healthiest adults; approximately two-fifths were judged relatively free of health problems.[6] These differences are shown in table 11 for men and women combined since the effect of family deprivation did not vary by sex.

The principal class difference in health problems by economic hardship occurs in the category of behavior disorders. Serious problems in one or more areas of adult life were more prevalent among the offspring of nondeprived parents in the middle class, and among the deprived of working-class origin. This difference also appears in heavy drinking up to 1964. Data were obtained from the medical record completed in 1953–54, from a question on the 1958 interview, and from a home interview in 1964. Men and women were assigned to one of five amount-frequency categories: problem, heavy, moderate, light, and abstinence. Slightly more than a third of the adults were classified as problem or heavy drinkers.

Table 11

Table 11	Diagnostic Classification of Men and Women (1954) by Economic Deprivation and Class Origin, in Percentages			
	Middle Class		Working Class	
Health Groups	Nondeprived	Deprived	Nondeprived	Deprived
Relatively symptom free	11	38	18	13
Anxiety and tension states	11	7	27	21
Psychosomatic illness	29	21	36	17
Behavior disorders	26	7	9	25
Somatic illness (serious)	20	19	9	17
Psychotic reaction	3	7		8
	100	99	99	101
Total no. of cases	35	42	11	24

Note. Two childhood categories in the original classification were deleted from the table.

The heavy drinkers, problem or otherwise, were more common among adults with nondeprived backgrounds in the middle class (43% vs. 24%), and the difference was slightly larger among women, while the contrast is reversed in the lower strata (36% vs. 45%). Lack of self-control or discipline is frequently implicated in life problems of various sorts, and appears as a distinguishing characteristic of heavy drinkers. The problem drinkers among the Oakland males were characterized in adolescence by an excessive tendency to express needs and impulses directly, and ranked high on self-indulgence, negativism, and rebelliousness.[7] These attributes have been linked to conditions that may have been concentrated, for different reasons, in the nondeprived middle class and in the deprived working class, including deficiencies in parental regulation, in self-discipline, and in acceptance of responsibility. As Block observes, children who acquire the disciplines of a productive life are likely to have parents who display these qualities in their own lifeways as parents, companions, and workers. "The contribution of parents is to provide both illustration and motivation, guiding the child toward certain forms and timing of behavior and away from the 'natural' state of unmodulated and immediate response" (Block 1971, p. 263).

One might argue that adult situations are the primary source of variation in health states, not family background or experience, and that the observed connection between adult health and family origin (social class and economic deprivation) occurred through differences in achieved status. Indeed, numerous studies have reported a relation between intergenerational mobility or achieved status and indicators of psychological well-being—a relation that applies to the Oakland sample as well, though questions can be raised about the causal sequence. (For a review of the literature and data on the Oakland subjects, see Elder 1969b and 1970.) Is adult status or health the primary antecedent factor, or is it best to think of the relation as reciprocal? In any case, the Oakland men who achieved higher status in their worklife, relative to the position of their fathers, ranked considerably higher on productive capacity, responsibility, morale, and sense of purpose than the nonmobile, while the latter were more often viewed as brittle, easily frustrated, self-defeating, etc. Status variations were much less consequential for the psychological health of the women.

The likelihood of good health in Stewart's classification is correlated with adult status in each of the background groups, defined by social class and economic deprivation, but status does not account for our findings on adults from the middle class. Though family deprivation makes a difference in psychological well-being among men, it had no appreciable effect on their occupational attainment. Even marital achievement among women, which is correlated with economic deprivation, does not account for the more positive health of women from deprived families.

Persisting health problems of one sort or another generally imply difficulties in coping with life situations, but they do not identify underlying modes of relating to the environment, to setbacks, or to accomplishments, or modes of managing inner feelings, impulses, or needs. There is no single path to psychological misfortune, to a failure of hope, trust, and efficacy in adaptation, though failure generally augments a regressive tendency in the interactional history of person and environment. When adaptive capacities are not up to environmental deprivations or demands, the individual may enter a "vicious circle of social causation," encountering "failures that make him hesitant to try. What to others are challenges appear to him as threats; he becomes preoccupied with defense of his small claims on life at the expense of energies to invest in constructive coping. And he falls increasingly behind his fellows in acquiring the knowledge and skills that are needed for success on those occasions when he does try" (Brewster Smith, in Clausen 1968, p. 277).

These processes are reversed through successful management of life's problems. Mastery strengthens faith in one's ability to cope, in personal efficacy and hopeful outcomes, and leads to the gratifications of productive engagement. As a general rule, "when mastery of a problem does occur, the state of the organism is superior to its state prior to the time of initial confrontation, in the sense that if the same problem arises again, the organism will be able to deal with it more efficiently than before" (Scott and Howard, in Levine and Scotch 1970, p. 272). Adaptive capacities which maximize competence in problem situations reflect this process of productive engagement, an active coping orientation to the environment: coordination of personal needs, and their satisfaction, with reality demands; a capacity for sustaining effort and relationships, even in the face of obstacles; resilience and flexibility in the ability to learn and grow from mistakes, from setbacks; and a capacity to plan and mobilize resources according to internally established principles. The presence or absence of health problems, however classified, tells us very little about these attributes of the individual's response to life's problems and their relation to the Depression experience.

Two factors are of interest in the following discussion of adult psychological competence. The first is the predominant orientation of transactions between self and situations, ranging from an active, coping response to passivity and a preoccupation with matters of self-defense. The second is the transient nature of distress symptoms in the Depression. Emotional tension aroused by difficult situations is unlikely to emerge as persistent symptoms when problems are effectively coped with. Symptoms in this case reflect an underlying process of problem solving. If our assumptions are correct concerning the adaptive potential of middle-class offspring, stress in the Depression should be most transitory and least predictive of corresponding states in adulthood among these sons and daughters of deprived parents. Greater continuity would be expected among the offspring of nondeprived families and more generally among adults with backgrounds in the working class.

As our first source of data on adult competence we selected a set of five-point ratings from Reichard's assessment of the dynamic and cognitive aspects of psychological functioning. These aspects are described as ego strength, personal integration, utilization of endowment, capacity for growth, and acceptance and realistic handling of impulses. All ratings were based on typescripts of the 1958 interview; inter-rater agreement for the scales averaged .72. Ego strength refers to the capacity to assume responsibility, to show persistency and resilience in efforts, to postpone immediate pleasures for the sake of internally established values. In commerce with life situations, competence is demonstrated by tolerance of frustrations and the resilience to rise above setbacks. Integration is manifested in the life of a person who adjusts flexibly to changing internal and external circumstances and impresses others as stable and predictable; he combines insight with realistic management of impulses, effective use of innate potentials, and coordinated efforts in the accomplishment of desired goals. Utilization of endowment refers to the relation between the promise of childhood

Personality in Adult
Experience

aptitudes and their fulfillment in adult experiences, with emphasis on vocational roles. Growth potential in the range of human life takes into account the ability to profit from experience, to surmount personal and environmental handicaps, to solve major life tasks. Lastly, acceptance and realism in impulse management indicates an awareness of needs and a flexible, prudent capacity to express, suppress, or sublimate them in accord with social appropriateness.

In combination, these interrelated attributes describe a competent response to life situations. Adult offspring of the deprived middle class are exemplars of this adaptive stance; they were judged more favorably on psychological competence and health than any other group in the sample. Since these results were similar for men and women, we combined the sexes in each of the deprivational class subgroups, as shown in table 12.

Table 12   Clinical Ratings of Men and Women on
                  Psychological Functioning, by Economic
                  Deprivation and Class Origin, in
                  Mean Scores

Clinical Ratings (Reichard, 1958)	Middle Class		Working Class	
	Nondeprived (N = 25)	Deprived (N = 30)	Nondeprived (N = 11)	Deprived (N = 26)
Ego strength	3.24	3.82	3.32	3.06
Ego integration	2.84	3.43	2.86	2.33
Utilization of endowment	2.73	3.40	3.59	2.71
Capacity for growth	2.54	3.27	2.50	2.40
Acceptance and realistic handling of impulses	2.46	3.22	2.32	2.27

Note. The difference between group means (nondeprived vs. deprived) is statistically significant (p < .05) on all five ratings for the middle-class subjects. Only "utilization of endowment" varied significantly by deprivation among the working-class subjects.

The sons and daughters of the deprived middle class rank well above the nondeprived of similar origin on ability to surmount difficulties and profit from experience, to postpone immediate gratification for the benefits of long-range accomplishment, and to use talents to their fullest advantage. Of these adaptive strategies, use of endowment has special significance. The more able in the deprived middle class were also the more highly motivated, in line with the presumed effect of status loss on motivation. Folk accounts of hardship as a spur to ambition find modest support in these lives, which escaped the dual handicap of a lower-status home and limited ability.

These differences also appear in the family correlates of two contrasting personality types which were identified in a factor analysis of adult Q-sort profiles (see note 5).[8] One type, which includes a fourth of the sample, is most appropriately described as "nonresilient" or vulnerable. The men in this sample were seen as basically anxious and hostile, preoccupied with personal adequacy, uncomfortable with uncertainty, inclined to withdraw in adverse situations, and defensive. Among women these attributes were coupled with a persistent need for reassurance, moodiness, self-pity, and concern with social impressions. The other type, indicating a healthy, resilient personality, included a third of the adults. The men ranked high on independence and responsibility, gave impressions of a productive, zestful life, and expressed themselves in an assertive, sex-appropriate manner. They ranked lower than any other personality type on predispositions to failure in demanding situations, on reluctance to act, to pity self, or to escape from adversity. Resourcefulness, dependability, and a sense of meaning in life were outstanding qualities of the resilient women. They were described as warm, vital persons with an understanding nature.

An adaptive, competent self stands out among the offspring of middle-class homes, and especially among the sons and daughters of deprived parents (45% vs. 32% of the nondeprived). Few adults from the middle class were characterized as vulnerable or brittle, but those who were were mainly the offspring of nondeprived parents (25% vs. 9%). Neither profile, mastery or otherwise, varied appreciably by family deprivation among adults from the working class; 43 percent were typed as nonresilient and 16 percent as mastery-oriented.

From the data examined to this point, we can identify three relatively distinct groups with respect to adult health. Ranked from high to low on health and competence, they are: deprived middle class, nondeprived middle class, and working class. The superior health of adults from the deprived middle class bears little resemblance to their Depression experience or to traditional thinking on stress and illness. Some growth-promoting experiences in family deprivation were expected among these adults, owing to their family resources and adaptive potential, but deprivation was not expected to have a general positive effect on adult health.

Another way of viewing this effect is to focus on adults from relatively well-off families in the middle class (the nondeprived) and their surprising resemblance on symptoms and adaptive deficiencies to working-class offspring. They were a privileged group in the Depression and entered adult roles at a relatively late age. Why are these adults not the healthiest, most competent members of the Oakland cohort? It seems that a childhood which shelters the young from the hardships

Personality in Adult Experience

of life consequently fails to develop or test adaptive capacities which are called upon in life crises. To engage and manage real-life (though not excessive) problems in childhood and adolescence is to participate in a sort of apprenticeship for adult life. Preparedness has been identified repeatedly as a key factor in the adaptive potential and psychological health of persons in novel situations; ill health among rural factory workers, for instance, has been found to vary with their preparation for such work.[9]

On most indicators, health status in adulthood is negatively related to family deprivation in the working class, but the association is surprisingly weak and unstable when we consider the array of stress factors in the deprived working class: broken families, heavy drinking, unemployment, the stigma of public relief, etc. The average family income in this stratum was substantially lower than that of nondeprived families in the working class. Yet despite these differences and the greater prevalence of emotional distress among children in deprived households, variations in family deprivation made little reliable difference in adult health. The most salient factor in the health of these adults is their origin in the working class. In the Depression, working-class children were lower than middle-class children on resources which tend to enhance adaptive prospects in adult life—intelligence, aspirations, and social rewards in peer associations and school.

The health outcomes we have observed suggest that indicators of emotional stress during the Depression were mainly transient responses to problem situations among persons from the deprived middle class. On self-reports and mother's observations, they ranked considerably higher on symptoms of stress such as hypersensitivity, emotionality, and anger than the nondeprived, and yet their health status as adults is more positive. In the light of this apparent reversal, we recall signs of adaptive variations in the 30s, in active, social responses versus passive withdrawal, which favored the adult prognosis of children from the deprived middle class (chapter 6). The nondeprived who felt unhappy and socially rejected by classmates were oriented to a fantasy world of imaginary friends; they generally preferred these friends to age-mates and ranked among the most unhappy, passive, and unpopular adolescents in the sample, according to field observations. By contrast, social unhappiness was not expressed in withdrawal or passivity among children in the deprived middle class; and it did not lessen their social interests or popularity among peers.

A more direct test of the "transient response" concept is provided by a comparison of the relation between adolescent and adult psychological states among persons from nondeprived and deprived families. Self-report scales were selected for this analysis from each of the two periods: the adolescent's report of emotional states in the junior high years, as measured by indices of emotionality and social unhappiness (described in chapter 6); and three scales from the Minnesota Multiphasic Personality Inventory, administered in the 1953–54 follow-up—Rosen's anxiety reaction scale, the Iowa manifest anxiety scale, and Barron's scale of ego strength. Correlations between the two sets of scales were calculated only for the offspring of middle-class parents, since few adults from the working class completed the inventory.

Psychological continuity from adolescence to middle age is more pronounced among adults from relatively well-to-do families than among the offspring of deprived parents. In the former group, high scorers on emotional tensions during the 30s (e.g., "Do you worry a good deal about things that might happen which you would not like?") showed some tendency to maintain this position on anxiety scales over twenty years later and to rank low on adaptive capacities (indexed by Barron's measure of ego strength). These patterns were reversed among the sons and daughters of deprived, middle-class parents. That is, high scorers on emotionality in adolescence were less likely than their opposites to rank high on the adult anxiety scales and low on adaptive capacities.[10] This difference and corresponding results on social unhappiness can only be regarded as suggestive in view of the small number of cases and our weak measures of adolescent health. Nevertheless, the data do point to a number of resourceful, competent adults among persons who grew up in deprived families and showed signs of emotional disturbance as adolescents.

If the experience of economic deprivation was an instrumental factor in developing the adaptive capacities of some middle-class children, we know little about the processes or mechanisms in this outcome; about the kinds or configurations of experience in the Depression; or about the specifics of interaction between deprivational conditions and adaptive repertoires in the life course. Detailed information would be needed on family situation, parents, and child—before, during, and after the Depression—to fill in these lacunae. More generally, we find that such linkages have been neglected in longitudinal research, and especially in cases of divergent lines of development. Explanation of psychological patterns in the life course has taken a back seat to preoccupation with the childhood predictors of adult outcomes and modes of psychological continuity. For example, Anderson found (from the analysis of longitudinal data) that a significant number of adolescents who had experienced difficulties in family and school demonstrated unexpected competence in "meeting their obligations and responsibilities" as young adults. "Putting them on their own," he concludes, "brought out qualities which had not appeared to the same

Personality in Adult
Experience

degree in their early school and home experiences. It is difficult to determine how much of this is the result of growth and how much the result of actual change in the situation."[11] Nevertheless, it is clear that ex post facto accounts of this sort do not help much in understanding such outcomes. We would need to know something about how these individuals differed in the course of development and life situations from persons who showed a high degree of stability on problematic coping between adolescence and adulthood.

Parenthood as Problem Situation and Growth Experience

When we think of a common life experience which tests adaptive capacities, the transition to parenthood immediately comes to mind. This event, even more than marriage, signifies entry into the responsibilities of adult life. Few events bring greater change or more novel demands in the lives of young adults. Change is especially dramatic for the working woman who suddenly finds herself unprepared for the obligations, restrictions, and adjustments which infant care and rearing entail. Problems tend to arise from the abrupt curtailment of extra-familial activities, from the unexpected demands of child care, the constraints of reduced income, and loss of accustomed companionship and sex life. As a form of group expansion, parenthood puts to a test the ability to manage finite or limited resources—time, energy, knowledge, and income. Adaptive needs are mirrored by recognized deficiencies in each of these respects. The firstborn thus creates a new situation, which is soon defined as a problem when customary patterns and resources are found wanting or inappropriate.[12]

Parenthood has special significance to the sons and daughters of deprived parents in the Oakland cohort. More than other members of the sample, they derived much satisfaction from family activity and were likely to regard children as one of the most valuable aspects of their marriage. But equally important is the parallel between the social requirements and constraints of parenthood and those of economically deprived households in the Depression. The former event increases consumption demands while the latter reduced supplies in meeting family needs, but the adaptive problem in both situations entails "getting along on less," that is, developing new forms of resource management and application. Increased labor demands in the household are also common to both situations, and would have similar consequences in the lives of the Oakland women; increased involvement in the household at the expense of social activities in the community. Assuming that household responsibilities generally included child care, realistic preparation for maternal activity was a potentially common experience among women who grew up in deprived families. In these respects, the Depression experience can be viewed as an apprenticeship for the adaptive requirements of parenthood.

Beyond the matter of preparation, one would expect value commitments to be a factor in how responsibilities are managed. Sacrifice is presumably most acceptable and self-fulfilling when the activity itself is meaningfully related to a valued goal or state; compare, for instance, the birth of an unwanted child with the birth of a child in a family where parental sentiments coincide with social expectations. But we cannot assume that acceptance of parenthood was linked with family deprivation. When we asked about the importance of family and children in the 1964 survey, the initial problems of parenthood for most adults had long been solved or bypassed. A majority, in fact, had experienced the full range of child-rearing tasks, from infancy through adolescence. At this stage the valuing of children could be viewed as an outgrowth of success in child rearing.

We first asked parents at what age their children were most enjoyable or the greatest problem; what parental experiences were most gratifying or most stressful. In order to ensure some commonality in parental experience, we excluded all adults from the analysis who did not have a child who was at least sixteen years of age in 1964. The second set of questions focused on a sense of adequacy in coping with parental problems, with emphasis on its relation to experiences in the Depression and life course. How was a person's life changed by "having children"? Each component of the parental experience—situation, sense of adequacy, and personal growth or change—was viewed from the respondent's perspective.

Both fathers and mothers were more likely to associate a particular age of their children with troubles than with enjoyment. Most mothers were unable to identify any one age period as the most satisfying—"a joy at all times" roughly describes their sentiments. Infancy was least satisfying, according to its few nominations, followed by the years of secondary school (table A–30). If we consider both joys and problems, latency or the grade school period stands out as the most satisfying age for parents, while late adolescence, equivalent to senior high through advanced education, lives up to its popular image as the most troublesome time, especially for fathers.

The most difficult age was not a likely candidate for the most pleasurable, though a third of the parents did select the same general age on both criteria. This concurrence in peak experience, positive and nega-

     Personality in Adult Experience

tive, increased sharply from adults who favored the preadolescent years to those who expressed greatest satisfaction with the teen or adolescent period (from 24 to 48 percent).

Parental satisfactions were associated with the rewards of being needed or feeling useful; with the fascination of seeing a child grow, mature, acquire new skills, etc.; and with the child's progress from dependence to self-reliance and independent mastery. These experiences were the most frequently mentioned sources of gratification when the Oakland parents were asked (in an open-ended question) to describe experiences which made a particular period of child rearing unusually satisfying. Approximately a third of the responses were assigned to each category. As might be expected, parental usefulness declined in prevalence by age of child, from 75 percent in the preschool/infancy category to 22 percent in the junior high years, with no mentions for the oldest children. Self-reliance of the child, on the other hand, more than trebled in frequency of mention from the youngest to the oldest age groups (20 to 66 percent). "Growth experience" was most often cited by parents who found greatest pleasure in their children at the latency or junior high age—approximately 48 percent.

More than any other age, "latency" offers multiple parental satisfactions and minimizes the contrasting problems of extreme dependency and independence. Rapid growth, a need and respect for parents, and modest self-reliance without excessive peer pressure—these and other rewards are combined in unique fashion within the grade school age. Difficulties with children of preschool age or younger were mainly restricted to the child's dependence on parents—his timidity, lack of understanding, inability to communicate, to care for self, etc.; and to demands on parental resources—time, energy, finances, etc. (46 percent of each type). The first problem was rarely cited for older children, though an expanded set of demands emerged in the junior high years as a difficult problem for parents; these include peer pressures, participation in unsupervised activities, school problems, economic needs, etc. No other problem came close to independence conflicts in assessments of children in high school; three-fourths of the parents cited difficulties of this sort.

Neither the type of parental problem nor the time period defined as most stressful or pleasurable were reliable indicators of subjective competence as a mother or father. Parents who felt the early years were more satisfying than adolescence did not view themselves as less able in the parental role than adults who enjoyed their children at all ages, or most of all as teenagers. The valuing of children and family activity was also unrelated to evaluation of adequacy. Our measure of competence in this analysis is a four-response question which asked each adult (in 1964) whether they had ever felt inadequate as a parent. With the exception of three respondents, all parents acknowledged that they had felt inadequate on at least some occasions; 26 percent replied "lots of times," 16 percent "fairly often," and 55 percent "once in a while." We shall interpret the latter response as a generalized sense of parental adequacy.

We looked for the origins of parental adequacy in four variables of childhood: class background, family deprivation, household responsibilities, and family size. Class differences in parental example and competence, family stability, and problem-solving skills all favor a middle-class background in the etiology of parental adequacy. Experiences analogous to parenthood were associated with membership in deprived families, with household chores, and with a number of siblings; a girl's child-care duties, for instance, are likely to increase with the number of younger siblings in her family. The data, however, show no evidence of these linkages, except in number of siblings; subjective adequacy was directly related to family size among women, even with class origin and adult education controlled. Only children were less likely than women with two or more siblings to report that they seldom felt inadequate (33 vs. 70 percent). On the debit side, neither family deprivation nor household chores were correlated with parental competence among men or women, and the effects of family status were just the reverse of our prediction. Parents who felt most effective were more often the children of low- than of high-status parents. Perceived inadequacies or shortcomings, in other words, were more frequently cited by the offspring of middle-class homes.[13]

On the surface, at least, the distribution of parental adequacy by class background did not mesh with known sources of interpersonal competence and is at variance with our findings on psychological health. From another angle, however, the acknowledgment of frequent shortcomings can be interpreted as sensitivity to the multidimensional complexities and limitations of parenthood. "Being a parent" is likely to be viewed as a broader, more variegated and challenging task by the well-educated adult from a middle-class home, an activity mainly geared to the developmental needs of the child. Perceived inadequacies would arise from these sensitivities and standards of excellence. Adult correlates of parental inadequacy in the Oakland sample generally correspond with this interpretation; shortcomings are most frequently reported by the college-educated adult in the upper middle class, regardless of background in the Depression or number of children in the family of procreation. Both educational attainment and class position are predictive of acknowledged limitations in the parental role among men and especially women.[14] The meaningfulness of this asso-

Personality in Adult
Experience

ciation is evident in a sampling of reasons which were offered for expressed deficiencies: the inability to protect children from making mistakes or harming themselves; difficulty in understanding or communicating with offspring; problems in motivating, guiding, and disciplining. The vast majority of reasons describe problems that are inherent in a developmental, child-sensitized form of upbringing.

In this regard, it is worth noting a parallel finding from a survey of American housewives (Lopata 1971, chap. 4). The problematic aspects of motherhood increased by educational level, even though objective difficulties were greater among mothers with less schooling. The latter frequently denied having any problems at all, or referred to the perfunctory routine of "bringing up kids." "Problems faced by this segment of the population are feared, not tackled, and best not even mentioned. It takes the confidence of at least partial competence and a breadth of perspective for a person to admit having problems in fulfilling the obligations of a whole complex of changing social relations and social roles" (ibid., pp. 212–13). The seemingly infinite dimensions of child rearing, of elasticity and expandability, do have psychological risks, however, in an exaggerated investment of ego and time. Slater parodies this tendency in his spoof of the middle-class fetish in child rearing: "In our society, it is as if every middle-class parent were determined to rear a John Stuart Mill; it turns one a bit queasy to see them walking about with signs on them so their three-year olds will learn to read, or complaining that their children are not learning enough in nursery school" (Slater 1970, p. 66).

Views of parental adequacy and experience are not likely to remain constant as demands and skills change from the anticipatory stage of parenthood to the youngest child's departure from home. Romantic images of parenthood tend to stress the rewards of having children: personal enrichment and self-fulfillment, among others. The makings of a crisis or problem are seen in the clash between this imagery and the realities of parental responsibility which call for substantial adjustments in priorities and life style. These realities and their personal consequences appear to be most salient to couples in adapting to their firstborn (see note 12). A more balanced view, between self-benefits and responsibility, would be expected among the Oakland parents during the middle years of life.

To avoid prestructured replies, we asked each parent an open-ended question on the most important way in which their lives or personalities had been changed by having children. Responses were then sorted into conceptually homogeneous categories. Half of the adults stressed some aspect of personal gain, apart from additional responsibility, such as the development of greater insight, tolerance, and understanding; the excitement, interest value, and youthfulness of being with children; and a sense of accomplishment, fulfillment, a richer life, etc. A third mentioned aspects of responsibility: the developmental task of guiding, disciplining, or shaping young lives, and the maturing influence of this experience; or the burdens of this task, phrased in terms of personal constraints and limitations—more concerns, less freedom, etc. An equal number of responses were assigned to each category. The remaining answers were too vague, general, or idiosyncratic to permit classification.

Though responsibility was mentioned more often by men than by women, this impact was associated with feelings of inadequacy in each sex group: two-fifths of the adults who felt inadequate "lots of times" compared to a fourth of the parents who acknowledged such feelings only occasionally. Awareness of parental shortcomings is thus related to the belief that child bearing is a demanding activity. In the judgment of an experienced father of three children, "one becomes a more mature adult by having children."

Experiences in the Depression have more to do with evaluations of parental experience than variations in adult status and circumstance. While adults in the upper middle class were more aware of their deficiencies as parents than persons of lower status, they did not differ on their interpretation of how children change an adult's life. An emphasis on parental responsibility, as challenge or burden, is related to family deprivation, not to adult or family status. Responsibility stands out among the childhood experiences of adults who grew up in deprived families, and they tended to stress this aspect of their experiences as parents; personal gratification or enrichment was cited more often by the offspring of nondeprived homes. Among adults who mentioned one of these two effects, responsibility appears mainly in the deprived group (49 percent versus a fifth of the nondeprived); similar differences were obtained on both the burdensome and challenging aspects. The continuing influence of family hardship is most evident among women; all but one of the adults who saw motherhood in terms of added responsibility were daughters of deprived parents in the middle and working class.

One may be tempted to view these interpretations of parental experience as reflections of interpersonal competence; on intuitive grounds, we sense an important difference in the psychology of an adult who feels he has gained understanding and emotional vitality from rearing his children and one impressed by the constraints of the parental role. The critical flaw in this judgment is that views of parenthood are likely to tell us at least as much about the meaning of preadult experiences as of parental experience. Whether recognized and desired or not, a parent's childhood intrudes in the present through interpretations that

Personality in Adult Experience

inform and structure his own behavior in child rearing. Responsibility, its constraints and challenge, is part of this framework among the off-spring of deprived families. Conditions in the 30s heightened their obligations to the family, and value commitments of this sort are expressed in adult values. Men who prize dependability in children, for instance, were likely to have handled work roles in the 30s as members of deprived households (see chapter 4). Self-oriented concerns were more possible for children in the nondeprived middle class, and their subsequent interpretation of personal growth in parenthood is generally compatible with this background.

Reviewing the Past

Different issues on the Depression experience are posed by looking forward and backward in the life span. Up to this point we have mainly proceeded from conditions in the 30s, from family deprivation, adaptations, and related meanings, to their manifestations in adult personality and life experience. Another way of viewing conditions in the Depression is to determine their meaning in adult memories. To what extent and how are they remembered and acknowledged? Are there differences in the chronology of life satisfactions between adults from deprived families who remember traumatic events in the Depression and those who recall no particular hardship? Does the acknowledgment of severe hardships signify a belief that life has become more satisfying since the 30s? By viewing Depression experiences from the perspective of middle age, we should gain more insight into their effect on the life course of emotional satisfaction.

Prior to the 1958 interview, each participant in the follow-up was asked to chart the high and low points in his or her life, using a ten-point scale for each year. The most positive evaluation is indicated by a score of 10. To increase the stability of these ratings, we averaged values in each of three time periods: the Depression decade, 1940–49 and 1950–58. Memories of the Depression experience were solicited by an interview question. All recollections were coded in terms of the implied impact of family hardship on the respondent:[15] severe—family hardships were described as very difficult, as causing much suffering; moderate—some hardships reported, though not extreme; and no recalled or reported adverse effect. Of the 88 codable responses, 15 percent were assigned to the extreme category and 17 percent to the moderate category. The large percentage of adults who gave no indication that life in the 30s was adversely affected by economic conditions may be attributed in part to ineffective probes, defensiveness, etc. Especially painful experiences were common among adults in the extreme category: the humiliation of having to wear cardboard in the soles of shoes, haughty relatives or neighbors, the shame of being on relief or of seeing father unemployed, not having enough fuel to heat the house, having to double up with grandparents, the deterioration of parental morale and health.

Memories of hard times were associated with objective deprivations and the feeling that life had become more rewarding since the Depression. Heavy economic loss, father's unemployment, and dependence on public assistance were common events in the early life history of adults with vivid memories of the Depression's impact. All members of the "extreme" group experienced at least one of these conditions, and a majority at least two. A relatively common impression among these respondents is described by a sales manager, the son of a man who lost his hardware store in the Depression as well as most of his savings. "The Depression had a big effect at the time. I think it set my father back quite a bit. Don't think he's ever fully recovered from it. The Depression years very definitely stick out. It was like starting life over again, as folks lost everything they had." Memories of moderate difficulty or stress were more evenly divided among the offspring of non-deprived and deprived homes.

Memories of the Depression seem to have functioned as a standard for evaluating subsequent life experiences. If life bottomed out in the 30s, the only viable option for evaluative change in later life was an upswing in fortunes. In fact, a sense of psychological well-being or satisfaction did increase from the 30s to middle age among men and women who remember severe hardships; from a low point in the Depression decade to a high point thereafter ($\overline{X}$s $= 5.5$ vs. 6.3). The opposite trend appears among adults who recalled no adverse effect; in this group, the years of secondary school were substantially more rewarding than experiences in the 1940s and 50s (from 6.8 to 5.4). Differences in adult status and social mobility did not account for these gradients, even though a positive trend in life satisfaction is slightly related to a pattern of intergenerational mobility.

Memory may increase understanding and acceptance of past experiences which cannot be changed—conflicts, humiliations, missed opportunities, etc. Thinking about the past leads to "reconsideration of previous experiences and their meanings," "often with concomitant revised or expanded understanding. Such reorganization of past experience may provide a more valid picture, giving new and significant meaning to one's life" (Butler 1963). Life reviews may also yield defensive illusions of the good or triumphal past; and greater preoccupation with fantasies of the past than with current realities. Illusions of this sort, denial, selective recall, and other mental sleights of hand are

Personality in Adult
Experience

implied by disparities between memories and Depression realities, but it is extremely difficult, with available information, to explain why some adults from deprived families readily divulged past hardships and others did not. More clinical evidence and expertise would be needed to interpret the psychological significance of these incongruities.

The risk in using memories for a description of emotional well-being in the Depression is illustrated by the reports of two men from deprived working-class families. Both were employed in lower middle class jobs in 1958 and were rated equally high on defensiveness by trained clinicians. One of the respondents had nothing to say or report on his more painful experiences in a family which had lost nearly two-thirds of its income by 1934. When asked how the Depression had affected his family, he described his father (a self-employed craftsman) as doing well. He claimed good fortune as a boy in not having to do without basic necessities, as many others had to, and remembered his adolescence as a very "happy" time. But an interviewer in 1934 pictured the father as "quite discouraged" and preoccupied, tending to isolate himself from family members for long periods. The family had just lost its rented home and was forced to move into the cramped quarters of a relative. Reports from the mother described her son as tense, quick to anger, and ashamed to bring friends home. On the positive side, the boy was well liked by his classmates and achieved some prominence in student activities. These social experiences were the "good times" in his adult memories. The other adult remembered his family and social life as we know it from materials collected in the 30s; a severe loss of income followed by mother's illness, occasional heavy drinking by father, the boy's work, and a limited social life.

Beyond their personal significance, images of the Depression have implications for the transmission of this experience to the offspring of Depression children. The Oakland parents who fail to recall the rigors of childhood in the 30s obviously have a different story to tell their children than adults who vividly recall hardships. Nothing has been recorded about the moral and social meanings of the Depression among families of the Oakland adults—the frequency with which Depression experiences are discussed with children, the use of Depression examples to underscore values, etc. However, suggestive evidence along this line is reported by a 1965 survey of 171 University of California students who were born in the mid-40s, a period which coincides with the childbearing years of the Oakland cohort. The frequency with which parents discussed experiences in the Depression was correlated with degree of hardship, as perceived by offspring, and both factors were predictive of youth who believed that parents used aspects of the Depression experience to emphasize certain values.[16] These students were also most likely to claim that much of their knowledge of the Depression was learned from parents and that they had been personally influenced in this respect. Prominent value influences included a greater appreciation of social issues, of contemporary opportunities and advantages, and of the need for economic security.

Failure to make deprivations in the 30s visible and understandable to children is evident in the lives of some adults in the Oakland sample who became aware of what these conditions "really meant" relatively late in life. In the case of at least two deprived middle-class families, parents appeared to shield their offspring from the meaning of family changes. The son of one of these families recalled that he did not "fully realize there was such a thing going on," though the father lost his clothing store and the mother had a nervous breakdown. "I didn't realize it at the time, but there came the day when my mother couldn't take it any more, and it was my father's inner strength, determination, and optimism that kept things rolling along."

In the experience of the Oakland adults, the emotional trajectory of life, whether up or down, is related to memories of the Depression. In general, life is on the upswing for adults who remember the Depression as a traumatic experience, regardless of differing achievements in family or occupational roles; their adult years are rated higher on satisfaction than their childhood years in the Depression. Is this upward trend more generally linked to deprivational conditions in the 30s? Are adults from deprived families more likely than the nondeprived to regard the Depression as the lowest point in life?

To compare trends in life gratification, we assigned each adult to one of three categories according to ratings on the life chart; a low point in the Depression decade to a high in the adult years (upward); the opposite pattern from high to low (downward); and a mixed or residual category. An upward trend was reported by 60 percent of the men and by 42 percent of the women; the downward group includes a fourth of the men and 40 percent of the women. Though men from deprived families were no higher on achieved status than the nondeprived, they were most likely to report an upward trend in life satisfaction from the Depression to middle age (81% vs. 47%). Likewise, high points in adult life were more often reported by women from deprived homes, from 54 percent to a third of the nondeprived. These differences were found among the offspring of both middle- and working-class families.

The relation between economic deprivation and life trends in satisfaction implies an intervening perception of the family situation as a stressful experience. While much evidence indirectly describes this definition of the situation, the Oakland respondents were never adequately questioned in the 30s on their perception of family well-being, on the

Personality in Adult
Experience

extent to which parents had a difficult time in making ends meet. The most appropriate index of perceived distress is provided by a question on mother's emotional state ("I wish mother were happier," in the senior high questionnaire). Most children who wished mother were happier were members of deprived families and tended to describe themselves as less happy and accepted by peers when compared to other children (chapter 6). Girls were more disturbed by mother's unhappiness than boys and, indeed, were more likely to reflect this stress in their life evaluations as adults. The worst years of life for these women extended from junior high to the end of senior high; thereafter, ratings of satisfaction increased through the 1950s. Nearly three-fourths of the daughters with unhappy mothers showed this upward trend, while the opposite trend was more common among the daughters of happy mothers; slightly more than half of these women located the high point of life in the Depression decade. In contrast to these variations, the Oakland men showed no reliable differences in life evaluation by perception of mother.

Through memories and actual experiences in the 30s, hardships in the Depression made a substantial difference in the way the Oakland adults have charted their life gratification. The observed variations are consistent with the theory that Depression experiences established a frame of reference for defining life periods as relatively good or bad times. From a relative perspective, adults who remember what it was like to have very little in the 30s appear to be more appreciative of their life situation in the more affluent, secure years of the 40s and 50s.

Perspectives on Politics and the Future

Adult health, the meaning of parenthood, and reviews of the past all refer to the personal experience of individuals. In each case we have examined ways of viewing and responding to life's problems, their relation to aspects of the Depression experience and to psychological consequences in adulthood. But the implications of economic hardship, for problem definition and response, extend beyond personal experience to generalized beliefs on focal issues in the 30s and to preferred lines of governmental response to the economic standstill. Collective endorsement of a more hopeful approach to the economic crisis is expressed in the unprecedented electoral shift to the Democratic party in 1932.

The life span of the Oakland cohort traverses an extraordinary range of focal orientations in American society, from the isolationism and domestic preoccupations of the 20s and 30s to involvement in World War II, to the birth of the United Nations, the postwar reconstruction of Europe, the specters of international communism and nuclear war. The decade of the 30s was a formative stage in the political maturity and social awareness of the Oakland adults. Where parents suffered unemployment and heavy economic losses, domestic and economic problems were of paramount concern. In the midst of crisis, a vote for Roosevelt expressed a desire for change for the better. The parental vote and shifts to the Democratic party have enduring implications for "children of the Depression" in the well-known pattern of intergenerational continuity in party affiliation; in the mature years of life, children tend to follow the party affiliation of their parents.[17]

These considerations suggest four adult perspectives on matters which are likely to be associated with economic hardship in the 30s: preference for the Democratic party, greater concern over America's domestic than international problems, preoccupation with economic problems on the domestic front, and an optimistic outlook toward the economic opportunities of contemporary youth. The political effect is based on the assumption of continuity in party preference between adolescence and middle age among the Oakland adults, regardless of intergenerational change in status, and yet we know from a number of studies that class position, among other factors, makes a difference in party preference. As in the case of values, political continuity may be dependent on the degree of social continuity. This qualification also applies to sensitivity regarding economic problems. The connection between economic deprivation and an optimistic outlook for young people is based on comparisons between the Depression experience and the present. As they view the present and the future, adults with a background of family hardship should be especially aware of the economic advantages and opportunities of their own children and of young people in general.

We have noted two plausible linkages between economic deprivation and preference for the Democratic party in the Oakland sample: the parental example or influence in politics, and the sensitizing effect of economic conditions and political climate in focal issues and politics. This effect extends beyond the family and applies especially to the late adolescent years of political awareness, the late 30s. However, these years do not correspond to the age at which a new generation is thought to be most vulnerable or receptive to political change—the age of majority and full citizenship responsibilities. The Oakland adults attained voting age in the early 40s, not in the Depression. Nevertheless, voting studies during the 40s and 50s indicate that Democratic ties were more likely to be developed by people who came of voting age

Personality in Adult
                                                Experience

during the Depression decade and early war years than by persons in adjacent historical periods.[18] This effect should be most evident among the offspring of deprived families in the Oakland sample.

Expressions of political change in family life have special relevance to members of the sample since they were dependents throughout the 30s. The presumed shift of deprived parents to support for Roosevelt runs counter to known bases of party choice. For instance, the heaviest losses in the middle class were concentrated among men who have traditionally supported the Republican party as advocating individualism and free enterprise. In the Oakland sample, these include self-employed businessmen, brokers, and real estate operators. There is evidence, from the Lynds' study of Middletown (1937, p. 473), that many traditional Republicans switched their support to Roosevelt through the 1936 elections, if only reluctantly.[19]

The ideal approach for identifying the political impact of parental shifts in party preference would include measurements of parents' party preference and issue orientations before, during, and after the 30s, along with information on their offspring's social-political attitudes in the Depression and party preference in adulthood. Our only option, however, was to use data from adult follow-ups (1958–64); suitable data on politics were not collected in the 30s. Retrospective reports in these follow-ups provided information on the father's party preference in the Depression; 61 percent of the fathers were described as Republicans, 30 percent as Democrats, and the remainder as independents or other. Support for the Democratic party came mainly from men with a Catholic or foreign background. But even with adjustments for class and religion, this political preference increased with income loss. A third of the deprived fathers in the middle class were described as Democrats, when adjustments were made for religion and ethnicity, compared to only 13 percent of the nondeprived. In the working class, the Democratic proportion ranged from 62 percent in the deprived group to a third of the nondeprived.

If economic loss was a causal factor in the Democratic preference of fathers, its effect should be mediated in part by discontent with the status quo or living conditions. We assume in this case that dissatisfaction is related to both deprivation and affiliation with the Democratic party. The best available indicator of discontent is the interviewer rating on mother's dissatisfaction with her lot; this rating was correlated with economic loss in the middle class (see chapter 3), and is also predictive of father's preference for the Democratic party. Economic deprivation did not affect father's politics among families in which mother was highly dissatisfied with her status. The largest variation in party preference emerged between extreme groups on both measures of

deprivation. Under conditions of nondeprived status and relative satisfaction, the Democrats claimed only 5 percent of the fathers compared
to 54 percent in the deprived, dissatisfied group. From these differences
we conclude that deprivation, in its objective and subjective forms, was
an important factor in the Democratic appeal to fathers in the Oakland
sample.

The significance of these differences is seen in the degree of political
continuity across the two generations; father and offspring agree on
party preference in four out of five cases, and most children of deprived
fathers in both the middle and the working class (slightly more than
80 percent) are Democrats. The popularity of the Democratic party
among children of deprived families holds despite their upward mobility. Whether high or low in class position, Catholic or Protestant, the
offspring of deprived parents rank consistently higher than the nondeprived on preference for the Democratic party (see table A–31).

The politics of adults from deprived homes adds support to our
expectation that domestic problems, especially those of an economic
nature, would be of great concern to them. During the 1958 interview,
each respondent was asked for his views on the most important problems facing the nation, and on what should be done to insure peace.
These problems were coded into homogeneous categories. Despite the
"Cold War" climate of the 50s and related international conflicts, only
a third of the respondents mentioned international problems of one
kind or another, including global war. At the head of the list of domestic problems was a perceived decline in the moral quality of life, with
emphasis on excessive materialism (36 percent), followed by economic
problems—wasteful spending, taxation, the possibility of recessions or
another depression (32 percent); and racial unrest, conflict, discrimination, etc. (28 percent). Issues akin to McCarthyism, such as communist or subversive influences on the home front, were mentioned by less
than 10 percent of the sample. The Eisenhower years were generally
good from the workingman's standpoint, despite ups and downs, and
only a sixth of the Oakland adults expressed any concern over prospects
of a severe recession or depression. Sensitivity to this issue shows little
relation to the severity of past hardships in the Great Depression.

Only issues of a domestic nature (spending, taxation) varied by
experiences in the Depression; no variations were found in concern
with international issues. The big problem to adults from nondeprived
homes in both social classes was moral decay; materialism and related
ills were placed at the top in a ranking of all domestic issues, while
problems of governmental expenditures and taxation were placed at the
bottom. Nearly half of the adults criticized manifestations of materialism in American life—"the greed for money." Though members of a

Personality in Adult
Experience

generation which is commonly stereotyped by the attractions of money and property, their views on materialism have much in common with those held in the 1970s by youth from the upper middle class. As one youth put it, not immodestly, my parents' concerns are "money and security"; I intend to make mine "freedom and learning."[20] We have no basis for concluding that money and possessions are unusually important in the life styles of adults from deprived circumstances in the Depression, though it is apparent that they were less inclined to stress the evils of materialism than the nondeprived. Only a fourth of the deprived cited issues of this sort. In the economic realm, slightly more than a third of the offspring of deprived families focused (to an equal degree) on wasteful government expenditures and the inequities of taxation, followed closely by racial problems and materialism, compared to only a tenth of the nondeprived. Of all the issues mentioned, only economic issues extended uniformly across political parties. With the data at hand, we cannot do justice in any sense to the complexity of attitudes toward economic issues and their relation to aspects of the Depression experience. Nevertheless, the differing points of emphasis by economic conditions generally parallel common observations.

An inward-looking perspective on national problems is reminiscent of the depressed, isolationist 30s, and yet we find no evidence of deprivational experiences in this outlook. Our finding is based on the analysis of issues (noted above) and by a comparison of three general approaches to the quest for peace that were mentioned in the 1958 interview: isolation—strengthen the United States and stay out of world entanglements; internationalism—material assistance to other countries, international exchange of citizens, strengthen the United Nations, etc.; and a dual focus on domestic and international efforts. Isolationism was the least popular of the strategies (21 percent), followed by a balanced effort at home and abroad (27 percent), and internationalism (35 percent). Sentiments favoring involvement in world affairs, whether coupled with domestic programs or not, were unrelated to experiences in the Depression. These views do not, however, show the more discriminating order of priorities. Values are a matter of choice among alternatives, and no attempt was made by the interviewers to force this choice.

When we turn to the adults' outlook for young people of the late 50s, including offspring, the dominant theme shifts from problems to opportunities. By and large, both men and women in the Oakland cohort have made a much better life for themselves than they knew in the Depression, at least in terms of economic welfare. The late 40s were good times for the most part, though not as rewarding, in their judgment, as the late 50s for young people starting out life. Three-fourths of the respondents in the 1958 interview felt that opportunities to get ahead were greater for young people then than they had been a generation before. Opportunities were either better or the same; poorer life chances were seldom mentioned.

Optimism—a durable feature of parental thinking on the future of children—typifies the outlook of parents in the Oakland sample. More significant and consequential, however, are the specific desires which parents would like to see fulfilled in their children's lives. One theory views such desires as an expression of felt deprivations in the parent's own life. This linkage is documented in a 1971 study by the explicit hope of some parents that their "activist" college offspring "would be more successful than they had been in leading self-fulfilling, socially responsible lives rather than participating in the 'rat race,' the suburban way of life" (Flacks 1970, p. 347). This theory also appears in many folk interpretations of the behavior of Depression-reared parents. Thus children are indulged because parents want to provide them with all of the things they were deprived of in childhood. Parental wishes are linked to the problematic aspects of life in the Depression. Along this line, one would expect "economic security," "a good education," and "emotional health and happiness" to be among the most prominent desires of the Oakland adults who grew up in deprived families. However, only the latter wish was mentioned with any frequency by parents who were asked (in the 1964 follow-up) what they most wanted for their children. The four most popular desires were "emotional health and happiness" (82 percent), "physical health" (48 percent), "occupational, marital success" (46 percent), and "maturity, responsibility" (28 percent). The two health goals were the only desires which were more frequently mentioned by adults from deprived families.[21] Good health is important in scarcity and in affluence, but it is in times of abundance that emotional well-being can be granted priority.

Personality in Adult
Experience

The Depression
Experiences in
Life Patterns

IV

We have come to see that the biographies of men and women, the kinds of individuals they have become, cannot be understood without reference to the historical structures in which the milieux of their everyday life are organized. Historical transformations carry meanings not only for individual ways of life, but for the very character— the limits and possibilities of the human being.

C. Wright Mills, *The Sociological Imagination.*

10

Children of the Great Depression

We have followed a group of children from their preadolescent years early in the Depression to their middle-age years, tracing step by step the ways in which deprivation left its mark on relationships and careers, life styles and personalities. The documentation of specific effects has at times entailed a painstaking examination of somewhat fragmentary data on diverse aspects of life experience, often requiring many qualifications. This effort has posed at least as many questions for subsequent inquiry as it has answered.

In this final chapter, we return to main themes in the biographies of individuals and cohorts that experienced the Great Depression. We shall consider, first, the advantages and limitations of the approach here followed as a basis for generalization on the effects of the Depression. It will be well to have in mind our choice of historical time, geographic location, and strategies in carrying out the investigation. Only then can we examine the degree of fit between our findings and the adaptational framework that has guided the analysis. This degree of fit is the focal point of the second part of the chapter. In the third and final section, we shall identify general themes of change since the Depression, using materials that extend well beyond the present study: marriage and family, children's role in the family and community, aspects of work and achievement among the young, and the collective experience of Depression and postwar generations. The relation between social change and the family still represents a largely unexplored territory.

We cannot ignore certain consequences of the Great Depression in other industrial countries that had profound implications for members of the Oakland cohort in World War II. The rise of the Nazi movement is the major example. What do we know about the degree and duration of economic stagnation in the United States relative to conditions in Great Britain, Canada, and Germany? Since this question takes us well beyond the concerns of the present study, it is briefly dealt with in Appendix C.

The Approach and
Other Options

Family adaptations have been viewed in this study as a primary link between economic hardship and the individual—his behavior, personality, and life course. Members of the cohort were born in the early 20s to Caucasian parents in the middle and working classes and spent their childhood and adolescent years in the urban milieus of the San Francisco Bay area. A majority grew up in households which lost heavily in the Depression, including a substantial proportion from the middle class. Economic loss is related to social factors that specify contrasting experiences in the Depression (occupation, education, ethnicity, etc.), but these factors do not identify variations in conditions of life with sufficient accuracy; for example, many of the professional fathers in the Oakland sample lost heavily through unemployment, economic cutbacks, etc. Our approach, then, has been to focus directly on variations in economic hardship (as measured by income loss between 1929 and 1933) among families that were located in the middle and working classes in 1929.

An alternative design might compare the effect of childhood experiences in the Depression and in the postwar era of prosperity. A comparison group would be identified by persons born *after* the economic crisis. One handicap with this type of analysis is that there are many differences between the two childhood eras other than those related to the state of the economy; it would be difficult indeed to disentangle relative deprivation or prosperity from other factors, especially those unique to the epoch. By assessing the effects of economic loss in a single cohort, we have examined the differential effect of the same historical event. The common birthdate means that members of the sample entered the Depression and started out life at approximately the same age.

The advantage of confining analysis to a single birth cohort is countered by its limitations for generalization. At least one comparison group which is either older or younger than the Oakland cohort is needed to place life patterns in context and to provide insight on the generality of our findings. From the evidence at hand, we would expect widely varied experiences and outcomes in the Depression across different age groups. Differences in structural constraints and opportunities are known to have varied from year to year in the 30s. Also, age variations can be viewed as a factor in the adaptive potential of the young in situations of socioeconomic change and deprivation. The family dependency of preschool children (circa 1930) would make them more vulnerable than members of the Oakland cohort to the pathogenic effects of economic hardship, while members of an older cohort, with birthdates around 1914, would be under obligation to help struggling parents with family support and would be severely limited in options for employment and advanced education. As one "veteran" put it: "The essence of being in your twenties in the Thirties was that no matter how well tuned up you were, you stayed on the ground. Many of us stayed on the ground, or just above it, for ten years."[1]

In these respects, it is apparent that some risks encountered by older and younger cohorts were generally minimized in the age group of the Oakland children. They were not old enough in the early 1930s to be drawn into full-time roles in family support, and they left home during the incipient stage of war mobilization and economic recovery. The critical phase of intellectual development and social dependency had passed when they entered the 30s; they were old enough to be aware of the crisis besetting their families and the country, and to assume important roles in the household economy. If one were to select an optimum age at which to pass through the Depression decade, it would not differ much from that of the Oakland sample.[2] We must recognize, of course, the undeniable suffering of some of the Oakland parents.

In future research on individuals and families in the Depression, we would favor a cohort which includes the Oakland parents as well as younger adults born during the first decade of this century. In the present study we could not do justice to the life course of the Oakland parents; the appropriate data were simply not available. The fathers were not interviewed at any point, and the mothers were interviewed only during the first half of the 30s. We could not adequately chart the economic history of families from 1929 to the end of the 30s and into the war years, or trace its impact to household composition and residential patterns, modes of family maintenance, marriage and parent-child relations. With family data of this kind we could at least begin to delineate patterns of economic change in the 30s, the timing and nature of recovery, and their implications for family change.

Knowing what we do about the lives of the Oakland children, there is every reason to expect more profound consequences in the latter stages of the parents' lives. Under what conditions did severe economic hardship lead to disabilities that persisted well beyond the 30s, to a sense of inferiority, a chronic state of poor health, a deep-seated fear of economic insecurity? To some of the Oakland fathers, economic hardships meant despair and helplessness, illness, and alcoholism; and to mothers, emotional distress, humiliation, and a heavy family burden. But their psychology and life pattern in the 40s and 50s, relative to conditions in the Depression, remain a mystery.

This unexamined period is matched by the early life course of the parent generation. To understand why parents responded as they did to

Children of the Great
Depression

crisis situations in the Depression, we would need to know something about their economic and social standards, sex-role values, and preparedness for the adaptive requirements of economic hardships. Inquiry along these lines would take us back to the social history of the grandparent generation, to emigration from Europe, the rural-urban transition, the parents' sociocultural and economic environment during childhood and adolescence.

Relations between the grandparent and parent generations bring into focus the kin network, a sorely neglected aspect of family life in the Depression and more generally in times of crisis. What were the implications of relative isolation from kin for the adaptation of nuclear units to severe economic deprivation? for units with origins in the middle class compared to families of lower status? How did economic aid and kin obligations affect alignments and alienation within the kin system? And what were the social and emotional effects of newly formed three-generation households? Answers to these and related questions bear upon an important theoretical issue: the relative strength and weakness of the nuclear family in adapting to crises in the urban-industrial environment.[3]

Any interpretation of results on the Oakland cohort must take into account its childhood setting and social composition. There is, as we have noted, a fair degree of resemblance between economic change in Oakland and in other large American cities during the 30s, but objective economic indicators cannot be used with confidence to make valid comparative statements of the impact of the Depression and related experiences. Sociopolitical conditions and subjective reality also must be considered. Beyond matters of place, the social characteristics of the sample are sufficient to restrain tendencies to generalize. By and large, neither wealthy nor very poor families (pre-1929) are represented in the sample. Most of the adults are products of the lower-middle and working classes. Throughout the analysis we have given special emphasis to children of the middle class and to the effects of economic loss in their lives, in contrast to the large body of research on children in situations of prolonged, extreme deprivation. The range of social experience among middle- and working-class families offered a broad perspective to our assessment of economic deprivation in the life course. Another important feature of the sample is its ethnic composition. A substantial number of immigrants from Southern Europe and the Scandinavian countries settled in Oakland during the early 1900s and are represented in our sample. The black population of the city is largely a post-Depression phenomenon resulting from the westward movement of Southern blacks to wartime industries.

Two other issues of importance concern the size and representativeness of the sample. Given the option, we would have preferred a larger sample to ensure more stable measurements and greater flexibility in analysis. Nevertheless, the sample is large for long-term studies. Representativeness was subordinated to residential permanence in setting up the longitudinal design. As a group, however, the Oakland children closely resembled their school classmates on socioeconomic characteristics. All of these considerations, as well as problems distinctive of long-term longitudinal research, have led us to emphasize the suggestive or heuristic aspects of the study. Many additional studies on both similar and different groups—of sharecroppers, farmers, racial minorities, etc.—are needed for an adequate understanding of the human implications of the Depression mosaic.

Limitations are inevitably encountered in the fixed body of data collected before, during, and after the 30s. Retrospective materials are useful in life histories and are often essential to fill the unfortunate number of lacunae, but they are generally a poor substitute for contemporaneous information. No amount of ingenuity can satisfactorily compensate for inadequate statistical information on unemployment among Americans in the 30s, a deficit which also applies to Canada. We have faced similar problems in tracing the effects of economic loss and unemployment in the lives of the Oakland adults. Given our ideal of collecting data to answer preformulated questions, such deficiencies generate some doubt about an investigation which was not envisioned by the original project staff. But if we view the Oakland archive in terms of its potential for this line of approach, *relative* to other options, we can appreciate its resources as a unique opportunity. With this in mind and respect for the archive's limitations, our guideline has been to make the best of what we have.

Depression Experiences in Personality and the Life Course

Drastic change and adaptive responses provided the focus for our effort to link economic loss among families in the Depression with personality and careers. An extraordinary cultural lag occurred when customary adaptive techniques proved ineffective for coping with urgent problems. Family income in the Oakland sample declined approximately 40 percent between 1929 and 1933, a change which shifted households toward a more labor-intensive economy. More goods and services were pro-

Children of the Great Depression

duced by family members to meet their own needs. Coupled with this transition were new ways of applying resources and skills to problems, especially through the enlarged family roles of mother and children; adjustments in marital influence and child control; and social strains that developed from the uncertainty, frustration, and adaptive requirements of discordant change and deprivation. These conditions, as proposed linkages between economic loss and the child, were grouped under three general categories: change in the *division of labor*, change in *family relationships*, and *social strains*.

Viewing deprivational situations among the Oakland children in terms of these three conditions, we assumed that their experiences, personality, and life prospects were influenced by environmental changes which accompanied economic loss. This perspective is consistent with the view that children are brought up, intentionally or otherwise, for conditions of life experienced by parents. But the nature of conditions is open to question. Do they represent life situations shaped by the temporary forces of economic depression, or projections onto the future which are based on Depression realities of scarcity and economic insecurity (hence the necessity to maximize forms of economic security), or the anticipation of attractive options in a more abundant life? In the first category we find an array of unintended consequences issuing from family adaptations. Modes of family maintenance—dependence on public assistance, aid from kin and friends, mother's employment, and children's roles in the household economy—constitute responses to family survival requirements in the most basic sense, but they also structured the interactional environment and learning experience of children. We have less evidence of the second type of social condition, which depicts (unconsciously or not) the future in terms of the present (Depression realities), although it does appear in case materials. For example, some Oakland parents encouraged their sons to find economically secure jobs, advice which turned out to be more appropriate for the depressed 30s than for the postwar era of prosperity. Deliberate socialization is consistent with this situation and with the anticipation of a new and more promising world.

Economic loss in the Depression generally produced a disparity between situation and person which called for new adaptations. We assumed that responses to deprivational situations, from autonomous and resilient coping to defensiveness and withdrawal, hinged on adaptive potential involving both personal resources (intellectual skills, etc.) and environmental support within the family; and that children from the middle class ranked higher than those from the working class on the capacity to adapt to change and adversity. Problem-solving resources and support for adaptive responses tend to increase with class position. Middle-class children and parents also rank higher on intellectual resources, and their conceptions of reality are more conducive to effective adaptation in situations of change and uncertainty. In view of these considerations, we expected economic deprivation to influence more adversely the psychological health and life course of children from the working class.

The last factor to be noted in our assessment of economic deprivation in personality and the life course is the circumstance under which Depression experiences are most likely to persist into the adult years. Though few issues have aroused more interest than that of the Depression's legacy, minimal attention has been given to the situations and linkages which affect continuity in the life span. From little more than intuition and self-reflection, hard times during the Depression have been linked to an extraordinary work commitment, a self-conscious desire for security, an inability to partake of pleasure or leisure without guilt feelings. In the realm of child-rearing aspirations, the most popular folk theory asserts that Depression-reared parents strive to endow their offspring with a life free of the hardships and suffering they knew as children; to wit, "We search for affluence with neurotic intensity so that our children will not have to go through what we went through."[4] As soon as we think about conditions leading to such outcomes, we become aware of complexities associated with situational variations in adult life. Are these outcomes more a consequence of adult status, of membership in the upper middle-class, than of early experiences in the Depression? Most informal statements on Depression effects are restricted to this sector of the class structure.

The problem, then, is to specify conditions in the life course which are most likely to favor continuity from the Depression to middle age. Childhood lessons seem most likely to have application to the adult years when situations in each time period are relatively similar. As a general rule, the data supported this hypothesis among men in the Oakland sample; the main effect of deprivation on values occcurred among men who did not achieve higher status than that of their fathers. Status differences among women made little difference in continuities from the Depression since family roles established an overriding bond with the past.

We have briefly identified three general elements in our analysis of the Oakland cohort from 1929 to the mid-60s: proposed *linkages between economic loss and the individual* which structured situations in the 30s (change in the division of labor, change in family relationships, and social strains); variations in *adaptive potential*

Children of the Great Depression

as a determinant of response to situational change and its psychological impact; and *adult situations*, relative to experiences in the 30s, as a factor in psychological continuity or the enduring effects of the Depression experience. We used modes of adaptive potential and life situations to specify conditions in which family deprivation would be *most* and *least* likely to have certain psychological effects in adulthood. On the assumption that adaptive resources are associated with family status, we expected economic hardship to have less pathogenic consequences for adult health among offspring of middle-class families than among adults from the lower strata. And, as we have noted, adult situations (defined by mobility, etc.) made a difference in the relation between family deprivation and the values of men.

The utility and limitations of this general model are most readily seen by tracing relations between economic deprivation, personality, and aspects of the life course. To do so, we have organized our findings in terms of the three linkages, beginning with adaptations in the division of labor.

Economic loss and father's unemployment in the middle and working class were correlated with downward mobility in occupational status, though most deprived families eventually recovered their social position by the early 40s. Unemployment always meant loss of income, but many families, especially in the middle class, received heavy economic losses without joblessness. As the supply of income and savings diminished, families cut back on expenditures, in part by using labor to meet consumption needs, and developed alternative forms of economic maintenance. These options included employment of mother, aid from kin, and dependence on public assistance; reliance on these forms of support was especially prevalent in the working class. Children were most likely to participate in the household economy of deprived families, with girls specializing in domestic tasks and boys in economic roles. Boys sought employment in response to both family and personal needs.

In the area of family relationships, mother's centrality as decision maker and emotional resource is the primary theme among deprived households. Severe economic loss increased the perceived power of mother in family matters within the middle and working class, and diminished father's social prestige, attractiveness, and emotional significance, as perceived by sons and daughters. These conditions weakened father's role as a control figure for the children and the effectiveness of parental control in general, though especially in relation to sons; and encouraged dependence on persons outside the family. More than other children, the sons and daughters of deprived parents sought companionship and counsel among persons outside the home, especially among teachers and friends. Only in the area of occupational choice was the deprived father especially salient to boys, and this finding is restricted to the middle class.

Roles in the deprived household and the matricentric family joined forces in structuring a conducive environment for traditional sex roles and an accelerated movement toward adulthood. Scarcity and labor-intensive adjustments had the effect of lowering adultlike responsibilities toward childhood. Girls were drawn into a household operation which was controlled by mother, whether employed or not, and were oriented toward a domestic future by this experience and constraints on advanced education. The daughters of deprived parents were most likely to favor domestic activities, adult company, and grown-up status in adolescence, and, if middle-class, to marry earlier than their nondeprived middle-class contemporaries. Family deprivation lessened prospects for education beyond high school. In the middle years of life, a deprived background made a difference in the commitment of women to family life, parenthood, and homemaking in general. Each of these values was linked with family deprivation in the 30s through household responsibilities in a mother-centered household. Family-centered values and a view of life which entails responsibility (e.g., the belief that children mainly change the ways of adults by adding responsibilities) emerged as dominant perspectives in the lives of women who grew up in deprived households.

Family conditions associated with economic loss served to liberate boys from parental controls; oriented them toward adults and adult concerns, including the problem of earning a living; and stressed responsibilities in life. Economic hardships emancipated boys through the autonomy and obligations of work roles, and a household arrangement in which father had less say in family matters than mother. Work roles involved boys from deprived homes in adultlike experiences beyond family boundaries, enlarged their sphere of know-how, and brought greater awareness to matters of economic independence and vocation. These experiences, and the realities of family hardship, accelerated movement toward the adult world. Interest in the company of adults, the desire to be an adult, vocational thinking, and crystallized goals were associated with economic deprivation. In adult life, vocational crystallization tended to minimize the educational disadvantage of family deprivation in worklife and achieved status, regardless of class origin. Value priorities in the deprived group include job security over the potential benefits of occupational risk, responsibility in views of parenthood and children, and satisfactions in the world of family life. However, these values, as well as minimal interest in leisure activity, were related to family

Children of the Great
Depression

deprivation mainly among men who did not advance above their father's status.

It is apparent that many features of child socialization in deprived situations have no clear reference to parental intentions on preparing offspring for the future. Rather they emerged from adaptations to family requirements. Some if not most Depression children were brought up differently from the way in which their parents were raised, but parental intention is much less credible as a source of this difference than structural change and adaptations centering on family needs. In fact, adaptations of this sort may work at cross-purposes in socialization with parental plans or visions for the child. This may have been the case in the domestic upbringing of girls in deprived middle-class homes, and their preference for marriage over advanced education or training. Some unintended consequences of socialization are also illustrated by Farber's study of eighteenth-century Salem. Farber found that "artisan families were responsible for the socialization of persons who were motivated in the extreme for upward social mobility" (1972, p. 201). In this stratum, achievement striving developed out of a way of life that stressed family and kinship as a means of ensuring security of livelihood and status. Such unintended effects on achievement motivation were also evident in the Depression experience, from the incentive value of status loss to pressures to rely on personal resources in getting ahead.

A psychic connection between family deprivation and the Oakland children developed out of social strains and comparisons. Family losses made status or identity uncertain through discordant change on dimensions of family status, among family members (the shift toward female dominance), and between families. Self-consciousness, emotional sensitivity, and emotionality are thought to arise in ambiguous situations, and were found to be correlated with economic deprivation in both social classes, though especially among girls. These emotional states linked conditions of life in deprived families with a relatively early marriage among the daughters of middle-class homes. Family losses increased judgment errors among the Oakland children regarding their status in the eyes of age-mates; they believed that they were held in lower esteem than was actually the case. This perception, whether valid or not, was real in its consequences through conflict with self estimates; it aroused critical attitudes and sensitivity toward evidence of social elitism and seemed to foster recognition striving among the boys. Another consistent motivational effect of status change in economic loss is the association between ability and achievement motivation, a relation which we interpreted as an index of the degree to which ability is applied or used. In both middle and working classes, achievement motivation was more highly correlated with ability among the offspring of deprived families than among the nondeprived. Lastly, felt hardships in the 30s established a psychological framework or contrast experience which made life appear to be on the upswing between childhood and middle age. Having met difficult times as a child, the offspring of deprived families were more likely than the nondeprived to feel that life had become more abundant and satisfying.

The final point to be noted on specific relations between economic deprivation and the Oakland cohort concerns adaptive potential in life achievement and health. Middle-class offspring were brighter, more ambitious in goals, and received greater support in problem solving and achievement than the sons and daughters of working-class homes. These differences parallel class variations in the adult status attained by men through education and worklife, and by women through marriage; and they partially account for the more negative effect of economic deprivation among the children of working-class parents. For the most part, however, personal assets in life achievement, which were unrelated to economic loss (intelligence, physical attractiveness of women, etc.), minimized handicaps associated with family situation and limited education.

The implications of class background for adult life are more pronounced in matters of health and well-being. Despite contrary outcomes in the Depression, the overall impact of family deprivation was generally positive among middle-class offspring, with negative outcomes most evident among adults from the working class. Men and women from the deprived middle class were *more* likely to be judged relatively free of symptoms than the nondeprived, and were also rated higher on ego strength, integration of impulses and strivings, utilization of personal resources, and capacity for growth. They were characterized as more resilient, more self-confident, and less defensive. On the other hand, most adults of working-class origin showed some impairment, with evidence of psychological health slightly more prevalent in the nondeprived group.

Summary

Three points summarize the enduring effects of the Depression experience among the Oakland adults: *the paths through which they achieved adult status, as against level of status; adult health and preferences in ways of responding to life's problems; and values.* On the first point, we conclude that family deprivation made life achievement more dependent on effort and accomplishments outside the educational system. While men from nondeprived families ranked

Children of the Great Depression

slightly higher on educational attainment, worklife assets and experiences counted for more in the deprived group. Likewise, the educational handicap of family deprivation was neutralized by women through their social accomplishments in marriage. The favorable career stage of the Oakland cohort in the 30s must be regarded as a key factor in the life accomplishments of adults who grew up in deprived families, when compared to the life course of the non-deprived. Historical research, cited in chapter 7, suggests that the occupational chances of young workers (born in the first decade of the twentieth century) were limited by conditions in the Depression, especially when they had little in the way of formal education and job skills.

On the second main effect, there is evidence that adult health is negatively related to economic hardships, as was forecast by some analysts in the 30s, though only among the offspring of working-class homes. The opposite relation appears among children of the middle class. The influence of economic hardship was also expressed in sensitivity to economic matters on the domestic scene and in ways of responding to them. Preference for the Democratic party, which is almost entirely limited to the deprived group, can be viewed as a crude index of focal concerns and preferred tactics in national politics.

Lastly, it is clear that economic hardship experienced in the Depression made an enduring contribution to views on "things that matter" in life. The one common value across men and women is the centrality of the family and the importance of children in marriage. Though men from deprived homes did not rank family above work, their priorities and those of women with similar backgrounds exemplify the familistic aura of the postwar years. The parental family in deprived situations did not present an attractive model for emulation, but it socialized girls for a domestic life and projected an adaptive image in difficult times.

Other values which have been attributed to Depression-reared men were linked to economic hardship in the Oakland cohort. Job security is perhaps the best example, though it was seldom given priority among the more able, successful adults. Security concerns emerged among men from deprived homes who were vulnerable to economic fluctuations in the sense that they faced certain limitations in talents and options. Economic hardship made work important, focused attention on getting a job, and presumably inspired hard work, but there is no evidence in our data that work matters more to men from deprived families, relative to other activities, than it does to other men. The valuation of work over family and leisure among highly successful men owes more to their accomplishments than to their background in the Depression.

The Depression Experience in Life Patterns

Economic values from the Depression experience have not received their due in our analysis for lack of appropriate information. This is unfortunate since there is probably a higher ratio of speculation to evidence on this presumed legacy of the 30s than on any other "effect." There is reason to expect economic deprivation to heighten belief in the "power of money," as suggested by the prevalence of monetary rewards in child rearing among families in the lower strata, but we lack evidence at present of a relation between materialistic attitudes and experiences in the 30s. "Depression" rationales for current economic habits in retrospective reports are no substitute for the results of a longitudinal analysis.

By stressing economic deprivation in personality and the life course, we have given little recognition to conditions of life in the nondeprived group and their enduring consequences. The nondeprived have simply represented a comparison group, and yet we might just as well have stressed the effects of economic well-being in the Depression. The findings can in fact be interpreted from this perspective, and we have done so at appropriate points. No comparison yielded more substantial differences in life pattern than the comparison between deprivational groups in the middle class. The relatively nondeprived generally grew up in families headed by fathers who remained employed throughout the 30s; some even improved their earnings and social position. For the most part, household needs did not require employment of the mother or substantial contributions by the children. In most respects, both family situation and opportunities seemed to ensure maximum life chances for these "children of plenty" in an era of generalized privation. And yet from the evidence at hand, this promise does not appear to be fulfilled in their adult lives, at least when compared to the adult experience of children from deprived homes. Beyond the generally acknowledged human costs of economic hardship, especially in the lower strata, the Depression may yield some insights on the social psychology of material abundance, a condition of no small significance in the American experience.[5] Scarcity and abundance are inevitable points of contrast as we move to an overview of central themes from the Depression experience.

Central Themes from the Depression Experience

An enduring theme of the Depression experience is its alien nature in American life and psychology, despite recurring hard times and the millions of Americans who have known only poverty.[6] It was alien to the social character and institutions shaped by an economy geared to abundance, with its image of unlimited resources, continuing growth and vitality, and equality of opportunity; to the prosperous, flush times of the 20s or New Era which "made the crackup especially painful";[7] and to the postwar years of prosperity. The Depression imposed its scarcity regime and disciplines on a society accustomed to a "politics of abundance," a policy of increasing wealth to benefit all rather than dividing or redistributing a fixed sum; and although it produced some conditions that approximate life situations in a scarcity economy, adaptive strategies (most notably on the national level) remained faithful to the abundance philosophy. Roosevelt, whom Potter aptly describes as an "apostle of abundance," set forth a New Deal for the American people which expressed his optimistic faith in the potential of the economy to benefit all, labor and management, rural and urban residents, old and young. Instead of pitting one class against another, efforts were made to balance their interests by introducing new factors into the equation which would increase the fund of economic well-being. It is by this politics of abundance or, in Potter's words, "this stratagem of refusing to accept the factors given, of drawing on nature's surplus and on technology's tricks, that America has often dealt with her problems of social reform" (Potter 1954, p. 121). It is also a key to the psychology of renewed hope and solidarity which spread across the land during the unparalleled Hundred Days, following FDR's inauguration in an atmosphere which one journalist likened to that of a "beleaguered capital in wartime."[8]

Beyond the clash between economic scarcity and a culture shaped by abundance, one senses a contradiction between the quest for central themes from the Depression experience and our respect for its complex diversity—across age, class, ethnic, and residential categories. Economic deprivation and its socioeconomic context (urban-industrial, class stratum, etc.), the cultural heritage, and political response all entered into the structuring of American lifeways in the 30s.[9] Scarcity alone says far too little about the context in which it occurred. Social trends, which Potter linked to economic growth and abundance, were established when the country entered the Depression; for example, the trend toward autonomy, equality, and companionship among family members (decline of the authoritarian regime); expansion of women's sphere of activity and opportunity, including education, work, and politics; and prolongation of the dependency years for the young (especially in the middle class) through extension of public education (mandatory or otherwise), age restrictions on entry into the labor force, and delay of civic responsibilities.

The Depression Experience in Life Patterns

In this context, severe economic losses produced some conditions which resemble aspects of life in an economy of scarcity, according to the Oakland data, but in forms responsive to the peculiar constraints and options of an urban-industrial setting. The household economy became more labor-intensive and service-oriented, as children were involved in productive roles according to traditional gender prescriptions, including some adult obligations. Labor surplus and scarce jobs had the effect of encouraging school attendance. If economic hardship lowered adultlike responsibilities and productive status toward childhood, it did so in only a limited fashion, since legal safeguards on dependency remained intact—school attendance and child labor laws, the age of majority, etc.

In view of the changes during the Depression, the family qualifies as an unusually promising area in which to investigate patterns of change and continuity from the 30s to the postwar decades of abundance. However, any attempt to do so must take into account the distinctive biography of each cohort, defined by birthdates before 1933. What were the particular constraints, options, and incentives encountered by these cohorts as they passed from childhood to adolescence and then to phases of adult life? "To some extent each generation is bounded in its career choices by its peculiar biography" (Hill 1970, p. 322). These choices appear in entering the labor market, the timing of marriage and parenthood, the number and spacing of children, the number and types of job changes by the husband, the timing of the wife's entry into the work force, and the scheduling of acquisitions—homes, durables, life insurance and investments. To determine why certain options are preferred over others, we would need to consider the historically-bounded childhood experience and socialization of each cohort.

We shall first take up the question of what can be said, with evidence or informed speculation, regarding the Depression's impact on marriage and family. Beyond this area, suggestive themes are indicated by a comparison of the early life experience of Depression children and their offspring in the postwar era of relative prosperity. This contrast centers on the family role of children, from active contribution to surplus status in an overmanned environment; aspects of occupational attainment for middle-class children, from opportunity to the issue of incentives; and the profound disparity in collective experience between Depression-reared parents in the middle class and their offspring, a disparity accented by contrasts between the sacrificial life in scarcity and war, and the "unearned" affluence of the young.

Marriage and Family

With few exceptions, periodic dislocations or crises in American life have not been linked to secular change in the family system. While studies have been conducted on families in crisis situations generated by depression and war, they were not designed to answer questions on the long-term impact of period-specific events in family life. The big picture before us is evolutionary change; the emerging types of family life and their relation to evolutionary change—the effects of urban-industrial growth, separation of the production function from households, etc. (see, e.g., Smelser 1967).

During World War II, Burgess and Locke formulated a still influential thesis which charts a major transformation in the American family. As restated in 1971, it holds that "the family has been in transition from a traditional family system, based on family members playing traditional roles, to a companionship family system, based on mutual affection, intimate communication, and mutual acceptance of division of labor and procedures of decision-making. The companionship form of the family is not conceived as having been realized but as emerging" (Burgess et al. 1971). Prominent aspects of this family type—mutuality of affection, equality, and autonomy—are embodied in the more experimental forms of family life in the 70s. Among the proposed sources of family change, organizational trends in society, from individuated-entrepreneurial to welfare-bureaucratic settings, are singled out for special emphasis by Miller and Swanson, and conceptually linked to patterns of child rearing. They speculate that "children reared in welfare-bureaucratic homes will be encouraged to be accommodative, to allow their impulses some spontaneous expression, and to seek direction from the organizational programs in which they participate" (Miller and Swanson 1958, p. 58). This upbringing is contrasted to the regime of entrepreneurial homes which regards self-discipline, autonomy, and mastery as valued qualities.

Following the organizational thesis, we would expect the Depression experience to be an important etiological factor in the newer family modes since it gave birth to prominent features of the welfare state as we know it today. While Miller and Swanson did not explore this connection, it is a key element in Farber's interpretation of family change: by heightening discontent with traditional lifeways, the Depression encouraged breaks with the past and the emergence of new family models (Farber 1972). The collapse of socioeconomic security in the older generation led to a search for new ways of organizing and justifying life, to an emphasis on companionship and affection as the basis of family relations. According to Farber, these focal concerns are rooted in "conceptions of the role of the family associated with the welfare state, equalitarianism and cultural pluralism, and the personal freedom afforded by modern urban society. The diffusion of the new

The Depression Experience in Life Patterns

family models was furthered by the enactment of governmental programs in the 30s to permit security in retirement and in time of personal crisis" (Farber 1972, pp. 208–9). Farber extends his analysis to offspring of the Depression generations who are critical of prevailing models of the family, both traditional and Depression-generated, and relates this sentiment to awareness of the human costs of bureaucracy (loss of control over one's destiny, cost-efficiency, impersonality, etc.) and their reflection in family life.

Farber could not do justice, within his context, to relations between the Depression experience and family change, or to the process by which new family types emerged from the 30s, if in fact they have. Indeed, it is difficult to find any support for Farber's thesis in the Oakland cohort. *Signs of family change among the offspring of deprived families are consistently in a conservative direction, toward traditional values and relationships.* Traditional family preferences among women are related to childhood experiences in economically deprived households. For both men and women of deprived origins, a high priority on family life is distinguished by the value of "having children," not by the importance of marital understanding or companionship. Neither education nor occupational status account for this value orientation among children of the Depression. One might regard the marital life of men from deprived homes as evidence of the companionship model; having grown up in families in which women played a major role, they were most likely to share decision-making authority with their wives. However, their mothers generally exercised greater influence in the 30s than their wives in the 60s.

From sketchy evidence, it appears that noteworthy change toward the companionship model occurred at an earlier point, in the child cohort of World War I which reached marital age in the early 30s. If we compare three generations in the Minneapolis area (defined by marriage in the first decade of the twentieth century, in the early 1930s, and in the early 1950s), discontinuity shows up only between the first two generations (Hill 1970, chap. 2; Hill and Aldous, in Goslin 1969). This change, which centers on normative models regarding the performance of marital and parental roles, is distinguished by greater equality and sharing in marriage, a more accepting attitude among women toward maternal ways, less punitive and more supportive relations with children, greater tolerance of sex play and curiosity among children, more flexibility in obedience demands, and a greater willingness to allow children to make their own decisions. This picture must be qualified by its dependence on retrospective data of uncertain validity, but an equally important issue, for our purposes, is the precise source of change. Why did it occur between young couples of the 30s and their parents, the grandparent generation? One factor is the educational advantage of the middle generation; this generation ranked substantially higher on education than the grandparent generation, and closely resembled the youngest generation in educational accomplishments.

After a period of uncertainty, it is now clear that conditions in the Depression profoundly influenced the timing of events in the family life cycle or, to use Reuben Hill's phrase, "the strategy of life cycle management." *Delays occurred in the timing of marriage, parenthood, and material acquisitions among cohorts that attained marital age in the 30s.* But this change was *not* accompanied by corresponding adjustments in preferences or values on the desired number of children.[10] Value change in consumership is less striking and convincing than behavioral change associated with the timing of acquisitions. These conclusions are worth noting as relatively firm generalizations on the Depression experience in family life.

The demographic depression in the mid-30s and the upsurge of annual birth figures following World War II, a baby boom which continued through 1957, brought out more clearly than ever before the inadequacy of change in crude fertility rates as a measure of general demographic trends. The baby boom encouraged speculation concerning a general increase in completed family size among American women and related change in values: Did women in the postwar decade aspire to a larger number of children than women in the 20s or 30s? The hazard in seeking answers to such questions by studying change in annual birth figures (period rates) is that the birth figures reflect the *timing* of family formation and completion, as well as possible change in size of family. In order to determine what is happening in a particular fertility trend—is it a function of a change in timing, in ultimate family size, or both?—it is necessary to compare the cumulative fertility rates for cohorts of women with variations in annual birth rates. Cohort analyses indicate that conditions in the Depression led to delays in the timing of marriage, and to postponements in childbearing which were most often "made up" by the younger cohorts of women. The timing of marriage stands out as the most important determinant of the childbearing schedule across cohorts of American women in this century. The making up of postponed births is generally regarded as a major factor in the baby boom, along with a decline in marital and parental age among younger women. Ryder speculates that the "succession of depression and then prosperity" called out responses which resemble a decision strategy for managing a new situation in the life course: "The response with the least consequences, a change in the time of marriage, is the first undertaken; that with the greatest consequences, a change in the number of children, is the last undertaken" (Ryder 1967, pp. 18–19).

Few effects of the Depression have had a more pervasive impact on American life than its contribution to the baby boom. As the children born in the boom moved through the age structure, they placed extraordinary demands on educational facilities and resources at the primary, secondary, and higher-education levels. Efforts to alleviate the shortage of personnel led to a surplus as the wave passed through. By the 1970s the demand was felt in the job market, in greater competition for jobs and limited options owing partly to the economic recession. The consequences of the baby boom are analogous in some respects to the effect of an expanding family size on the social experiences and opportunities of dependents; unless resources and opportunities keep pace, additional births reduce the share of each child. Children born in the mid- to late 30s may have been handicapped by family hardships, unlike the postwar group in the middle class, but they came of age at a time when the demand for workers more than equaled their relatively small numbers.

Consumption patterns are linked to the pace of family formation, to marital age and the timing of childbearing, and were responsive in like manner to economic constraints in the Depression. In Reuben Hill's comparison of family consumption across three generations, intergenerational change is linked to differences in the historical context of marriage and to the secular trend toward greater prosperity and a planned economy (Hill 1970). Hill's average grandparent was married in 1907, the parent in 1931, and the member of the third generation in 1953. Career strategies in the grandparent generation were distinguished by relatively modest goals, by a cautionary approach to the development of resources, and by limited aspirations for self and children. "Prudence" describes the strategies employed by the parent generation, especially in family planning and acquisitions, material and security. Forward planning is most evident in the generation which married in the 50s. These couples acquired security provisions (life insurance and retirement) more rapidly, were most advanced in the timing of home ownership, and were also most likely to rely upon credit in the acquisition of automobiles and durable goods. To achieve a more complete picture of these differences within the life cycle, let us refer to Hill's cogent summary.

The grandparent generation entered marriage at a late age and, lacking knowledge and competence in family planning methods, bore more children at closer intervals over a longer period of time than its generational successor. At the mercy of an unplanned economy and limited occupational opportunities, this generation shifted jobs infre-

289

quently while remaining in the blue collar class, acquired home and adequate amenities only after children were launched. Unprotected by life insurance over most of its career and prevented from building a nest egg for retirement after launching children because of the economic depression, this generation launched its children into marriage later and over a longer period of time with altogether a longer period of childbearing, childrearing and leave taking. Educational aspirations for its children were lowest of the generations with most of its children over achieving these goals.

[The parent generation] entered marriage during the Great Depression at a prudent age for marriage, spaced children farthest apart and closed their families early with the smallest total number of children, [and] augmented the family income by the early reentry of the wife into the labor force to take advantage of war-born opportunities for employment. Deferred from military service because of age and family responsibilities, the breadwinner upgraded his occupational position by shifting jobs frequently. Home ownership was postponed latest of the generations whereas children were launched nine years earlier, thus enabling this generation to be in a position to be helpful financially to both grandparent and child generation.

Couples of the married child generation entered marriage youngest at slightly more modest jobs than their parents when they married, but with more than half of its wives working and expecting to remain in the labor force. Although they have the highest aspirations for their children, they have spaced them closest together of the generations, and have expectations of a larger family size than their parents. . . . it leads the generations year by year in its acquisitions of housing amenities and durable goods, in its occupational advancement, and in its rapidly advancing income level. [Pp. 310–11]

In keeping with Farber's analysis, a new model of life cycle management is indicated among couples who married in the early years of the Depression, one which is linked to the security provisions that developed out of this era through New Deal legislation. However, the relation of companionship values to the Depression experience and to the security benefits of the welfare bureaucracy is not clear, especially among couples that felt the hardships of severe deprivation. These conditions often brought instrumental values to the fore and severely strained the fabric of companionship. Indeed, loss of companionship and affection has been attributed to the trauma of Depression life. If some families were brought together in closer harmony by common hardship, more were undoubtedly strained to the breaking point and beyond. In any case, the evidence suggests that social and economic security favors the emergence of companionship values and their expression in family relationships. Historically, ideologies of personal choice, equality, and mutuality have emerged and spread most rapidly within the middle classes of society.

Economic conditions in the Depression, followed by the demands of war, produced noteworthy change in women's activities, both within the home and in the larger community—a behavioral development (especially in family influence, shared tasks, and gainful employment) which far exceeds known evidence on corresponding value change.[11] This cultural lag also appears in the lives of the Oakland women who grew up in deprived homes; though distinguished by a traditional conception of woman's role, their sphere of activity is broader and does not differ markedly from that of other women in the cohort. But what about the sex role concepts of their daughters who came of age in the late 50s and 60s? Inferential evidence suggests that they most likely resembled their mothers in the centrality of marriage, family life, and children, at least through 1967. Most college women in the mid-60s expressed this kind of outlook.[12] Generational differences would be more likely among the few daughters who entered college in the 1970s, in view of the heightened consciousness, ferment, and protest among educated women over traditional sex-role constraints and the generalized minority group status of American women.

Children's Role in Family and Community

What changes have occurred in the relation of children to family and adult life since the Depression? Using a broad framework which is not restricted to monetary considerations, let us consider some implications of productive and nonproductive status among the young, as they relate to the 30s and the 70s. The labor-intensive economy of deprived households in the 30s often brought older children into the world of adults, if we are to judge from childhood experiences in the Oakland cohort. These children had productive roles to perform. But in a more general sense they were needed, and, in being needed, they had the chance and responsibility to make a real contribution to the welfare of others. Being needed gives rise to a sense of belonging and place, of being committed to something larger than the self. However onerous the task may be, there is gratification and even personal growth to be gained in being challenged by a real undertaking if it is not excessive or exploitative. Thus we are not referring here to the desperate situation of many Depression children who lived a life not unlike that of the children of Mayhew's London poor—the offspring of the costermongers who worked the streets of mid-nineteenth-century London selling fruit, vegetables, and fish (Mayhew 1968). For most of the Oakland children in deprived families, especially in the middle class, productive status in

Children of the Great Depression

the household economy did not require an educational sacrifice or even a noteworthy limitation on social contacts with age-mates. Our point is that economic losses changed the relation of children to the family and adult world by involving them in needed work which contributed to the welfare of others. Much of this work entailed "people services," in contrast to gainful employment. Similar change is noted in the vast literature on families and communities in natural disasters; the young often play vital roles in the labor-intensive emergency social system.

Since the Depression and especially World War II various developments have conspired to isolate the young from challenging situations in which they could make valuable contributions to family and community welfare. Prosperity, population concentration, industrial growth with its capital-intensive formula, and educational upgrading have led to an extension of the dependency years and increasing segregation of the young from the routine experiences of adults. In this consumption-oriented society, urban middle-class families have little use for the productive hands of offspring, and the same applies to community institutions. Unlike the outmoded "one-room schoolhouse," an under-manned institution from the adult standpoint, most contemporary schools are organized around the educational contributions of adults; little is formally expected of children in educating their peers, whether younger or comparable in age. An important exception is seen in experimental schools that are organized around the principle of "children teaching children."[13]

From the perspective of children and their productive potential, our urbanized, affluent society represents an overmanned environment; the young are members of a surplus category which is mainly restricted to vicarious contact with the occupational routines of life. Some important implications of this situation are suggested by Roger Barker's insightful research on the inhabitants of undermanned and overmanned behavior settings; in the former environment, inhabitants were found to engage in difficult and important actions more frequently—they are "busier, more vigorous, more versatile, and more oriented vis-à-vis the settings they inhabit, and more interdependent" (Barker 1968, p. 190). Noting that undermanned settings are becoming less prevalent in American society, Barker points out that its historically distinctive features are rooted in an idea which relates undermanned settings to a way of life—the land of opportunity, people of plenty, and the free frontier; it is the idea that "there has been a superabundance of goals to be achieved and an excess of tasks to be done in relation to the nation's inhabitants, and that these have been important influences on the American society and people" (ibid., p. 189).

The Depression Experience in Life Patterns

This society of abundance can and even must support "a large quota of nonproductive members," as it is presently organized, but should it tolerate the costs, especially among the young; the costs of not feeling needed, of being denied the challenge and rewards which come from meaningful contributions to a common endeavor? This question emerged at the 1970 White House Conference on Children relative to the issue of age segregation. In recognizing the need to bring adults "back into the lives of children" and children back into the lives of adults, the conference report urged that ways be developed for "children and youth to engage in meaningful activities in the world of adults."[14] Some parents, as children of the Great Depression, sense this problem of isolation from the workways of the community in their uneasiness over a beneficent life that has required so little from their own children.

Opportunity and Incentives in Life Prospects

What young Americans in the 30s lacked was opportunity, not desire or ambition; their life prospects depended on access to scarce resources, on advanced education and a good job. Shortly after the Depression decade, Margaret Mead brought to mind another constraint on the American version of life opportunity, a constraint stemming from a presumed decline in economic expansion: "Has the American scene shifted so that we still demand of every child a measure of success which is actually less and less possible for him to attain? . . . Have we made it a condition of success that a son should reach a position higher than his father's when such an achievement (for the many) is dependent upon the existence of a frontier and an expanding economy?"[15] This question is pertinent to the achievement possibilities of contemporary youth in the upper middle class, especially as members of the baby boom cohort. But in another sense their achievement may be less a matter of opportunity than of incentive. For this was, in Edward Shils's words, "a uniquely indulged generation. . . . A life beyond the dreams of avarice seemed to have become accessible to those whom fortunes of birth—in time and status—had favoured."[16]

Does a childhood of abundance weaken traditional incentives in occupational life—the incentive of economic gain, for instance, or even the value of social prestige? This outcome is suggested by the implications of reward satiation for learning and motivation. Also, time represents an important constraint on the gratification obtained from goods, according to Staffan Linder, an economist. He argues that we derive less satisfaction from the possessions we acquire as their volume increases; that we acquire them with little thought or knowledge, give less effort to their maintenance, and spend too little time on a single item to develop an appreciation of any of them (Linder 1970).

In view of these considerations, we would expect parents who grew up in the depressed 30s to assign greater priority to finances and possessions than their adult offspring, and in particular to place greater value on economic gain in their worklife. While relevant evidence is weak on generations in the middle class, it is at least suggestive of this difference.[17] Apart from generational change, it is clear that economic factors have low priority on value in the job choices of present-day college students, according to a major study in progress.[18] By and large, the students surveyed in the study did not have to buck financial problems, thanks to scholarships, loans, and parental support. Unlike the parents who knew hardships in the past, the students were inclined to take for granted a reasonable or comfortable standard of living. Earnings and prestige were not the important considerations in choice of a job. Their outstanding priority centered on the job's growth potential and its contribution to others.

As yet, we do not know how or whether the work preferences of postwar cohorts are related to values and Depression experiences in the parent generation. Nevertheless, job priorities do appear to have changed since the 20s, and significantly so, if we are to judge from studies of the American worker. In a recent survey, both blue- and white-collar workers described a rewarding job as one that offers a chance for personal growth and achievement, the opportunity to perform well and to contribute something unique.[19] Just as good times enable workers and students to value such factors, the return to bad times (a recession or depression) would again give priority to the bread-and-butter issues which had special significance to men in the Depression (see chapter 1, note 25).

Collective Experience in History

On the topic of central themes in American life since the 30s, we have explored perspectives from the historical worlds of Depression and postwar abundance, using the vantage point of marriage and family, the role of children in family and community, and life prospects. These points of comparison highlight suggestive lines of continuity and change, but they neglect what some might regard as a more significant comparison; on the social-political experience and generalized perspectives that reflect lives lived interdependently at different points in history.

This interdependence is noteworthy in the Great Depression and World War II since major crises generally produce experiences that are widely shared. Collective experience is revitalized when problems are interpreted within the framework of a national crisis, an emergency of such proportion that it threatens the common way of life. National survival thus transcends the special and divisive interests of individuals and groups, of social strata and regions. Americans were drawn into the nation's struggle for survival in both crises; the struggle became their civic obligation and their personal hardships part of the nation's experience.

Rooted in this experience is a psychic framework of self-sacrifice and earned success in the nation's cause which still finds expression in views of contemporary events and developments. Sacrifice was highlighted in the Depression during Roosevelt's first term through the psychology of war and mass mobilization, whereas specialized class interests, conflicts, and politics came to the fore as the economic crisis receded. World War II did not bring hardship or devastation to as many homes as did the Depression, and its sacrificial claims were muted for the majority by renewed prosperity, but the two crises are strikingly similar in their psychological themes—the national emergency and the super-ordinate goal of survival, the forging of national solidarity through appeals and coercion which subordinated personal and group interests to the higher cause, mass mobilization of citizen talents and contributions in the national effort, and the pride that came from participation in a collective effort that eventually prevailed.[20]

Prominent issues and experiences in this epoch of Depression and war are seen in the ideological orientation of the Old Left, with its roots in the economic and political milieu of the 30s. Consistent with its past in the New Deal era, the Old Left has sought amelioristic change (socioeconomic, racial) through established institutions and the democratic process; to a significant degree, its response has been structured and informed by a national framework and especially by the national interest (Mauss 1971). During the early 30s and World War II, action "in the national interest" generally called for closing the ranks (putting aside internal differences) to do battle with a common threat or enemy. In the Old Left, this appeal gained priority over the issue of fundamental reform during the war and is expressed more generally by support for war efforts which purport to defend the Free World from the communist threat of world domination. Through its sense of history and optimistic futurism, the movement has shown a deep-seated faith in centralized government, based on democratic principles, as a vehicle for social, racial, and economic reforms. It has also strongly favored the integrationist goal in race relations.

Children of the Great
Depression

Some analysts view the New Left of the 60s (Students for Democratic Action), which emerged from the civil rights movement, as an extension of the Old through family socialization and ideology (Mauss 1971; cf. Altbach and Peterson 1971). Studies have found that a large proportion of student activists are offspring of parents with leftist beliefs, though not necessarily as extreme, especially on approved tactics. In ideology, the connection is traced from the Old Left's criticism of inequalities in the distribution of income and wealth to the New Left's attack on inequalities in the distribution of power, manifested by oppression and alienation. Whatever their similarities, the differences are of greater interest since they are most apparent on themes that were especially characteristic of life in the Depression and Second World War—national solidarity at the expense of grass-roots reform, governmental action in the national interest, centralized power in government. In the New Left we find a rejection of Cold War psychology and American imperialism abroad through military intervention and economic exploitation; support for pluralist forces in society; and an attack on the oppressive, antidemocratic tendencies of centralized power in bureaucracies—government, business, military, even labor.

The years between '29 and '46, as individual and collective experience in two major crises, are known to Americans born after World War II only from what they have read, seen, or heard. But even among the knowledgeable, one would expect some difficulty in understanding and appreciating the "nation-saving" priorities that prevailed at the time. The culture of these times warrants examination in the context of contemporary intergenerational relations. We need to know more about differences between younger and older Americans concerning the appropriate response to appeals that are clothed in the national interest, and about the implications of sacrifice and accomplishment in the biography of Depression cohorts. This biography is unique in the sense that widespread hardship, which enhanced the value of material goods and the desire for children, was soon followed by an economic upswing that often turned these values into reality. In one life span, Americans had moved from scarcity to abundance, from sacrifice to the freedoms made possible by prosperity.

The change in life situation had a good deal more to do with war-generated prosperity and the business cycle than with individual talent or effort; but the important question is how it was (and still is being) interpreted, especially by parents to their children. The experience of Depression cohorts is such that members are apt to interpret their good fortunes as a legacy or gift to the next generation. As a point of contrast, we need only compare the probable relation between young adults who were born into well-to-do homes in the postwar years and their

The Depression Experience in Life Patterns

children. Not having faced poverty or hardship as children, they would be most unlikely to regard a life of plenty as their special contribution to the welfare of the coming generation.

As a prominent factor in the Great Depression, inequality in the distribution of income and wealth has again emerged as a compelling issue, and will most certainly be among the leading political concerns in the coming decades, both at home and in relations between nations. No lessening of the basic pattern of inequality in the United States has occurred, at least since World War II—and some would say since the end of World War I.[21] In any case, the absolute dollar gap between rich and poor Americans has widened during the past decade, and so has the economic gap between societies. Renewed sensitivity to the need for radical change in this area has come at a time of increased awareness that economic growth and consumption have foreseeable limits in the planetary ecosystem. Though alien to a culture of abundance, to the idea of increasing the cake for all (which too readily ignores the notion of fair shares), this image of limited resources has much in common with the realities of Depression life in the 30s; with the problem of "making the best of what we have." For children of the Depression generations and especially for their children, some disciplines practiced in the 30s—frugality, conservation, and so forth—are likely to become imperatives in the years ahead.

Children of the Great Depression

Appendixes

Appendix A   Tables

Appendix A contains tables A–1 through A–33. Tables 1 through 12, without the prefix "A," are to be found in the text. See list of tables, page vii above, for page numbers.

Table A-1

Comparison of Selected Cities in the Depression on Indicators of Economic Change

Number of Building Permits Issued

City	Number of Building Permits Issued 1929	Number of Building Permits Issued as Percentage of 1929 Total			
		1931	1933	1935	1937
Oakland	4,264	64%	40%	90%	119%
San Francisco	5,505	95	62	74	106
Los Angeles	31,722	80	50	68	104
Detroit	26,554	38	15	38	62
Cleveland	9,863	67	30	36	48
Atlanta	2,946	110	60	79	73
Philadelphia	10,388	53	34	42	113

Note.   Figures cover new building and repairs to old buildings, but exclude data on installation permits which are not strictly building operations. The totals reported for 1929 and subsequent years represent the number of buildings covered by permits issued, rather than the number of permits.

Source: "Statistical Abstracts of the United States": 1931, pp. 871–73; 1935, pp. 789–91; 1939, pp. 867–68.

Net Sales in Retail Trade

City	Net Sales in Retail Trade 1929	Net Sales in Retail Trade as Percentage of 1929 Total	
		1933	1935
Oakland	204,437	51%	69%
San Francisco	499,060	51	60
Los Angeles	914,071	50	65
Detroit	882,087	42	62
Cleveland	534,241	52	67
Atlanta	165,107	57	83
Philadelphia	1,122,168	46	59

Source: "Statistical Abstracts of the United States": 1931, pp. 326–28; 1935, pp. 781–82; 1939, pp. 854–55

Number Employed in Retail Trade

City	Number Employed in Retail Trade 1929	Number of Employed as Percentage of 1929 Total	
		1933	1935
Oakland	16,392	66%	98%
San Francisco	44,562	68	88
Los Angeles	74,938	75	107
Detroit	68,315	69	100
Cleveland	46,347	73	103
Atlanta	18,495	73	106
Philadelphia	102,318	69	89

Source: "Statistical Abstracts of the United States": 1931, pp. 326–28; 1935, pp. 781–82; 1939, pp. 854–55.

Table A-2   Sources of Family Support by Social Class, Economic Deprivation, and Paternal Employment[a]

Social Class, 1929, and Economic Deprivation	Number of Cases	Sources of Family Support (Percent)	
		Mother employed 1934	Received Money from Relatives or Boarders, 1929–33
Middle class			
Nondeprived	46	9	7
Deprived			
Father employed	29	39	17
Father unemployed	33	21	27
Working class			
Nondeprived	21	19	10
Deprived			
Father employed	23	30	26
Father unemployed	24	37	25

[a] To carry out this three-way division of each social class, we included all of the Oakland cases that had socioeconomic information. Some of these Ss did not continue in the study beyond 1935 and thus are not included in the basic adolescent core sample of 167. This procedure applies to tables A-2, A-3, and A-4.

Table A-3   Assistance from Public Agencies in
                   Two Time Periods, by Social Class and
                   Economic Deprivation

| Social Class, 1929, and Economic Deprivation | Number of Cases | Assistance from Public Agencies (Percent) | |
		1929–33	1934–41
Middle class			
Nondeprived	46	2	4
Deprived			
Father employed	29	—	9
Father unemployed	33	21	48
Working class			
Nondeprived	21	4	15
Deprived			
Father employed	23	13	15
Father unemployed	24	46	60

Table A-4   Interviewer Mean Ratings of Mothers by
                   Social Class, Economic Deprivation, and
                   Paternal Unemployment

Ratings and Social Class, 1929[a]	Nondeprived	Deprived and Unemployed	Statistical Significance
Dissatisfied with lot			
Middle class	3.3	4.5	$p < .01$
Working class	3.9	4.2	
Feelings of inadequacy			
Middle class	3.2	3.7	$p < .10$
Working class	3.8	3.6	
Fatigued, tired			
Middle class	3.4	4.0	$p < .01$
Working class	3.8	3.8	
Feels secure, confident			
Middle class	4.0	3.4	$p < .01$
Working class	4.0	3.7	
Unkempt in appearance			
Middle class	3.2	3.8	$p < .01$
Working class	4.1	4.0	
Total number of cases			
Middle class	46	33	
Working class	21	24	

[a] The seven-point ratings are an average of ratings
made by the interviewer in 1932, 1934, and 1936. A
high score on each rating is described by its title.
Thus a score of 7 is the highest rating possible on
dissatisfaction with lot.

Table A-5   Ratings of Girls' Dependability and Industry in 1937 by Work Status and Domestic Chores in 1936

| Selected Situation Ratings, Fall 1937 | Mean Scores | | | P Values for Subgroup Comparisons: T-Tests |
	Work and Chores N = 17 (A)	Chores N = 25 (B)	Neither N = 21 (C)	
Dependable	55.5	50.2	49.1	A > B** A > C**
Resists authority	43.8	49.0	52.7	A < C**
Industrious	56.5	47.8	48.0	A > C**

** $p < .01$

Note.   Group A includes girls with a job who had scores of 3–5 on the household task index; Group B includes unemployed girls with scores of 4 and 5 on the task index; and Group C includes girls who did not have a job and scored 0–2 on the task index. No differences between groups B and C are statistically significant at .05 level.

Table A-6   Social Independence of Children as Reported by Mother, by Social Class, Economic Deprivation, and Sex, in Percentages

| Status | Went out with friends[a] on weekend evenings | | Went out with friends[a] on school evenings | |
	Boys	Girls	Boys	Girls
Middle class				
Nondeprived	28 (28)	35 (17)	32 (28)	24 (17)
Deprived	43 (28)	57 (21)	54 (24)	29 (21)
	−15%	−22%	−22%	− 5%
Working class[b]				
Nondeprived	33 (9)	64 (11)	22 (9)	45 (11)
Deprived	47 (17)	46 (24)	61 (18)	32 (25)
	−14%	18%	−39%	13%

[a]   "Friends" includes boys and girls.

[b]   Though percentage differences are consistent across the two items, the number of cases in the nondeprived working class is too small to provide reliable values.

Table A-7   Parental Competence, Traditionalism, and Role Performance as Determinants of Mother Dominance in Economically Deprived Middle- and Working-Class Families

Potential Sources of Marital Power[a]	Correlates of Mother Dominance in Deprived Families	
	Middle Class (Min. N = 35)	Working Class (Min. N = 32)
Parental competence		
Mother has more education than father	.09	−.26
Father's age	.23	.06
Foreign-born parents (as index of traditionalism)	([b])	−.08
Role performance		
Family downward mobile	.42 p < .01	.18
Unstable work life	.23	.39 p < .05
Mother employed, 1934	.10	.06

[a]   Relative education includes five categories: father two levels above mother on the Hollingshead index, father one level above mother, equal, mother one and then two levels above father. With the exception of father's age, all other items were dichotomized. Unstable or disorderly worklife refers to change in line of work, movement up and down in status structure, etc.

[b]   The number of subjects with foreign-born parents in the middle class is too small to permit analysis.

Table A-8 — Associational Preferences of Boys and Girls by Class and Deprivation (1933–34)

Social Referent	Boys			Girls		
	Average Rank: ($\overline{X}$)	Effects[a] of Low Status	Effects[a] of Deprivation	Average Rank: ($\overline{X}$)	Effects[a] of Low Status	Effects[a] of Deprivation
Father	1.84	− .17	− .26	2.17	− .21	− .07
Mother	2.29	+ .06	+ .10	2.21	+ .18	+ .13
Groups of friends	2.71	+ .05	+ .34	2.13	− .03	+ .25
Best friend	2.22	+ .06	+ .23	2.43	+ .19	+ .18

Note. Each respondent was asked whether he would prefer the company of father, mother, a group of friends, or a best friend on a trip to the circus. Three preference levels were provided for each referent—first, second, and third choice. The highest rank is scored "1," the lowest, "3."

[a] A positive value for the effect of social class indicates that working-class respondents ranked the referent higher (toward a score of "1") than middle-class subjects. That is, the average rank for the working class is higher than the middle-class mean. Similarly, a comparable effect of deprivation would indicate that children in the deprived group ranked the referent higher than members of the nondeprived category. The approximate number of boys in each group is 41 and 22 for middle and working class, and 29 versus 34 for the nondeprived and deprived categories. Figures for comparable groups among girls are 33 and 34 on social class and 23 versus 42 on deprivation.

Table A-9 — Persons Preferred by Children as Sources of Advice and Assistance (1933–34) by Family Social Class and Economic Deprivation

Family Social Class and Economic Deprivation	Number of Respondents	Persons Turned to,[a] in Percentages				
		Father	Mother	Siblings	Teachers	Peers
Middle class						
Nondeprived	40	50	70	13	5	5
Deprived	47	43	83	23	23	19
Working class						
Nondeprived	18	33	67	11	11	6
Deprived	33	36	88	21	24	27

[a] Since the respondent could check more than one person, the percentages total more than 100 percent.

Table A-10

Boys' and Girls' Relations to Parents in
High School, by Economic Deprivation,
Maternal Dominance, and Family
Class (1929)

Relations to Parents (Nine-point ratings)	Correlation Coefficients (r)		
	Economic Deprivation: Percent Loss, 1929–33[a]	Maternal Dominance: (scores of 1–5)	Family Class, 1929 (high score = high status)
Boys (min. N = 34)			
Closer to mother	.22	.38 p < .05	.11
Attracted to mother	.11	.25	.41 p < .01
Attracted to father	−.10	.10	.49 p < .01
Girls (min. N = 33)			
Closer to mother	.41 p < .01	.40 p < .01	−.24
Attracted to mother	.21	.30 p < .05	.13
Attracted to father	−.20	−.08	.18

[a] We used the full distribution of cases on percent income loss (instead of the usual dichotomous measure) for two reasons. The distribution resembled a normal curve, and the income figures were sufficiently accurate to justify its use on the small number of cases with family ratings.

Table A-11

Daughters' Adult Evaluation of Parents in
the Depression, by Economic
Deprivation and Family Class,
in Percentages

Evaluation, 1958	Economic Deprivation, 1929		Family Class, 1929	
	Nondeprived (N = 16)[a]	Deprived (N = 28)[a]	Middle Class (N = 24)[a]	Working Class (N = 23)[a]
Fairly good or very good understanding of daughter				
Mother	62	57	58	57
Father	73	44	54	50
Favorable impression of parents qua parents				
Mother	87	56	64	60
Father	87	52	64	67

[a] Subgroup Ns vary by no more than one case across the four items.

Table A-12 | Positive Evaluation of Mother and Father as Parents (1958) by Closeness to Mother in Adolescence

Sex of Adult	Positive Evaluation of Parents in Adulthood (correlation coefficients–r)	
	Mother	Father
Men (N = 45)	.01	.06
Women (N = 42)	.19	− .28

Note: "Closer to mother than to father" is measured by a nine-point rating; and positive evaluation of parents by four-point items.

Table A-13 | Emotional State of Boys and Girls by Economic Deprivation and Social Class (Junior High Period), in Mean Scores[a]

Indicators of Emotional State	Boys		Girls	
	Middle Class	Working Class	Middle Class	Working Class
Social well-being				
Nondeprived	8.7	9.0	9.4	8.7
Deprived	8.6	8.7	8.4	7.8
			ND > D**	MC > WC*
Emotionality				
Nondeprived	2.5	2.5	3.1	3.9
Deprived	2.1	2.8	2.9	3.9

* $p < .05$ (test of difference between means, e.g., nondeprived vs. deprived).

** $p < .01$

[a] The minimum number of cases in the nondeprived and deprived groups is 25 and 24 for middle-class boys; 7 and 24 for working-class boys; 15 and 23 for middle-class girls; and 10 and 23 for working-class girls.

Table A-14   Classmate Exclusiveness as Perceived by Boys and Girls, by Economic Deprivation and Social Class (High School Period), in Mean Standard Scores

Economic Deprivation by Social Class	Perceived Exclusiveness	
	Boys	Girls
Middle class		
Nondeprived	48.9 (26)	44.0 (15)
Deprived	49.5 (24)	52.7 (23)
Working class		
Nondeprived	50.0 (8)	47.3 (10)
Deprived	52.3 (14)	52.1 (24)
Nondeprived vs. deprived		ND < D p < .05

Table A-15   Adult Observers' Mean Ratings of Well-Groomed Appearance, by Economic Deprivation and Social Class (Junior High Period)

Social Class and Economic Deprivation	Well-Groomed Appearance	
	Boys	Girls
Middle Class		
Nondeprived	57.1 (28)	61.2 (18)
Deprived	52.5 (30)	53.3 (29)
		ND > D*
Working Class		
Nondeprived	51.8 (10)	50.2 (10)
Deprived	48.1 (21)	47.2 (30)

*   p < .05 (t-test)

Note.   This scale was selected from the set of Free-Play Ratings which were made by staff observers at the Institute of Child Welfare.

Table A-16   Adult Observers' Mean Social Ratings of Boys and Girls by Economic Deprivation and Social Class (Junior High Period)

Social Status[a] by Economic Deprivation	Boys		Girls	
	Middle Class	Working Class	Middle Class	Working Class
Social leader				
Nondeprived	50.2 (28)	41.2 (10)	51.3 (18)	47.4 (10)
Deprived	50.2 (30)	52.3 (21)	48.5 (29)	47.3 (30)
		ND < D*		
Popular				
Nondeprived	50.2 (28)	44.8 (10)	52.4 (18)	50.4 (10)
Deprived	52.6 (30)	52.3 (21)	48.3 (29)	50.0 (30)
		ND < D*		

* $p < .05$ (t-test)

a   Free-Play Ratings. These ratings are described in Appendix B.

Table A-17   Emotional and Social Correlates of Social Fantasy by Sex and Economic Deprivation (Junior High Period)

Emotional and Social Status[a]	Correlations (r) with Index of Social Fantasy			
	Boys		Girls	
	Nondeprived (N = 30)	Deprived (N = 36)	Nondeprived (N = 24)	Deprived (N = 43)
Social well-being	−.41	−.40	−.19	−.16
Emotionality	.60	.06	.42	.02
Popular	−.29	.19	−.32	.08
Popular with boys	−.33	.13	−.22	.15
Popular with girls	−.31	.14	−.25	.08

a   All indicators except the last two on popularity with each sex apply to the junior high years. "Popular" refers to a Free-Play Rating; the other two popularity scales were drawn from the 1937 Situation Ratings (see Appendix B). Only the difference between r coefficients for "emotionality" among boys is statistically significant at the .05 level.

Table A-18   Mental Ability and Academic Aptitude of Boys and Girls, by Economic Deprivation and Social Class, in Mean Scores

Social Class and Economic Deprivation	Mental Ability: IQ[a]		Academic Aptitude[b]	
	Boys	Girls	Boys	Girls
Middle class				
Nondeprived	118.4 (28)	116.2 (16)	4.6 (28)	5.0 (14)
Deprived	115.9 (28)	109.0 (25)	4.5 (28)	4.7 (22)
		ND > D*		
Working class				
Nondeprived	109.5 (7)	105.3 (10)	4.1 (7)	4.6 (9)
Deprived	113.1 (16)	107.2 (25)	4.0 (14)	4.6 (25)

* $p < .05$ (two-tailed t-test). Comparison of middle- and working-class children produced a significant difference only on mental ability. With boys and girls combined, the difference was significant at the .01 level.

a   Scores on Stanford-Binets in 1933 and 1938 were averaged before means were calculated.

b   This measure included an average of two seven-point ratings on academic interest and performance. These were made by three teachers who knew the adolescents well in high school.

Table A-19   Motivational Orientations of Boys, by Economic Deprivation and Social Class, in Mean Scores

Social Class and Economic Deprivation	Need for Achievement[a]	Need for Power and Status[b]	Prestige of Occupational Interests (1938)[c]
Middle class			
Nondeprived	2.4 (27)	47.2 (25)	47.3 (23)
Deprived	2.4 (25)	54.7 (24)	48.8 (19)
Working class			
Nondeprived	1.5 (7)	44.8 (6)	42.0 (7)
Deprived	2.2 (15)	50.0 (15)	43.1 (10)
Comparisons by			
Economic deprivation		ND < D*	
Class			MC > WC*

    * $p < .05$ (t-test)

    a   Need for achievement is measured by a five-point rating; a score of "one" indicates a low need. In order to make a high value equivalent to a strong need to achieve, we reversed the scores.

    b   Need for power and status is indexed by a summation of scores on two motivational ratings: need for social recognition and social control. Scores were also reversed on these ratings in order to make a high value equivalent to a strong need. Values on each rating were first summed and then standardized.

    c   Level of occupational goal is measured by the occupational level scale in the Strong Vocational Interest Blank which was administered to the boys in 1938.

Table A-20   Timing of Career Establishment by Economic Deprivation and Class Origin (1929), in Percentages

Time of Career Establishment[a]	Middle Class		Working Class	
	Nondeprived	Deprived	Nondeprived	Deprived
Before 1945	9	25	25	39
1945–48	39	55	38	31
1949 +	52	20	38	30
	100 (23)	100 (20)	101 (8)	100 (13)

    a   Refers to the year when subject entered a line of work which was followed for at least six years.

Table A-21   Average Number of Jobs and Employers by Class Origin (1929), Economic Deprivation, and Time Period, in Means

Class Origin and Economic Deprivation	Jobs		Employers	
	1940–46	1946–55	1940–46	1946–55
Middle class				
Nondeprived (N = 23)	2.00	2.92	1.96	2.38
Deprived (N = 18)	2.56	2.94	2.17	2.53
Working class				
Nondeprived (N = 8)	2.13	2.38	2.12	2.00
Deprived (N = 13)	4.00	2.75	3.85	2.67

Note.   The only statistically significant difference between nondeprived and deprived groups (with class groups combined) is the variation on average number of jobs before 1946, $p < .05$.

Table A-22   Achievement Motivation and Intelligence in Occupational Mobility, by Class Origin and Deprivation, in Mean Scores[a]

Class Origin and Economic Deprivation	Achievement Motivation[b]			Intelligence (IQ)		
	Mobile	Non-mobile		Mobile	Non-mobile	
Middle class						
Nondeprived	2.6 (11)	2.3 (12)		123.1 (11)	112.8 (12)	M > N**
Deprived	2.8 (11)	1.9 (9)	M > N*	119.9 (11)	113.7 (9)	
Total sample						
Nondeprived	2.6 (14)	2.2 (15)		119.4 (14)	111.6 (17)	M > N**
Deprived	2.7 (19)	1.9 (12)	M > N*	117.4 (21)	113.2 (13)	

* $p < .05$ (two-tailed t-test)

** $p < .01$

a   Mobile and nonmobile men differ significantly on achievement motivation only in the deprived group, and on IQ only in the nondeprived group. Both differences apply both to the middle class and to the total sample.

b   Scores were reversed on achievement motivation in order to make high values equivalent to a strong need to achieve (5 = high, 1 = low).

Table A-23 — Relation between Occupational Attainment (1958) and Selected Antecedent Factors by Economic Deprivation and Class Origin: Multiple Regression Analysis

Factors	Middle Class Origin				Total Sample			
	Nondeprived (N=23)		Deprived (N=20)		Nondeprived (N=31)		Deprived (N=34)	
	r	beta	r	beta	r	beta	r	beta
Achievement need (5 = high, 1 = low)	.13	.19	.32	.27	.07	.07	.33	.27
Intelligence (IQ)	.60	.62	.28	.20	.50	.52	.19	.09
Family status (1929) (5 = high, 1 = low)	—	—	—	—	.14	.04	.32	.27
	$R^2 = .39$		$R^2 = .14$		$R^2 = .26$		$R^2 = .19$	

Table A-24 — Selected Determinants of Activity Preferences among Oakland Men: Zero-Order Correlations and Partial Regression Coefficients in Standard Form (beta). N = 46

Determinants	Work		Family		Leisure	
	r	beta	r	beta	r	beta
Adult social class (1958) (5 = high, 1 = low)	.29	.27	−.15	−.17	−.39	−.39
IQ (1933–38)	.32	.25	−.16	−.08	−.24	−.16
Economic deprivation[a]	.01	−.02	.30	.33	−.30	−.26
Class origin (1929) (5 = high, 1 = low)	−.10	−.19	.01	.14	.14	.17
	$R^2 = .14$		$R^2 = .18$		$R^2 = .29$	

[a] Economic deprivation was treated as a dummy variable with nondeprived status scored 0 and deprived status, 1.

Table A-25

Preference for Job Security over Risk/Greater Gain, by Adult Status, Intelligence, and Family Background: Partial Regression Coefficients in Standard Form (beta)

Determinants of Security Preference	Prefers Job Security over Risk N = 37	
	r	beta
Low adult status (1958)	.22	.20
Low ability (IQ, 1933–38)	.46	.45
Economic deprivation	.19	.27
Working class origin (1929)	.05	−.07

Note. All items in this analysis have been dichotomized and scored 0 and 1. High scores correspond with item descriptions. Preference for job security is indicated by valuing job security and a reasonable income more than a less certain job with the possibility of greater reward (1) versus "the opposite choice" (0); low adult status (1958) refers to class categories of III, IV, and V versus I and II; low ability refers to IQ scores below the median; economic deprivation contrasts the deprived with the nondeprived; and working class in 1929 refers to categories IV and V on the Hollingshead Index.

Table A-26

An Intergenerational Comparison of Educational Attainment for Married Daughters, Their Parents, and Their Husbands

Educational Attainment	Percentage Distribution			
	Father	Mother	Daughter	Husband
College graduate	15	10	11	36
Some college	10	8	31	18
High school graduate	14	21	58	39
Some high school	22	19	—	7
Nine years or less	39	32	—	—
Unknown	—	10	—	—
	100 (72)	100 (72)	100 (72)	100 (72)

Table A-27   Married Women's Status in Adulthood by Class Origin and Economic Deprivation

Status in Adulthood	Middle-Class Origin		Working-Class Origin	
	Nondeprived (N = 13)	Deprived (N = 20)	Nondeprived (N = 11)	Deprived (N = 23)
Completed education by age of 20 (percent)	23	45	80	78
Own education (percent)				
College graduate	23	15	—	9
Some college	54	35	9	17
Less than college	23	50	91	74
Husband's education (percent)				
College graduate	54	55	18	22
Some college	—	30	9	17
No college	46	15	73	61
Wife's education less than husband's (percent)	46	75	27	30
Husband's occupational status, 1958 ($\bar{X}$)[a] (1 = high, 7 = low)	2.8	2.2	4.1	3.2
Social class, 1958 ($\bar{X}$)[a] (1 = high, 5 = low)	2.6	2.2	3.5	3.0

[a]   None of the differences between deprivational groups on mean occupational status and social class are statistically significant beyond the .05 level.

Table A-28   Activity Preferences of Women by Economic Deprivation, in Mean Scores

Economic Deprivation	Family	Work	Leisure	Community
Nondeprived (N = 20)	3.4	2.0	1.5	1.6
Deprived (N = 32)	4.8	1.6	1.5	1.0
	ND < D*			

* $p < .05$ (two-tailed t-test)

Table A-29   Years of Full-Time Employment for Women by Class Origin and Economic Deprivation, in Percentages

Years of Full-time Employment	Middle Class		Working Class	
	Total	Deprived	Total	Deprived
Before 1946				
None	27	25	14	12
One-four	46	40	50	52
Four +	27	35	36	36
	100 (33)	100 (20)	100 (36)	100 (25)
1946–1955				
None	54	45	56	50
One-four	30	40	24	29
Four +	15	15	21	21
	99 (33)	100 (20)	101 (34)	100 (24)

Table A-30   Age at Which Children Were Most Enjoyable and Greatest Problem (1964), by Sex of Parent, in Percentages

Age Period	Children Most Enjoyable		Children Greatest Problem	
	Men	Women	Men	Women
No particular period	20	61	13	20
Infancy	3	5	10	12
Preschool	19	7	16	2
Grade school	23	12	3	7
Junior high school	16	10	10	24
Senior high school +	19	5	48	34
	100 (31)	100 (41)	100 (31)	99 (41)

Note.   All subjects included in the table had their first child before the age of twenty-eight. Their oldest child at the time of the 1964 survey was at least sixteen years of age.

Table A-31 Political Party Affiliation of Oakland Adults (1958–64) by Selected Factors in a Multiple Classification Analysis,[a] in Percentages

Class Origin and Economic Deprivation	Republican	Democrat
Middle class		
Nondeprived (N = 33)	79	9
Deprived (N = 41)	54	32
Working class		
Nondeprived (N = 13)	74	23
Deprived (N = 24)	48	41
Grand percent[b]	61	27

[a] Three variables, not shown in the table, were included as controls in the analysis: adult class, religion, and sex.

[b] For the total sample, the relation between economic deprivation and party preference (Republican vs. Democratic/Independent) yielded a χ^2 value of 7.17, 1 df, $p < .01$.

Table A-32 Percentage Distribution of Families of Adolescents in Three Samples by Parental Nationality, Household Structure, and Father's Occupation

Background Factors	Oakland Growth Study, 1934	Junior High Students, 1934	High School Students, 1934
Parents native-born	72	68	—
Household structure intact	74	84	75
Father's occupation			
Professional, managerial	27	19	25
White-collar, small businessman, etc.	36	33	33
Blue-collar	31	36	28
Total number of cases	167	951	1,722

Table A-33   Intelligence and Family Characteristics of Subjects in the Adolescent and Adult Samples

Characteristics	Adolescent Sample	Adult Sample
IQ		
120	31	30
110–119	30	31
100–109	26	26
< 100	13	12
	100	100
Social class in 1929[a]		
Upper middle (I + II)	19	19
Lower middle (III)	38	37
Working (IV + V)	43	44
	100	100
Household structure		
% intact	74	74
Parental ethnicity		
% with native-born parents	72	74

[a] Based on Hollingshead's two-factor index (education and occupation).

Sample
Characteristics,
Data Sources,
and
Methodological
Issues

The purpose of this appendix is to provide greater detail on the Oakland sample, on the selection of participants and their resemblance to classmates, and on the educational environment; to describe major sources of data in the 1930s and in the subjects' adult years; and to review issues pertaining to measurement error, external validity, and analytic procedures. Before getting into these matters, some background points are worth noting in relation to a research strategy which entails the use of available data.

Available data, collected for other purposes, are typically only an approximation of the data the researcher would collect in a design of his own choosing. The present study did not have an option other than the use of archival data. Cost is a consideration in this form of secondary research, although the more important issue is whether the investment is likely to prove worthwhile under the constraints of past decisions, resource allocations, and knowledge limitations. The greater the time span covered by the materials, the more likely one is to feel these constraints, owing to change in research techniques. Up to a point, the suitability of archival materials can be improved through recoding procedures, aggregation across time periods, etc. In the Oakland study, these materials were incomplete in areas germane to our conceptual model. The effect of constraints in sample design and data collection have been noted at various points in the preceding analysis.

The Oakland Sample and Its Educational Setting

The Oakland Growth Study began in January 1931, when fifth-grade children from five schools in the northeastern sector of Oakland were selected for a projected longitudinal analysis of mental, social, and physical development in a normal sample of boys and girls. Selection was based on two criteria: willingness to participate, and anticipated permanence of residence in the area. This selection produced a sample of 84 boys and 83 girls which was studied continuously from 1932 to 1939 (the end of high school). All of the children were white, over 80 percent were Protestant (only four children were Jewish, and 12 percent were Catholic), and approximately three-fifths of the families were intact and were headed by native-born parents.

Despite the use of procedures that do not ensure a representative sample, families in the Oakland sample closely resemble families of other students who were enrolled in the junior and senior high schools attended by the subjects. Questionnaire surveys of all students enrolled in these schools in 1934 collected data on parental nationality, household status, and fathers' occupation. According to the comparison shown in table A–32, families in the Oakland sample were only slightly higher on occupational status. The adolescent sample of Oakland children is also comparable on these background factors to subjects who were followed up in the adult years (see table A–33).

Neoprogressive concepts of education were prominent in the climate and philosophy of the secondary schools attended by the Oakland children. Both the junior and senior high school advocated the philosophy that schools should minimize class differences among students and educate the whole child, with emphasis on social development and adjustment, tolerance, and good citizenship. The schools were linked to the School of Education at the University of California and served as experimental institutions in the neoprogressive movement of the 1930s. As might be expected, traditional academic subjects and intellectual excellence received greater stress in the high school.

In the early 30s, the physical plant of the junior high school was severely overcrowded, serving over a thousand students, a majority of whom were taught in portable structures. The staff included thirty-four teachers and four counselors. The temporary buildings were heated by small coal stoves and were furnished by undersized chairs and desks from elementary schools. Children who were unable to obtain adequate meals at home were offered free or low-cost meals in a cafeteria that was located in one of the portable buildings. A clubhouse established by the Institute of Child Welfare (now Human Development) at Berkeley was used by staff members for naturalistic observations of the study members, but all children were welcome. It quickly became a popular setting for peer groups and social activities.

The transition between junior and senior high school brought significant change in the social experiences of children in the study.

Upon leaving the security of familiar surroundings and friends, they entered a larger school which was highly regarded for its college preparatory program and diversified curriculum in the arts, natural sciences, and social studies. Students were recruited from all areas of Oakland. In this school of some nineteen hundred students and staff members (at the time the subjects were in high school), social training and citizenship education were mainly extracurricular activities. The teaching staff ranked high on quality: two-fifths of the teachers had postgraduate degrees, and nearly 90 percent had engaged in at least some advanced work while teaching at the school. Within the community, the school was recognized for its excellent record of placing qualified students in the state university.

"Undemocratic" patterns in social activities received much criticism from staff and student leaders. Particular attention was given to ways of minimizing social distinctions in group discussions involving both students and teachers. One outcome of this exchange entailed a set of dress codes for girls. They were required to wear skirts and middy outfits from the second week of school, and the rule was enforced by a student "Middy Board." To avoid the social consequences of worn clothing, some of the boys from more deprived families decided to wear their R.O.T.C. uniforms. Monday was designated "civilian clothes day," a day when students could choose what clothes they wanted to wear.

Data Collection
in the 1930s

The depth and wealth of longitudinal data on children in the Oakland study offered an unusual opportunity for the present research. While the data were not collected for the explicit purposes of this study, we were fortunate that the program of data collection was broad and obtained economic information at two crucial points on families in the study, 1929 and 1933. Four sets of data are used extensively in the analysis: interviews with mothers in 1932, 1934, and 1936; questionnaires administered to the children in junior and senior high school; ratings of family relations in the senior high period; and staff ratings of behavior. The first two sets were not coded in a form that was usable in the present analysis, and thus required considerable preparation. This task involved trained coders, a computer programmer, and the author over a two-year period. Much of the available information on family relations and parental personality is drawn from these data sets. Unfortunately interviews were not conducted with the fathers, and mothers were seldom asked questions about their husbands. An overview of these data sets is provided below.

Interviews with
Mothers

A staff member of the Institute of Child Welfare visited each family on an annual basis and recorded observations of family life in a log. These qualitative materials were found to be an invaluable source of insights and illustrations for the analysis, but they were not sufficiently systematic to permit codification. Systematic home interviews were conducted only in 1932, 1934, and 1936. The first and last interviews obtained information on child-rearing practices, family relationships, and peer activities. This was supplemented by economic and occupational data in the 1934 interview.

The staff member who interviewed the mothers also rated them on personal characteristics, using a seven-point scale. Examples of scales used in the present analysis include dissatisfaction with lot, feelings of inferiority, fatigue, and personal appearance. To improve the stability of each scale, we averaged the three ratings on each characteristic.

Questionnaires from
Children

Two types of questionnaires were administered to the children: a questionnaire on social and emotional behavior that was administered seven times between 1932 and 1938; and the Strong Vocational Interest Blank in 1938. The latter provided data on occupational goals and is too well-known to justify description at this point. The first questionnaire is one of the more important sources of data in our analysis, and was specifically designed for the Oakland study by Caroline Tryon.[1] The respondents were told that the questions "are to help us find out what people think and the things they wish to do. There aren't any 'right' or 'wrong' answers. Each person will answer differently. Just try to put down what you really think and wish." Topics covered by questions include the emotional climate of the home, parent-child relations, relations with peers, and self-attitudes. In order to obtain more stable measures, we averaged all dichotomous and ordinal-response categories for the seventh and eighth grades, and for the eleventh and twelfth grades. Instruments for each of these periods are labeled in the analysis as the junior and senior high questionnaires.

Ratings on Family Relations

The children's perceptions of parents and family relationships were also measured by nine-point ratings in the senior high period. In this period, three trained judges were presented with an identical set of data on each subject—including parental interviews, self-reports, classmate impressions, and staff observations—and were asked to sort independently a set of interpersonal statements into nine ordered categories, ranging from 1 (uncharacteristic) to 9 (most characteristic).[2] The judgments on each statement were then averaged to obtain each subject's score. The average reliability of the composite Q-set for each of the periods was slightly less than .70. Examples of ratings used in the present analysis are "feels closer to mother than to father," "perceives father to be an attractive man," and "feels that father is a respected man as judged by societal standards."

Staff Ratings

Three sets of staff ratings are used in the present study: Free-Play ratings for the junior and senior high periods; situation ratings obtained in 1937;[3] and ratings of needs which refer to the high school years.

During semiannual visits to the Institute of Child Welfare for physical and mental examinations, the children were rated by observers on a wide range of social behavior and personal attributes in free social situations (hence, Free-Play ratings). These trips were made by small same-sex groups—usually six or eight of the children would come together. The setting was the playground of the institute. The time was either arranged as an informal lunch period or as a picnic in which the children and at least two members of the staff participated. The staff members were well known by the children and related to them as interested, friendly adults. Systematic observations made during the period were recorded afterward on comment sheets and rating schedules. Reliabilities for at least two observers were generally above .70 across the 40 seven-point scales for each year. The annual ratings were averaged for the junior and senior high periods.

The situation ratings, representing the average judgments of three staff members, were based on intensive observations of behavior in a specially designed clubhouse where the subjects and their friends met in mixed groups. The clubhouse was maintained on the property of the junior high school, and later for a year on the grounds of the senior high school. When the children moved to high school, a number of supplementary activities—dances, trips, and parties—were arranged to facilitate staff observations. The seven-point scales measured a wide range of behavior, including responsibility, industry, and popularity. Reliability coefficients for the three raters were generally greater than .75.

Three staff members under the supervision of Else Frenkel-Brunswik rated the children on a set of needs, using intuition and materials obtained from observation, questionnaires, and interviews. Three of the ratings are directly relevant to the motivational effect of status loss in the Depression: need for recognition—"desire to excite praise and commendation, to command respect, social approval, prestige, honor, and fame;" need for control—"desire to control one's human environment by suggestion, persuasion, and command"; and need for achievement—"desire to attain a high level of objective accomplishments, to increase self-regard by successful exercise of talent, to select hard tasks." The judges were instructed to base their judgments on assumed motivation instead of on social technique. Attained status in aggression, leadership, or social acceptance was thus excluded from consideration. The intensity of need for social recognition, for instance, does not "necessarily describe the actual prestige or social status which characterize the position of the child relative to the group, but describes rather how strongly the child is motivated by the goal of social prestige. Such an urge may sometimes be openly displayed; in other instances, however, it may be blocked from any behavioral outlet."[4] The ratings varied from 1 (highest intensity) to 5 (lowest intensity). Reliabilities for the three judges were approximately .70.

Data Collection in the 1940s to 1960s

A systematic effort to obtain data or establish contact with members of the Oakland study was made at two points in the 1940s: a short questionnaire survey of occupational interests and activities in 1941, and contact through phone calls or letters in 1948. Two major follow-ups were made in the 1950s, and these were followed by a mailed questionnaire in 1964. Seventy-six women and sixty-nine men participated in at least one of these major follow-ups. This sample does not differ from the adolescent sample on IQ, family social class in 1929, ethnicity, and household structure (see table A-33).

In the first follow-up (1953-54), the subjects were interviewed extensively, participated in a thorough physical examination and a psychiatric assessment, and completed a series of personality inventories. Apart from the life-history information collected at this point, we used the psychiatric assessment as one measure of psychological health in adulthood (see chapter 9). A lengthy interview was conducted in the second follow-up (1957-58). The interviews included five or more sessions of two or three hours each covering recollections of adolescence, perceptions of parents, marital relations, occupational and family information, and memories of the Depression. Retrospective ratings of each year in the life cycle up to 1958 were also obtained from the subjects at this time. The third follow-up (1964) relied primarily on a mailed questionnaire. From all of these data, family and occupational histories were constructed for each subject up to 1958. These histories ordered the adult data according to both chronological age and year since the subjects were approximately the same age. One can move from age at first marriage, for instance, or of entry into a stable career line to the approximate year and back again without too large a sacrifice in accuracy. Occupational and family histories are the main sources of data for analyses of the life course of men and women which are reported in chapters 7 and 8.

Measurement Error, External Validity, and Analytic Procedures

The preceding description of the archival data has special significance for the relation between input quality and outcomes in the data analysis. The results of our analysis are limited by how well we have measured key variables and even more fundamentally by our assumptions concerning relevant variables and their interrelations. If, for example, our hypothesized linkages between economic deprivation and outcomes in the life course are incorrect, in the sense that they provide a poor map of reality, no amount of thoroughness in measurement would salvage the results; estimation of the wrong model will yield misleading or meaningless estimates. Also, our retrieval operations and adaptation of materials from the Oakland archive were structured by questions based on the adaptational model. But the foremost problem in the archival work centered on matters of measurement; the availability of indicators of variables in the analytic model, and their adequacy. We sought consistent measures with a high degree of internal validity, in the sense that they describe what we think they are describing, but we have had to settle for less in some cases with appropriate allowances in the analysis and interpretation.[5]

Appendix B

Errors in measurement arise from situational factors which make for unstable or inconsistent values relative to the "true" value, across place, time, and source (mother, child, etc.), and from limitations in the measurement device itself. Transitory factors can produce variations in scores which have no correspondence to the "true" value. This unreliability may occur, for instance, through the effect of a respondent's mood on reported family relationships, or the difference in interviewing style, or observational context. Wherever possible and appropriate, the following procedures were employed to cope with this measurement problem. To maximize the stability of observed values in the 1930 data, we averaged scores or used composites which were based on the repeated application of the same measurement device within two time periods, junior—and senior—high school. As noted in the preceding section, this procedure was applied to questionnaire data from the children, to interviewer ratings of the mothers, to the observational ratings in general, and to clinical judgments on case materials (the ratings of family relationships and needs). The most reliable measures in the data archive are those based on staff observations.

When the option was available, we used multiple indicators of the same dependent variable. This strategy served our theoretical interests in some instances by enabling a comparison of different views of the same behavior (see chapter 6), but it was also a way of dealing with the uncertain reliabilities of single indicators. For example, the psychological states associated with economic deprivation may partly reflect the peculiarities of a measurement device, such as the type of questions which comprise the index. We would have greater confidence in these results if they also emerge from analysis with other measures of psychological health. This approach was employed in our assessment of economic deprivation in adult health (chapter 9).

Frequently in the childhood period and especially the adult years we were limited to single-item indicators of both independent and dependent variables. This type of index was used in analyses of children's roles in the household economy (as the report of mother on children's financial help and gainful employment), of marital power in the family of origin, and of children's attitudes generally. With few exceptions, aspects of careers, attitudes and perceptions in adulthood were measured by indexes which were also based on data from only one self-report item. A few measures even combined the limitations of a single item with the problematic validity of retrospective reports. We gained some insight on the adequacy of these measures from their correlation with other indexes, from the extent to which the relations correspond with theory and with empirical evidence in

Sample Characteristics,
Data Sources

the research literature. The accumulated evidence on sex differences, for example, provides a basis for evaluating the Oakland findings on sex differences in the 30s and adult years. The literature on class variations in the psychic effects of economic deprivation, on family adaptations to economic hardship, and on status attainment also offers standards of comparison in relation to the Oakland results. Despite measurement level handicaps, these results do largely support the theoretical frame of the study and correspond with findings in the relevant literature.

The very nature of a longitudinal study makes generalizations hazardous. The Oakland sample was not formed by using the procedures of probability sampling, and thus we do not know its population. In fact, the sample is most accurately described as a particular universe of fifth-grade students in the northeastern sector of Oakland (1931), defined by residential permanence and a willingness to cooperate. By virtue of their membership in the study, the Oakland children had experiences which were not generally available to classmates, including frequent physical and personality assessments, friendly contact with adults in nonauthority roles, special recreational and educational trips, etc. Without a control group, there is no satisfactory method for identifying the impact of reactive measurements and unique project experiences. Nevertheless, we have sought a rough estimation of the study's external validity through comparisons with other research. We were able to do so in a number of areas, as noted above, but the effort was handicapped by lack of a comparable study. Up to the present, no other study had investigated the effects of the Depression experience in the life course.

Apart from an unlikely replication of the Oakland analysis on a sample of Americans in the same age group, a comparison of this cohort with another appears to be the most promising source of evidence on the generalization boundaries of the Oakland research. A longitudinal study with this design is presently underway; the Oakland sample will be compared with a younger cohort (birthdates, 1928–29) over four decades, from 1929 to 1970. Comparisons will also be made between members of these cohorts and their offspring who were recently interviewed. Plans call for an investigation of the linkage between the Depression experience and intergenerational similarities and variations in value orientations and politics. If all goes well, this analysis should substantially enlarge our current understanding of the Depression experience in the course of individual lives and social history.

Traditionally, level of measurement and sample characteristics have received considerable weight as underlying assumptions in the use of analytic techniques and tests of significance, in decisions regarding statistical analysis. Parametric statistics offer an important advantage over nonparametric statistics in their greater power, but they require a level of measurement (interval or ratio) which is all too rare in sociological research. If we favor the use of parametric statistics, as we have in this study, what are the consequences of violating the assumption on level of measurement? An assessment of such violations leads to the conclusion that "under almost any conceivable research situation, [parametric] statistical tests are robust enough to allow the researcher to use them with little fear of gross errors regardless of whether or not he has an interval or ratio scale so long as his ordinal measure is monotonically related to the underlying true scale."[6] In regression analysis, the normality assumption mainly applies to the dependent variable, while measurement error affects estimates through the independent variables.

Though most indicators in the Oakland archive are either nominal or ordinal in level of measurement, parametric statistics were used wherever, in our judgment, there was an analytic advantage in doing so and serious errors seemed unlikely. To minimize such errors, we generally compared the results of analyses which employed both parametric and nonparametric measures, i.e., cross-tabular analyses and ordinal measures of association with the results of correlational analysis. The path-analytic technique, which can handle dichotomous or dummy variables, was employed to test the linkage model[7]—to obtain estimates of the main effects of economic deprivation (non-deprived versus deprived) and its indirect effects through family adaptations in the Depression.

The patterning of relationships received higher priority in our evaluation of results than isolated statistical tests. While specific hypotheses were proposed as we outlined the analytic structure of the study, our interpretation of findings focused on a broader frame; for example, on linkages between the division of labor and power in the family, the comparative effects of family deprivation in status attainment and adult health, etc. Tests of significance have been used sparingly as a minimum criterion for determining reliable, non-chance findings, despite the non-probability sample.[8] Statistically significant findings in a relatively small sample do indicate sizable effects or differences, and are helpful in this respect as an evaluative standard. Another useful index of reliable findings in the analysis, that of consistency, entailed the comparison of results based on different indicators of the same concept, and of outcomes from theoretically related analyses. Each method was viewed simply as a guideline for evaluating the results.

Sample Characteristics,
Data Sources

Appendix C   On Comparisons of the Great Depression

In reflecting upon their Depression experience, Americans inevitably make comparative judgments: "Conditions were not as bad for us as they were for other families," or "They were worse," or "We were all in the same boat." They might also recall differences between groups or categories of Americans, between classes, old and young, the Anglo-Saxons and the ethnics, the assembly-line workers and the craftsmen. But few are likely to compare living conditions in America of the 30s with those in contemporary Germany, Canada, or England. Unlike World War II, the Great Depression is not familiar to the average American as an international crisis; only with wars and threats of war did overseas matters gain prominence among public issues. The remembered smallness or simplicity of Depression life owes something to its domestic boundaries.

But to understand the depressed 30s in America, its antecedents, developments, and aftermath, we are necessarily drawn to the international field; to war mobilization and the effects of World War I, to American dominance and interdependence in the world economy, to the diffusion of reformative models, the rise of fascism, the recovery impetus of World War II. Little is known, at present, about the comparative dimensions of the Great Depression; a comprehensive, sociohistorical study along these lines has yet to be accomplished.[1] Nevertheless, there is no lack of comparative statements on widely varied aspects of the Depression, with or without appropriate efforts in documentation. Some comparisons rely solely upon economic indicators as measures of impact, as if to assume that a social problem or crisis is an objective given, or that the same rate of unemployment has similar meaning in different sociohistorical contexts. Striking developments in the 30s, such as the rise of a new perceived reality in the United States and Germany, add considerable weight to the assumption that a "social problem exists primarily in terms of how it is defined and conceived in a society instead of being an objective

330

condition with a definite makeup" (Blumer 1971). The mood of a people follows no uniform relation to objective hardships. In this respect, Gorer argues that while objective deprivations were more severe in the U.S., the collective mood was less hopeful in England: "the sullen despair continued until the war became inevitable" (Gorer 1967, p. 16). Even the use of different economic criteria can lead to opposing interpretations of the Depression's impact. Thus the conclusion that the United States was hit harder by the Depression than Germany is generally supported by economic measures, though not by commonly cited unemployment rates.

Some clarity may be gained by viewing comparative statements in relation to a general model of the Depression as a collective stress or crisis situation. One skeleton example would be to regard the collective response of the populace as a function of interpretations and objective features of the situation. Four objective dimensions are especially appropriate to the Depression: scope, speed of onset, duration of impact, and degree of social preparedness.[2] The first three factors (as indicators of situational demand) and social preparedness influence lines of response directly and indirectly through shared definitions of the situation. Comparative assessments of the Depression generally make reference to one or more of these situational variables. Scope refers to the proportion and distribution of the population afflicted by the event; in the case of the Depression, to the prevalence and distribution (social and geographic) of unemployment, relative income loss, etc. This criterion appears in Galbraith's judgment that the Great Depression outranks World War II in the panoply of crises in American life (only a minority of Americans experienced severe wartime hardships, losses, etc.).[3]

Substantial inter-country differences in the Depression's speed of onset and duration have been noted for some time. The general economic trough occurred later, the slump persisted longer, and the decline in national income was greater (close to 50 percent) in the United States and Canada, than in Great Britain, Germany, and Australia. The underlying causal factors extend beyond our limited interest in the Depression's relative impact. However, two issues are worth noting. The first is the potential impact of national differences in social preparedness on the duration of the crisis—a point we shall take up in relation to sociohistorical factors in adaptive capacity. The second issue is the international consequences of the drastic slump in the U.S. economy. By the late 20s, industrial production for the U.S. had climbed to over two-fifths of the world total, to nearly twice the combined figure for Great Britain and Germany. Shocks from the '29 Crash

On Comparisons of the
Great Depression

and the severe decline in international trade were keenly felt by countries, such as Australia, that were vulnerable to fluctuations in overseas factors.

With its sociohistorical aspects, social preparedness has special significance for accounts of the Depression's relative impact. Relevant considerations include the pace of recovery from World War I, dependence on exports of agricultural goods, relative prosperity in the 20s as a contrast to economic decline, and the availability of adaptive mechanisms which are suited to the emergent requirements of a depressed economy (public security provisions). Barton's definition of a "prepared" social system is especially germane to common weaknesses in pre-depression America and Canada; a system is well prepared for a given type of collective problem situation "if it has well-defined roles for individuals, for which they are adequately trained, with these roles integrated in workable organizations and plans" (Barton 1969, p. 41). In the 20s, the United States and Canada were "decentralized in an age of increasing centralization, and riding hard for a fall."[4] Both countries lacked a tradition of state responsibility and appropriate mechanisms of coordination and control; both nations were backward, from a comparative perspective, in the importance of the public sector and its social legislation. If "no major country in the world was so ill-prepared as the United States to cope" with the Depression, as Leuchtenburg asserts,[5] Canada was at least a close second. While the two countries shared many features of being ill prepared, Patterson's comparative study (see note 1) suggests that Canada probably suffered more, owing to its fixed costs, high provincial debts, and heavy dependence on the export of staples.

A gradual impact of relatively long duration permits the development of adaptive measures through trial and error, despite low preparedness, as in the American version of the Great Depression. The Depression thus differs from a nuclear attack, with its sudden onset and short duration, coupled with low preparedness. We can best illustrate the problems and issues one encounters in comparative assessments of the Depression's impact by focusing on indicators of scope and preparedness, and their relation to collective interpretations and response.

The most common measures of the Depression's relative impact deal more or less directly with the matter of scope, and are compromised by a discouraging list of qualifications. Unemployment rates illustrate this point. An international comparison of these rates is handicapped by inter-country inconsistencies in the definition of unemployment, in the timing and sources of data collection. In addition, the consequences of unemployment depend on the economic and technological stage of the country, on urban-industrial development and the importance of the public sector. Some of these problems can be minimized, as seen in Schedvin's analysis, through the use of data from comparable sources in societies that rank in the upper category of industrialization, as shown in figure 10. Estimates for all countries except the U.S. and Japan (official) are based on trade union returns. The most one can claim for these figures is that they indicate an approximate order of the countries on one measure of the Depression's scope. On Schedvin's comparison of declines in real national product, industrial production, and national expenditure, the United States ranked slightly higher on impact than Germany and considerably higher than Great Britain.

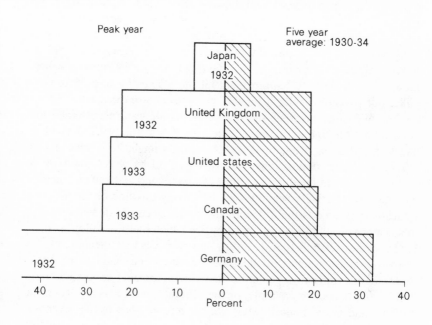

Figure C-1   Unemployment Rates in Five Countries

Sole reliance on unemployment data as an index of the Depression's impact tends to yield a misleading picture of economic well-being among families that did not experience periods of joblessness. This applies, in particular, to the economic situation of self-employed businessmen; some of these men in the Oakland study, who lost most of their income, were able to maintain their commercial activity in some fashion. The tendency for unemployment figures to exaggerate assessments of class differences is seen in Runciman's analysis of class relations in England's depression (circa 1931); these figures, which

On Comparisons of the
Great Depression

declined sharply by occupational status, were presented as primary evidence for the conclusion that manual workers were harder hit by the Depression than were clerical workers, as a group (Runciman 1966, p. 81). In any case, this interpretation applies only to the objective condition of unemployment, for Runciman's analysis leads to an opposing conclusion on the class distribution of perceived well-being or relative deprivation. "During the Depression . . . relative deprivation among manual workers and their families appears to have been low in both frequency and magnitude"; depressed economic conditions had the effect of restricting their social comparisons to the working class, unlike periods of rising prosperity and the war years (ibid., p. 64). By contrast, a broader and more demanding frame of social comparison in the middle classes (the contrast with relatively high status before losses) made social declines especially real and traumatic. Along this line, Schoenbaum's observation on Nazi Germany may also apply to other industrial societies: "Unemployment hit the blue collar and white collar alike, but psychologically it hit the white-collar worker harder."[6]

One might further argue that the more people were accustomed to good times and high expectations, the greater was the psychological effect of bad times. Canadians and Americans might be singled out in this respect; both populations were very well off by world standards in 1929, were conditioned by a culture of abundance and self-reliance, and suffered relatively heavy losses. Following this line of thought, Leuchtenburg asserts that "Americans experienced the depression as much more of a shock than did countries which had not enjoyed the boom of the1920's."[7] It is doubtful, however, whether meaningful, comparative assessments of shock or impact can be made at present, except in extreme cases, given the many unknowns and contextual variations. One thinks, for example, of the different mix of factors (chronic political and moral malaise, etc.) which were at work in the psychological climate of Germany (1929–32), the context of Nazi extremism —a climate which Grunberger describes as "a mood of living in an *Endsituation* (final situation), which presaged either chaos or an 'ineluctable transformation.' "[8] Clearly, what little we know about cross-national differences in the Depression crisis, in psychic impact and economic conditions, does not help much in understanding the political realities of the time.

A striking expression of these realities is seen in the rapid expansion of centralized governmental power. Effective emergency action in the crisis required superordinate goals, control, and sacrifice; and in the United States, as well as other hard-hit countries (especially Germany), this action was shaped by the imagery and machinery of wartime mobilization. An early version of this political response appeared in

Herbert Spencer's thesis (*Principles of Sociology*) that war causes an expansion of governmental regulation and political change in the direction of totalitarianism. Sorokin later extended Spencer's thesis to all major disasters or crises of national scope—to famine, economic collapse, war, pestilence. Ranging over a vast array of historical and comparative materials, Sorokin identified this emergent response to crisis as one of the strongest "inductive generalizations in history"; "the main effect of calamities upon the political and social structure of society is an expansion of governmental regulation, regimentation, and control of social relationships and a decrease in the regulation and management of social relationships by individuals and private groups" (Sorokin 1937, p. 122). Such developments have taken different forms, depending on context, and are generally restrained by a tradition of democratic rule. Yet the private world of the individual American was controlled by government to an unusual degree in the Depression during Roosevelt's first term of office.

Lessons from mobilization in World War I, on the psychology and machinery of wartime mobilization, were freely adapted to the problems of national recovery in the New Deal. "There was scarcely a New Deal act or agency that did not owe something to the experience of World War I" (Leuchtenburg 1964, p. 109).[9] The success of this experience and the urgency of the Depression crisis sustained belief that the "nation at war for its survival" was the only superordinate idea that could develop the necessary unity and coordination in sacrificial effort and commitment. As one New Dealer put it: "The fact is that only war has up to now proved to be such a transcending objective that doctrine is willingly sacrificed for efficiency in its service."

The superordinate goal of "nation saving" through mobilization techniques adapted from World War I is most clearly embodied in two New Deal Agencies: the National Recovery Administration (designed after the War Industries Board of World War I) and the popular Civilian Conservation Corps. Roosevelt recruited veterans of the war effort to direct or staff both agencies. Under the heavy hand of General Hugh Johnson, implementation of NRA mandates illustrates the profound implications of war psychology for relations between the state and individual liberties; honor gained in sacrifice and cooperation for the national interest, the social penalty for nonconformists and "slackers"— the uncooperative were on the "other side." Nowhere is the mass psychology in conformity pressures more clearly stated than in the words of Bernard Baruch, who first proposed the idea of an NRA insignia that later took the form of the "Blue Eagle"—a "badge of honor" for cooperation in the NRA campaign. In reference to wartime, Baruch observed that "if it is commonly understood that those who are cooperating are soldiers against the enemy within and those who omit to act are on the other side, there will be little hanging back. The insignia of government approval on doorways, letterheads, and invoices will become a necessity in business." In this martial spirit of the times, the consumer power of housewives was mobilized by the slogan "Buy now under the Blue Eagle." More generally, in the early years of Roosevelt's first term, many acts which did not fit the New Deal plan for recovery were regarded as disloyal, even as sabotage. Labor strikes were so interpreted from the New Dealers' view of the national interest. Such constraints and pressures were softened and excesses corrected as the crisis diminished.

Just as mobilization in World War I provided a model for coping with the Depression, mobilization under the New Deal developed techniques and resources that prepared America for the emerging fascist threat in Europe. This connection is most readily seen in the Civilian Conservation Corps, an agency whose objectives (to instill "martial virtues in the nation's youth," etc.) were carried out by the army; "CCC recruits convened at army recruiting stations; traveled to an army camp where they were outfitted in World War I clothing; were transported to the woods by troop-train; fell asleep in army tents to the strain of 'Taps' and woke to 'Reveille.' " Despite fears of military control and militarism in this peacetime army, the program gained widespread favor through its image of shepherding the nation's youth and physical resources. Few congressmen, however, were unaware of CCC veterans as a potential military nucleus in case of war. As the nation entered the Second World War, mobilization analogues of the NRA and CCC emerged with their message of solidarity, sacrifice, and commitment in a transcendent cause.

Notes

Full facts of publication (subtitles, places of publication, names of publishers, etc.) are given only for works not listed in the Select Bibliography.

1 The Depression Experience

1 Mitchell, *Depression Decade* (1947); Sternsher, *Hitting Home* (1970), pp. 20–21; and Huntington, *Unemployment Relief and the Unemployed* (1939), p. 6.

2 Eugene Smolensky, *Adjustment to Depression and War, 1930–1945* (San Francisco: Scott, Foresman, 1964), p. 7. Inequality in the distribution of income, a major cause of the Depression, increased in the 1930s. "In 1929 the distribution of income was, by American standards, extremely uneven, giving much too much to persons at the top of the income scale and too little to those at the bottom. The situation grew worse during the depression as unemployment hit low-income families the hardest. It was not until World War II created a great demand for labor to meet production requirements that average- and low-income families began to enjoy better incomes." Thomas C. Cochran, *The Great Depression and World War II* (San Francisco: Scott, Foresman & Co., 1968), p. 2. See also Douglass C. North, *Growth and Welfare in the American Past* (Englewood Cliffs, N.J.: Prentice-Hall, 1966), pp. 174–80.

3 Harvey Swados, ed., *The American Writer and the Great Depression* (Indianapolis: Bobbs-Merrill, 1966), p. xii.

4 Milton Meltzer, *Brother Can You Spare a Dime? The Great Depression, 1929–1933* (New York: Knopf, 1969), p. 3. For a study which shows how individuals reconstruct the past to fit the present, see Fred Davis, *Passage through Crisis* (Indianapolis: Bobbs-Merrill, 1961).

5 Thomas Lask, "Surfacing in the Thirties" (a review of Albert Halper's *Good-Bye, Union*

Square [Chicago: Quadrangle, 1970]), *New York Times*, 6 November 1970.

6 Herbert J. Gans, *The Levittowners* (New York: Pantheon, 1967), p. 201.

7 Robert A. Nesbit's statement of Max Weber's question on the rise of capitalism, a specific case of a more general class of questions on social change: "What are the conditions under which actual social change takes place in the history of a given social institution or given mode of social behavior?" *Social Change and History* (1969), pp. 275, 277.

8 The approach is consistent with the "new social history," with history "from the bottom up." See the work of Stephan Thernstrom, *Poverty and Progress* (1964) and *The Other Bostonians* (1973); of Philip Greven, *Four Generations* (1970); and of Richard Sennett, *Families against the City* (1970). For a critical overview of developments in social history, see Hobsbawm, "From Social History to the History of Society" (1971).

9 According to Thomas, social science "must reach the actual human experiences and attitudes which constitute the full, live and active social reality beneath the formal organization of social phenomena. . . .A social institution can be fully understood only if we do not limit ourselves to abstract study of its formal organization, but analyze the way in which it appears in the personal experience of various members of the group and follow the influence which it has upon their lives." In Volkhart, ed., *Social Behavior and Personality* (1951), p. 146. See also Herbert Blumer's penetrating critique of *The Polish Peasant* in *An Appraisal of . . . "The Polish Peasant"* (1939).

10 There is a substantial literature on the response of children to crises. Important studies include Freud and Burlingham, *War and Children* (1943); Martha Wolfenstein and Gilbert Kliman, *Children and the Death of a President* (Garden City, N.Y.: Doubleday, 1965); and Coles, *Children of Crisis* (1967).

11 Crisis phenomena are generally subsumed by the concept of social strain in theories of social change and collective behavior. See Neil J. Smelser, *Theory of Collective Behavior* (New York: Free Press, 1963). In the following section of the text, we shall draw upon W. I. Thomas's theory of crisis situation and adaptation. Most of the relevant essays can be found in Volkhart, ed., *Social Behavior and Personality* (1951). For an extension of this perspective, see Mechanic, *Medical Sociology* (1968), chap. 9. Thomas's view of the adaptational process draws upon elements of

Darwin's adaptive variation-selection process. For an application of the latter to culture-personality relations, see Robert A. LeVine, *Culture, Behavior, and Personality* (Chicago: Aldine, 1973).

12 For a creative theoretical contribution on this topic, see Norma Haan, "Proposed Model of Ego Functioning: Coping and Defense Mechanisms in Relationship to IQ Change," *Psychological Monographs* 77 (1963), Whole No. 571. Another valuable contribution is provided by Daniel R. Miller and Guy E. Swanson, *Inner Conflict and Defense* (New York: Holt, 1960).

13 Other studies of the family in the Depression include Cavan and Ranck, *The Family and the Depression* (1938); Komarovsky, *The Unemployed Man and His Family* (1940); and Bakke, *Citizens without Work* (1940). The Social Science Research Council sponsored a series of studies on social aspects of the Depression, including a well-known volume on the family: Stouffer and Lazarsfeld, *Research Memorandum on the Family in the Depression* (1937).

14 For the classic study on this consequence of extreme deprivation, see Jahoda, Lazarsfeld, and Zeisel, *Marienthal* (1970)—an English version of a book published some thirty years earlier in German.

15 Inkeles, "Social Change and Social Character" (1955), esp. pp. 14–15. In a more recent essay, Inkeles examines at some length the unintended consequences of social change in child socialization ("Society, Social Structure, and Child Socialization," in Clausen 1968, pp. 75–93). See also LeVine, *Culture, Behavior, and Personality* (note 11 above), esp. chap. 7, "The Applicability of a Darwinian View."

16 See Daniel R. Miller, "Personality as a System," in Raoul Naroll and Ronald Cohen, eds., *A Handbook of Method in Cultural Anthropology* (Garden City, N.Y.: The Natural History Press, 1970), pp. 509–26. This essay is an excellent source on method in formulating linkages between social structure and personality. Also relevant is Elder, "On Linking Social Structure and Personality" (1973).

17 A link between the "Depression trauma" and work orientation among British manual workers is discussed in a speculative essay by Geoffrey Gorer, "What's the Matter with Britain?" (1967).

18 Theoretical and methodological issues in the comparative study of age groups are cogently discussed in Riley, Johnson, and Foner, *Aging and Society* (1972), vol. 3, esp. chap. 2; and in Hyman, *Secondary Analysis of Sample Surveys* (1972), esp. pp. 274–90.

19 The primary source on instruments and data collected in the 1930s is Harold E. Jones, "Procedures of the Adolescence Growth Study," *Journal of Consulting Psychology* 3 (1939): 177–80. A comparable source on the adult years is John A. Clausen, "Personality Measurement in the Oakland Growth Study," in James E. Birren, ed., *Relations of Development and Aging* (Springfield, Ill.: Charles Thomas, 1964), pp. 165–75.

20 The estimates are based on data and sources reported by Cabell Phillips, *From the Crash to the Blitz, 1929–1939* (New York: Macmillan, 1969), p. 34. Data on taxpayer returns were obtained from the *Statistical Abstracts of the United States, 1935*, p. 182; *1939*, p. 183.

21 See Edgar J. Hinkel and William E. McCone, eds., *Oakland, 1858–1938* (Oakland, Calif.: Oakland Public Library, 1939).

22 Frederick Wyatt, "A Psychologist Looks at History," *Journal of Social Issues* 17 (1961): 66–77.

23 In this respect, Easterlin's warning to analysts of economic series closely parallels our research experience: "A scholar interested in quantitative study of an extended historical period is ill advised to have strong preconceptions about data requirements and statistical methodology. All too soon he will find himself pushed to the brink of despair by the fragmentary nature of the data and by problems of conceptual and statistical comparability. He must be prepared, moreover, to become a producer as well as a consumer of historical series." Easterlin, *Population, Labor Force, and Long Swings in Economic Growth* (1968), p. 7. Kai Erikson observes that "working with historical materials requires an approach to data tempered by a kind of skepticism and uncertainty." "Sociology . . ." (1970), p. 335.

24 In recent years, for instance, studies of relevance to the Depression have been conducted on the social-psychological effects of plant shutdowns. Aiken, Ferman, and Sheppard, *Economic Failure, Alienation, and Extremism* (1968); Slote, *Termination* (1969). A thorough review of research in the Depression on the psychological effects of unemployment is reported by Zawadski and Lazarsfeld in "The Psychological Consequences of Unemployment" (1935).

25 A sharp downturn in the economy would drastically alter the social world of many children from the upper classes, beyond its effect on the family environment. "The collapse of the counter-culture of the 1920s in the face of economic depression suggests that one must eschew any linear theory of societal change. The

cultural revolt of the present period presupposes economic stability and affluence, conditions which, given the cyclical behavior of capitalist economies, should not be taken for granted." Milton Mankoff and Richard Flacks, "The Changing Social Base of the American Student Movement," in Philip G. Altbach and Robert S. Laufer, eds., *The New Pilgrims: Youth Protest in Transition* (New York: David McKay, 1972), pp. 56–57.

26 William Kessen, "Research Design in the Study of Developmental Problems," in Mussen 1960, pp. 36–70. Ever conscious of the unique value and limitations of their data, longitudinal researchers tend to conduct their inquiries in the spirit set forth by Kessen. Concerning their study of the Fels subjects, Kagan and Moss state: "We view this research report primarily as a source of new hypotheses and not as an almanac of facts. It is an invitation to our colleagues to select ideas according to their taste and to submit to more rigorous testing the provocative hunches uncovered by this investigation." *Birth to Maturity* (1962), p. 19. In relation to the Oakland study, see Jack Block, *Lives through Time* (1971), an extraordinary study of personality change among members of both the Oakland and the Guidance samples at the Institute of Human Development.

2 Adaptations to Economic Deprivation

1 Subjective deprivation, a perceived disparity between expectations and attainment, and the resulting discontent are widely regarded as major forces in the emergence of social movements. In this vein, Hal Draper suggests the student movement of the thirties was partly a consequence of social and economic decline among middle-class families. "A whole section of the American middle class was being declassed; and the student movement was in part a result of this declassment." "The Student Movement of the Thirties: A Political History," in Simons 1967, p. 156. Much of the discontent associated with declassment may have been expressed in the dramatic shift in party preference from Republican to Democratic between 1928 and 1932. An important question for the present study is how parental discontent and party preference were expressed in the political socialization of children. We shall briefly touch upon this question in the concluding pages of chapter 9, using the limited data available.

2 Gerhard Lenski brought the phenomenon of status incongruence to the attention of researchers in his article "Status Crystallization: A Non-vertical Dimension of Social Status,"

American Sociological Review 19 (1954): 405–13.
On the effects of status incongruence, see
Malewski, "The Degree of Status Incongruence
and Its Effects" (1966). See also Thomas
F. Pettigrew, "Social Evaluation Theory:
Convergence and Applications," in D. Levine, ed.,
Nebraska Symposium on Motivation, 1967
(Lincoln: University of Nebraska Press, 1967).

3 Marvin S. Olsen and Judy Corder Tully,
"Socioeconomic-Ethnic Status Inconsistency and
Preference for Political Change," *American
Sociological Review* 37 (1972): 560–74.

4 Though conditions in the family favored the
employment of women, there was considerable
resentment among unemployed men toward
women "who cheated them out of employment."
Edwin C. Lewis, *Developing Women's
Potential* (Ames: Iowa State University Press,
1968), p. 151.

5 Albert K. Cohen, Foreword to Frank Musgrove,
Youth and the Social Order (Bloomington:
Indiana University Press, 1965), p. ix. Pertinent to
this point is Ralph Linton's observation that
societies may refuse to give formal recognition to
adolescence in one of two ways. "The child
status with its patterns of submission and
dependence may be extended upward to include
the adolescent period, or the adult status with
its multitude of social obligations may be
extended downward to include it." "Age and Sex
Categories" (1942).

6 Cyril S. Smith, *Adolescence* (London: Longmans,
1968), p. 7.

7 John Dewey, *The Child and the Curriculum*
(Chicago: University of Chicago Press, 1956),
p. 35.

8 See Beatrice Whiting, ed., *Six Cultures: Studies of
Child Rearing* (New York: Wiley, 1963).

9 But see Cecile T. LaFollette, *A Study of the
Problem of 652 Gainfully Employed Married
Women Homemakers* (1934); Esther E. Prevey,
"A Quantitative Study of Family Practices
in Training Children in the Use of Money,"
Journal of Educational Psychology 36 (1945):
411–28; Dale B. Harris, "Work and the
Transition to Maturity," *Teachers College Record*
63 (1961): 146–53; and Murray A. Straus,
"Work Roles and Financial Responsibility in the
Socialization of Farm, Fringe, and Town
Boys" (1962).

10 Komarovsky's study, as well as most other studies
of family life in the Depression, did not
obtain data on families before the Depression or
economic crisis. However, Komarovsky
demonstrates considerable skill in attempting to
reconstruct family life.

11 Among urban Mexican-American families, the patriarchal ideal is shifting toward a norm of equality. See Joan W. Moore, *Mexican-Americans* (Englewood Cliffs, N.J.: Prentice-Hall, 1970), chap. 6.

12 This relation is also shown in a more recent study: Charles E. Bowerman and Glen H. Elder, Jr., "Variations in Adolescent Perception of Family Power Structure," *American Sociological Review* 29 (1964): 551–67.

13 George Herbert Mead, *Mind, Self, and Society* (Chicago: University of Chicago Press, 1934), p. 162. The assumption that social conflict increases consciousness of behavior is found in the writings of a large number of social theorists, including George Simmel, George Herbert Mead, and Karl Marx. In the words of Park and Burgess, "only where there is conflict is behavior conscious and self-conscious." See Robert E. Park and Ernest W. Burgess, *Introduction to the Science of Society* (Chicago: University of Chicago Press, 1921), p. 578.

14 The best single source is Bakke, *Citizens without Work* (1940). One could argue that conditions in the Depression simply augmented the degree of status ambiguity which is generally characteristic of a mobile, achievement-oriented society. Eric Larrabee observes that "we are anxious about status because it is problematical, which is another way of saying that the system no longer works. We are no longer bound by birth or bankroll to a fixed place in it, and there is opportunity—though no requirement—for the individual to escape. In this disorderly turmoil it is difficult to discover who one is." *The Self-Conscious Society* (Garden City, N.J.: Doubleday, 1960), p. 44. Likewise C. Wright Mills claims that the United States is more like a society in which prestige is unstable and ambivalent than a society with a definite, stable system of prestige. When "the individual's claims are not usually honored by others," the social world constitutes a "maze of misunderstanding, of sudden frustration and sudden indulgence, and the individual, as his self-esteem fluctuates, is under strain and full of anxiety." Mills, *White Collar* (1951), p. 240.

15 Milton M. Gordon, *Assimilation in American Life* (New York: Oxford University Press, 1964), p. 57. There is a sizable literature which shows that status inconsistency is related to emotional stress, but little is known about how parental status incongruence affects children. For studies of adults, see Jackson, "Status Inconsistency and Symptoms of Stress" (1962); Jackson and Burke, "Status and Symptoms of Stress" (1965); and a literature review by Robert

L. Kahn and John R. P. French, Jr., "Status and Conflict," in McGrath 1970, chap. 14.

16 See Jahoda et al., *Marienthal* (1970); and Stuart T. Hauser, *Black and White Identity Formation* (New York: Wiley, 1971). Hauser observes that "the configuration of identity foreclosure is defined by *stasis*, a marked diminution of change in all facets of multiple self-images. Inherent in this stasis of self-images is the individual's experience—conscious—of the restricted alternatives" (p. 109).

17 From a time series analysis of educational data, Ferriss found support for two hypotheses on the relation between economics and persistence in school: "When the family financial need becomes greater, as occurs during depressions, the student will be pressed into employment and will drop out of school," and, "When unemployment increases, jobs are less plentiful, and the more marginal workers, such as an enrolled student, will be more likely to remain a student than enter the labor market; conversely, when jobs are plentiful, the more marginal worker will be attracted to employment and hence the enrolled student will drop out of school to take a job." Abbott L. Ferriss, *Indicators of Trends in American Education* (New York: Russell Sage Foundation 1969), p. 25.

18 Beran Wolfe, "Psycho-analyzing the Depression," *The Forum*, April 1932, p. 212.

19 Alexander H. Leighton, *My Name is Legion* (New York: Basic Books, 1959).

20 The following analysis borrows extensively from Mechanic's stress-adaptation model. See chapter 9 of his *Medical Sociology* (1968); and his essay "Some Problems in Developing a Social Psychology of Adaptation to Stress," in McGrath 1970, pp. 104–23.

21 See Straus, "Communication, Creativity, and Problem Solving Ability of Middle- and Working-Class Families in Three Societies (1968). See also Lloyd Rogler and August B. Hollinghead, *Trapped: Families and Schizophrenia* (New York: Wiley, 1965); and Dohrenwend and Dohrenwend, *Social Status and Psychological Disorder* (1969).

22 Melvin L. Kohn, "Class, Family, and Schizophrenia: A Reformulation," *Social Forces* 50 (1972): 295–304.

23 In Anna Freud's study of children during the London Blitz, the effect of destruction and death on children was found to be contingent on the parents' response to these events. See Freud and Burlingham, *War and Children* (1943).

24 Stuart Wolf, "Life Stress and Patterns of Disease," in Harold I. Lief, Victor F. Lief, and

Nina R. Lief, eds., *The Psychological Basis of Medical Practice* (New York: Harper and Row, 1963).

25 Hinkle and Wolff, "The Nature of Man's Adaptation to His Total Environment and the Relation of This to Illness" (1957); and L. E. Hinkle, Jr., et al., "An Investigation of the Relation between Life Experience, Personality Characteristics, and General Susceptibility to Illness," *Psychosomatic Medicine* 20 (1958): 278–95.

26 I. Gregory, "Anterospective Data Following Childhood Loss of a Parent. II. Pathology, Performance and Potential among College Students," *Archives of General Psychiatry* 13 (1965): 110–20.

3 Economic Deprivation and Family Status

1 One would need to know a great deal more than we currently know about the frames of reference that structure judgments in order to make headway on this problem. In a pioneering study on the psychology of status, Herbert H. Hyman found income alone to be a relatively poor indicator of satisfaction with economic status. Dissatisfied persons ranged in income from $336 to $4,000, the satisfied from $900 to $6,100. One person who earned only $336 a year claimed that she would be "joyous" over an income of $900. By contrast, a person who earned slightly less than $4,000 aspired to an income of $25,000. See "The Psychology of Status" (1942). On the psychophysical values of status change, see Harry Helson, *Adaptation-Level Theory* (New York: Harper and Row, 1964). Prestige and economic frames of reference are structured by class position, and we shall use social class in 1929 as an indicator of the context in which economic loss occurred.

2 See also Jacqueline D. Goodchilds and Ewart E. Smith, "The Effects of Unemployment as Mediated by Social Status," *Sociometry* 26 (1963): 287–93.

3 Social class (1929) is measured by the Hollingshead index which is based on both father's education and his occupation. On both dimensions, scores range from 7 (unskilled, some grade school) to 1 (higher executives, professional training). Occupational rank is weighted by a factor of 7; education by a factor of 4. The range of total scores is divided into five status categories. The major division in this study is between middle-class (I, II, III) and working-class (IV, V) families. *In correlational analyses, we shall reverse the scores on occupation, education,*

*and social class in order to make a high
score equivalent to high status.*

4 Miller has described lower-class life as "crisis-like, constantly trying to make do with string where rope is needed." S. M. Miller, "The American Lower-Class: A Typological Approach," in Reissman et al. 1964, p. 147.

5 E. J. Hanna et al., *Report and Recommendations of the California State Unemployment Commission* (San Francisco, 1932), p. 171.

6 Age of father is perhaps most important as a determinant of success in obtaining a new job after losing employment. See Aiken et al., *Economic Failure, Alienation, and Extremism* (1968), p. 36. On national variations in unemployment by industries and type of occupation, see Broadus Mitchell, *Depression Decade: From New Era through the New Deal, 1929–1941* (New York: Rinehart and Co. 1947), esp. p. 98.

7 The prevalence of hard times among families of entrepreneurs in the "old middle class" is also reported in a retrospective study of adults, some of whom had grown up in the Depression era. They were asked, "During the years you were growing up, did your parents ever have a hard time making ends meet?" Hard times were most frequently reported by the offspring of unskilled fathers, followed by small-scale entrepreneurs, and low-status sales personnel. Langner and Michael, *Life Stress and Mental Health* (1963), pp. 231–32.

8 A systematic record of adjustments in expenditure is not available for the Oakland families. However, data on recreational patterns do show an inverse relation between commercial forms of entertainment and economic deprivation. For instance, the percentage of parents who attended the movies at least twice a month is inversely related to deprivation in both social classes; from 49 to 24 percent among fathers in the middle class, and from 38 to 13 percent in the working class. Similar differences were found for mothers. Given the cross-sectional nature of these data, there is no way to determine the extent to which economic loss accounted for *reductions* in expenditures for commercial entertainment.

9 In 1929, economic statistics for Oakland place the minimum cost of living for a laborer with three children at $118 per month. Even if we subtract the decline in cost of living, the monthly figure is far above $45 per month.

10 See Norman M. Bradburn and David Caplowitz, *Reports on Happiness: A Pilot Study of Behavior Related to Mental Health* (Chicago:

Aldine, 1965). An extension of this research is reported in Bradburn, *The Structure of Psychological Well-Being* (1970).

11 See H. Kornhauser, "Attitudes of Economic Groups," *Public Opinion Quarterly* 2(1938): 260–68.

12 Multiple classification analysis permits the use of categorical independent variables, such as neighborhood status, in a regression analysis, and enables simultaneous control of all test factors by statistically adjusting subclass percentages for the effects of all variables together. No assumptions concerning the linearity of the effects of each factor are required; no estimates of interaction effects are obtained. See J. W. Morgan et al., *Income and Welfare in the United States* (New York: McGraw-Hill, 1962), Appendix E.

13 Case studies presented by Bakke in *Citizens without Work* (1940) and by Angell in *The Family Encounters the Depression* (1936) are a rich source of qualitative data on this association. More recent data on social participation may be found in Hallowell Pope, "Economic Deprivation and Social Class Participation in a Group of 'Middle Class' Factory Workers," *Social Problems* 11 (1964), esp. p. 297.

4 Children in the Household Economy

Epigraph: From Margot Hentoff's review of Laura Ingalls Wilder's "Little House Books" ("Kids, Pull Up Your Socks: A Review of Children's Books," *The New York Review of Books*, 20, April 1972, p. 15). Wilder's story of Laura Ingalls, beginning with her early childhood in a pioneer family (circa 1860s) may appear to have little relevance to the experience of urban children in the Depression. But there are some important similarities, as we shall see. On social roles, children in deprived families had more in common with Laura Ingalls than with contemporary children in affluent families, a point implied in Hentoff's thoughtful question: "How, in *this* world, are we going to be able to give the young back their sense of worth?" (p. 15).

1 See Talcott Parsons, "Age and Sex in the Social Structure of the United States," in C. Kluckhohn and H. A. Murray, eds., *Personality in Nature, Society, and Culture*, 2d ed., rev. (New York: Knopf, 1953), pp. 269–81.

2 A durable belief in research on work roles assumes that tasks shape behavior. However, empirical knowledge on this problem is still very rudimentary. For provocative work in this area, see Breer and Locke, *Task Experience as a Source of Attitudes* (1965).

3 Systematic information on type of job, hours, and wage was not obtained from the Oakland children or from their parents. As a result, we are unable to determine the prevalence of examples cited in this paragraph.

4 In a cross-cultural study, Minturn and Lambert found that a child receives strong pressures to assume responsibility if his mother is making a contribution to the family economy. *Mothers of Six Cultures* (1964), p. 271. See also Prodipto Roy, "Adolescent Roles: Rural-Urban Differences," in Nye and Hoffman 1963, pp. 165–81.

5 James H. S. Bossard, *Parent and Child* (Philadelphia: University of Pennsylvania Press, 1953), chapter 6. A relation between pressures to assume responsibilities and size of family was found by Minturn and Lambert (1964), p. 271.

6 All four variables in this standard regression analysis are dichotomies; economic deprivation, nondeprived vs. deprived; family size, less than three children vs. three or more; work experience for boys, yes vs. no; and domestic chores for girls, scores of 0–2 vs. 3–5. Deprivation and family size are correlated .33 and .30 with boys' work, and .42 and .16 with girls' chores.

7 All reported differences by family deprivation and work status are statistically significant at the .05 level. Economic aspirations were indexed by an item on the junior high questionnaire which asked the respondents whether they wanted to have more spending money than their classmates (a gradient scale with scores ranging from 1 to 5). Desire for control was indexed by the average ratings of trained judges who read observational and self-report materials in the high school period on each child in the sample. Values on the scale range from 1 to 5. A more detailed description of this and other motivational ratings may be found in Appendix B.

8 Esther E. Prevey, "A Quantitative Study of Family Practices in Training Children in the Use of Money," *Journal of Educational Psychology* 36 (1945): 411–28.

9 The economic support of boys in nondeprived families is similar in this respect to that of urban boys in Straus's study (1962). In both groups, over a third received pay for doing chores around the house.

10 For a description of this statistical technique, see chapter 3, note 12.

11 Glen H. Elder, Jr., "The Depression Experience in Family Relations and Upbringing," unpublished manuscript, spring 1966.

12 It is most unlikely that the observers' rating of industrious behavior was influenced by knowledge of the boys' work status. All the Situation

Ratings were based on observed behavior in school-related activities.

13 The classification was performed by Dr. Barbara Kirk, director of Counseling Center, University of California, Berkeley. Four categories were used: strongly domestic, probable domestic, mixed domestic-career, career. The first two categories defined a preference for the domestic role.

14 For both sexes, mean scores on adult orientation are 52.4 for the employed and 46.1 for the unemployed categories.

15 Desire for adult status was indexed by a question in the junior high questionnaire: "Do you want to be a grown-up man or woman?" A majority of the children gave an affirmative response (67 percent), and the percentage increased by family hardship. In terms of percentage difference, the effects of class and deprivation are identical (14 percent).

5 Family Relations

1 In a study of family reactions to troubles of various sorts, Koos found that a relatively permanent loss of paternal authority resulted in every family in which father was seen as having failed to meet the demands of the crisis situation. See Earl L. Koos, *Families in Trouble* (1946). Corresponding effects of leadership failure in crisis situations are provided by two experimental studies: Hamblin, "Leadership and Crisis" (1958); and Bahr and Rollins, "Crisis and Conjugal Power" (1971). Related to this perspective on leadership is the "status threat" hypothesis proposed by Short and Strodtbeck to account for the differential involvement of gang boys in delinquent activity. James F. Short, Jr., and Fred L. Strodtbeck, *Group Process and Gang Delinquency* (Chicago: University of Chicago Press, 1955), p. 245.

2 See Blood and Wolfe, *Husbands and Wives* (1960); and Lee Rainwater, *Behind Ghetto Walls* (Chicago: Aldine, 1970). Marital power is by no means a simple function of socioeconomic and educational factors, as studies by Komarovsky (*Blue-Collar Marriage*, 1962, chap. 10) and Scanzoni (*Opportunity and the Family*, 1970, chap. 6) show. On this point, see also Hyman Rodman, "Marital Power in France, Greece, Yugoslavia, and the United States," *Journal of Marriage and the Family* 30 (1967): 320–24. Other factors which are pertinent to the analysis are noted in the following discussion in the text.

3 Reuben Hill and Donald A. Hansen, "The Family in Disaster," in Baker and Chapman 1962;

Bahr and Rollins, "Crisis and Conjugal Power" (1971).

4 David M. Heer, "Dominance and the Working Wife," *Social Forces* 36 (1958): 347; Blood and Wolfe, *Husbands and Wives* (1960), p. 42.

5 This relationship is reported by Blood and Wolfe, pp. 37–38; and by Komarovsky, *Blue-Collar Marriage* (1962), p. 229.

6 Komarovsky, *The Unemployed Man and His Family* (1940), chap. 3. For a pioneering study of male dominance ideology in power relations, see Lois W. Hoffman, "Effects of Employment of Mothers on Parental Power Relations and the Division of Household Tasks," *Marriage and Family Living* 22 (1960): 27–35.

7 Jane Addams, "Social Consequences of Business Depression," in Felix Morley, ed., *Aspects of the Depression* (Chicago: University of Chicago Press, 1932), p. 13.

8 See Murray A. Straus, "Conjugal Power Structure and Adolescent Personality," *Marriage and Family Living* 24 (1962): 17–25.

9 Charles E. Bowerman and Glen H. Elder, Jr., "Variations in Adolescent Perceptions of Family Power Structure," *American Sociological Review* 29 (1964): 551–67.

10 Members of the study were surveyed by a mail questionnaire in 1964. The power item includes five response categories; "much more" and "somewhat more" responses were combined for both mother and father dominance. The five-point scale is used in all correlational analyses.

11 A high score on family status (5) equals high status. The original status scores were reversed in order to achieve this correspondence.

12 See William T. Smelser, "Adolescent and Adult Occupational Choice as a Function of Family Socioeconomic History," *Sociometry* 26 (1963): 393–409.

13 Mean scores for girls in the middle class are 4.1 and 5.3 for the two deprivational groups, and 3.7 and 5.2 for the two groups in the working class. For both social classes, average conflict scores for the two deprivational groups of boys are 4.9 and 5.5.

14 For boys, the correlation between perceived conflict and mother's power is $-.20$; for girls, $-.09$.

15 See Martin Gold, *Status Forces in Delinquent Boys* (Ann Arbor, Mich.: Institute for Social Research, 1963); Glen H. Elder, Jr., "Family Structure and the Transmission of Values and Norms in the Process of Child Rearing," Ph.D. diss., University of North Carolina, 1961, chap. 10; Travis Hirschi, *Causes of Delinquency*

(Berkeley: University of California Press, 1969), chaps. 6 and 8; and Albert Bandura, "Social-Learning Theory of Identificatory Processes," in Goslin 1969, p. 241.

16 Reference here is to the social power or resource theory of identification; the primary model selected for emulation is the person who controls rewarding resources. See Bandura, in Goslin 1969, pp. 229–30.

17 See Charles E. Bowerman and John W. Kinch, "Changes in Family and Peer Orientation of Children between the Fourth and Tenth Grades," *Social Forces* 37 (1959): 206–11. A review of this literature is provided by Willard W. Hartup, "Peer Interaction and Social Organization," in Mussen 1970, pp. 429–36.

18 This finding is drawn from ongoing research directed by the author. On the importance of extrafamilial persons to ambitious youth from the lower class, see Robert A. Ellis and William C. Lane, "Structural Supports for Upward Mobility." *American Sociological Review* 28 (1963): 743–56; and Elder, *Adolescent Socialization and Personality Development* (1971), pp. 91–94.

19 Father's attractiveness among girls correlated − .25 with perceived conflict and .14 with family status. Among boys, the same analysis yielded r correlations of − .08 and .49.

20 With the effects of mother dominance partialled out, the correlation between deprivation and closeness to mother dropped to .27.

21 We compared mother-dominated families with households in which father was at least equal on power in the deprived and nondeprived groups. For both classes, the average percentage difference was 17 percent.

22 As mentioned in chapter 4, independence striving among adolescents is not incompatible with a desire for adult recognition and acceptance on the one hand, and peer involvement on the other. See C. M. Lucas and J. E. Horrocks, "An Experimental Approach to the Analysis of Adolescent Needs," *Child Development* 31 (1960): 479–87.

23 Using reports from mothers in the 1936 interview, we find that a tendency to question parental judgment increased from nondeprived to deprived status among boys in the middle class (8% vs. 23%) and in the working class (25% vs. 46%). Among girls, the nondeprived were less inclined to accept parental authority in the middle class (25% vs. 19%) and in the working class (38% vs. 29%).

24 Two questions from the 1964 questionnaire were used in the analysis: "Which parent was more strict with you?" and "Compared with

parents of other boys and girls you know, would you say your parents were stricter, or less strict?" On the first question, the five responses ranged from "father always" (a score of 1) to "mother always" (score of 5). The five response categories on the second question ranged from "parents less strict" to "parents much more strict." The five-point index of mother's power correlated .36 with mother's relative strictness among girls, and .02 among boys (both tau_c coefficients). Mother's power was negatively correlated with parental strictness only among boys ($-.16$ versus .02 for girls).

25 Thirty percent of the daughters of dominant mothers participated in these activities on school nights and with a group of both boys and girls in the evening, in comparison to 44 percent of the girls with more influential fathers.

26 Two sets of data were used to index heterosexual experience. In the 1936 interview, mothers were asked whether their son or daughter made phone calls to members of the opposite sex. Responses to this question were supplemented by retrospective information on heterosexual experience in the 1958 interview. Two measures of dating were constructed from replies to open-ended questions (1958): age at first date or heterosexual affair (senior high or later versus junior high school); and amount of dating (from little or none, to moderate and considerable). Girls were more likely to initiate phone contacts with the opposite sex (42% vs. 22%), especially in the nondeprived group. Among boys this form of contact increased by economic deprivation in the middle class (13% vs. 26%) and in the working class (12% vs. 38%). These differences were reversed for girls: 64% vs. 50% in the middle class and 40% vs. 28% in the working class. An early age at first date and considerable dating were correlated with deprivation only among boys ($tau_c = .36$ and .16). Corresponding values for girls were close to zero. In both sex groups, the relation between these indicators and family status did not differ from chance.

27 The only information available on sexual behavior was obtained in the 1958 interview. Despite the questionable validity of this recall, the correlates of acknowledged premarital sex are consistent with previous research. Reported coitus before marriage was correlated with low family status in both sex groups ($tau_c = -.37$). With class controlled premarital intercourse was only slightly more prevalent in the deprived than in the nondeprived group (less than 10 percent for both sexes).

28 A useful source of documents on American attitudes toward success and failure in the

Depression is provided by Rosemary F. Carroll, "The Impact of the Great Depression on American Attitudes toward Success: A Study of the Programs of Norman Vincent Peale, Dale Carnegie, and Johnson O'Connor," Ph.D. diss., State University of Rutgers, 1968. The research literature on unemployment in the Depression is another source of information on the tendency of men to blame themselves. See Zawadski and Lazarsfeld, "The Psychological Effects of Unemployment" (1935).

29 Subjective deprivation is a likely outcome of subordination to wife when men use male dominance as a basis for self-evaluation. This standard may represent status before the Depression, as well as men in the Depression who maintained their dominant position in family affairs. For a provocative discussion of relative deprivation and its social consequences in disaster situations, see Barton's analysis of the altruistic community, in *Communities in Disaster* (1969), chap. 5.

30 For an excellent synthetic analysis of research and theory on marital integration, see Levinger, "Marital Cohesiveness and Dissolution" (1965).

31 Alice S. Rossi, "Naming Children in Middle-Class Families," *American Sociological Review* 30 (1965): 503.

32 The relation between economic deprivation in the Depression and weak attachment to kin among men is not explained by differential intergenerational mobility. Neither upward nor downward mobility accounts for the attitudes of men from deprived families.

33 See Bert Adams, *Kinship in an Urban Setting* (Chicago: Markham, 1968).

34 Ibid., chap. 4.

35 A thorough review of the literature on intergenerational relations is provided by Marvin B. Sussman, "Relationships of Adult Children with Their Parents in the United States," in Shanas and Streib 1965.

36 This exchange brings to mind Marcel Mauss's brilliant essay *The Gift* (London: Cohen and West, 1954). Using materials on archaic societies, Mauss examined the social significance of gifts or presents "which are in theory voluntary, disinterested and spontaneous, but are in fact obligatory and interested. The form usually taken is that of the gift generously offered; but the accompanying behavior is formal pretence and social deception, while the transaction itself is based on obligation and economic self-interest" (p. 1).

37 See John A. Penrod, "American Literature and the Great Depression," Ph.D. diss., University of Pennsylvania, 1954.

6 Status Change and Personality

Epigraph: A comment made by Frank Jones on the contemporary painter Marshall Glasier. The quotation was drawn from Hans Gerth and C. Wright Mills, *Character and Social Structure* (1953), p. 91.

1 The relation between self-orientations and motivational tendencies is briefly developed by Frank Miyamoto in "Self, Motivation, and Symbolic Interactionist Theory" (1970). Miyamoto assumes that "the need to see oneself as favorably viewed by others is generally the most critical of the self-orientations"; that motivational tendencies centering on self-definition predominate when "one's position in social relations or the appropriate line of action are in any degree problematic"; and that self-feelings are prominent when emotional states "are regarded as offering a better guide to action than evaluations or cognitions" (pp. 280–84). Status loss in the Depression created problems and activated motivational tendencies in all three domains of self-orientation.

2 Herbert Blumer's concept, "sense of group position," has particular utility in the study of status change among families. Though initially proposed in an essay on intergroup relations and prejudice, it seems equally useful in understanding the behavior of family members during periods of drastic change. See "Race Prejudice as a Sense of Group Position" (1958).

3 From his New Jersey research during the Depression, James Plant found that teachers often had difficulty in obtaining information about the home situation from their students. "Well, we know they are having an awful time but they never say anything to us about it. We can never get them to admit they are having any troubles at home." *Personality and the Cultural Pattern* (1937), p. 207.

4 In his well-known looking-glass model of the self, Cooley observed that social reference frequently takes the form of a definite impression of how one's self appears to others, and the imagined effect of this impression on others. There are three distinguishable components of this orientation: "the imagination of our appearance to the other person; the imagination of his judgment of that appearance; and some sort of self-feeling, such as pride or mortification." See Cooley, *Human Nature and the Social Order* (1922), pp. 183–84.

5 These adaptations to deprivation are an abbreviation of more complex models developed by Parsons and Horney. See Talcott Parsons, *The Social System* (Glencoe, Ill.: Free Press, 1951),

p. 259; and Karen Horney, *The Neurotic Personality of Our Time* (New York: W. W. Norton, 1937), pp. 167–87.

6 Each item includes a five-point gradient scale, with values ranging from 1 to 5 (least to most characteristic). The question on social rejection was reverse-scored in order to form an index on which a high score signifies social well-being.

7 Working-class children did score higher on emotionality than middle-class children, but the difference was statistically reliable only among girls ($\overline{X} = 3.6$ vs. 4.8, $p<.05$).

8 No check was scored 0, one check was given a score of 1, and two checks were scored 2. Values on the items were first summed and then standardized.

9 This example was drawn from R. E. Brownlee, "Developing the Core Curriculum at University High School," *University High School Journal* 19 (1940):48. A thorough overview of the schools attended by the Oakland children is reported in John Geyer, "Claremont Junior High School and University High School in the 1930s," unpublished working paper, Institute of Human Development, University of California, Berkeley, 1964. Both schools were deeply influenced by the progressive education movement, and bear some resemblance in philosophy and practice to John Dewey's original experimental school in Chicago. For a recent account of this school, see K. C. Mayhew and A. C. Edwards, *The Dewey School* (New York: Atherton Press, 1966).

10 In their analysis of survey data on residents of Manhattan in New York City, Srole and his associates concluded that wives tend "to be more vulnerable psychologically than the husbands to conflicts generated in their relationships to each other. In that case, and other factors being equal, it could be hypothesized that marital strains are potentially more unbalancing for women than for men." Srole et al., *Mental Health in the Metropolis* (1962), p. 177.

11 Girls are more likely to be concerned about their appearance than boys, and for good reason: it is a major source of feminine status and selection into the leading crowd. In a nationwide sample of adolescents, 61 percent of the girls felt that they worried most about their appearance—clothes, looks, etc.—compared to only 11 percent of the boys. Data obtained from tables 152, 155, 164, and 167 in *A Study of Boys Becoming Adolescents* (Ann Arbor, Mich.: Survey Research Center, Institute for Social Research, 1960); and from tables 7 and 10 in Elizabeth Douvan, *A Study of Adolescent Girls* (ibid.,

1957). In James Coleman's study of adolescents, good clothes were among the most frequently mentioned qualities for a girl's entry into the leading crowd, while students placed it near the bottom as a status-conferring asset for boys. See James Coleman, *The Adolescent Society* (New York: The Free Press of Glencoe, 1961), p. 31. The psychological significance of clothes for the self-image is explored by Gregory Stone in "Appearance and the Self," in Arnold Rose, ed., *Human Behavior and Social Processes* (Boston: Houghton Mifflin, 1962), pp. 86–118.

12 These measures were selected from a set of peer nominations on a "Guess who" instrument. Each child was asked to match statements (such as "Here is a student who is well-dressed") to actual classmates. Ratings were obtained each year during the junior high period. On well-groomed appearance, peer reputation in 1934 was moderately correlated with the adult or staff rating among boys ($r = .58$), and a similar relationship was obtained among girls. For a detailed description of the "Guess who" technique, see Caroline M. Tryon, "Evaluations of Adolescent Personality by Adolescents," *Monographs of the Society for Research in Child Development* 4, no. 4 (1939).

13 For the junior high period, the index of social well-being and the adult rating of well-groomed appearance were correlated .26 among boys and .38 among girls. The greater significance of attractive grooming for the sex-typed appeal of girls is shown in the following correlations: Well-groomed appearance correlated .60 with an adult rating of feminine appeal but only .29 with masculine appeal. Both sex appeal scales were drawn from the Free-Play set of ratings.

14 Class differences in grooming and physical attractiveness were more prominent in high school among the girls than were the effects of economic deprivation. The daughters of middle-class parents were rated significantly higher on both aspects of appearance than girls from the working class. See Elder, "Appearance and Education in Marriage Mobility" (1969).

15 In the junior high period, mean scores on social fantasy were 2.42 and 2.93 for boys and girls in deprived and nondeprived families, $p < .05$. Scores were only slightly higher among middle-class respondents. For the senior high period, nondeprived boys in both social classes reported a stronger preference for social fantasy than boys from deprived families (average $\overline{X}$s = 3.63 vs. 2.78, $p < .05$). The average score for girls ($\overline{X} = 2.76$) did not vary by economic deprivation or social class.

16 The measure used in this comparison is a Situation Rating, *group* vs. *self-interest*, which is based on observations during the high school years (see Appendix B for a complete description). A high score on the rating indicates a cooperative orientation toward others, a willingness to subordinate personal desires for the benefit of the group. In both social classes, members of deprived families were rated significantly higher on group interest than the offspring of nondeprived families (overall difference, $p < .05$). On standardized scores, differences were most pronounced among boys; 46 vs. 55 for nondeprived and deprived groups in the middle class ($p < .01$), and 45 vs. 51 for comparable groups in the working class ($p < .05$).

17 See William T. Smelser's report on boys in the longitudinal sample of the Guidance Study—which is also based at the Institute of Human Development, Berkeley—"Adolescent and Adult Occupational Choice as a Function of Family Socio-Economic History," *Sociometry* 26(1963): 393–409.

18 The other five need ratings include: aggression—"the desire to deprive others by belittling, attacking, ridiculing, deprecating"; succorance—"the desire for support from outside"; escape—"the tendency to escape all unpleasant situations, to avoid blame, hardship"; abasement—"the tendency to self-deprecation, self-blame, or belittlement, to submit passively to external forces"; and social ties—"the desire to join groups, to live socially, to conform to custom."

19 Scores on this scale have been interpreted as an index of aspiration level, although its validity in this respect has not been convincingly demonstrated. Along this line, Darley suggests that a value on the scale indicates "the degree to which the individual's total background has prepared him to seek the prestige and discharge the social responsibilities growing out of high income, professional status, recognition, or leadership in the community." See John A. Darley, *Clinical Aspects and Interpretation of the Strong Vocational Interest Blank* (New York: Psychological Corporation, 1941), p. 60. For our purposes, we shall interpret scores as an indication of the prestige level of the respondents' occupational interests.

20 These tendencies refer to ratings of recognition, control, and aggression. For deprived and nondeprived groups, need for aggression correlated $- .19$ with social well-being in the deprived group of boys and .01 in the nondeprived group. The other two ratings showed comparable differences, none of which is statistically significant (strong need = high score for this analysis).

21 See S. G. Jaffe and Joseph Sandler, "Notes on Pain, Depression, and Individualism," in *Psychoanalytic Study of the Child*, no. 20 (New York: International Universities Press, 1965), p. 396.

22 The average *r* correlation for the relation between dissatisfaction and the two motivational ratings is .15 for the total sample and .23 for the middle-class boys (strong motive = high score).

23 Ratings of recognition and control needs did not vary by economic deprivation when maternal dissatisfaction and criticism were controlled. However, the sons of dissatisfied and critical mothers scored markedly higher on these measures of ambition than the sons of more contented mothers in both the deprived and nondeprived groups. These differences are not large enough to be statistically reliable, owing partly to the small subgroups.

24 This index was constructed by Mary C. Jones. For the original analysis, see "A Study of Socialization Patterns at the High School Level" (1958).

25 The maximum weight assigned to news items in each of the categories is as follows: student leadership—fifteen points for student body president; athletics—ten points for athletic star with statewide recognition; intellectual recognition—six points for editor of the daily newspaper; arts and drama—five points for achieving summer scholarships to Arts and Crafts College; interest club—two points for president; and miscellaneous—ten points for election as "King of the Carnival."

26 The adolescents were asked whether they resembled a student who is a leader ("The girls [boys] all do what she [he] wants them to do") and a student who is "the most popular girl (boy) in school." Following these questions, they were asked whether they "wanted to be like these youth." A score of five equalled "yes" and "no" a score of one. The two items on perceived status were summed to form an achievement scale, and the same procedure was followed in constructing an index of desired status. The measure of social aspiration was obtained by subtracting the former index from the latter.

27 All probability values reported in this paragraph are based on one-tailed *t*-tests.

28 Even when studies are explicitly designed to test a theory, indicators frequently bear little relation to the concepts they are intended to measure. Research on the self is an example. As Schwartz and Stryker note, "The important problem faced by social psychologists dealing in self theory has to do with the measurement of

the meaning that individuals attribute to themselves as objects. Sociologists have not dealt sufficiently with that meaning and its dimensions." Michael Schwartz and Sheldon Stryker, *Deviance, Selves, and Others*, Rose Monograph Series in Sociology, no. 1 (Washington, D.C.: American Sociological Association, 1971), p. 36.

7 Earning a Living

Epigraphs: Both quotations were drawn from Studs Terkel's *Hard Times* (1970). The son's observation is from page 345; the garbage worker's from page 35.

1 The growing significance of formal education in the careers of men is shown by data on a nationwide sample of men in 1962. Blau and Duncan systematically compared four age groups on the relation between educational and occupational attainment: 55 to 64 (age 16 in 1913–22); 45 to 54 (age 16 in 1923–32); 35 to 44 (age 16 in 1933–42—includes men who are the same age as the Oakland subjects); and 25 to 34 (age 16 in 1943–52). While the influence of social origins on occupational attainment remained relatively constant across the four groups, the latter has become increasingly dependent on educational level. This impact is mainly restricted to ultimate occupational achievement, as against early worklife experiences. Blau and Duncan, *The American Occupational Structure* (1967), chap. 5. Also see A. J. Jaffe and W. Adams, "College Education for U.S. Youth: The Attitudes of Parents and Children," *American Journal of Economics and Sociology* 3 (1964): 269–84.

2 Broadus Mitchell, *Depression Decade: From New Era through the New Deal, 1929–41* (New York: Rinehart and Co., 1947), p. 371. Defense spending reached $6.2 billion a year by 1 January 1941. By the end of the year, the annual rate had risen more than threefold. The index of industrial production, which averaged 87 between 1930 and 1939, climbed sharply to 174 in the early months of 1942. See Mitchell, pp. 371–77.

3 It is estimated that approximately three-fourths of the boys who reached the age of 16 between 1933 and 1942 entered the armed forces. See Blau and Duncan, 1967, p. 197. Despite much speculation to the contrary, there is no reliable evidence that educational benefits in the GI bill equalized opportunities for men coming from diverse socioeconomic backgrounds (see Blau and Duncan, p. 179). Charles Nam estimates that approximately 7.5 percent of the men who completed their first year of college between 1940 and 1955 did so as a result of the GI bill.

359

See "Impact of the GI Bills on the Educational Level of Male Population" (1964).

4 All of the boys in the adolescent sample completed high school, and thus represent a select subgroup of students who entered secondary school in the Oakland school system during the Depression.

5 Each draftee's term of service was extended by Congress (13 December 1941) to six months after the end of World War II.

6 Occupation and educational status are measured by seven-level scales originally designed by August Hollingshead. Educational attainment: professional training; college graduate; some college; high school graduate and business school; some high school—approximately 10–11 years; 7–9 years of school; and under seven years of school. Occupational attainment: higher executives, proprietors of large concerns, and major professionals; business managers, proprietors of medium-sized businesses, and lesser professionals; administrative personnel, small independent businessmen, and minor professionals; clerical and sales workers, technicians, and owners of little businesses; skilled manual employees; machine operators and semiskilled employees; and unskilled employees.

7 In subsequent analyses, occupational status in adulthood will refer to the social prestige of the 1958 job. Status of the first job after formal education has very limited value, owing to the disruptive impact of the war and the low coding reliability on type of job in the early work history.

8 See O. J. Harvey, D. E. Hunt, and H. M. Schroder, *Conceptual Systems and Personality Organization* (New York: Wiley, 1961), p. 11.

9 This adjustment could be interpreted as a reduction of dissonance issuing from the disparity between family resources and standing, on the one hand, and conceptions of self and future, on the other. In addition to the lowering of goals, dissonance might have been reduced by shifting future-dependence from family to personal talents. Adjustments of the latter type appear to fit the data better since economic loss did not adversely affect level of achievement motivation or goal. The assumption that vocational decision making is motivated by the need to minimize dissonance is consistent with our hypothesized relation between economic deprivation and crystallization. For a discussion of the dissonance interpretation, see Thomas L. Hilton, "Career Decision-Making," *Journal of Counseling Psychology* 9 (1962): 291–98.

10 I am deeply indebted to Dr. Barbara Kirk, director of the Counseling Center at the University

of California (Berkeley), for her generous professional assistance on the clinical analysis.

11 Donald E. Super and Phoebe L. Overstreet, *The Vocational Maturity of Ninth Grade Boys* (New York: Columbia Teachers College, Bureau of Publications, 1960), p. 63.

12 This sequence refers to a career which Harold Wilensky has defined as "a succession of related jobs, arranged in a hierarchy of prestige, through which persons move in an ordered (more-or-less predictable) sequence." See his "Orderly Careers and Social Participation" (1961).

13 An r correlation of $-.22$ between vocational maturity (clinical measure) and entry into a career line after 1948 among men from the middle class. Late entry was of course most common among men who completed their education in the postwar years.

14 In recent years the remembered past has been used creatively as a source of information on the life course and its meaning. See Butler, "The Life Review" (1963); and M. A. Lieberman and Jacqueline M. Falk, "The Remembered Past as a Source of Data for Research on the Life Cycle," *Human Development* 14 (1971): 132–41.

15 We are referring here to Maslow's hierarchy of basic needs: physiological needs, safety, belongingness and love, esteem, and self-actualization. Maslow, *Motivation and Personality* (1954), esp. chap. 5.

16 This measure of achievement motivation indexes the desire to excel on hard tasks, and should be distinguished from ratings of the desire for recognition and mastery, which were found to be significantly related to economic deprivation (chap. 6). The relation between social striving and occupational attainment is examined subsequently within the broader context of ambition and the utilization of ability.

17 With a substantial increase in the complexity of analysis, it is possible to include symmetric relations in path models. An early source on nonrecursive models is A. S. Goldberger's *Econometric Theory* (New York: Wiley, 1964). For sociological examples, see Kenneth C. Land "Significant Others, the Self-Reflexive Act and the Attitude Formation Process: A Reinterpretation," *American Sociological Review* 36 (1971): 1085–98.

18 Bruce K. Eckland, "Academic Ability, Higher Education, and Occupational Mobility," *American Sociological Review* 30 (1965): 744.

19 Occupational mobility was measured by cross-tabulating father's occupational status in

1929 with the subject's status in 1958, as indexed
by Hollingshead's seven-level scale. The ages
of the father and son at these two points were
similar—approximately 38 years. On the basis of
this cross-tabulation, three mobility patterns
for the total sample were identified: upward,
stable, and downward. One modification in this
classification was required for seven men
from "professional" families who were still in
this general stratum in 1958. From a close
examination of work history information, we
found that these men differed substantially
from their fathers on status and authority in the
work setting. In one case, the son of a high
school teacher achieved a postgraduate degree in
engineering and advanced to a high-level
position as one of the directors of research and
development in a large aircraft company. In
another, the son of a field engineer who was
employed by a local industrial construction
firm achieved the status of a certified public
accountant and worked his way up to the
vice-presidency of a large branch bank. Six men
from professional families were downwardly
mobile, and all but one were at least two levels
below their father's occupational status.

20 Bernard C. Rosen, "The Achievement Syndrome:
A Psychocultural Dimension of Social
Stratification," in Atkinson 1958, pp. 500–508.

21 Another way of looking at the influence of
vocational crystallization is to partial out its
effect on the relation between achievement
motivation and occupational attainment. To do
this, we focused on the group in which desire to
excel was most predictive of adult status—
men from deprived families. With vocational
maturity controlled, the relationship was reduced
by a fourth, from an r of .33 to an r of .25.
By controlling intellectual ability as well, the
relationship dropped to .20, a value which is still
stronger than the correlation for men in
the nondeprived group.

22 Melvin L. Kohn, "Social Class and Parent-Child
Relationships: An Interpretation," *American
Journal of Sociology* 68 (1963): 471.

23 Kohn, *Class and Conformity* (1969).

24 Leonard I. Pearlin and Melvin L. Kohn, "Social
Class, Occupation, and Parental Values:
A Cross-National Study," *American Sociological
Review* 31 (1966): 466.

25 The classic study on deprivation as a reinforcer
of motivation is Gewirtz and Baer, "Deprivation
and Satiation as Social Reinforcers on Drive
Conditions" (1958). The assumed adjustment of
adaptive mechanisms to the satisfaction of
the more basic need follows Maslow's theoretical
position: "The person will *want* the more basic

of two needs when deprived in both." *Motivation and Personality* (1954), p. 99. One of the clearest illustrations of this form of adaptation is seen in Jahoda et al., *Marienthal* (1970).

26 Riesman, *The Lonely Crowd* (1950), p. 345. Many unanswered questions remain in the Depression's impact on the meaning of leisure to "veterans" of this historical period. Wecter concludes that "on no aspect of American life did the Depression have a more striking effect than the use of leisure." Dixon Wecter, *The Age of the Great Depression* (1948; Chicago: Quadrangle, 1971), p. 219. The relation between economic affluence and leisure time is explored by Linder in *The Harried Leisure Class* (1970).

27 Adult social class in 1958 is correlated .29 with valuation of work. Similar results were obtained in relation to occupational mobility.

28 The family as an "emotional haven" was conceptually developed by Talcott Parsons and Renee Fox in "Illness, Therapy, and the Modern Urban American Family" (1952).

29 This is not to say that the quality of married life does not influence valuation of family activity. In fact, men who reported marital disagreements on economics, child rearing, friends, and other matters, and those who found little happiness in marriage, were unlikely to value family activity (average $r = -.28$). However home unhappiness does not account for the relation between deprived status in the 30s and family preference. Men from nondeprived and deprived homes were equally likely to rate their marriage as happy.

30 The five response categories for each aspect of the job were scored as follows, and then summed to form the three indexes: "like it very much"—3; "like it somewhat"—2; "neither like it nor dislike it"—1; and "somewhat dislike it" and "dislike it very much"—0. Since each of the clusters includes three items, the scores range from 0 to 9. Mean scores on the Extrinsic, Mobility and Prestige, and Intrinsic indexes are 6.1, 6.4, and 5.2 respectively.

31 Potter, *People of Plenty* (1954), p. 205. The quotation is from Simon Nelson Patten, *The New Basis of Civilization* (New York: Macmillan, 1907), pp. 87–88.

32 Despite its low salience, "the security and comfort of a home" was placed in either fifth or sixth position by a larger proportion of men from non-deprived families (53% vs. 33% of the deprived group). By contrast, "standard of living" was more often assigned to last place by the offspring of deprived families (81% vs. 47%).

33 For a discussion and extension of Easterlin's utility theory, see Hawthorn, *The Sociology of*

Fertility (1970). I am indebted to Reuben Hill for noting some implications of Easterlin's theory for the Oakland data.

34 The security motive in preference for a large family is discussed by Lois Hoffman and Frederick Wyatt in "Social Change and Motivations for Having Larger Families: Some Theoretical Considerations," *Merrill-Palmer Quarterly* 6 (1960): 235–44.

35 Joseph Adelson, "Is Women's Lib a Passing Fad?" *New York Times Magazine*, 19 March 1972. Adelson's conclusion—that Women's Lib is a temporary aberration—is at least faithful to his generation's experience with family life and women's roles.

36 On the transmission of authority patterns from one generation to the next, see Ingersoll, "A Study of the Transmission of Authority Patterns in the Family" (1948); and Leslie and Johnsen, "Changed Perceptions of the Maternal Role" (1963). The lack of substantial carry-over in parental roles across two generations is reported by Bronson et al., "Patterns of Authority and Affection in Two Generations" (1959).

37 Leonard S. Cottrell, Jr., "Interpersonal Interaction and the Development of the Self," in Goslin 1969, p. 564.

38 The research literature remains unclear on the precise sources of discrepant reports by husband and wife. See Donald H. Granbois and Ronald P. Willett, "Equivalence of Family Role Measures Based on Husband and Wife Data," *Journal of Marriage and the Family* 32 (1970): 68–72.

39 The other three response categories are "husband more than wife," "equal," and "wife more than husband." Though values on economic power ranged from 2 to 10, the respondents were distributed across only four categories, from 3 to 6. Values on child-rearing influence ranged from 3 to 15, with all cases falling between 7 and 13. The average score on economic power is 5.1; on child rearing, 10.1.

8 Leading a Contingent Life

Epigraph: Lorine Pruett, "Why Women Fail," in Samuel D. Schmalhausen and V. R. Calverton, *Women's Coming of Age* (New York: Liveright, 1931), p. 252. See also Pruett's sociological analysis of women in the Depression, *Women Workers through the Depression* (1934).

1 To Farber's concept of the "family as a set of mutually contingent careers," we would add the obvious point that social dependence in marriage is generally not equal. See "The Family

as a Set of Mutually Contingent Careers," in Foote 1961, pp. 276–97.

2 "As recently as 1936, 72 per cent of a Gallup poll sampling disapproved of married women working if their husbands could support them. In 1938, 90 per cent of a sample of men said married women should not work, and 88 per cent of a sample of women agreed that married women should give up their jobs if their husbands wanted them to." Bernard, *Women and the Public Interest* (1971), p. 149.

3 A significant analysis of the two-role pattern in the life course of women is provided by Alva Myrdal and Viola Klein in *Women's Two Roles: Home and Work* (London: Routledge and Kegan Paul, 1956).

4 See Lee Burchinal, "Adolescent Role Deprivation and High School Marriage," *Marriage and Family Living* 21 (1959): 378–94; and Floyd Martinson, "Ego Deficiency as a Factor in Marriage," *American Sociological Review* 20 (1955): 161–64.

5 The life patterns of women in the Oakland sample are described by marital age and marriage mobility in the following papers by the author: "Role Orientations, Marital Age, and Life Patterns in Adulthood" (1972); and "Marriage Mobility, Adult Roles, and Personality" (1970). We shall draw upon these papers throughout the chapter.

6 Change in the employment situation of women since 1940 and the effects of maternal employment are covered in Nye and Hoffman, eds., *The Employed Mother in America* (1963).

7 These patterns are adapted from Mary C. McMulvey, "Psychological and Sociological Factors in Prediction of Career Patterns of Women" (1961). For a more detailed examination of women's career patterns, see Bernard, *Women and the Public Interest* (1971), chaps. 8 and 9.

8 This interpretation finds support in the "ego deficiency" factor identified by Floyd Martinson. I prefer to place this factor within the framework of self-other relations. See Martinson, "Ego Deficiency as a Factor in Marriage," *American Sociological Review* 20 (1955): 161–64.

9 The median number of children for middle-class offspring is 3.2 for the nondeprived group and 2.7 for the deprived; in the working class, median values for each group are 2.0 and 2.3.

10 This follows from the negative relationship between deprived status and the educational level of the middle-class subjects. For the total sample, family deprivation is moderately predictive

of husband's occupational status ($r = .23$). With class origin and deprived status defined as givens in a regression equation, the addition of the subjects' education made no appreciable difference in the main effect of family deprivation.

11 Kingsley Davis, *Human Society* (New York: Macmillan, 1949), p. 404.

12 Jerome K. Myers and Bertram N. Roberts, *Family and Class Dynamics in Mental Illness* (New York: Wiley, 1959), p. 159.

13 The following analysis in the text draws extensively upon an earlier paper by the author, "Appearance and Education in Marriage Mobility" (1969).

14 Two measures of appearance were selected from observational ratings of the women during the high school years: well-groomed appearance, and physical attractiveness. These and other ratings were made by staff members in a playground setting during semiannual visits to the Institute of Child Welfare (see Appendix B for a description of the Free-Play ratings). The two or more staff members in attendance were well known by the girls and related to them as interested, friendly adults. Observations during these sessions were recorded afterwards on comment sheets and on seven-point scales (inter-rater reliabilities above .80). Physical attractiveness represents an average of scores on the following scales: attractive coloring, features, and physique; thin-to-fat, femininity of physique and behavior, pleasing expression, and sex appeal. To increase the stability of the judgments, scores on each scale were averaged for the high school period. The two scales were first related to marriage mobility for all women in the sample, and then compared with higher education in marital achievement within groups defined by class origin and economic deprivation.

15 Social striving among peers was measured by a five-point rating of the desire for social mastery; "a desire to control one's human environment by suggestion, persuasion, or command" (see Appendix B for a more complete description of measurement procedures). This motivational tendency represents an average of the ratings made by three judges on the basis of observational materials from the senior high period. Subtle indirect cues as well as overt features of behavior were used to infer the underlying motive. A nine-point index of high aspiration for adult status was selected from the California Q set (see Appendix B), which provided ratings for the high school period. The index represents an average of ratings by three judges.

16 Apart from Lopata's research (*Occupation: Housewife*), evidence on the persistence of this

ideology may be found in a number of articles in Athena Theodore, ed., *The Professional Woman* (Cambridge, Mass.: Schenkman, 1971). See especially the article by Margaret M. Poloma and T. Neal Garland, "The Myth of the Egalitarian Family: Familial Roles and the Professionally Employed Wife." p. 741–76.

17 To illustrate his concept of "cultural lag," William F. Ogburn frequently used examples of the uneven rates of change in the family system. Many changes in the family "seemed to be due to the economic factor which removed production activities such as spinning, weaving, soapmaking, tanning of leather from the household and put them in factories, thus taking away many of the household duties of the wife. Yet the ideology of the position of the wife persisted. It was said that woman's place was in the home." Ogburn, "Cultural Lag as Theory," *Sociology and Social Research* 41 (1957): 169. For a collection of Ogburn's writings on social change, see *William F. Ogburn on Culture and Social Change: Selected Papers*, edited with an introduction by Otis Dudley Duncan (Chicago: University of Chicago Press, 1964).

18 Margaret J. Zube, "Changing Concepts of Morality: 1948–69," *Social Forces* 50 (1972): 385–93. The *Ladies Home Journal* is one of the most traditional of women's magazines in this age of women's liberation. According to a recent editorial, approximately one-fifth of American women are readers. All quotations in this paragraph are drawn from Zube's article.

19 Correlations with family and work preference are as follows: educational level ($r = -.32$ and .17); full-time employment in 1964 ($r = -.26$ and .42); number of children ($r = .15$ and .05); and husband's status, 1958 ($r = .11$ and $-.11$). Employed women in 1964 had less children and were married to lower-status men (average $r = -.25$).

20 The two indices are identical to those which were constructed for men in chapter 7. Economic power represents the summation of scores on two five-category items: the expenditure of money and the selection and purchase of a car. Child-rearing power was determined from responses to three five-response items: how children should be disciplined, when they should date, the practice of religious training. Responses to each item ranged from "husband always" (score of 1) to "wife always" (a score of 5); thus the higher the score, the greater the respondent's perceived influence in her own marriage. Mean scores for economic and child-rearing power are 4.6 and 9.2 with standard deviations of 1.2 and 1.4.

21 The overall importance of the housewife role to married women in Lopata's sample closely resembles the attitudes of the Oakland women. Seventy-four percent of the women ranked mother first in importance among the roles of women, followed by wife and housewife (61 and 58 percent). Four-fifths of the 568 women, including 100 who were employed, did not regard "the importance of female participation in the life of the society sufficiently to remember such obligations in answers to open-ended questions. They limit women to home roles, regardless of their age or actual involvement in the family institution." (*Occupation: Housewife*, p. 47–48)

22 Years of full-time employment from 1946 to 1955 were negatively related to husband's occupational status (1958) and number of children ($r = -.16$ and $-.06$). The latter factors were more negatively related to full-time employment at the time of the 1964 survey ($r = -.26$ and $-.24$).

23 Disenchantment in marriage tends to increase over time with degree of segregation in the activities of husband and wife. See Jan Dizard, *Social Change in the Family* (1968).

24 Reuben Hill and Joan Aldous, "Socialization for Marriage and Parenthood," in Goslin 1969, p. 893. Hill and Aldous make special reference here to a pioneering study of marital adjustment: Ernest W. Burgess and Leonard S. Cottrell, Jr., *Predicting Success or Failure in Marriage* (New York: Prentice-Hall, 1939).

25 On a ten-point scale (1964), reported marital happiness increased in prevalence by social class ($r = .22$), and a similar relation was found among men in the sample.

26 A three-item index was constructed from the women's responses to three interrelated aspects of their husbands' job: income, social prestige, and future prospects. Responses to each item were scored as follows and then summed: "Like it very much," 3; "Like it somewhat," 2; "Neither like it nor dislike it," 1; and "Somewhat or very much dislike it," O. Scores thus ranged from 0 to 9. For the total sample, the index was correlated with social class in 1958 ($r = .28$) and with economic deprivation ($r = .14$). The latter relationship is due entirely to the association between deprivation and marital achievement. For a more detailed analysis of marriage mobility and its attitudinal correlates, see Elder, "Marriage Mobility, Adult Roles, and Personality" (1970).

27 Joseph Adelson, "Is Women's Lib a Passing Fad?" *New York Times Magazine*, 19 March 1972, p. 94.

28 Harold L. Wilensky, "The Uneven Distribution of Leisure: The Impact of Economic Growth on Free Time," *Social Problems* 9 (1961): 53.

9 Personality in Adult Experience

Epigraph: From Frank Barron, *Personal Soundness in University Graduate Students* (Berkeley: University of California Press, 1954).

1 The past decade has witnessed a significant shift in the study of psychological functioning from an emphasis on mental illness to an emphasis on mental health. See, for instance, Bradburn, *The Structure of Psychological Well-Being* (1969); and Sanford, *Self and Society* (1966). The role of values in conceptions of mental health is discussed by M. B. Smith in " 'Mental Health' Reconsidered: A Special Case of the Problem of Values in Psychology," *American Psychologist* 16 (1961): 299–306.

2 Langner and associates have found that "a child whose parents are in a low-income bracket has more than twice the chance of being psychiatrically impaired than a child whose parents are in a high-income bracket." Thomas S. Langner et al., "Children of the City: Affluence, Poverty, and Mental Health," in Allen 1970, chap. 10, p. 194. The significance of this result for our purposes is that the economic effect was most severe among children whose parents had very little education.

3 A detailed description of procedures used in classifying the subjects is available and may be obtained through the Institute of Human Development (Berkeley). An earlier analysis of the antecedents of psychosomatic illness in adulthood is reported by Louis Stewart in "Social and Emotional Adjustment during Adolescence as Related to the Development of Psychosomatic Illness in Adulthood," *Genetic Psychology Monographs* 65 (1962): 175–215.

4 Coding procedures are described by Suzanne Reichard in *Dynamic and Cognitive Personality Variables*, Memorandum on the Oakland Growth Study (Berkeley: Institute of Human Development, University of California, 1961).

5 In Block's project, three trained judges reviewed interview material on each case, and then arranged a set of 100 statements (e.g., "genuinely submissive") in nine piles such that the extreme piles included statements which were least or most characteristic of the person. Ratings of the judges on each case were averaged to obtain a single description. Common personality types were then generated by factoring Q correlations which index the degree of resemblance between Q-sort descriptions. For a detailed account of the

judging process, see Jack Block, *Lives through Time* (1971), chap. 3.

6 The difference in percent symptom-free between the nondeprived and deprived groups (middle class) is statistically reliable ($\chi^2 = 7.2$ *l d.f.*, $< .05$).

7 Mary C. Jones, "Personality Correlates and Antecedents of Drinking Patterns in Adult Males," *Journal of Consulting and Clinical Psychology* 32 (1968): 2–12.

8 These types were identified in an early stage of analysis. More recently, in *Lives through Time*, Block systematically compared personality types which were generated by factoring conjointly two sets of Q descriptions for the junior high period and middle age (circa 1958). This procedure generated five types of personality development among the males and six types among the females. With Professor Block's generous assistance, a special effort was made to link these personality types with economic deprivation and class origin. In the final analysis, differences between the two studies proved to be too large to overcome; no reliable conclusions could be drawn from the results. Two points are worth noting in this respect. Block's sample includes members of the Guidance sample (located at the Institute of Human Development) as well as members of the Oakland study, and thus each personality type includes a very small number of the Oakland subjects. But, more importantly, a large number of the Oakland subjects in Block's analysis did not fall into any personality type. For example, 28 percent of the men were classified as residuals. These cases are likely to include subjects who were characterized by substantial personality change between preadolescence and middle age, since the simultaneous factoring of Q formulations at two points in time would tend to maximize personality continuity and coherence.

9 John Cassel, "Physical Illness in Response to Stress," in Levine and Scotch 1970, p. 197.

10 These differences in the total group were most pronounced among the men. A comparison of the adult correlates of emotionality (junior high period) shows the following differences between the male offspring of nondeprived ($N = 18$) and deprived families ($N = 26$): anxiety reaction ($r = .38$ vs. $-.27$); Iowa manifest anxiety ($r = .27$ vs. -20); and ego strength ($r = -.44$ vs. $.36$). Consistency of direction is the main point to note across these comparisons in view of the small subgroups. On the adolescent index of social unhappiness, these comparisons yielded an average difference between correlations of .34.

11 John E. Anderson, "The Prediction of Adjustment over Time," in Ira Iscoe and Harold W. Stevenson, eds., *Personality Development in Children* (Austin: University of Texas Press, 1960), pp. 28–72, esp. p. 68. In regard to Anderson's observation, Levine and Scotch note that unwarranted beliefs about stress include the assumption that "events stressful for an individual must lead to disruptive or pathological consequences." Levine and Scotch, eds., *Social Stress* (1970), p. 9. Emphasis on dimensions of psychological stability or continuity over time is found in Kagan and Moss, *Birth to Maturity* (1962); and in Block, *Lives through Time* (1971).

12 A series of studies have assembled evidence on entry into parenthood as a problem or crisis situation. See LeMasters, "Parenthood as Crisis" (1963); and Daniel Hobbs, Jr., "Parenthood as Crisis" (1965). From her in-depth survey of housewives, Lopata concludes that "the event causing the greatest discontinuity of personality in American middle-class women is the birth of the first child, particularly if it is not immediately followed by a return to full-time involvement outside the home. It is not just a 'crisis' which is followed by a return to previous roles and relations, but an event marking a complete change in life approach." *Occupation: Housewife* (1971), pp. 200–201.

13 Parental adequacy in relation to family status (1929): ave. tau_c for men and women $= -.18$. Compare with tau_c of $.28$ for the association between family size and adequacy among women.

14 For women, perceived adequacy is correlated $-.12$ with their education and $-.29$ with their class position in marriage (tau_c coefficients). These relationships were slightly weaker among men. In studies of parenthood as a crisis, effective resolution of problems is generally related to marital satisfaction, and we find a similar, though weak, relation among the Oakland parents between reported marital happiness in 1964 and perceived parental adequacy (average $tau_c = .07$).

15 Two coders applied these categories to each of the interview transcripts and achieved agreement on slightly more than four-fifths of the cases. Differences were discussed and reconciled.

16 The ethical impact of parental interpretations of historical experiences is one of the least explored problems in socialization. Note, for example, the implied linkages in the family experience of Andrew Goodman, a college boy who, as a civil rights worker, was murdered by whites in Mississippi. Shortly after his death his mother wrote: "How many times had Bob and

I talked about the Great Depression, just to help our boys understand suffering they had never seen or experienced? How many times had we talked about Nazi brutality, because we believed it had to be the business of everyone, even of our children, who could not remember it? Those terrible things were the great truths of our generation, Bob's and mine. If my son now felt that a fight for human dignity in Mississippi was his business—the business of his generation—was I to say, 'No, no, I lied when I said a person must act on his beliefs." Mrs. Robert W. Goodman, as told to Bernard Asbell, "My Son Didn't Die in Vain," *Good Housekeeping* 161 (May 1965): 160.

17 See Herbert H. Hyman, *Political Socialization* (Glencoe, Ill.: Free Press, 1959).

18 Anne Foner, "The Polity," in Riley et al. 1972, pp. 140–44. See also Angus Campbell et al., *The American Voter* (New York: Wiley, 1960), pp. 153–55.

19 Even residents of staunchly conservative Orange County (California) gave Roosevelt a plurality of votes in 1932. Democrats outnumbered Republicans in registration for the election of 1936, an unprecedented event in local history. However, this change did not alter the basic conservative stance of the county. "The Great Depression, with its consequent expansion of the governmental role, shook the faith for a time but did not fundamentally alter it." Robert L. Pritchard, "Orange County during the Depressed Thirties: A Study in Twentieth-Century California Local History," in Sternsher 1970, pp. 247–64.

20 The quotation is drawn from a survey of 171 University of California students (1965).

21 The average percentage difference by family deprivation for the two health objectives is 16 percent.

10 Children of the Great Depression

1 Hugh MacLennan, "What It Was Like to Be in Your Twenties in the Thirties," in Victor Hoar, ed., *The Great Depression: Essays and Memoirs from Canada and the United States* (Toronto: Copp Clark Publishing Co., 1969), p. 145.

2 In a comparison of five-year cohorts, Leonard Cain found that the largest percentage gain among persons with at least one year of college and with college degrees was made by the 1921–25 cohort, the group to which the Oakland adults belong. Leonard D. Cain, Jr., "The 1916–1925 Cohort of Americans" (1970).

3 Using data on middle-class families in a Chicago neighborhood (1870s and 1880s), Richard Sennett challenges the presumed adaptive functions of the nuclear family in the urban-industrial environment. He claims that the family was used more as an emotional haven from the hostile city environment than as an adaptive mechanism. Sennett, *Families against the City* (1970). For a recent overview of social history on the family, see Tamara K. Hareven, "The History of the Family as an Interdisciplinary Field" (1971).

4 Hoar (see note 1), p. iv.

5 Of relevance here is Barton's theoretical work on relative deprivation (1969).

6 This paragraph and the following are indebted to aspects of Potter's essay *People of Plenty* (1954). Though seemingly unpromising for a study of abundance, the American Depression is actually very much a product of twentieth-century abundance; productivity outstripped consumer demand or purchasing power. Moreover, Potter's own analysis shows that one can gain valuable insight into the workings of a culture of abundance during a period of economic scarcity. An important distinction between the poor in times of general prosperity and depression is made by Michael Harrington in his forceful documentation of poverty in the affluent postwar years, *The Other America* (1962). See also a report by the Child Study Association of America, *Children of Poverty—Children of Affluence* (New York, 1967).

7 "Unaccustomed to prolonged adversity, Americans experienced the depression as much more of a shock than did countries which had not enjoyed the boom of the 1920's." William E. Leuchtenburg, "The Great Depression," in C. Vann Woodward, ed., *The Comparative Approach to American History* (New York: Basic Books, 1968), p. 297.

8 The analogy is attributed to Arthur Krock of the *New York Times*. "The tide turned with Roosevelt's swift and decisive action as he took office. Despair turned into hope, and faith and confidence reached a peak as the Hundred Days came to an end." Cabel Phillips, *From the Crash to the Blitz, 1929–1939* (New York: Macmillan, 1969), p. 128.

9 Human costs of the Depression owe much to the conflict between scarcity conditions and lifeways fashioned in an abundance culture. During an era of unparalleled economic growth (1820–1930), when the potentialities of natural abundance were being developed, belief in equality of opportunity, unconstrained by legal impediments or position, fostered commitments

to the unattainable ideal of mobility for all and justified a low standard of living as a penalty for the unsuccessful. Responsibility for failure to rise or achieve was thus assigned to the individual. In the Depression, the jobless and economically deprived often acted as if they were exempt from mobility or livelihood barriers of a sociolegal nature, even though such freedom has meaning only in a context of positive opportunity. Structural barriers to economic well-being did not deter men from blaming themselves for failing to meet such goals. See Potter, *People of Plenty*, p. 93.

10 Judith Blake, "Family Size in the 1960's—A Baffling Fad?" *Eugenics Quarterly* 14 (1967): 60–74.

11 Despite the large number of women who entered wartime industries, a comparison of national surveys before and after the war shows no meaningful increase in support for careers among married women. Linda B. Dahl, "Effects of World War II on Attitudes toward Women in the Labor Force," M.A. thesis, University of North Carolina, 1971. In reference to the 40s and the impact of World War II, William Chafe concludes that "women's sphere had been significantly expanded, yet traditional attitudes toward women's place remained largely unchanged. . . . The 'lag' between cultural norms and everyday behavior said a great deal about what happened (and did not happen) in the 1940's." *The American Woman* (1972), pp. 188–89.

12 Joseph Katz and associates, *No Time for Youth* (San Francisco: Jossey-Bass, 1968).

13 A report of one such school in California stresses the minimal expense of this organizational principle in upgrading the educational process (Ralph J. Melaregno and Gerald Newmark, "Tutorial Community Project, Report of the Second Year, July 1969–August 1970," Santa Monica: System Development Corporation, n.d.).

14 *Report to the President*, White House Conference on Children (Washington, D.C., Government Printing Office, 1970), pp. 248–49.

15 Margaret Mead, *And Keep Your Powder Dry* (New York: William Morrow and Co., 1942), pp. 68–69.

16 Edward Shils, "Plenitude and Scarcity," *Encounter*, May 1964, p. 44.

17 Flacks, "Social and Cultural Meanings of Student Revolt" (1970). In a lower social stratum (defined by grandparents in the working class), Bengtson and Lovejoy report no change in materialistic values across three generations of

Southern Californians, "Values, Personality, and Social Structure" (1973).

18 David Gottlieb, "Youth and Work," unpublished manuscript, Pennsylvania State University, 1972.

19 Stanley E. Seashore and J. Thad Barnowe, "Demographic and Job Factors Associated with the 'Blue Collar Blues,' " unpublished manuscript, Institute for Social Research, Ann Arbor, Mich., 1972.

20 On the use of war analogues in social mobilization during the Depression, see Leuchtenburg, "The New Deal and the Analogue of War" (1964). Sorokin observes that "in all the measures of the New Deal there is scarcely one that does not find its prototype in the expedients invented in the remote past for coping with similar emergencies." *Man and Society in Calamity* (1942), p. 134. On the relation between superordinate goals and group solidarity, see Muzafir Sherif, "Superordinate Goals in the Reduction of Intergroup Tensions," *American Journal of Sociology* 53 (1958): 349–56.

21 For an up-to-date appraisal, see Letitia Upton and Nancy Lyons, *Basic Facts: Distribution of Personal Income and Wealth in the United States* (Cambridge, Mass.: The Cambridge Institute, 1972).

Appendix B   **Sample Characteristics, Data Sources, and Methodological Issues**

1 Caroline Tryon, *U.C. Inventory 1: Social and Emotional Adjustment*, Rev. Form (Berkeley: Institute of Child Welfare, University of California, 1939).

2 See Jack Block, *The Q-Sort Method in Personality Assessment and Psychiatric Research* (Springfield, Ill.: Charles C. Thomas, 1961). I am indebted to Dr. Block for permission to use these *Q*-sort data. See also Block's *Lives through Time* (1971).

3 The Free-Play and Situation ratings are described by Francis Burk Newman in "The Adolescent in Social Groups: Studies in the Observation of Personality," *Applied Psychology Monographs* 9 (1946); 1–94. On the rating of needs or drives, see Else Frenkel Brunswik, "Motivation and Behavior," *Genetic Psychology Monographs* 26 (1942): 121–265.

4 Frenkel Brunswik, "Motivation and Behavior," p. 144.

5 On validity and reliability, see Samuel A. Stouffer, *Social Research to Test Ideas* (New York: Free Press of Glencoe, 1962), p. 265.

6 George W. Bohrnstedt and T. Michael Carter, "Robustness in Regression Analysis," in Herbert

375

L. Costner, ed., *Sociological Methodology 1971* (San Francisco: Jossey-Bass, 1971), p. 131.

7 Otis D. Duncan, "Path Analysis: Sociological Examples," *American Journal of Sociology* 72 (1966): 1–16; K. C. Land, "Principles of Path Analysis," in Edgar F. Borgatta, ed., *Sociological Methodology 1969* (San Francisco: Jossey-Bass, 1969), pp. 3–37.

8 This use of statistical tests is consistent with David Gold's interpretation in "Statistical Tests and Substantive Significance," *American Sociologist* 4 (1969): 43.

Appendix C   On Comparisons of the Great Depression

1 William E. Leuchtenburg, "The Great Depression," in C. Van Woodward, ed., *The Comparative Approach to American History* (New York: Basic Books, 1968), p. 312. In reference to the surge of interest in comparative history, James Patterson asserts that "few historians are actually writing it, and fewer still succeed in arriving at meaningful comparison." "Federalism in Crisis: A Comparative Study of Canada and the United States in the Depression of the 1930's," in Hoar (1969), p. 1 (see note 1, chap. 10). The problems entailed in arriving at meaningful comparisons on economic indicators are briefly discussed by C. B. Schedvin, *Australia and the Great Depression* (Sydney: Sydney University Press, 1970), pp. 43–46.

2 These dimensions are drawn from Allen Barton's skillful analysis of disaster research, *Communities in Disaster* (1969), p. 41. Barton does not focus on societies as a unit of analysis, but his elaborate conceptual framework has much to offer comparative studies of the Great Depression. The four dimensions are only a small fragment of Barton's model. Apart from the references cited, economic data on Germany were obtained from C. W. Guillebaud, *The Economic Recovery of Germany, 1933–1938* (London: Macmillan, 1939), esp. appendix table 6.

3 John Kenneth Galbraith, *American Capitalism*, 2d ed. (Boston: Houghton Mifflin, 1962).

4 Patterson (see note 1 above), p. 5.

5 Leuchtenburg (see note 1 above), 297.

6 David Schoenbaum, *Hitler's Social Revolution: Class and Status in Nazi Germany, 1933–1939* (Garden City, N.Y.: Doubleday, 1966), p. 9.

7 Leuchtenburg (see note 1 above), p. 297.

8 Richard Grunberger, *The Twelve-Year Reich: A Social History of Nazi Germany, 1933–1945* (New York: Holt, Rinehart and Winston, 1971), p. 10.

9 Leuchtenburg, "The New Deal and the Analogue of War" (1964), p. 109. All subsequent quotations in the text are drawn from this essay.

Select Bibliography

This bibliography includes only those works cited in the text and notes that bear most directly upon the study and its implications. Methodological and statistical references that pertain to the Oakland Growth Study and data analysis are not listed here, since they are readily accessible to the reader under the notes to Appendix B, "Sample Characteristics, Data Sources, and Methodological Issues." Needless to say, no restricted bibliography could do justice to the full array of social historical work on the Great Depression, and reviews in the literature make such coverage unnecessary. (See Sternsher's essay in *Hitting Home*, cited here, for a brief introduction.)

Aiken, Michael;
Ferman, Louis A.;
and
Sheppard, Harold L.
1968
Economic Failure, Alienation, and Extremism. Ann Arbor: University of Michigan Press.

Allen, Vernon L., ed.
1970
Psychological Factors in Poverty. Chicago: Markham.

Altbach, Philip G.,
and Peterson, Patti
1971
"Before Berkeley: Historical Perspectives on American Student Activism." *Annals of the American Academy of Political and Social Science* 395:1–14.

Angell, Robert Cooley
1936
The Family Encounters the Depression. New York: Charles Scribner's Sons.

Atkinson, John W., ed.
1958
Motives in Fantasy, Action, and Society. Princeton: Van Nostrand.

Bahr, Stephen J.,
and Rollins, Boyd C.
1971
"Crisis and Conjugal Power." *Journal of Marriage and Family* 33:360–367.

Baker, George, and
Chapman, D. W., eds.
1962
Man and Society in Disaster. New York: Basic Books.

Bakke, E. W.
1940

Citizens without Work. New Haven: Yale University Press.

Barker, Roger
1968

Ecological Psychology. Stanford: Stanford University Press.

Barton, Allen
1969

Communities in Disaster. Garden City, N. Y.: Doubleday.

Bengtson, Vern L., and Lovejoy, Chris
1973

"Values, Personality, and Social Structure: An Intergenerational Analysis." *American Behavioral Scientist* 16:880–912.

Bensman, Joseph, and Vidich, Arthur J.
1971

The New American Society. Chicago: Quadrangle Books.

Bernard, Jessie
1971

Women and the Public Interest. Chicago: Aldine.

Bird, Caroline
1966

The Invisible Scar. New York: McKay and Co.

Blau, Peter M., and Duncan, Otis Dudley
1967

The American Occupational Structure. New York: John Wiley and Sons.

Block, Jack (in collaboration with Norma Haan)
1971

Lives through Time. Berkeley: Bancroft Books.

Blood, Robert O., Jr., and Wolfe, Donald M.
1960

Husbands and Wives. Glencoe, Ill.: The Free Press.

Blumer, Herbert
1939

An Appraisal of Thomas and Znaniecki's "The Polish Peasant in Europe and America." New York: Social Science Research Council, Bull. 44.

1958

"Race Prejudice as a Sense of Group Position." *Pacific Sociological Review* 1:3–7.

1971

"Social Problems as Collective Behavior." *Social Problems* 18:298–306.

Bowerman, Charles E., and Glen H. Elder, Jr.
1964

"Variations in Adolescent Perceptions of Family Power Structure." *American Sociological Review* 29:551–67.

Bradburn, Norman M.
1969

The Structure of Psychological Well-Being. Chicago: Aldine.

Breer, Paul E., and Locke, Edwin A.
1965

Task Experience as a Source of Attitudes. Homewood, Ill.: Dorsey Press.

Bronson, Wanda S.; Katten, Edith S.; and Livson, Norman
1959

"Patterns of Authority and Affection in Two Generations." *Journal of Abnormal and Social Psychology* 58:143–52.

Brunswik, Else Frenkel
1942

"Motivation and Behavior." *Genetic Psychology Monographs* 26:121–265.

Burgess, Ernest W.; Locke, Harvey J.; and Thomes, Mary Margaret
1971
The Family: From Tradition to Companionship. 4th ed. New York: Van Nostrand.

Butler, Robert N.
1963
"The Life Review: An Interpretation of Reminiscence in the Aged." *Psychiatry* 26:65–76.

Cain, Leonard D., Jr.
1970
"The 1916–1925 Cohort of Americans: Its Contributions to the Generation Gap." Paper presented at the annual meeting of the American Sociological Association, Washington, D. C., September 1, 1970.

Cavan, Ruth S., and Ranck, Katharine H.
1938
The Family and the Depression: A Study of 100 Chicago Families. Chicago: University of Chicago Press.

Chafe, William Henry
1972
The American Woman: Her Changing Social, Economic, and Political Roles, 1920–1970. New York: Oxford University Press.

Christensen, Harold T., ed.
1964
The Handbook of Marriage and the Family. Chicago: Rand McNally.

Clausen, John A., ed.
1968
Socialization and Society. Boston: Little, Brown and Co. (See especially chap. 7, by M. Brewster Smith, "Competence and Socialization," and chap. 2, by Alex Inkeles, "Society, Social Structure, and Child Socialization.")

Coles, Robert
1967
Children of Crisis. Boston: Little, Brown and Co.

Cooley, Charles H.
1922
Human Nature and the Social Order. New York: Charles Scribner's Sons.

Dizard, Jan
1968
Social Change in the Family. Chicago: Community and Family Study Center.

Dohrenwend, Bruce P., and Dohrenwend, Barbara S.
1969
Social Status and Psychological Disorder: A Causal Inquiry. New York: John Wiley and Sons.

Easterlin, Richard A.
1961
"The American Baby Boom in Historical Perspective." *American Economic Review* 51:869–911.

1968
Population, Labor Force, and Long Swings in Economic Growth: The American Experience. New York: National Bureau of Economic Research.

Elder, Glen H., Jr.
1968
"Achievement Motivation and Intelligence in Occupational Mobility: A Longitudinal Analysis." *Sociometry* 31:327–54.

1969a
"Appearance and Education in Marriage Mobility." *American Sociological Review* 34:519–33.

379

1969b   "Occupational Mobility, Life Patterns, and Personality." *Journal of Health and Social Behavior* 10:308–23.

1970   "Marriage Mobility, Adult Roles, and Personality." *Sociological Symposium* no. 4:31–54.

1971   *Adolescent Socialization and Personality Development.* Chicago: Rand McNally.

1972   "Role Orientations, Marital Age, and Life Patterns in Adulthood." *Merrill-Palmer Quarterly* 18:3–24.

1973   "On Linking Social Structure and Personality." *American Behavioral Scientist* 16:785–800.

Erikson, Kai 1970   "Sociology and the Historical Perspective." *American Sociologist* 5:331–38.

Estvan, Frank 1952   "The Relationship of Social Status, Intelligence, and Sex of Ten- and Eleven-Year-Old Children to an Awareness of Poverty." *Genetic Psychology Monographs* 46:3–60.

Farber, Bernard 1972   *Guardians of Virtue: Salem Families in 1800.* New York: Basic Books.

Festinger, Leon 1957   *A Theory of Cognitive Dissonance.* Evanston, Ill.: Row, Peterson.

Flacks, Richard 1970   "Social and Cultural Meanings of Student Revolt: Some Informal Comparative Observations." *Social Problems* 17:340–57.

Foote, Nelson N., ed. 1961   *Household Decision-Making.* New York: New York University Press.

Freud, Anna, and Burlingham, Dorothy T. 1943   *War and Children.* New York: International Universities Press.

Fromm, Erich 1941   *Escape from Freedom.* New York: Farrar and Rinehart.

Gerth, Hans, and Mills, C. Wright 1953   *Character and Social Structure. New York:* Harcourt, Brace and World.

Gewirtz, Jacob L., and Baer, Donald M. 1958   "Deprivation and Satiation as Social Reinforcers on Drive Conditions." *Journal of Abnormal and Social Psychology* 57:165–72.

Ginsburg, S. W. 1942   "What Unemployment Does to People: A Study in Adjustment to Crisis." *American Journal of Psychiatry* 99:439:46.

Glaser, Barney G., and Strauss, Anselm L. 1964   "Awareness Contexts and Social Interaction." *American Sociological Review* 29:667–79.

Glaser, Daniel, and Rice, Kent 1959   "Crime, Age, and Employment." *American Sociological Review* 24:679–89.

Goode, William J. "The Theory and Measurement of Family
1968 Change." In *Indicators of Social Change:
Concepts and Measurements*, edited by Eleanor
Bernert Sheldon and Wilbert E. Moore. New
York: Russell Sage Foundation.

Gorer, Geoffrey "What's the Matter with Britain?" *New York
1967 Times Magazine* 31.

Goslin, David A., ed. *Handbook of Socialization Theory and Research.*
1969 Chicago: Rand McNally. (See especially
chapters by Reuben Hill and Joan Aldous,
"Socialization for Marriage and Parenthood";
and by Leonard Cottrell, "Interpersonal
Interaction and the Development of the Self.")

Gouldner, Alvin, and *Notes on Technology and the Moral Order.*
Peterson, William Indianapolis: Bobbs-Merrill.
1961

Greven, Philip J., Jr. *Four Generations: Population, Land, and Family
1970 in Colonial Andover, Massachusetts.* Ithaca and
London: Cornell University Press.

Hamblin, Robert L. "Leadership and Crisis." *Sociometry* 21:322–35.
1958

Hansen, Donald A., "Families under Stress." In *The Handbook of
and Hill, Reuben Marriage and the Family*, edited by Harold T.
1964 Christensen, chap. 19. Chicago: Rand McNally.

Hareven, Tamara K. "The History of the Family as an Interdisciplinary
1971 Field." *Journal of Interdisciplinary History*
2:399–414.

Harrington, Michael *The Other America.* New York: Macmillan.
1962

Hawthorn, Geoffrey *The Sociology of Fertility.* London: Macmillan
1970 and Co.

Heer, David M. "The Measurement and Bases of Family Power."
1963 *Marriage and Family Living* 25:133–39.

Hill, Reuben *Families under Stress.* New York: Harper and
1949 Bros.
1970 *Family Development in Three Generations.*
Cambridge, Mass.: Schenkman.

Hinkle, L. E., Jr., and "The Nature of Man's Adaptation to His Total
Wolff, H. A. Environment and the Relation of This to Illness."
1957 *A.M.A. Archives of Internal Medicine* 22:449–60.

Hobbs, Daniel, Jr. "Parenthood as Crisis: A Third Study." *Marriage
1965 and Family Living* 27:367–72.

Hobsbawm, E. J. "From Social History to the History of Society."
1971 In *Historical Studies Today*, edited by Felix
Gilbert and Stephen R. Graubard, pp. 1–26.
New York: W. W. Norton.

Hoffman, Lois W. "Effects of Employment of Mothers on Parental
1960 Power Relations and the Division of Household
Tasks." *Marriage and Family Living* 22:27–35.

Huntington, Emily H.   *Unemployment Relief and the Unemployed.*
                1939   Berkeley and Los Angeles: University of
                        California Press.

Hyman, Herbert H.   "The Psychology of Status." *Archives of*
                1942   *Psychology* 38, no. 269.
                1972   *Secondary Analysis of Sample Surveys: Principles,*
                        Procedures, and Potentialities. New York: John
                        Wiley and Sons.

Ingersoll, Hazel L.   "A Study of the Transmission of Authority
                1948   Patterns in the Family." *Genetic Psychology*
                        Monographs 38:225–302.

Inkeles, Alex   "Social Change and Social Character: The Role of
                1955   Parental Mediation." *Journal of Social Issues* 11,
                        no. 2: 12–23.

Jackson, Elton F.   "Status Inconsistency and Symptoms of Stress."
                1962   *American Sociological Review* 27:469–80.

Jackson, Elton F.,   "Status and Symptoms of Stress: Additive and
and Burke, Peter J.   Interaction Effects," *American Sociological*
                1965   *Review* 30:556–64.

Jahoda, Marie;   *Marienthal.* Chicago: Aldine.
Lazarsfeld, Paul F.;
and Zeisel, Hans
                1970

Jones, Mary C.   "A Study of Socialization Patterns at the High
                1958   School Level." *The Journal of Genetic*
                        Psychology 93:87–111.

Kagan, Jerome, and   *Birth to Maturity.* New York: John Wiley and Co.
Moss, Howard
                1962

Kasl, Stanislav, and   "Effects of Parental Status Incongruence and
Cobb, Sidney   Discrepancy on Physical and Mental Health of
                1967   Adult Offspring." *Journal of Personality and*
                        Social Psychology Monograph 7, no. 2, pt. 2.

Kirkendall, Richard S. "The Great Depression: Another Watershed in
                1964   American History?" In *Change and Continuity*
                        in Twentieth-Century America, edited by John
                        Braeman, Robert H. Bremner, and Everett
                        Walters. New York: Harper and Row.

Knudsen, Dean O.   "The Declining Status of Women: Popular Myths
                1969   and the Failure of Functionalist Thought."
                        Social Forces 48:183–93.

Kohn, Melvin L.   *Class and Conformity: A Study in Values.*
                1969   Homewood, Ill.: Dorsey Press.

Komarovsky, Mirra   *The Unemployed Man and His Family.* New
                1940   York: Columbia University Press.
                1962   *Blue-Collar Marriage.* New York: Random House.

Koos, Earl L.   *Families in Trouble.* New York: King's Crown
                1946   Press.

LaFollette, Cecile T.
1934
A Study of the Problems of 652 Gainfully Employed Married Women Homemakers. New York: Teachers College, Columbia University.

Langner, Thomas S., and Michael, Stanley T.
1963
Life Stress and Mental Health. New York: Free Press.

LeMasters, E. E.
1963
"Parenthood as Crisis." *Marriage and Family Living* 25:196–201.

Lenski, Gerhard
1954
"Status Crystallization: A Non-vertical Dimension of Social Status," *American Sociological Review* 19 (1954): 405–13.

Leslie, Gerald R., and Johnsen, Kathryn P.
1963
"Changed Perceptions of the Maternal Role." *American Sociological Review* 28:919–28.

Leuchtenburg, William E.
1964
"The New Deal and the Analogue of War." In *Change and Continuity in Twentieth-Century America,* edited by John Braeman, Robert H. Bremner, and Everett Walters. New York: Harper and Row.

Levine, Sol, and Scotch, Norman A., eds.
1970
Social Stress. Chicago: Aldine (See especially chapter 10, by R. Scott and A. Howard, "Models of Stress.")

Levinger, George
1965
"Marital Cohesiveness and Dissolution: An Integrative Review." *Journal of Marriage and the Family* 27:19–28.

Linder, Staffan B.
1970
The Harried Leisure Class. New York: Columbia University Press.

Linton, Ralph
1942
"Age and Sex Categories." *American Sociological Review* 7:589–603.

Lipset, Seymour M., and Todd, Everett C.
1971
"College Generations—from the 1930s to the 1960s." *The Public Interest* 25:99–113.

Lopata, Helena Z.
1971
Occupation: Housewife. New York: Oxford University Press.

Lynd, Robert S., and Lynd, Helen Merritt
1937
Middletown in Transition: A Study in Cultural Conflicts. New York: Harcourt, Brace, and Co.

McClelland, David C.
1961
The Achieving Society. Princeton, N. J.: Van Nostrand.

Macfarlane, Jean W.
1964
"Perspectives on Personality Consistency and Change from the Guidance Study." *Vita Humana* 7:115–26.

McGrath, Joseph E., ed.
1970
Social and Psychological Factors in Stress. New York: Holt, Rinehart, and Winston.

McMulvey, Mary C.
1961
"Psychological and Sociological Factors in Prediction of Career Patterns of Women." Ph.D. dissertation, Harvard University.

Malewski, Andrzej
1966
"The Degree of Status Incongruence and Its Effects." In *Class, Status, and Power*, edited by Reinhard Bendix and Seymour M. Lipset, 2d ed., pp. 303–8. New York: Free Press.

Mannheim, Karl
1952
"The Problem of Generations." In *Essays on the Sociology of Knowledge*, translated and edited by Paul Kecskemetic, pp. 276–322. London: Routledge and Kegan Paul.

Maslow, Abraham H.
1954
Motivation and Personality. New York: Harper and Row.

Mauss, Armand L.
1971
"The Lost Promise of Reconciliation: New versus Old Left." *Journal of Social Issues* 27:1–20. (The entire issue is devoted to Old and New Left.)

Mayhew, Henry
1968
London Labour and London Poor. Vol. 1. New York: Dover. (Originally published by Griffin, Bohn, and Co. in 1861–62.)

Mechanic, David
1968
Medical Sociology. New York: Free Press.

Miller, Daniel R.
1970
"Personality as a System." In *A Handbook of Method in Cultural Anthropology*, edited by Raoul Naroll and Ronald Cohen, pp. 509–26. Garden City, N. Y.: The Natural History Press.

Miller, Daniel R., and Swanson, Guy E.
1958
The Changing American Parent. New York: John Wiley and Sons.

Mills, C. Wright
1951
White Collar. New York: Oxford University Press.
1959
The Sociological Imagination. New York: Oxford University Press.

Minturn, Leigh, and Lambert, William
1964
Mothers of Six Cultures. New York: John Wiley and Sons.

Mitchell, Broadus
1947
Depression Decade: From New Era through the New Deal, 1929–1941. New York: Rinehart and Co.

Miyamoto, Frank
1970
"Self, Motivation, and Symbolic Interactionist Theory." In *Human Nature and Collective Behavior: Papers in Honor of Herbert Blumer*, edited by Tamotsu Shibutani, pp. 271–85. Englewood Cliffs, N. J.: Prentice-Hall.

Mogey, John M.
1957
"A Century of Declining Paternal Authority." *Marriage and Family Living* 19:234–39.

Moss, J. Joel
1964
"Teenage Marriage: Cross-National Trends and Sociological Factors in the Decision of When to Marry." *Acta Sociologica* 8:98–117.

Mussen, Paul H., ed.
1960
Handbook of Research Methods and Child Development. New York: John Wiley and Sons.

(See especially William Kessen, "Research Design in the Study of Developmental Problems.")

1970   *Carmichael's Manual of Child Psychology.* New York: John Wiley and Sons.

Nam, Charles
1964   "Impact of the GI Bills on the Educational Level of Male Population." *Social Forces* 43:26–32.

Nesbit, Robert A.
1969   *Social Change and History.* New York: Oxford University Press.
1970   *The Social Bond.* New York: Knopf.

Nye, F. Ivan, and Hoffman, Lois W., eds.
1963   *The Employed Mother in America.* Chicago: Rand McNally.

Ogburn, William F.
1964   *William F. Ogburn on Culture and Social Change: Selected Papers.* Edited and with an Introduction by Otis Dudley Duncan. Chicago: University of Chicago Press.

Parsons, Talcott, and Fox, Renee
1952   "Illness, Therapy, and the Modern Urban American Family." *Journal of Social Issues* 8:31–44.

Perry, Stewart E.; Silber, Earle; and Bloch, Donald A.
1956   *The Child and His Family in Disaster: A Study of the 1953 Vicksburg Tornado.* Washington, D.C.: National Research Council, Study no. 5.

Plant, James
1937   *Personality and the Cultural Pattern.* New York: The Commonwealth Fund.

Potter, David M.
1954   *People of Plenty.* Chicago: University of Chicago Press.

Pruett, Lorine
1934   *Women Workers through the Depression.* New York: Macmillan.

Rahe, Richard H.
1969   "Life Crisis and Health Change." In *Psychotrophic Drug Response: Advances in Prediction,* edited by Philip R. A. May and J. R. Wittenborn. Springfield, Ill.: Charles C. Thomas.

Reissman, Frank; Cohen, Jerome; and Pearl, Arthur, eds.
1964   *Mental Health of the Poor.* New York: Free Press.

Riesman, David
1950   *The Lonely Crowd.* New Haven: Yale University Press.

Riley, Matilda White; Johnson, Marilyn; and Foner, Anne
1972   *Aging and Society: A Sociology of Age Stratification.* Vol. 3. New York: Russell Sage Foundation.

Rosenberg, Morris
1965   *Society and the Adolescent Self-Image.* Princeton, N. J.: Princeton University Press.

Rossi, Alice S.
1964   "Equality between the Sexes." *Daedalus* 93:607–52.

Runciman, W. G.
1966
Relative Deprivation and Social Justice. Berkeley and Los Angeles: University of California Press.

Ryder, Norman B.
1965
"The Cohort as a Concept in the Study of Social Change." *American Sociological Review* 30:843–61.

1967
"The Emergence of a Modern Fertility Pattern: United States, 1917–66." Paper presented at a conference on "Fertility and Family Planning: A World View," University of Michigan, 15–17 November 1967.

Sanford, Nevitt
1966
Self and Society. New York: Atherton Press.

Scanzoni, John H.
1970
Opportunity and the Family: A Study of the Conjugal Family in Relation to the Economic-Opportunity Structure. New York: Free Press.

Sennett, Richard
1970
Families against the City. Cambridge, Mass.: Harvard University Press.

Shanas, Ethel, and Streib, Gordon F., eds.
1965
Social Structure and the Family: Generational Relations. Englewood Cliffs, N. J.: Prentice-Hall.

Sherif, Muzafir
1958
"Superordinate Goals in the Reduction of Intergroup Tensions." *American Journal of Sociology* 53:349–56.

Simons, Rita J., ed.
1967
As We Saw the Thirties. Urbana: University of Illinois Press. (See especially Hal Draper's essay, "The Student Movement of the Thirties: A Political History.")

Slater, Philip
1970
The Pursuit of Loneliness. Boston: Beacon Press.

Slote, Alfred
1969
Termination: The Closing at Baker Plant. Indianapolis: Bobbs-Merrill.

Smelser, Neil J.
1967
"Sociological History: The Industrial Revolution and the British Working-Class Family." In *Essays in Sociological Explanation,* by Smelser. Englewood Cliffs, N. J.: Prentice-Hall.

Sorokin, Pitirim A.
1942
Man and Society in Calamity. New York: E. P. Dutton and Co.

Spiegel, John P.
1968
"The Resolution of Role Conflict within the Family." In *A Modern Introduction to the Family,* edited by Norman W. Bell and E. F. Vogel, pp. 361–81. New York: Free Press.

Srole, Leo; Langner, T. S.; Michael, S. T.; Opler, M. K.; and Rennie, T. A. C.
1962
Mental Health in the Metropolis. New York: McGraw-Hill.

Sternsher, Bernard
1969
The Negro in Depression and War: Prelude to Revolution, 1930–45. Chicago: Quadrangle Books.

1970
Hitting Home: The Great Depression in Town and Country. Edited by Bernard Sternsher. Chicago: Quadrangle Books.

Stotland, Ezra
1969
The Psychology of Hope. San Francisco: Jossey-Bass.

Stouffer, Samuel A., and Lazarsfeld, Paul F.
1937
Research Memorandum on the Family in the Depression. New York: The Social Science Research Council.

Straus, Murray A.
1962
"Work Roles and Financial Responsibility in the Socialization of Farm, Fringe, and Town Boys." *Rural Sociology* 27:257–74.

1968
"Communication, Creativity, and Problem Solving Ability of Middle- and Working-Class Families in Three Societies." *American Journal of Sociology* 73:417–30.

Sullivan, Harry Stack
1947
Conceptions of Modern Psychiatry. New York: Norton.

Super, D. E.; Starishevsky, R.; Matlin, N.; and Jordan, J. P., eds.
1963
Career Development: Self-Concept Theory. Princeton, N. J.: College Entrance Examination Board.

Taft, Philip
1964
Organized Labor in American History. New York: Harper and Row.

Terkel, Studs
1970
Hard Times. New York: Pantheon.

Thernstrom, Stephan
1964
Poverty and Progress: Social Mobility in a Nineteenth-Century City. Cambridge, Mass.: Harvard University Press.

1973
The Other Bostonians: Class and Mobility in the American Metropolis, 1880–1970. Cambridge, Mass.: Harvard University Press.

Thomas, Dorothy S.
1927
Social Aspects of Business Cycles. New York: Knopf.

Thomas, William I., and Znaniecki, Florian
1918–20
The Polish Peasant in Europe and America. Vols. 1 and 2. Chicago: University of Chicago Press.

U. S. Department of Health, Education, and Welfare
1968
Perspectives on Human Deprivation. Washington, D.C.: U.S. Government Printing Office.

Volkhart, Edmund H., ed.
1951
Social Behavior and Personality: Contributions of W. I. Thomas to Theory and Research. New York: Social Science Research Council.

Warner, William F.
and Abegglen, James
1963

Big Business Leaders in America. New York: Atheneum.

Weinstock, Allan R.
1967

"Family Environment and the Development of Defense and Coping Mechanisms." *Journal of Personality and Social Psychology* 5:67–75.

Wilensky, Harold L.
1961

"Orderly Careers and Social Participation: The Impact of Work History on the Social Integration of the Middle Mass." *American Sociological Review* 26:521–39.

Wolff, Sula
1969

Children under Stress. London: Penguin Press.

Zawadski, B., and
Lazarsfeld, Paul F.
1935

"The Psychological Consequences of Unemployment." *Journal of Social Psychology* 6:224–51.

Zollschan, George K.,
and Hirsch, Walter, eds.
1964

Explorations in Social Change. Boston: Houghton Mifflin. (See especially David Kirk's essay, "The Impact of Drastic Change on Social Relations: A Model for the Identification and Specification of Stress.")

Index

Detroit, in Depression, 19
Dewey, John, 342, 355
Dickens, Charles, 3
Dislocations, socioeco-
nomic. *See* Depres-
sion, Great; Crisis
situation
Division of labor in the
family, 25, 28, 49–50,
278–79; children's
roles in, 28, 64–70;
mother's employment
in, 28, 50–51, 67
Dizard, Jan, 237, 368
Dohrenwend, Barbara S.,
241, 344
Dohrenwend, Bruce P.,
241, 344
Domesticity: in adoles-
cence, 79–80; and
adulthood of female
subjects, 212, 223–25,
279; and father ab-
sence, 239; and mari-
tal age, 216; postwar,
5, 221–23, 238–39,
291, 374; and work-
life, 231–34
Douvan, Elizabeth, 355
Draper, Hal, 341
Drinking, heavy: of
father, 61; and family
hardship, 244–45; and
occupational mobility,
193; and wife domi-
nance, 91
Duncan, Otis Dudley,
158, 359, 367, 376

Easterlin, Richard A., 5,
157, 195, 340, 363–64
Eckland, Bruce K., 361
Economic conditions, in
Depression, 3–4, 18–
19, 45–46, 332–34
Economic deprivation,
7–9, 24, 45–49; and
family social class,
45–46, 114–15, 235;
interpretations of, 16,
53, 59, 104–5, 132–33;
and opportunity, 33–
34, 134–36, 154, 165,
293
Economic inequality,
297, 337
Economy, planned,
289–90

Educational change by
generation, 210–11
Education: of father, 49;
of female subjects,
208–9, 210–11, 225;
of male subjects, 154,
156, 158, 160–62, 204.
See also Schools;
Occupational status;
GI Bill
Edwards, A. C., 355
Elder, Glen H., Jr., 36,
105, 123, 136, 137–38,
153, 172, 176, 193,
215, 246, 339, 343,
348, 350, 351, 356,
365, 366, 368
Emigration, 8, 57, 274
Environments, over-
manned vs. under-
manned, 285, 292–93
Erikson, Kai, 340
Estvan, Frank, 58

"Failure of complemen-
tarity," 31, 50, 54, 60,
118
Falk, Jacqueline M., 361
Family adaptation, 11–
12. *See also* Family
maintenance
Family conflict: and
attraction to parents,
100, 351; and emo-
tional state of subjects,
129; and hardship,
91–94, 101; and har-
mony, 94, 106
Family maintenance, 25,
26, 28, 49–53, 278–79;
children's roles, 28,
64–70; expenditures,
25, 94, 346; harmony
and conflict, 94; and
heavy drinking, 61;
mother's employment,
28, 50–51, 67; and
social defenses, 26, 53,
59–60. *See also*
Household
Family models, new,
286–87
Family size, 56, 68–70,
255.
Family structure. *See*
Family maintenance;

Harris, Dale B., 342
Hartup, Willard W., 98, 351
Harvey, O. J., 360
Hauser, Stuart T., 344
Hawthorn, Geoffrey, 363–64
Health: of fathers, 58, 60; literature on, 34–40, 241–43; of mothers, 54–57; "proneness thesis" of ill health, 37–38; of subjects as adults, 243–51, 261–62, 365; of subjects as children, 122–30, 356
Heer, David M., 84, 90, 350
Helson, Harry, 345 n.1
Hentoff, Margot, 64, 347
Heterosexual activity, 76–77, 103–4, 352
Hill, Reuben, 11, 12, 16, 25, 44, 210, 285, 287–88, 289–90, 349, 364, 368
Hilton, Thomas L., 360
Hinkel, Edgar J., 340
Hinkle, L. E., Jr., 38, 345
Hirsch, Walter, 31
Hirschi, Travis, 350
History: inductive generalizations in, 335; new social, 338, 373; oral, 4
Hoar, Victor, 372, 373
Hobbs, Daniel, Jr., 371
Hobsbawm, E. J., 338
Hoffman, Lois W., 348, 350, 364, 365
Hollingshead, August B., 344, 345, 360
Hollingshead Two Factor Index, 47, 159, 211, 345–46
Home: security of, 193, 226, 228; tranquillity of, 197, 221, 238
Homemaking: learning role of, 79–80; satisfaction with, 229–31, 238
Horney, Karen, 354–55
Horrocks, J. E., 351
Household: as emotional haven, 186, 193, 197; as labor-intensive

economy, 25, 64, 203, 222, 279, 285. *See also* Family maintenance; Fertility; Values
Household chores of children, 28, 29, 64–69; and family-centered values, 225–26; and homemaking, 230; and money, 72–74
Howard, A., 247
Hunt, D. E., 360
Huntington, Emily H., 18, 337
"Husband-oriented," 206, 233, 237–38
Hyman, Herbert H., 23, 339, 345, 372

Income loss. *See* Depression, Great; Economic deprivation
Independence, social, 29, 76–79, 86, 102–3
Industry of subjects, 75
Ingersoll, Hazel L., 364
Inkeles, Alex, 13, 339
Institute of Human Development. *See* Oakland Growth Study
Iscoe, Ira, 371

Jackson, Elton F., 343
Jaffe, A. J., 359
Jaffe, S. G., 141, 358
Jahoda, Marie, 35, 339, 344, 363
Japan, 333
Johnsen, Kathryn P., 364
Johnson, General Hugh, 335
Johnson, Marilyn, 339, 372
Jones, Frank, 118, 354
Jones, Harold E., 340
Jones, Mary C., 135, 358, 370
Jordan, J. P., 165

Kagan, Jerome, 341, 371
Kahn, Robert L., 343–44
Kasl, Stanislav, 32, 38
Katten, Edith S., 364
Katz, Joseph, 374

family, 197–99. *See also* Maternal dominance

Marital happiness: female subjects, 236–38, 368; male subjects, 193–94, 363

Marriage: age at first, 157, 207; and antecedents, 203–4, 213–17; companionate, 286, 287, 290; early, 216–17; timing of, 208–9

Martinson, Floyd, 365

Marx, Karl, 343

Maslow, Abraham H., 190, 294, 361, 362–63

Materialism, as domestic problem, 265–66

Maternal dominance: and adult offspring, 108–10; emotional centrality, 99–102; and adult daughter, 225–26; and family conflicts, 91–94; and parental control, 30, 86, 102–3; socioeconomic determinants of, 87–91. *See also* Marital decision-making

Matlin, N., 165

Mauss, Armand L., 295–96

Mauss, Marcel, 353

Mayhew, Henry, 291

Mayhew, K. C., 355

Mead, George Herbert, 343

Mead, Margaret, 293, 374

Meals in school, 321

Measurement problems, 21–23, 326–29

Mechanic, David, 36, 37, 338, 344

Meltzer, Milton, 337

Mental ability: and family background, 137; in male subjects, 174–76; and values, 184, 187, 188. *See also* Adaptive potential

Michael, Stanley T., 38, 346, 355

Middle class: "new," 158; "old," 48, 346

Middle-class standards, 16, 26, 44, 53, 55

"Middy Board," 332

Military service, 156, 159, 208

Miller, Daniel R., 286, 339

Miller, S. M., 346

Mills, C. Wright, 189, 269, 343, 354

Minturn, Leigh, 348

Mitchell, Broadus, 337, 346, 359

Miyamoto, Frank, 354

Mobility, downward occupational, 46, 123–24; and heavy drinking, 61, 193; and wife dominance, 91

Mobility, intergenerational occupational, 362; antecedents of, 173–83; and childhood factors, 188, 190–91; and psychological functioning, 192, 245–46

Mobility, through marriage, 217–20

Mogey, John M., 384

Moore, Joan W., 343

Morgan, J. W., 347

Morley, Felix, 350

Moss, Howard, 341, 371

Moss, J. Joel, 103, 157, 206

Mother: discontent of, 53–57; dominance of, 87–91; emotional centrality of, 99–102; in labor market, 50–51; martyr image of, 112–13. *See also* Significant others

Motivation: and definition of the situation, 146–47; and family conditions, 33, 120, 136–45; in marriage mobility, 219; in status attainment, 173–77; and work activity, 70

Multiple classification analysis, 56, 73–74, 347

Murray, H. A., 347

Musgrove, Frank, 342

Mussen, Paul H., 98, 341, 351